Yale Historical Publications, Miscellany, 124

NEW MASTERS

NORTHERN PLANTERS DURING THE
CIVIL WAR AND RECONSTRUCTION

Lawrence N. Powell

Yale University Press
New Haven and London
1980

Designed by Thomas Whitridge
and set in IBM Press Roman type by
A & B Typesetters, Inc., Concord, New Hampshire.
Printed in the United States of America by
Halliday Lithograph, West Hanover, Mass.

Published in Great Britain, Europe, Africa, and
Asia (except Japan) by Yale University Press,
Ltd., London. Distributed in Australia and
New Zealand by Book & Film Services, Artarmon,
N.S.W., Australia; and in Japan by Harper & Row,
Publishers, Tokyo Office.

Library of Congress Cataloging in Publication Data

Powell, Lawrence N
  New masters.

  (Yale historical publications: Miscellany; 124)
  Bibliography: p.
  Includes index.
  1. Plantations—Southern States—History. 2. Cotton growing—Southern States—History.
3. Afro-American agricultural laborers—Southern States—History. 4. Southern States—
History—1865–1877. I. Title. II. Series.
  HD1471.U5P68   338.1'0975   79-64226
  ISBN 0-300-02217-4

    Grateful acknowledgment is made to Kent State University Press
for permission to use Lawrence N. Powell, "The American Land Company
and Agency: John A. Andrew and the Northernization of the South,"
Civil War History 21(Dec. 1975):293-308, portions of which appear
in chapter 1.

To My Parents

Stewart N. Powell
Elizabeth G. Powell

Contents

Tables

Preface

My interest was first drawn to the subject of northern planters by Willie Lee Rose's study of the South Carolina Sea Islands during the Civil War.[1] Here was a fascinating history, brilliantly told, of how the liberators and the liberated first tried to resolve what freedom meant in one part of the Cotton Kingdom. Of all the familiar Reconstruction characters who turned up in her story, it was the free enterprisers from the North, the planter-missionaries, who intrigued me the most, for they attempted to grapple with the major questions confronting the nation after it determined to abolish chattel slavery. How was the transition to be made from slave labor to free labor, from a paternalistic economy to a marketplace economy? How were the country's divergent labor systems going to be nationalized and brought into reasonable harmony? Admittedly, white and black southerners eventually answered these questions for themselves, although not without some outside guidance and assistance. But no one who has ever read Professor Rose's book will doubt that rich insights can be gleaned from studying how the free-labor system evolved in the hands of men whose prejudices were not with the old order.

It was exciting, therefore, to discover that northern planters were by no means confined to Port Royal, that they ranged throughout most of the South during the early years of emancipation, and that there were profitable opportunities for further investigation of this subject if the relevant material could be brought together. To be sure, it would be a somewhat different kind of study. By and large, it would have to focus on men with less idealism and different commitments and take into account the constant presence of suspicious and sometimes hostile southern whites. This latter situation was never really a problem for the newcomers on the Sea Islands, or rather it was less of a problem partly because they confronted the people they displaced only during the Thermidorian phase of the revolution at Port Royal.

On the whole, the subject seemed worth pursuing. It promised to shed light on the limitations of liberal reform during a critical stage of the country's evolution into a mature industrial society, and it held forth the possibility of illuminating important aspects of the Old South's metamorphosis into the New South. Finally, it struck me as an interesting chapter in the larger story of North-South relations, one that I have tried to tell in human terms, and that I feel is really what the study is all about.

One thing became clear: These Yankee planters were much more numerous than has been generally imagined. The more I researched, the more ubiquitous they became. Northern planters were coming into the low country of South Carolina and Georgia at such a rapid rate shortly after the war that reporters spoke nonchalantly of the day when "a pleasant Yankee colony," if not a skirmish line, would reach all the way from Charleston to Fernandina, Florida.[2] Moreover, a visitor to Macon, Georgia, in August 1865 found "northern men in all of the out of the way places" doing "almost all the business."[3] It was apparently not much different in Alabama. According to John T. Trowbridge, "men from the Middle States and the great West were everywhere buying and leasing plantations, hiring freedmen, and setting thousands of ploughs in motion."[4] At the beginning of 1866 Louisiana supposedly "was fast becoming 'Northernized,' " especially in the cotton parishes. Yankees, in fact, were said to be "doing most of the cotton-planting" along both banks of the Mississippi River, and by late 1865 they had already begun to pour into the interior "in large numbers, with the intention to lease plantations and go to cotton raising."[5]

It is exceedingly difficult to determine the precise number of northerners who were engaged in southern planting during the Civil War and Reconstruction. The only hard data we have is a sample of 524 northern planters that I have compiled for six states of the lower South, roughly for the period 1862-76 (see appendix). It had to be mined the hard way. Because most of the new planters came and went between 1860 and 1870 (for reasons that will become apparent later), the U.S. Census was of no help.[6] Thus, all that is available in the way of estimates of the total northern planter population is a few impressionistic appraisals, and these vary widely. Yankee newcomers in Alabama, for example, said that five thousand northerners moved to the state shortly after Appomattox, not less than three thousand of whom were "engaged in the cultivation of cotton."[7] A northern editor in Vicksburg reckoned that nearly ten thousand former Union soldiers had settled in Mississippi, and that nearly half of them were in his immediate vicinity alone. John Trowbridge tells us that by 1866 fifty thousand northern men had put down stakes in Louisiana since the firing on Fort Sumter, and that most of them were in planting.[8] There are no estimates (or at least none that I have run across) for the remaining states of the former Confederacy, but one student of Reconstruction believes that "thousands of soldiers immediately turned planters without returning home, and thousands of other Northerners came South to buy or rent cotton lands."[9] It would be nice to use one of these estimates as a basis for extrapolating the total Yankee planter population in the South during these years. But none of the estimates is reliable enough to yield a result not open to the charge of speciousness.

If guesses are all we have to go on, I might as well go on record as saying that I think that anywhere from twenty thousand to fifty thousand northerners tried their hands at planting during the period under consideration. This is admittedly only a hunch, but it is an informed hunch, and I feel comfortable with the estimate. These newcomers turn up in too many disparate sources to have been a paltry presence in the South in these years. The northern planting class was, in fact, as numerically significant as any group of Reconstruction actors. Members of this group probably outnumbered Yankee schoolmarms (whom Henry L. Swint estimates to have totaled five thousand),[10] for the simple reason that profit has usually been a stronger motive than philanthropy. They also exceeded the number of Freedmen's Bureau agents; and they surely bulked larger than carpetbagger officeholders, who were largely recruited from the ranks of northern planters.[11] They probably outnumbered scalawag politicians as well. Northern planters were one of the largest categories of *dramatis personae* in the Reconstruction drama. Yet they have not been studied to any significant extent.

Obviously, I could not investigate all of the northern planters, which is why this study confines itself principally to those in the states of the lower South. For my purposes these states include South Carolina, Georgia, Florida, Alabama, Mississippi, and Louisiana. I have occasionally used material from other states, but only when I thought it necessary to illustrate an important point in the most effective way. Although this study ostensibly embraces the years 1862 through 1876, most of the action takes place before 1868; most Yankee planters left the South before Radical Reconstruction was fairly under way. Finally, I am concerned here chiefly with northern cotton planters, though, again, when it served the purpose at hand I sometimes looked at newcomers who cultivated rice and sugar. The realities of the situation necessitated this focus on cotton. "They hav'n't got sugar on the brain," said a Louisianian of the northerners in his state shortly after the war; "it's cotton they're all crazy after."[12] The following pages should make abundantly clear just how obsessed Yankees were with growing cotton during the early years of emancipation.

I have accumulated many debts in the course of preparing this study. I would like to thank the manuscript librarians at Cornell University, Duke University, Emory University, Harvard University, Louisiana State University, the University of Florida, the University of Michigan, the University of North Carolina, the Library of Congress, and the South Caroliniana Library. Thanks are also due to the staffs at the Georgia Historical Society, the Massachusetts Historical Society, the Minnesota Historical Society, the Missouri Historical Society, the Historical Society of Pennsylvania, the Alabama Department of Archives and History, the Georgia Department of Archives and History, the Iowa Department of Archives and History, the Mississippi Department of Archives and History, and the South Carolina Department of Archives. The late Herman Kahn of the Archives of Yale University and Michael Musick and Mrs. Elizabeth Holcamper of the National Archives gave very generously of their time. Elizabeth Potter and her staff at the Essex Institute made my visit with them a memorable one. A special word of thanks is due Professor William Childers at the University of Florida for placing valuable research material at my disposal. Patricia Clark of the Papers of Andrew Johnson also supplied me with helpful items. To Thomas R. Morse of Concord, Massachusetts, I am grateful for a copy of his father's memoirs.

Several people have given valuable assistance at various stages of the book's progress. For their reading of drafts of the manuscript, I wish to thank John Boles, Robert Byrd, Carla Carr, Daniel Crofts, William Ferris, Eric Foner, Steve Goodell, Julie S. Jones, William S. McFeely, Clarence L. Mohr, Willie Lee Rose, Michael Sherry, and Carol Wasserloos. Special mention should be made of Marie Caskey, Steven Hahn, Peter Ripley, Michael Wayne, and, especially, James Caskey, upon whose time and patience I have imposed rather selfishly. I am very much in their debt. It is hard to know how to begin thanking John Blassingame for all the ways he has helped me to see this project through. He has my lasting gratitude.

I owe a large debt to my dissertation adviser, C. Vann Woodward. He has given me encouragement and helpful criticism at every stage of this study and has had a major influence on my understanding of history. He once told me I should not be afraid to make a mistake. I have always appreciated his advice.

Thanks are also due to Ann Stoddard for her excellent job of typing the manuscript, to Sally Serafim of Yale Press for her copy editing, to John M. Espy for reading proofs, and to Charles and Louise Skirven for generously helping out with some of the expenses connected with the manuscript's preparation. A research grant from Yale University defrayed some of my travel expenses.

My wife, Diana, has been my best critic. She has not only listened to or read most of the study, but has revived my spirit on more than one occasion.

Of course, I am solely responsible for any errors of fact and judgment that remain in the book.

1 *"New Masters"*

The northern planter movement never wanted for enthusiasts. The Yankees who went south to raise cotton during the Civil War and Reconstruction had undertaken what they and their well-wishers conceived to be a magnificent mission. The newcomers, it was said, would help render the South loyal, "soften sectional asperities," perhaps make the nation more homogeneous, and surely would assist the former slave states with the difficulties of adjusting to a new system of labor.[1] This last service was rather crucial. If the sectional conflict was basically over rival economic systems, as many northerners at the time believed, the substitution of free labor for slave labor in the South was a matter of large consequence for the lasting peace and security of the Union. The North gave the question a lot of attention, though perhaps not as much as it should have. The victor tried many experiments in order to acquaint the vanquished with the operations of the modern marketplace. He introduced the practice of written labor contracts, mobilized military provost marshals to enforce them, and finally established a government agency—the Freedmen's Bureau—to supervise the transition to new ways of making a living. But a young, expansive capitalist North also concluded that its own people had special qualifications for the requirements of the hour. This was a people, after all, who could easily proclaim that in Reconstruction "the actual operations of business companies and the energetic prosecution of mercantile affairs will do more to heal existing difficulties than the speculations of politicians."[2] Government agents were only the referees of free labor in the South. Yankee planters were the pioneers.

This attempt to introduce free labor into the cotton South by way of northern enterprise was not without its ironies. It grew out of the federal government's ineffectiveness in dealing with the hundreds of thousands of slaves who emancipated themselves by fleeing to the invading Union armies or by refusing to flee from them. The administration in Washington had entered the war pledged to protect slavery where it existed and determined to restore the Union at all hazards. President Abraham Lincoln was not about to adopt any policies that might alienate the loyal border states, close the door to eventual compromise with the seceding states, or aggravate the racial anxieties of the northern states. He believed that a program of gradual, voluntary, and compensated emancipation, coupled with Negro colonization, would pacify the rebellious South at the same time that it removed the source of the original difficulty. Beyond that, the president preferred to leave the details of racial policy to those military commanders and civilian subordinates who had the prudence not to run too far ahead of public opinion.[3]

The result generally was a crazy-quilt policy regarding southern blacks. Some Union generals tried to exclude them from their lines or at least to allow fugitive slave hunters free access to them. A few bold officers sought to arm them and use them on foraging missions within their theaters of operation. General Benjamin F. Butler hit upon an expedient at Fortress Monroe, Virginia, in 1861 that was eventually adopted by many military commanders. He termed the fugitive slaves contraband of war and set them to work on military fortifications.[4] At this early date few northern officials thought to turn to private enterprise. A few even turned against it. Secretary of the Treasury Salmon P. Chase resisted the many proposals that vested business interests in the North brought forward for the employment of the thousands of slaves who stayed behind when the Union navy sailed into the Port Royal district of South Carolina in the fall of 1861. He chose instead to accept the plan offered by a young Massachusetts lawyer whose experience at Fortress Monroe entitled his opinions to a certain amount of respect. Edward L. Pierce believed that "not even the best of men . . . should be put in a position where there would be a conflict between his humanity and his self-interest." He persuaded the secretary that the plantations and the people now in the government's hands should be placed in the charge of the young idealists and schoolteachers whom the antislavery communities of Boston, New York, and Philadelphia were ready to send to the Sea Islands.[5]

As antislavery pressure and southern intransigence inched Congress and then the president toward the recognition that emancipation was at least a military necessity, federal policy regarding the contrabands began to assume more definite shape. Realities in the field also compelled some changes. The black population grew with every advance of the Union armies, jumping almost exponentially during and after the siege of Vicksburg, Mississippi, in the spring and summer of 1863. Federal officials quickly ran out of projects to keep the destitute slaves usefully employed. Herding the black refugees into contraband camps where disease and suffering shocked all decent observers scarcely helped the situation. If the North cared anything at all for such humanitarian credentials as it still possessed, the administration clearly needed a comprehensive policy that would show that liberation was a positive military asset, and that "the slaves could make the transition from slavery to freedom."[6] The policy was even more necessary from the standpoint of northern racial fears, which were more susceptible than ever to Democratic propaganda after Lincoln and his party had also decided that colonization was no longer practicable and that "the fate of the Negro race was to be settled largely in the South." The only way to scotch the widespread apprehension (especially in the Midwest) that emancipation would fill the free states with black paupers was to devise a strategy proving that they could be kept gainfully occupied in the South. The solution the administration finally hit upon in early 1863 was to mobilize the freedmen for war by arming the able-bodied ones and making the rest self-supporting on the southern soil. In late March of 1863 General Lorenzo Thomas, acting as "the president's emissary" and under instructions from

Secretary of War Edward M. Stanton, went to the Mississippi Valley to work out the details of this new policy of racial containment.[7]

The solution was only partial. The emphasis of the new program was to prove that the ex-slaves could earn their own way like other men and women and that the country could profit from cotton produced by black free labor; black soldiers originally were only supposed to perform garrison duty and protect the cotton producers on the plantations.[8] What the new policy left unsettled, however, was the question of who was to take charge of the plantations. Most of the plantations along the Mississippi River from above Vicksburg to Port Gibson had either been abandoned by their owners or confiscated by the government, except for the estates of a small but influential group of planters around Natchez and Vicksburg. General Thomas's initial intention was to appoint government overseers to manage the plantations on the government's hands, though he confessed "that this is a difficult subject to handle," and he offered his views "with diffidence."[9]

Thomas probably realized that neither government plantations nor home farms by and large had been managed very efficiently, through no fault of the freedmen or the officials immediately in charge. The problem was the government's tardy payrolls and its practice of depositing the wages of black laborers in a Quartermaster's fund, to be used for the care of the destitute.[10] This was hardly the way to inculcate the ethic of individual initiative. To men who believed that the prompt payment of wages could restore even "the muscle of all the disabled" freedmen, it made sense to bring private enterprise into the picture.[11] And if the political, moral, and military implications of emancipation compelled the federal government to demonstrate that the ex-slaves could be converted to free laborers in the South, what could be more natural than for it to seek assistance from northern enterprisers, who ostensibly knew something about operating a business with wage earners.

General Thomas quickly came around to this point of view, though not until he consulted with "several gentlemen of capital" who were in the Mississippi Valley at the time looking for cotton lands to cultivate. Less than two weeks after explaining his initial program to Secretary Stanton, the general said that his aim now was to prove that the freedmen could be "profitably employed by enterprising men."[12] Thomas resolved to rent the abandoned and confiscated plantations to "loyal" men of "pecuniary responsibility," and he appointed three commissioners of leasing to supervise the operation. No great supporter of Quartermaster rationing, he also directed that henceforth home farms and contraband camps were to serve as labor depots for the plantations and that the government was to work the freed people only when the number of "qualified lessees" proved insufficient. To set the whole operation in motion, the general proceeded to "give immediate publicity . . . to this place, in the hope of inducing persons of enterprise and capital to come here and engage in the matter." He offered them good terms. Yearly rent consisted only of a two-dollar tax on each four-hundred-pound bale of cotton produced. Northern planters were to help inaugurate the new order in at least part of the South.[13]

The administration in Washington had little difficulty endorsing General Thomas's plan. The program in the Mississippi Valley conformed in many of its essentials to the drift of federal policy elsewhere in the occupied Confederacy. General Butler and General Nathaniel P. Banks, with executive approval, had already instituted a wage system for the sugar plantations in the Department of the Gulf, though the presence there of many old slaveholders, whom Lincoln planned to use for restoring Louisiana to the Union, obviated the need for outside lessees.[14]

The case was quite different in the South Carolina Sea Islands. Here federal authorities relied almost exclusively on northern men. The Direct Tax commissioners for South Carolina, the administrators of the land forfeited by refugee southerners for the nonpayment of the direct tax recently levied by the federal Congress, believed that "the system of *free* labor . . . has not had even the semblance of a fair trial" at Port Royal,[15] and acting under the authority of congressional legislation enacted in 1861 and 1862, they commenced a series of land sales in March 1863 that continued on and off for many years. The first purchasers were principally the New England wing of the planter-missionaries, who had long been chafing at government control. They welcomed more favorable circumstances in which to prove their theory that free labor could grow more cotton, more cheaply, than slave labor. The largest buyer was a syndicate headed by Edward S. Philbrick, backed by wealthy northern philanthropists who shared his view that "there would be many advantages to private ownership if there were some assurance that the new owners would not be selfishly motivated."[16] Nor was this all. The tax commissioners also meant to carry out their congressional authority to establish a leasing system for most of the land that they set aside for "charitable, Educational, or police purposes." It was too late in the season to rent any acreage in 1863, and thus many plantations remained in the care of government superintendents. But in 1864 and thereafter, leases for school farms (as some of the plantations were called) were sold to the highest bidder at the periodic land auctions. These leases in some respects were more desirable than those available in the West. They ran for four years, not one season.[17]

This turn toward using northern planters to help settle "the question of Free Labor upon the cotton-fields of the South" obviously precluded more radical alternatives.[18] Federal authorities were reluctant to lease or sell subdivided plantation tracts to the freedmen, as a few northern idealists and many black people would have preferred. Authorities in the Mississippi Valley occasionally rented small parcels of land to black farmers, yet only to such ex-slaves as they felt possessed the funds and talents to make it through a season unassisted.[19] At Port Royal things were somewhat different. Before the Direct Tax Commission closed its books, the freedmen managed to purchase several thousand acres of Sea Island land and to lease a considerable amount in addition from both the government and private owners. But the acreage they acquired was always well below that purchased by northern immigrants, and this result was intended by a majority of the tax commissioners. They fought back an effort to apply the principle of western homesteading to the land at Port Royal because they "envisioned a mixed settlement" of white plantations and small black farms and believed that "the larger owners would be able to organize agricultural activities on their land and to provide employment for landless Negroes and those with limited acreage."[20]

The truth is, not many of the liberators had boundless faith in the freedmen's capacity for "self-directed" labor so soon after their emancipation. Slavery had been a poor school in which to learn the incentives of classical economics, and it was not generally expected that its pupils could escape "the evils of their former life" overnight. When in January 1865 General William T. Sherman set aside a strip of land along the southeastern seaboard for the exclusive occupancy of the thousands of slaves who followed his army to the sea, the news was generally greeted in the North with lamentation and deep foreboding. It was a great mistake in statesmanship, the New York *Times* said, for what the ex-slaves needed was not isolation and complete independence, but "all the advantages which the neighborhood of a superior race . . . would bring to them." And what they needed even more was the good example and friendly guidance such as Yankee employers could largely provide.[21] Few doubted, after emancipation, that the freedmen had some promise, provided that Yankee paternalism was allowed full scope. Many northerners even persuaded themselves that black people saw the situation this way, too. It would be hard to find a more popular northern conceit in these years than the conviction that the ex-slaves trusted the liberators, preferred Yankees as employers, and concluded to "go their bottom dollar on them."[22]

It was a good thing that black people thought as they did, northerners believed. All indications pointed to the conclusion that the old planting class could not be depended on for either industrious example or free-labor commitment. Ex-slaveholders seemed wedded to the idea that the black man would work only under compulsion. They were even disposed, some observers feared, to sabotage the entire free-labor experiment in order to vindicate their prejudices. When the old masters talked of free labor, they really meant slave labor, "only hired, not bought."[23] And how could men whose habits and customs were shaped by the old order readily grasp the requirements of the new order? The case seemed plain to all who had eyes to see. If the freedmen were ever to be transformed into productive free laborers within the South, the New York *Times* argued with unintended irony, "it must be done by giving them new masters"— northerners who had grown up with the wage system and were not discomfited by the vagaries of its operations. The ex-slaveholders needed practical examples of free-labor industry fully as much as the ex-slaves. An increasing number of northerners could imagine no better way to demonstrate for the South the workings of free labor than by putting the vanquished in direct competition with the victor. Yankee planters would attract the best hands, if not drive up wages throughout the former Confederacy.[24] The New York *Herald* claimed it had discovered the remedy for southern backwardness: "The prosperity of the South, of the planters and of the negroes depend alike on the emigration of the Yankees and Yankee energy."[25]

This logic had a seductiveness that sometimes overcame sober judgment. There were predictions that northerners would grow most of the South's cotton in the early postwar years. "Of this there can be no doubt," asserted a Massachusetts cotton agent who toured the late Confederacy shortly after Appomattox. It was also assumed that Yankee planters would increase the production of the staple and lower its price, which in turn would improve the country's balance of trade and hasten a return to hard money.[26] Even the textile interests of Boston were not inclined to question these assumptions, though they did doubt whether enough northern capital and enterprise could be conveyed to the South in season to make a difference. After the war they wanted to return to the system of growing cotton on government plantations, at least until the southern economy was able to function on its own.[27] But men who did not have to worry about keeping their spindles running were confident that the invasion of Yankee planters would be on schedule, particularly if it were properly organized. John A. Andrew, the celebrated Civil War governor of Massachusetts, took the needful steps. With a capital subscription of $35,000 from Boston and New York investors, in the fall of 1865 he organized the American Land Company and Agency in order to channel northern men and money into the southern plantation economy. It was his faith that the newcomers would literally "show the Southern people . . . how to cultivate cotton."[28]

There were admittedly some reservations about the Yankee planter movement. A few friends of the ex-slave failed to see the benefits of giving him "new masters" instead of a farm of his own.[29] Opponents of land monopoly also found it hard to applaud a development that appeared likely to perpetuate the system of large estates. Most of them seemed to favor carving up southern plantations for distribution to northern soldiers.[30] Warnings occasionally came from unexpected sources. "Let it be generally presumed by the ignorant Blacks of the South that a Yankee, *because* a Yankee, is necessarily their friend," the New York *Tribune* cautioned, and there would be the devil to pay. Some of the worst specimens of New England would descend on the South

> like locusts, starting schools and prayer meetings, at every cross-roads, getting hold of abandoned or confiscated plantations and hiring laborers right and left, cutting timber here, trying out tar and turpentine there, and growing corn, cotton, rice, and sugar which they will have sold at the earliest day and run away with the proceeds, leaving the negroes in rags and foodless, with Winter just coming on.[31]

These were strong words coming from a journal that was for the most part indefatigable in advertising the opportunities for fortune and philanthropy awaiting northern cotton growers in the postemancipation South. Like all other southern reforms of northern origin during the sectional crisis, the Yankee planter movement went forward with divine blessing and patriotic gratitude. Governor Andrew was sure that "since Divine Providence has put man into a mortal body, and into material relations, we propose a most profound missionary work." He was typical of the age.[32] Seldom in our nation's history has so much energy gone into arguing the patriotic duty of making a quick killing.

If the aim was to interest northerners in southern plantations, the propagandists could have put aside their moralizing and stated just the facts. Nothing excited northern acquisitiveness so much in the period from 1863 to 1868 as the prospect of turning a fast dollar from cotton-growing. Plantation lands could be bought or rented at prices well below prewar levels, cotton was selling at a record high, and labor was supposedly cheap and docile. From a modest outlay of capital, enterprising northerners might reap rich returns. And everyone had estimates to prove it.[33] The wartime stream of Yankees to Port Royal and the Mississippi Valley was considerable, even though it was said that nine-tenths of the applicants for plantations in the West in 1864 returned home "disgusted with the whole arrangement & with the bad faith" of the government.[34] No matter. The postwar current from the North ran just as swiftly, and much more deeply. Scarcely a railroad car or steamboat headed South in the winter of 1865-66 without a crowd of prospective cotton growers. A pleasing feature of sailing to the former Confederacy after Appomattox, one Boston man said, was that "nearly half the travellers in every boat are New Englanders."[35] The cotton rush was on.

Who were these northerners who went south during and after the war to raise cotton, and what were their motives and commitments? How did white southerners regard them and treat them? What did the freedmen actually think of them as employers? These are just some of the questions that the following pages attempt to answer.

2 *"A Short Road to Wealth"*

Northern planters are probably the least understood of all the major participants in Reconstruction. We know a great deal about the backgrounds and motives of the wartime missionaries at Port Royal and the handful of Wisconsin men who planted in the West at roughly the same time. We also know something about the various individual northern planters who published memoirs or attracted biographers. But the identities and motives of most of the Yankee cotton growers remain largely a mystery. Who were these men and where did they come from? Why did they move to the South and what were their ambitions for the region? Were they racial idealists or merely quick-kill artists? Did they plan to stay long? We need answers to these questions if we would understand the type of social system northern planters meant to establish in the postemancipation South.

One answer we can give immediately is that Yankee planters were young, well-educated men from business and professional backgrounds.[1] Over 90 percent of them had been in some line of business or in a profession; nearly one-fourth of them had attended college; and most of them were in their early thirties, the average age being thirty-three. Surprisingly, most were not ex-soldiers; only 40 percent of the Yankee planter class had served in the Union army. Except for the Far West (including the mountain states), all sections of the North were well represented. New Englanders comprised 40 percent of the total, but men from the midwestern and mid-Atlantic states were not far behind, with 33 and 26 percent, respectively. Moreover, the four states of Massachusetts, New York, Illinois, and Ohio accounted for nearly 70 percent of the total sample, but every free state sent emigrants to the cotton districts of the South. Generally, New Englanders predominated in the southeastern states, while midwesterners held the edge in the western cotton states. Where one planted cotton seems to have had a lot to do with where one's regiment or friends had served tours of duty. (Appendix, tables 1-4 and 14.) It was said that in New England, for example, "almost every family has some near relative, who, having laid down his arms, has established himself in the region with which the war made him acquainted."[2]

The first wave of northern planters came ashore at Port Royal, South Carolina. They were an exceptional group in many respects. Those who came from Boston under the auspices of the Education Commission represented "some of the choicest young men of New England fresh from Harvard, Yale, and

Brown, from the divinity schools of Andover and Cambridge, men of practical talent and experience."[3] They were from some of the best families in Boston, and they would go on to successful careers after they returned to the North. The contingent from the American Missionary Association had less impressive credentials, but they too had better than average educations. Over one-half of all the "Gideonites," as the early Yankees at Port Royal liked to call themselves, had attended college, and better than two-thirds of them were, or were about to become, professional men. Teachers and ministers were especially familiar figures on the Sea Islands during the war.[4] (Appendix, tables 5-7.)

The character of the population on the Sea Islands changed perceptibly after the federal government started selling and leasing plantations. The change was small at the first Direct Tax sale early in 1863; a high proportion of the purchasers were missionaries, chiefly from the Boston group. Two or three sutlers bought in, but "no dangerous speculators made their appearance."[5] (Appendix, table 6.) Strangers showed up in increasing numbers, however, at the well-advertised sales held during 1864 and 1865. The newcomers seem to have been businessmen from the New England and mid-Atlantic states, and they were somewhat older than the original invaders and not nearly so well educated. Having learned that the government was selling cotton lands at Port Royal for $1.25 per acre, they intended to head south as soon as they could put their business affairs in order; if that was impracticable, they meant to send an agent to act as proxy.[6] Midway through the Port Royal experiment the northern population on the Sea Islands began to assume a different character. (Appendix, tables 8-10.)

And Port Royal was not exceptional. It was simply being opened up to the same influences that shaped affairs in the West. At the beginning of 1864 businessmen also started crowding into the Mississippi Valley to take advantage of the newly established plantation leasing system. They came with good letters of recommendation and were said to be "most worthy, reliable and devoted men of pecuniary means to large extent," although there were some among them who merely wanted a place from which to ship illicit cotton. They came chiefly from the Midwest, where the program was well advertised. The promise of a $15,000 return from a $2,000 investment, which one of General Lorenzo Thomas's publicity agents never tired of repeating during his promotion tour of the Northwest, struck a responsive chord throughout the region.[7] But word reached the East, too, that the West was "the place to make a fortune," and New Englanders and New Yorkers were not left standing at the post. Some of the easterners had already attended the tax sales in South Carolina and had simply moved on to the Mississippi Valley after concluding that Port Royal was "played out." If the rising price of plantation lands did not frighten them off, the confusion surrounding the sale of land to the freedmen did.[8] But it was not inappropriate that they shifted their theater of operations. In the Mississippi Valley they were in familiar company, even if they could not always abide "the half civilized race of pork eating 'right smart' housiers [*sic*]."[9] Whether at Port Royal or in the Mississippi Valley, the northerners who came south during the latter years of the war were generally of a recognizable type. Over two-thirds of them were businessmen, usually in their early forties, who saw their opportunity and took it. (Appendix, tables 9-10.)

These wartime northern planters were overwhelmingly from civilian backgrounds. There were some Union veterans among the lessees in the Mississippi Valley, but their number was not large. The Direct Tax Commission for South Carolina tried to look out for the soldier interest by giving military personnel preferential treatment in the purchase of tax lands during the sales of 1864 and 1865. Union soldiers, sailors, and marines were required to pay only one-fourth of the purchase price immediately and the balance in three years. But speculators appear to have benefited the most from the military sales. If the soldiers were not already acting as fronts for business interests, they usually transferred their titles to civilians not long after the original purchase. When the unpaid balances started falling due in 1867, the tax commissioners wondered whether the government would ever realize anything close to the value at which the army, navy, and marine lands had been sold three years earlier. Many of the civilian speculators to whom the military buyers had sold out were now "disposed to shirk the payment of the three-fourths purchase money and bid in the property at a price much below that at the former sale."[10]

If civilian planters were ascendant during the war, Yankees with military experience had their day after the war. Most of the northerners who went into cotton-planting following Appomattox were Union veterans. They had much in common with the missionaries at Port Royal. They, too, were usually in their early thirties and well educated: one-third had had some college training. Quite a few of them, moreover, came from professional backgrounds. Lawyers, doctors, teachers, and engineers accounted for almost 60 percent of the total. It should cause no surprise that the overwhelming majority of the military contingent had been officers—and officers of high rank: almost 40 percent were at least majors when they left the military. (Appendix, tables 15-17.) There were many Union generals who took up planting after the war. The Mississippi Delta boasted of several brigade commanders, but in Alabama practically the entire federal command staff became cotton growers, occasionally with the aid of local authorities. The commanding general at Talladega, M. H. Chrysler, asked the provisional governor to help keep him in his present post, as he was "almost persuaded to allow [Alabama] . . . to adopt [him] as one of her own children."[11]

White officers of Negro troops also bulked large in the military contingent. Several officers of the 2nd United States Colored Troops (USCT) in Florida went into planting and they were joined by their counterparts from the Fifty-fourth and Fifty-fifth Massachusetts (Colored). They thought they "could make some money now speculating in cotton and other things."[12] In the western theater it was no different. Throughout the South USCT officers were "looking after land to buy or rent," and had "numerous opportunities to invest money in crops, land, etc."[13] One observer put their number in the hundreds. He was probably not exaggerating. About 12 percent of the former Union officers who went into cotton-planting appear to have served with black troops.[14] (Appendix, table 18.)

Federal authorities, in a small way, tried to accommodate the soldiers' interest in the South. In the Department of the Gulf all officers and men who wished to remain in the South could be discharged there with full pay and benefits, instead of having to return home. Several regiments took advantage of this arrangement because it gave them "some ready money" with which to get started in a new home.[15] Benjamin C. Truman, whom President Andrew Johnson sent to the South on a fact-finding mission, claimed he could name "thirty regiments one-half of whose officers and many of the men have returned to the South, and as many more that have left large numbers there upon being disbanded." In some outfits nearly all of the company commanders and several of the field officers stayed behind to plant cotton when their comrades returned home.[16] Having seen the country while on military campaign, they had resolved "to own a good farm down here somewhere" after the war. In fact, a few felt tempted to quit the military before the surrender in order to get into the planting business.[17]

Indeed, the prospects for cotton-growing seemed so favorable that some officers could not wait until their commissions expired to take advantage of the opportunity. In the Mississippi Valley, where it was said that even "corruption has become corrupted," the speculative climate demoralized practically everyone exposed to it.[18] "The military men," one lessee complained, "are, from all I can learn, deeper in this business [cotton speculation] than they are in putting down the rebellion."[19] Most of the corruption involved illicit trade in cotton, but some officers became planters on their own account. A major on General Ulysses S. Grant's staff, for example, leased a plantation near Vicksburg and "engaged largely in the business." If military responsibilities prevented close attention to plantation duties, there was always a brother or some near relative to manage the place.[20] Apparently even General Lorenzo S. Thomas, who had set up the leasing system in the department and was in charge of recruiting black troops, had an interest in his son's plantation in Concordia Parish, Louisiana, during 1864; the year before, young Henry Thomas had made good profits on a standing crop abandoned by its owner.[21]

Military officers were not alone in taking advantage of the leasing system. The men who administered the program often gave in to temptation. At one period two of the three commissioners in charge of leasing (including Judge Lewis Dent, General Grant's brother-in-law) were plantation lessees. Agents of the Commission on Leasing were no less active in renting property for which they were officially responsible.[22] James E. Yeatman advocated forbidding Commission officials and their relatives to lease plantations, and for a while at least the abuse was curbed when the Treasury Department temporarily took over the program.[23] But the closest scrutiny could not have stopped the practice of silent partnerships. The plantation leasing system bears a strong resemblance to those modern regulatory agencies that have been captured by the very interests they are empowered to police.

Official involvement in cotton plantations continued into the postwar period. Agents of the Bureau of Refugees, Freedmen, and Abandoned Lands, which Congress had established in March 1865 to ease the transition to free labor, sometimes had difficulty in keeping separate their private and public accounts. Their speculations evidently had the blessing of higher authorities. General Oliver Otis Howard, the Bureau commissioner, encouraged northern entrepreneurs to plant cotton because he wanted "to afford promptly as many examples as possible of the successful employment of negroes under a free labor system." So long as his agents did not prostitute official position for private gain, he had no complaint if they followed his advice, as many apparently did.[24] On their inspection tour in 1866 Generals James S. Fullerton and John Steedman, who admittedly were more interested in discrediting than in reforming the Bureau, turned up several cases of agents who had invested in cotton-growing. In Texas, Louisiana, and Alabama several subordinate agents were "engaged in planting." They usually hired a manager to run their places or simply furnished the planters the money with which to grow crops.[25] Few of the major officials of the state bureaus had plantation investments, though some were involved in buying cotton from the freedman. Higher-ups in the agency, such as General Davis Tillson in Georgia and General Wager Swayne in Alabama, usually waited until they left government service before they entered planting.[26]

A few prominent officials in the Southeast acquired planting interests before they left the agency, however, and they caused the Bureau considerable embarrassment. General Ralph Ely, in charge of the Edgefield district of South Carolina, apparently had a private interest in four plantations, two of which he leased from the government at an annual rent of $5,000 each. Three other plantations, which the freedmen worked on their own account, were also under his administration and one of these he later rented to a clerk in his office. The speculations evidently interfered with his duties. Freedmen in his jurisdiction suffering from a smallpox epidemic complained that he was never available to hear their grievances concerning the local hospital, "as he was absent attending to his plantations."[27] They might also have taken note of how the planting class in his district gave him high marks for his determined efforts to make the freedmen do their "duty."[28] General Ely resigned his commission in time to avoid arrest and trial for malfeasance. Shortly afterward, he led a colony of approximately one thousand ex-slaves from South Carolina to the lumbering and agricultural settlement that missionaries and former USCT officers had recently established at New Smyrna, on the Florida Atlantic coast. The enterprise did nothing to improve Ely's reputation. An inspector for the Freedmen's Bureau believed that Ely was using some of the rations supplied by the government to pay the laborers on a plantation that the general was working in partnership with a black woman. The colony did not last long. The threat of starvation forced most of the black settlers to seek plantation work in the interior.[29]

But it was the planting activities of agents in North Carolina that caused the Freedmen's Bureau the most serious embarrassment. Practically the entire agency in that state appears to have had direct or indirect interests in rice and cotton plantations, some of which belonged to large northern syndicates.[30] Even the Bureau commissioner for the state, Colonel Eliphalet Whittlesey, had an interest in a large plantation (named "Yankee Hall") operated by one of his officials, the Reverend Horace James, who had been in charge of freedman affairs in North Carolina during the war. The involvement of North Carolina agents surfaced after an overseer shot and killed one of the laborers who was attempting to escape from disciplinary labor. Generals Steedmen and Fullerton, who were in the state at the time all of the details came out, wasted no time in publicizing the incident. When added to the numerous cases of planter-agents who diverted unused government supplies to their own plantations, the affair precipitated a shake-up in the Bureau. Fifteen Bureau agents in North Carolina, including Whittlesey, were relieved of duty and court-martialed, although most of them were eventually acquitted.[31] In May 1866 General Howard prohibited Bureau agents from acquiring plantation interests within the limits of their jurisdiction. He was upset by the accusations against his agents. He thought they were being unfairly singled out. "All I can say," he explained to the president, "is that a great many—in fact nearly all—the officers of the government have invested their funds in planting or something else."[32] He might have had General Steedman himself in mind, for it was reported that the inspector was "largely interested in a plantation in Arkansas, which [was] worked by Negroes."[33]

But Freedmen's Bureau agents who speculated in plantations on the side differed from most Yankee planters only in their official positions. It bears repeating that northern cotton growers as a class were usually young professional and businessmen of good education. At the risk of oversimplification, one might say that the typical Yankee planter in the lower South in these years was probably a thirty-two-year-old lawyer from New England who had attended college and was just getting his career launched when the firing on Fort Sumter interrupted his plans.

One fact stands out: very few laborers and farmers from the North took advantage of the opportunities in southern cotton plantations during and shortly after the war. Only 5 percent of the northern planting class appear to have been farmers. (Appendix, table 3.) There was much talk at this time about how the South was soon to be flooded with mechanics and yeomen from the free states. There was also no end to schemes for planting the South with colonies of the "bone and sinew" of northern society. Occasionally these projects had successful outcomes, for every now and then one runs across reports of southern colonies of northern farmers, some of whom had combined their resources to operate cotton plantations successfully.[34] Yet such colonies were rare, rarer even than the handful of Yankee farmers who turned up on plantations in this period. Perhaps the explanation lies in the relative prosperity of northern agriculture during the war, when the European demand for American wheat increased the profits of farmers substantially, particularly in the Midwest. Many northern agriculturalists must have asked themselves what advantage there was in abandoning a good business for the promise of a better one. "No person as a 'Speculation' can afford to leave Iowa for any other region on Earth," one of her farming sons allowed. American farmers have seldom migrated to new territory when times were flush at home.[35]

Even if farmers had been in a mood to pack up and move, it is doubtful whether many of them could have afforded the luxury of a plantation speculation. Only relatively well-off farmers and laborers had the seed capital with which to begin a farm in the West;[36] fewer still could have borne the expenses of operating a cotton plantation. Even though the price of cotton land was depressed right after Appomattox, a considerable outlay of money was required to purchase and feed the stock, buy seed and implements, and pay and supply the laborers: estimates of yearly operating expenses, exclusive of rent or purchase costs, ran anywhere from $20,000 for a 500-acre plantation to over $50,000 for a 1,000-acre place along the Mississippi River.[37] Only a limited number of persons could absorb these expenses. Young farmers and mechanics who counted their capital in the hundreds of dollars were not able to take advantage of plantation speculations even in the best of times.[38] The only openings they found on cotton plantations were as overseers or even share-croppers, usually for Yankee planters.[39] Thus, this crusade to modernize southern cotton cultivation was undertaken largely by men who had little practical acquaintance with agriculture. Several Yankee planters could point to some practical farming experience and some might even have been gentlemen farmers, but most had no knowledge of farm management. It remained to be seen how they would adjust to the responsibilities of operating a large cotton plantation, where the work force sometimes numbered in the hundreds.

If the farming element among the Yankee planter class was disproportionately small, the same was not true for moneyed men. There are many indications that "substantial" businessmen were heavily interested in cotton plantations during and after the war. Some were older businessmen who had rented out their factories and wanted to retire in the South, partly for reasons of climate and health.[40] John Murray Forbes, who had diverted his profits from the China trade into western railroads, in 1865 intended to establish a settlement on the St. Johns River in northern Florida, along the lines of the Port Royal experiment (in which he had taken a large interest). It would be a "combination of Sea Island planting and a Sanatorium." The idea of a Florida colony was "an old dream of mine," he explained, "as I expect to pass the last winters of my life in some such climate."[41] Northern creditors of southern planters, on the other hand, were more interested in protecting old investments than in making new ones. They consequently felt they were "entitled to preference" from the federal leasing commissioners for the leases of plantations on which they held mortgages.[42] Several successful businessmen from Milwaukee, Wisconsin, moreover, became substantial planters in the area of Natchez, Mississippi, in 1864. Transplanted easterners, they had taken a large part in the development of the Badger State and had made "considerable personal fortunes" out of land speculation, flour milling, merchandising, banking, railroads, construction, breweries, and utilities. They were looking to diversify their portfolios.[43]

Sometimes northern business companies acquired plantation interests, and on an extensive scale. A produce commission merchant from Albany, New York, at one time had control of eleven plantations on the South Carolina Sea Islands. One northern company paid $100,000 in gold for an 18,000-acre Georgia Sea Island and intended to bring in 300 German immigrants to raise long-staple cotton.[44] These companies usually sent out agents to operate their plantations. One engine manufacturer from Indiana said that his motive in purchasing a plantation was as much to put a trusted agent "in the way of making money as anything. He is a faithful man, and has been in our employ for a long time. This is to be his reward."[45]

The commission house of Hoyt, Sprague & Company was probably the largest plunger in southern cotton plantations. The company was the New York firm of the youthful senator from Rhode Island, William Sprague IV, whose great wealth had earlier helped him win the governor's chair and the hand of Kate Chase, daughter of Secretary of Treasury Salmon P. Chase. The Sprague family fortune was in textile mills, and throughout the war the senator had fretted about how to keep them supplied with cotton. His hand could be seen in the early maneuvers to turn Port Royal over to private business interests. Although he prided himself on being the "first volunteer of the war," on at least one occasion he resorted to treason in order to keep his spindles running, helping to outfit a Confederate agent with the arms and ammunition necessary for the purchase of some Texas cotton.[46] Sprague's cotton operations after the war were no less substantial for being within the limits of the law. He had a large speculation going in Alabama in the summer following Appomattox. One of his partners in a scheme to buy up Confederate cotton was George Spencer, a future carpetbag senator from Alabama. Spencer figured "to make at least fifty-thousand dollars" out of the operation, but he would be "satisfied with half that amount."[47] Senator Sprague did not confine his southern investments to cotton. Through his New York partner, Edwin Hoyt, he was the largest purchaser of city lots at the Direct Tax sales in Fernandina, Florida, and the owner of several large Florida sawmills that he put in the charge of ex-Confederate generals.[48] But his largest southern investment was doubtless the leasing of thirteen river-bottom plantations in Mississippi and Louisiana shortly after the war. Again he relied on the management services of a former Confederate General, this time John Floyd King, son of Thomas Butler King, of the Georgia Sea Islands.[49]

The senator from Rhode Island was not the only New England textile manufacturer who resorted to growing cotton, either for himself or for the highest bidder. The lords of the loom were beginning to worry about their growing dependence on Indian cotton during the war. John Payson Williston, who had a large interest in cotton mills in western Massachusetts, was president of the Northampton Cotton Company, which leased plantations in Louisiana in 1864. He was also a shareholder in the Free Labor Cotton Company, which was founded by Edward Atkinson, a treasurer of six northern textile mills. Counting among its subscribers some of the leading cotton interests in Massachusetts, and capitalized at $115,000, Atkinson's company also operated in the Mississippi Valley during the war.[50] The largest textile baron of them all, Amos A. Lawrence, may have had an indirect interest in cotton plantations. His nephew, Frank W. Lawrence, who was among the original missionaries sent to Port Royal by the Boston Education Commission, had purchased two plantations at the first of the Direct Tax sales on the Sea Islands. At first skeptical of the venture because he feared the possibility of black land ownership, Amos Lawrence was soon prepared to advance money "for any other ventures in land which the younger Lawrence might see fit to undertake." He was certain the land would never decline in value.[51]

Port Royal, South Carolina, served as the base of operations for many northern cotton-growing companies. The syndicate for which Edward S. Philbrick was the agent was the largest of these, controlling some eight thousand acres of Sea Island cotton land.[52] But other northern concerns were not negligible operations. The Port Royal Cotton Company controlled 3,400 acres in the Sea Islands and boasted a capitalization of $150,000, apparently supplied by business interests in New York City. Its president and chief plantation superintendent was Dr. William J. Randolph, who had served in Thomas Wentworth Higginson's black regiment, the First South Carolina Volunteers. and had taken advantage of the military provision of the Direct Tax laws.[53] Another large outfit in the area was the Sea Island Cotton Company. It was the creation of a few wool growers from upstate New York and had a subscribed capital of $74,000. This amount quickly grew after the partners roped in the former

Republican congressman from their district, Alfred Ely of Rochester, who had been one of the picnickers captured by the Confederates at First Manassas. Ely had little trouble marketing the company's securities. In 1865 the firm paid a 25 percent dividend to its shareholders. The Sea Island company also added steadily to the land it controlled. What it could not buy directly at the Direct Tax sales, it leased or bought from other tax purchasers, mainly army veterans. On occasion it simply made the military purchasers agents of the company.[54]

Forming cotton-growing companies was a popular business during the war. Joint stock companies seemed to spring up overnight as news spread of the fabulous profits to be made in leasing plantations in the Mississippi Valley. Small investors in towns throughout the Midwest hurriedly put together cotton-growing companies and sent their agents south. Capitalized at $150,000, the Bellefontaine Cotton Company of Ohio wanted to lease four to five thousand acres of cotton land. Another Ohio company claimed to represent the investments of many farmers. Kenosha, Wisconsin, alone had two cotton companies which were said to be "composed of some of the most 'careful and substantial citizens.' "[55] The Ann Arbor Cotton Company represented the interests not only of the citizens of Ann Arbor, but of many officials of the University of Michigan. The company was the creation of Alexander Winchell, a professor of geology, zoology, and botany at the university. Though he had little personal capital to put into the venture, he discovered that raising money and getting a leave of absence from the university were not the serious obstacles he had feared. The Board of Regents "very readily" granted him a leave, and there were "plenty of men of capital who will furnish the means and go shares with me." The university regent to whom he had made a formal request for time off even subscribed money to Winchell's venture. The president of the university, Erastus O. Haven, signed on as secretary of the concern and was "one of the large stockholders in the Ann Arbor Cotton Company." In 1864 the company leased four Tensas Parish, Louisiana, plantations comprising two thousand acres in all.[56]

The Ann Arbor Cotton Company's plantation interests along the Mississippi River grew when it amalgamated with the "Association for Mutual Protection." This was a group of fifty planters on Lake Providence peninsula who had banded together for self-defense after General William T. Sherman had forbidden the use of his troops for the protection of government lessees. It included J. P. Williston's Northampton Cotton Company, a former president of the State Normal University of Illinois, and assorted lessees in the area.[57] The association had a stand of forty rifles and had "pledged the military ten percent of our crop for insurance against further raids."[58] Its constitution "embraced only the subject of protection from guerillas," but it was soon operating as a regular business company, with profit-sharing arrangements and procedures for executing plantation leases in the name of the "Planter's Association." It controlled twenty thousand acres and represented an investment of $150,000.[59]

The Sea Island Cotton Company also eventually enlarged its sphere of operations. Its officers had been troubled by the lack of specific authorization in its New York charter to grow cotton, and they wanted to get the statutes changed.[60] In 1866 they merged the Sea Island Company into the United States Cotton Company after securing "a contract with certain capitalists in Europe for a large amount of money to be used in a general cotton business." Old stockholders were awarded 50 percent additional shares in the new company, which hired a former Confederate general to market its securities in Europe. The United States Cotton Company apparently swallowed up the Port Royal Cotton Company as well. Captain William J. Randolph became one of the new concern's plantation superintendents.[61]

The forming of combinations to grow cotton was not confined to large investors. Nearly every Yankee plantation enterprise seemed to involve at least two partners, and usually three or four. They frequently styled themselves "John Lynch & Co.," "Smith, Wood & Co.," and other such designations, but they were invariably joint partnerships gotten up by the interested planters in order to specify in writing the division of the profits.[62] Sometimes these modest operations joined with similar northern enterprises, buying or renting adjoining plantations and forming themselves into small colonies. They did not have in view any business purposes. They simply desired agreeable society and the means for mutual defense, if that proved necessary. Thus there were the "Ohio Colony" in Mississippi, the "Gordon Colony" in northern Florida, and two or three like settlements of Illinois men in Dallas County, Alabama, to name only a few.[63] These small partnerships, moreover, generally consisted of friends and neighbors from the North and frequently of associates from the military. A few company commanders might join their battalion commander in a go at raising cotton, or a Union general might lead a group of his staff officers into the business. There were many variations.[64] But one fact stands out: wherever a group of Yankees were planting together it was likely that at least one pair of brothers, brothers-in-law, or cousins was among the number, occasionally shuttling in and out as relatives vied for positions on the plantation. There were some plantation ventures that were entirely family enterprises, or rather expressions of the American form of family capitalism.[65]

The partnerships and business combinations that Yankee planters formed so frequently were usually a matter of financial necessity. Except for the large investors, the young newcomers were generally men of "moderate means—not such as are called poor men or are they wealthy." Often they had to sell houses, mills, factories, and medical practices in order to "raise the means for this enterprise." If they had been in the military they might have put away a few thousand dollars from their salaries.[66] But whatever the source of their individual wealth they commonly found it expedient to combine their means with that of others in order to secure adequate operating capital. Even then they often had to look for some outside support. With his usual perspicacity, John Murray Forbes advised one young New Englander who was excited about cotton-raising to "get enough friends to unite with you to buy a considerable tract and let you manage it for a certain percentum of profits (if any!)."[67] If one moved in the right circles, enticing well-to-do friends into the venture was not a serious problem, for "there was no lack of capital to back such enterprises." Usually, though, it was some rich uncle, brother-in-law, or parent of one of the planting partners who acted as the banker.[68] Harriet Beecher Stowe, for example, sank $10,000 in a plantation venture in which her son had taken an interest after having been approached by two Connecticut veterans who had a line on a place in Florida but lacked the means to operate it. Frederick Stowe had become an alcoholic shortly after his discharge from the army for a head wound suffered at Gettysburg, and Mrs. Stowe thought that a stint at cotton-raising "might straighten Fred out."[69]

Thus far we have only treated the identities of the northern planters and given some idea of the types of business combinations and financial arrangements that characterized their operations.

But what of their motives? Obviously Harriet Beecher Stowe had more than purely a financial interest in her plantation investment. But she was exceptional. Almost every other northerner who invested in cotton plantations in these years looked chiefly to the speculative aspects. With the price of cotton at times reaching as high as $2.50 a pound, with good land selling and renting for a pittance, and with northern propagandists publicizing the fabulous profits awaiting men of enterprise, it is small wonder that Yankees saw cotton-raising as a lottery that had no losers. The newcomers commonly calculated their profits in the tens, even hundreds, of thousands of dollars, with the conviction of men who knew that such a chance comes but once in a lifetime. Cautious investors tried to guard against excessive optimism, exaggerating the costs of cultivation here, lowering the price of cotton there, but appetites for huge gains got the best of even their judgment. No one appears to have been satisfied with less than 100 percent return on his money. Everybody expected to make fortunes, and this was all the inducement most Yankees needed to try the experiment in free-labor cotton.[70] Cotton-planting, to most of them, was "a short road to wealth."[71]

The speculative motive was particularly strong during the war, especially in the Mississippi Valley, where officials had done everything they could to make the leasing of government plantations attractive.[72] The prevalence of speculators is too well known to require repetition, but it is helpful to keep in mind that the spirit in the West, and in Port Royal after 1863 for that matter, was largely an extension of the commercial spirit in the North. The war years were admittedly a time of great sacrifice, of "grand movements which are destined to signalize the age and purify the character of the strongest republic . . . that ever lived." But they were also a time when "keen and enterprising men having breadth of view and business sagacity are finding abundant occupation and abundant reward."[73] This fact was not lost on those northerners who came of age in the 1860s. Just as the crusade for human freedom neared culmination and swept before it a nation hitherto indifferent to any war aim save that of Union, some young idealists began to turn their thoughts in more worldly directions. One Wisconsin man started to wonder in the latter phases of the war whether he and his friends had overstated the case against "the 'almighty dollar' being the sole thing worthy of human worship" and had "fooled away valuable time trying to 'get up' brilliant editorials, and make 'powerful' 'briefs.'" After mature reflection on the subject, he now went "most emphatically for amending the old prayer 'give me neither poverty nor riches,' by striking the last two words. Yes, give me the dollar! and all other things shall be added unto me." He was seriously considering emigrating to the South.[74]

The speculative interest in cotton-growing was closely related to economic developments in the North during and shortly after the war. Throughout most of the war, times were unusually flush for northern businessmen. Rapidly advancing prices (the annual rate of inflation for the war period was almost 20 percent) boosted profits enormously because a variety of causes were acting to force down real wages. Lucrative war contracts and fluctuating gold prices created many instant millionaires. But the prosperity of the period was largely artificial. In most industrial sectors of the northern economy the rates of growth had actually fallen off. Profits were up everywhere, even in those industries such as textiles that were operating well below capacity, but nowhere were they so promising as in the areas of speculation. Relatively small amounts of capital went into expanding industrial capacity, but a large volume entered the stock market, the commodity market, the gold market, and gambling operations in general.[75] Cotton-growing in the South was one of the more attractive gambles of the period.

Sometimes speculators on Wall Street found plantation investments crucial to their operations. One of these investors was Langdon Williams, who bankrolled the cotton enterprise of two cousins in Louisiana, James D. Waters and George G. Klapp, of whom more later. Williams had looked upon his plantation speculation as a "campaign" and was "willing to abide the chances of war."[76] He was therefore doubly thankful for the profits from the 1864 crop, for the windfall allowed him to expand his operations at home. "I have been 'running a muck' with the money you sent up," he informed his cousins. "Have been buying gold stocks and coal stocks in the most promiscuous way." He was involved with a stockjobber who formed "many of these companies," got the stock at first prices, and then sold out most of his interest when the stock rose. "I have gone in 6 or 8 of these companies," Williams wrote.[77] But in this business the danger of being overextended was constant. When the price of gold began to decline as Union victory approached, Williams had difficulty raising the capital for planting operations in 1865. Since most of his certificates were already held as collateral for his many stock purchases (which he was unwilling to unload), he had to borrow on his father's stock in order to honor the first drafts from Louisiana. "I feel it to be (in these times) neck or nothing," he explained.[78] For the remainder of the planting season Williams manipulated his own securities deftly enough to worry through, and as the business climate dampened further after Appomattox, he had all the more reason to appreciate his cotton investments. He discovered that "there does not seem any prospect of another business."[79]

The thing that made cotton-planting so attractive to the speculative investor was that it seemed altogether more certain than any other gamble then available. The speculative mania of the war years created a great deal of investment uncertainty. Not only fluctuating prices but the conviction that a crash must inevitably accompany a return of peace discouraged businessmen from enlarging their legitimate operations. In order to hedge against inflation and the expected downturn in trade, the prudent entrepreneur sank his surplus profits in nonperishable goods and land.[80] The wool-growing interests that had formed the Sea Island Cotton Company knew that the unusually large profits from wool production and manufacture of the war period could not continue indefinitely. "When the War closes," one company official wrote, "the chances are that there will be a general bust up of affairs and we must be prepared for it so that we can pay all demands at any time."[81] One safeguard against the eventual crash was to divert profits into a related line of business, particularly if it held hope for a continuation of lucrative returns. Two New Yorkers who had raised wool in California during the war were "now anxious to transfer California enterprise into Alabama" and wanted five to ten thousand acres of plantation land.[82] Similar calculations may have influenced the merchants, bankers, and grain dealers from Milwaukee and its vicinity who rushed to lease plantations near Natchez not long after the area fell into Union hands. One Wisconsin businessman wrote to his brother stationed in Mississippi: "I hope you . . . may find your way to make a *pile*. Money will be a very convenient thing to have a year or two hence when the smash comes." All the talk about how the South was destined to displace the West in the affections of investors and immigrants was also making northern land speculators somewhat nervous. One large landowner in Minnesota thought seriously of moving south because he feared "the War would open up such a vast extent of attractive country that would draw much eastern and foreign emigration that would else come here."[83] If there was a coming thing among smart investors in this period, it would appear to have been the cotton lands of the South.

It is misleading, however, to emphasize unduly the presence of large capitalists and prosperous businessmen in the Yankee planter class. There is a sense in which we are justified in speaking of the push of distress as well as the pull of opportunity in accounting for the motives that gave rise to this movement. The fact is that there were many northern cotton growers who had gone south partly for reasons of economic hardship, for the war ruined more people than it made rich. The rising cost of living during the war years was no advantage to wage earners, salaried workers, and individuals on fixed incomes. "All we consumed went up in price," one prospective northern immigrant complained.[84] A Massachusetts engineer who was in the market for a cotton plantation had found his "expenses increased in a much greater ratio than my income. For this reason I desire to make a change." An Illinois family that leased a place in Mississippi had "the acquisition of years" swept away by the change in the currency.[85] Whitelaw Reid knew the difficulties of trying to live on a fixed income. He simply could not survive on his salary from the Cincinnati *Gazette*, for which he was a celebrated war correspondent. His postwar tour of the South as well as his position as librarian for the U.S. Congress were attempts to supplement a shrinking income. His cotton-growing enterprises in Louisiana a short while later, moreover, appear to have been an effort to put his financial difficulties permanently behind him.[86]

This way of looking at cotton-planting appealed strongly to Alexander Winchell, the geology professor who organized the Ann Arbor Cotton Company. A widower with three young children, Winchell had learned that "poverty is a threefold curse to the man of books." He found that lack of books, materials, and opportunity to travel hampered his scientific studies. Inflation had shrunk his regular professional income "to about one half its former value. I can barely make ends meet," he complained.[87] The establishment of the plantation leasing system in the Mississippi Valley seemed providential. Cotton-planting offered rewards more generous than any scientific or scholarly grant then available, and one or two good seasons, he thought, would enable him "to accomplish the main objects of [his] life." His obligations in the circumstances seemed clear. "If by devoting a year or two solely to money making I could clear any such sum [$14,500] ," Winchell confided in his diary, "it is my duty to do it." Many other educators felt the same, or at least concluded that their shrunken salaries seemed puny next to the fabulous profits of growing cotton.[88]

To the victims of inflation must be added the casualties of bankruptcy. The war began with an industrial and financial recession. The crisis lasted only until 1862, being quickly followed by a prosperity that some at the time thought embarrassing, but in 1861 alone it caused two thousand more commercial failures than had occurred during the Panic of 1857. Hardest hit were small businessmen.[89] One of these was a housebroker from Boston who accounted himself "worth in good property $100,000" when the war commenced. The crash ruined him. In 1861 his expensive residence "was *sold at auction*, by my creditors *over my head*, and myself, wife and children turned [out] *pennyless*." He came to Port Royal in 1863, apparently not entirely out at the elbows, bought a plantation at the tax sales and John Fripp's beautiful house from a military purchaser, and began doing business in an active way, cultivating cotton, selling lumber and ice, renting rooms, and merchandising to the freedmen. By 1866 he owned at least three Sea Island plantations and seemed on the way to financial recovery.[90]

There were other northerners who went into planting during the war in order to repair "fortunes ruined by this rebellion."[91] The Waters family of Salem, Massachusetts, had been drawn south for this very reason. William D. Waters, the father of the clan, was descended from a family that had a distinguished place in Salem's mercantile, maritime, and military history. Declining a college education in order to enter trade, he went to sea, first as a supercargo and then as a captain, retiring once his family began to grow. He thereupon founded first a cotton mill and then the Aqueduct and Turnpike Company, the chief supplier of Salem's water. His success won him two terms in the state legislature, and the family seemed to be prosperous until city authorities, during the war, decided to change from well water to pond water. The decision threw the Waters enterprise into insolvency proceedings and the matter was even taken up by the state legislature.[92]

The fall of the House of Waters dispersed the family throughout the South. Their plantation investments were far-flung. James D. Waters, one of the older sons, joined his Philadelphia cousin, George G. Klapp, in operating leased plantations in Concordia Parish, Louisiana, from 1864 to 1868, and they were spelled at various times by their younger brothers. In the Natchez area they met with good fortune, making the acquaintance of the Lorenzo Thomas family, who rented a neighboring plantation.[93] James Waters expected to make a great deal of money in his new situation, but he could not afford to be too voluble about his early success in Louisiana. Until his father's business (with which he had been connected) got a discharge from creditors, there was a danger that his profits from cotton-growing might be seized for the payment of old debts. "It is one blessing down here," James wrote of his new surroundings, "that I am clear entirely from that atmosphere [of debt], and the constant consciousness of obligation, which I could not avoid North."[94]

The elder Waters was initially not as successful when, in 1864, he went to South Carolina, where his youngest son, Clifford, was a government plantation superintendent. The crush of speculators at the tax sales had driven up land prices beyond his means, obliging him to search for business prospects in Florida. The family was also "full of schemes to start the shingle business in Florida and Georgia if [they could] raise the capital." In 1865, however, Waters succeeded in leasing two of Edward Philbrick's plantations, one of which he bought the following year.[95] The summit of the family's ambition was frankly "to make money," yet to do it not individually but collectively. "Our interests are all one," James Waters told his father, whom he never hesitated to supply with operating cash for the Port Royal venture. Whether in South Carolina or Louisiana, everybody's profits were intended to "forward the fortunes of the family" and enable them to "come together again."[96] They had high hopes of an eventual reunion, for they were sure that at least one of the clan would make a strike, and "if any of us do get up we will pull up the rest too, if it's a possible thing." They prided themselves on maintaining "the 'family interest' notion pretty well."[97]

The push of economic distress scarcely abated after the surrender. The slump that sober men had been expecting arrived on schedule. Early in 1865 wholesale prices dropped suddenly. The federal government helped the recession along. The ending of war contracts necessitated some economic readjustments, but the rapid liquidation of the federal deficit ("perhaps one seventh of national income") probably had a greater impact. The quick demobilization of the Union armies glutted the labor market—in realization of yet another northern apprehension—and the large influx of immigrants in 1866 and 1867 only aggravated the situation. The downturn at least had the virtue of being neither long nor severe. It lasted only until December 1867 and its effects were offset by the postwar upswing in building and railroad construction.[98] Yet the recession was hard enough on men who had to pick up careers that the war had cut short.

The economic downturn was certainly a disappointment to thousands of Union soldiers, the men comprising the majority of the northerners who entered planting after the war. They found business in the North dull as their date of discharge approached. Although they were anxious to get back home, many of them had no plans for the future and no guarantee that they could find work when they returned.[99] Freedmen's Bureau Commissioner Howard understood their situation. "Our volunteer officers are soon to leave the service," he wrote in vindication of his agents who were found to be speculating in cotton, "and like provident men generally, they seek to secure some livelihood."[100] Agents of the Freedmen's Bureau were perhaps more fortunately situated in terms of shaping their plans for civilian life than many Union officers. Most young majors and captains and colonels at the time seemed to be "speculating about the future." No one wanted to leave the service with "nothing of importance to fall back upon."[101]

The lack of civilian prospects troubled Lieutenant Colonel Charles F. Morse of the Second Massachusetts Infantry. It was galling that some of his subordinate officers had found good business positions while he had to "content [himself] for the present with looking forward to a very unsettled future."[102] Henry Lee Higginson, a fellow officer with whom Morse later teamed up in growing cotton in Georgia, was also no stranger to the vicissitudes of finding civilian employment. He had been discharged in 1864 for war wounds but had been unable to find employment in Boston, despite his Harvard education, Brahmin background, and business experience. That his father was a State Street broker undoubtedly helped young Higginson finally land a position with a Boston oil syndicate as manager of its operations in Ohio. But the job ended quickly. In the summer of 1865 he was out of work again, and having "nothing to do," he concluded that cotton-planting was an opportunity he could not pass up.[103] Higginson's postwar predicament was fairly common. Quite a few young veterans returned home only to discover that well-paying jobs were hard to come by. Captain Henry Thomas, General Lorenzo Thomas's son, realized his mistake not long after returning to the North in search of better openings. His brickyard business in Washington, D.C., was unremunerative, and he doubted that he was "Yank" enough to go into the speculations then available in government mules and wagons and come out whole. In 1866 he returned to Louisiana with his father to give cotton-raising another chance.[104] A former officer of black troops who had obtained a good overseer's job spoke for many of his class: "I think you will agree with me that I could hardly expect to do as well anywhere else as here."[105]

Possibly, professional men found the adjustment to civilian life especially difficult. Except for physicians, who had usually served as army surgeons and were therefore all the more skilled for the experience, most young professionals who had served in the army had lost valuable time and seasoning in their fields. Some of them had doubts about their ability to resume careers that the war had interrupted. Lawyers seemed particularly troubled by their prospects: legal business in the North was so flat after Appomattox that even a former U.S. senator considered trying to set up a practice in the South.[106] "Bred to the law," one Massachusetts officer explained, "I left but a small vacancy when I went away, and find on my return one or two members of the profession indifferently comfortable even in that space." He was debating whether to raise cotton and oranges in Florida, where he was stationed at the time. "I used to think that I couldn't content myself in the South," he confessed, "but if I can make any more money I may get to like it."[107]

Moneymaking was a serious matter to men who were about thirty years of age (as most of these newcomers were) and still not launched in a remunerative career. Young Union veterans realized that they had reached that stage of life when men of the American middle class were supposed to be well on their way to securing an "honorable independence." It was well understood that in most circumstances it was hard for young men to get started, but easy for them once a start had been made.[108] The thing that puzzled them was how to get it. The protagonist in Albion W. Tourgee's famous novel of southern Reconstruction said the answer was a new start in a new place. He returned from the service to find most of his law practice in the hands of competitors. He felt he was too old to begin anew. "Remember, I am over thirty now," he told his wife, "and we have only our house and the surplus of my savings in the Army . . . not anything like the competency I hoped to have secured by this time. . . ." He decided to invest his small means in a cotton plantation in North Carolina.[109]

In truth, it was this chance to secure a "competency," to be one's own man financially and in other ways, that made planting so attractive to large numbers of young professional and business men during and shortly after the war. Raising cotton was not only a way to make money but a way to make a lot of money, and thus to render oneself "independent of the weak sympathies of fellow mortals." A man might become fixed for life if only he had a modest capital, a few acquaintances of similar means and inclinations, and one or two wealthy friends or relatives willing to back the venture. This obviously was not an opportunity that young men without occupation or decent prospects could easily pass up. After all, they had grown up with an ideology that exalted the ideal of independence, and they realized that in their competitive world anyone who did not struggle to reach the top of the heap ran the risk of being buried somewhere near the bottom. At the time he was forming his cotton company, Professor Winchell could have been speaking for an entire generation of the American middle class: *"Each for himself* is the law of human scrambling."[110]

So it was not simply the push of economic distress—not simply the recessions that opened and followed the war and the inflation that came in between—that gave rise to the northern interest in southern plantations. It was also the pull of opportunity, a pull so strong that Yankees by the thousands would probably have gone south even if conditions at home had been more favorable. George C. Benham, for example, was not doing badly in his drugstore in 1865, but when an army friend showed him an estimate of what he could make in planting, Benham's business assumed a different aspect. "What a puny, sickly thing our drug store looked to me now . . . it looked *mean.*" Why plod along for twenty years in the drug business when he could gain "a fine competency" in four years in the planting business? The question seemed to answer itself.[111]

Thus, although hard times in the North were a factor of no small importance in the calculations of the newcomers, economic stringency only added urgency to a motive that was compelling in its own right. Insofar as northern planters had one overriding ambition, it was the pursuit of the main chance.

And yet the northern interest in cotton-planting occupied broader ground than merely the desire to make a quick killing. Many nonmaterial considerations entered into the decision to move south during and after the war. Even the goal of independence was not strictly a dollars and cents aspiration, though money was admittedly a large part of it. There were certain things about the social and physical basis of plantation life in the early years of emancipation that made cotton-growing appear to be an occupation that might be desirable in and of itself. Among the obvious attractions of planting were the prestige and power that usually attached to those who engaged in it and the advantage of healthy activity in a salubrious setting. To these had been added a motive that a military crusade for freedom had pronounced proper and meet: the chance to do something useful and philanthropic for a race of mankind that for over two centuries had been kept in degrading bondage.

One minor though not insignificant motive for emigrating to the South was the desire to live more simply and to escape the drabness of the office. More than one northerner gave up a professional position in order to enter into business in the cotton fields.[112] Eben Loomis jumped at the chance to be quit of his position as a computer at the United States Navy's Nautical Almanac office in Cambridge, Massachusetts, when his wife's uncle agreed to put up the capital for a southern venture. Though a scientist by training, Loomis was a nature lover by temperament. He had walked with Henry David Thoreau in Concord and had accompanied Walt Whitman through the Blue Ridge Mountains.[113] His new life as a cotton planter was rough and occasionally monotonous, "but it is not computing so I am satisfied." Fresh air was not all that he was after. He set great store by his independence. "I have nobody over me to say what salary I should get and when it shall be paid," he exulted about farming life. "If I fail I should do my own blaming, if I succeed I have myself to thank."[114]

George Benham also wanted the country life and a fuller scope for his sense of independence. But no 80-acre western farm could meet his requirements. He did not intend to exchange the monotony of filling prescriptions for the drudgery of slopping hogs. His bucolic tastes ran toward the mythic proportions of the "cavalier." He "fancied the grand sweep of an eleven-hundred-acre plantation, with a roll of laborers running up into the hundreds; riding on a fine horse, with a broad panama hat, and a ringing spur, under a Southern sky—that was the poetry of country life; that was the country life [he] had in mind."[115] Benham's fantasies must have been contagious. His neighborhood of Carroll Parish, Louisiana, had a number of northern planters who wanted to play Lord Bountiful. They styled their community the Empire of Carroll, founded a House of Hastings, and boasted often of the "notables of this Inland Empire." It was done in jest, but it nonetheless betrayed a strain of romanticism that was not uncommon among the newcomers. Only with difficulty could some northerners conceal their envy of plantation estates "fit for princes" and of the "lordly life" of the great planters.[116]

The appeal of the cavalier myth, however, was anchored in something more substantial than simple covetousness. Yankees who had lost status as well as money had special reasons for recalling fondly the leisured graces and aristocratic virtues of the old regime. Among a portion of the northern elite there was a strong resentment of the parvenues whom the fortunes of war and the cycles of business had recently pushed to the surface of American life. In Philadelphia, for example, a city that had had close ties with the large-scale planters of the Old South, a social uneasiness and a fear of the future were everywhere to be seen shortly after Appomattox. "The shoddies are the only ones who have any money," George Klapp wrote to his New England cousin, James D. Waters, who doubtless knew firsthand about such status anxiety. "The best and oldest families here are becoming reduced, and the sons are going to work in the counting houses of these very shoddyites," Klapp explained. Several of these displaced scions had larger aspirations than shopkeeping. A good bit of excitement broke out in some of the better circles of Philadelphia society whenever the subject of cotton plantations arose.[117] One of these Philadelphians suggested the reason. He said he wanted to grow cotton near Charleston, South Carolina, in order to get "clear of a class of the community [he] never admired."[118] But cotton-planting may not have been a very effective method of keeping the *nouveaux riches* at arm's length at this time. After all, several men of recent fortune were also heading south during and after the war partly with an eye toward acquiring the respectability of country gentlemen. No sooner had one "very fair specimen of the Connecticut Yankee" arrived in Natchez, Mississippi, for the purpose of planting cotton than he let it be known that he was "rather ambitious of getting into society" and wanted to be introduced around town.[119]

If some northerners were drawn to planting because of the status it might confer or restore, many others were attracted to it because of the power it promised. This had been the darker side of the cavalier myth, but perhaps the abolition of slavery had purged it of the despotic associations that had excited northern fear and repugnance before the war. In any event a host of former Union officers frankly saw in plantation lordship a way of holding on to certain aspects of military life. Often the veteran's first choice of an occupation was a commission in the regular army, even if it required a demotion in rank. "A permanent position in the army is a tempting bait to attract a young man," particularly if one's aim above all else was to "have some responsibility and not be altogether a subordinate."[120] It was hard for them to shake the habit of command that military life had ingrained in them. The experience of leading troops had changed some men almost beyond recognition. "Instead of the Bashful diffident boy that left you," an officer of black soldiers, Henry M. Crydenwise, informed his parents, "I am now a rabid strict disciplinarian accustomed to giving orders and having them obeyed and have about as much brass or as soldiers would term it, 'cheek' as the law allows." A New York colonel who commanded the militia in Memphis after its occupation, later marrying into an Alabama plantation, made a point of always galloping through the city streets—for "great men never go slowly." The bows and curtseys had "a strange effect" on him. "I don't know that I am as tall as the President but I feel a heap bigger," he wrote to his mother.[121]

Commissions in the regular army grew harder to get as the military forces were reduced to a fraction of their wartime strength. But plantation openings were plentiful enough and managing a farm of broad acres and large work forces seemed to offer possibilities for continuing to indulge habits of command acquired in the army. Thomas Wentworth Higginson, the New England abolitionist and writer who had raised the first regiment of black soldiers during the Civil War, recalled that "two years of army life . . . had so checked the desire for active literary pursuits" that he preferred to find some occupation in which he could have "the charge and government of men." His attitude, he said, "was really identical with that which led some volunteer officers to enter the regular army, and others to undertake cotton raising at the South." After the war Higginson followed a literary career anyway, but had he chosen to enter planting he would have found the transition easy.[122] One colonel of black troops who led some of his former officers and men into cotton-planting obviously had excellent advantages for making the change of command.[123]

The attractions of power also tempted several young New England patricians to shift from soldiering to planting after the surrender. These were men who before the war simply could not find an acceptable profession. None of the positions of leadership that had been the inheritance of persons of their background and temperament was any longer available to them, owing to the rise of new wealth and the democratization of the political culture. After searching for something to do, they became earnest transcendentalists and tried to obey Ralph Waldo Emerson's adjuration to cultivate the inner self while pursuing an active life. But this unattainable ideal only complicated the adjustment of young patricians to antebellum life and drove them still deeper into a morbid self-consciousness. The firing on Fort Sumter was something of "an answer to their prayers."[124] Henry Lee Higginson, a younger cousin of Thomas Wentworth Higginson, said later, "I always did long for some such War, and it came in the nick of time for me."[125] Not only did the experience of leading men in combat dispel their doubts regarding the ability of their class to assume and carry out their responsibilities as natural leaders, it also seems to have whetted their appetites for more duty along related lines. Cotton-planting was a popular enterprise among them after the war.

The war experience had other fateful consequences for these young transcendentalists. In the words of George Fredrickson, it caused them to shed "the whole Emersonian style of intellectuality." Having learned from camp life a new respect for the duty of bearing up manfully under disagreeable conditions, they had become reconciled to being useful citizens. One important aspect of this intellectual transformation, to quote Fredrickson again, was that "the War, as an experience of doing without thinking, had suggested that an unreflective activism was the best escape from the burden of self."[126]

Apparently one could bypass the military phase of the retreat from Emersonian precepts. Few New England transcendentalists agonized more painfully about their dilemma than young Clifford Waters of Salem. Raised on the writings of Emerson, Waters was not comfortable with his own emotions. On occasion he would grow enthusiastic about some question only later to feel disgusted "at having been betrayed into the slightest show of feeling."[127] Though the war made him restless, as it did many of his Harvard classmates, he never enlisted in the army; instead, he joined several of his friends who went to Port Royal after graduation in 1863 to become plantation superintendents. The Direct Tax sales of the plantations soon left him without a position and forced him to seek employment in his eldest brother's tea commission firm in Boston. He could not abide the "petty botherations" of the office. He suffered from nervous exhaustion, loss of appetite, and fainting spells, and he seemed at times near suicide. Moments of sublime exaltation would seize him and then give way to a feeling that "nothing but utter annihilation were to be desired."[128] What he needed most of all, he concluded, was "a harder and more active life, something to stir me up and make me take an interest in something besides myself." He admitted that he did not want to think, and he was sure his condition would improve if only he could "bourgeon out" as a cotton planter.[129] He eventually got the chance. He helped James Waters and George Klapp grow cotton in Louisiana during the 1865 and 1866 seasons and then assisted his father in running the family plantations at Port Royal.

Clifford Waters's desire to find suitable work did not countenance radical abolitionism. He was "very strong in his opinions of the darkies," and even after emancipation he thought not only that "they ought to be slaves but . . . also that they ought to have more protective laws than formerly."[130] The entire family seemed to hold the view that slavery was "a just and healthy institution if properly carried on."[131] They were somewhat more conservative than many men of their class and region. But if Clifford Waters had a dim view of black potentialities, his fellow plantation superintendents at Port Royal did not. Several were from abolitionist families, and most of the "Gideonites" held strong antislavery convictions. They had come south to prove beyond doubt that chaos would not result from emancipation and that the black man would work for a living. Even John Murray Forbes, the organizer of the syndicate that financed Edward Philbrick's operations, had undertaken the project more "with a view to seeing the experiment tried than to profit."[132] The missionaries who bought plantations at the tax sales admittedly had a larger pecuniary interest in black free labor than Forbes, but they too in the main were dedicated to proving that "the fundamental precept of classical economics, progress through enlightened self-interest, was altogether color-blind."[133]

There were in fact many northern plantation ventures in these years that were not business enterprises in the narrower sense. Edward Atkinson's Free Labor Cotton Company had higher aims than merely supplying cotton to northern textile mills. J. P. Williston's Northampton Cotton Company also was no mere speculation. Williston was an old Garrisonian and had been one of the leading spirits in the New England Emigrant Aid Company.[134] George L. Stearns was another wealthy philanthropist who took a real interest in the welfare of the freedmen. He leased two plantations in Tennessee during the war. In 1869 a group of Boston abolitionists and philanthropists established a "Southern Industrial School and Labor Enterprise" on a Georgia plantation and sent the former fugitive slaves William and Ellen Craft to manage it. Even antislavery organizations entered the field. The American Missionary Association and the American Freedmen's Union Commission both purchased plantations for resale to the ex-slaves.[135]

A sincere desire to forward the interests of the freedmen was not confined to wealthy philanthropists and antislavery societies. High purpose animated several of the Yankee planters. Even the Mississippi Valley—where it was said each season that the character of the lessees was improving—could boast of northerners who were mindful of the idealistic side of their enterprises. One of these was Thomas W. Knox, the war correspondent of the New York *World*, who teamed up with a fellow journalist to lease a plantation in 1864. "As a philanthropic undertaking, it was commendable," Knox wrote of his cotton enterprise. "As a financial experiment, it promised success. We looked at the matter in all its aspects."[136] There were many other Yankee planters both during and after the war who studied the matter from more than just the financial angle. Henry Lee Higginson and his partners exemplified the highest ideals of the northern planter movement. "We had done our best to upset the social conditions at the South, and helped free the negroes," he wrote, "and it seemed fair that we should try to help in their education."[137]

A desire to help the ex-slaves with the transition to freedom also influenced the motives of several former officers of black troops. Henry M. Crydenwise, a young farmer from upstate New York, represented one of the finer types of USCT officers who entered cotton-planting. Pious and right-thinking, he had risen from private to lieutenant in a New York regiment only to throw that over for a commission in a black regiment. A higher rank was a minor reason for the decision. While he was a private in Florida, Crydenwise had a perceptive eye for the independent gestures of which the slaves were capable, and he began to teach Sunday school classes for black children. He considered the command of black troops "a great field for Christian and philanthropic labor, a field where great good may be accomplished."[138] For a few months after the war he served as a Freedmen's Bureau agent in Alabama, work in which he took a strong interest. When he was discharged in 1866 he readily accepted an offer to become a plantation overseer in Mississippi. In so doing he believed he was "directed by a wisdom greater than [his own]."[139] Of course he had financial reasons for staying in the South. Most northern planters did. But Crydenwise and men like him believed that profit and philanthropy were not incompatible. The former lieutenant of a black regiment who had walked almost the entire length of Louisiana with forty of his men in search of an eligible plantation averred that "money is the main thing, though it is not all: here is work that is to be done in bringing up the freedmen to a standard of usefulness."[140]

Robertson and Garth Wilkinson James also looked on their planting enterprises as a chance to prove that "the freed Negro under decent and just treatment can be worked to profit to employer and employee."[141] The younger brothers of William and Henry James, they had received a remarkable education in Europe and America under the guidance of their father, Henry James, Sr., the Swedenborgian philosopher. "Above all they were taught that a mere money success was 'vulgar' and that they must never let themselves be 'gobbled up' by business or a profession." Schooled as well in New England abolitionism, chiefly at the academy of Frank Sanborn, a financial backer of John Brown, they enlisted as officers in two of the first black regiments, Garth as the adjutant with the Fifty-fourth Massachusetts and Robertson as a lieutenant with the Fifty-fifth. Garth was "vastly attached to the Negro-soldier cause," and he seems to have responded as positively to camp life as did other young New England intellectuals.[142] After their discharge Garth and Robertson joined five other Massachusetts men, mostly ex-Union officers, to form the Gordon colony, the Yankee planting community in northern Florida that they named in honor of the Massachusetts general, George H. Gordon, a brother-in-law of one of the planters. The enterprise had their father's financial blessing and a utopian purpose that set it apart from many plantation ventures of its kind. The young James boys (they were not yet twenty-one) intended to prepare the freedmen "to take part in the new heaven and the new earth" that Henry James, Sr., prophesied would "swim into reality" after slavery was abolished. In the eyes of some of its supporters the Gordon colony was an attempt to achieve "Swedenborg's New Jerusalem on earth" by means of the scientific principles of Charles Fourier.[143]

The James brothers were not entirely alone in this design. The South in these years attracted its share of professional visionaries. A surgeon to various black regiments, John Milton Hawks, had joined with associates from Port Royal in 1865 to organize the Florida Land and Lumber Company. The company attempted to establish a freedmen's colony in New Smyrna, Florida, presumably patterned after the cooperative community Hawks had tried to establish in California in 1851.[144] The lady whom some credited with starting the war, Harriet Beecher Stowe, did not have in mind "a mere worldly enterprise" when she financed her son Frederick's plantation. "I have had for many years a longing to be more immediately doing Christ's work on earth," she wrote to her brother. Her sympathies were with "that poor people whose cause in words I have tried to plead," and she now meant to do something to improve their lot.

Her sister Catharine Beecher was flirting with more grandiose schemes. She had a plan for establishing in each southern state a model agricultural institution run solely by women. The institutions would be based on the most advanced ideas of domestic industry.[145] Edward Daniels was yet another abolitionist with visionary ambitions for the reconstructed South. Having served as the state geologist of Wisconsin before the war and as a Union colonel during the war, Daniels in 1868 bought the Virginia estate once owned by George Mason, a founding father of the republic. Daniels was motivated by a desire to teach the freedmen the principles of scientific farming. He later organized his plantation along the lines of the cooperative community at Ripon, Wisconsin, where he had briefly lived in early life.[146]

The utopian vision certainly moved Charles Stearns. He was an old Garrisonian abolitionist and nonresistant from Massachusetts who had been a conductor on the Underground Railroad during his student days at Oberlin College. In the 1840s he had worked among black people in Canada and Michigan and had traveled as an evangelical missionary in Kentucky and Tennessee. He had once even gone to jail in Hartford, Connecticut, for his pacifist principles. These he had soon abandoned when he moved to Kansas in the 1850s, where border ruffians made things too warm for him to turn the other cheek. Stearns spent the war years in Colorado building up a prosperous business and agitating for freedom.[147] He had concluded well before the firing on Fort Sumter that when slavery ceased "it would be the duty of abolitionists to labor for the elevation of its former victims."[148] In 1866, together with some antislavery friends from Colorado, he bought a 1,500-acre plantation in Columbia County, Georgia, not far from the city of Augusta. Stearns was still enough of a nonresistant at this time to pledge his determination to prove "the superiority of moral means over brute force" in the governing of men. He also saw his plantation investment as a useful experiment for testing the practicability of the "cooperative principle." At least since the time of his editorship of a labor-reform journal in the 1840s, Stearns had been troubled by "the vast discrepancy between the profits of labor, and of capital," and he now meant to do something about redressing this imbalance.[149]

It would strain credulity to suggest that benevolent intentions toward the freedmen typified the purposes of the vast majority of Yankee cotton growers in these years. To be sure, nearly all northern planters tended to see eye to eye on the necessity for the ex-slaves to spend some time under the supervision of men like themselves. But whatever there was of genuine goodwill in northern paternalism was distinctly confined to the idealists. For every Charles Stearns there may have been ten like B. H. True, a Union captain who took up planting in Georgia after Appomattox. He told a congressional committee that he felt "as friendly toward" black people "as anyone can," yet he confessed that "there is an antagonism which we all have against the race; that I cannot get rid of; I do not believe any man can."[150] His was probably the usual attitude, judging from the many references to "niggers" and "darkies" in the letters of these men. It is saying nothing new to point out that most of the victors were in their own way as thoroughly imbued with the convictions and sentiments of white supremacy as were the vanquished.

But many Yankee planters had been made abolitionists "by the inexorable logic of events," and they tended to assume that their opinions on race were irrelevant in the economic sphere. This fact alone distinguished them in important ways from their southern counterparts. The new men often said that they welcomed emancipation and accepted the idea of black free labor. Their public statements of aims frequently expressed a desire to aid and protect the ex-slaves, to seek "the mutual profits of the freedmen and ourselves."[151] There was no conscious hypocrisy in this position. A belief in the inferiority of blacks did not prevent their acknowledging that the ex-slaves were human beings and thus entitled to enjoy those natural rights that were the birthright of every free laborer in the modern age—namely, the right to make contracts, accumulate property, be secure in family relations, and bargain for economic advantage in the marketplace. In time a portion of the Yankee planting class would come to advocate giving the former slaves civil rights, and a few would even say that they should be granted political rights as well, the aim in both cases being to enable the freedmen to become more secure in their natural rights.[152] But eventually another, and we may suspect, larger, portion of the same class would move in the opposite direction. Once the freedmen showed they were able to use the market to further their own interests—as against those of the new masters —Yankee paternalism would degenerate into a racism every bit as spiteful and vindictive as that of the old masters, and maybe more so. Most northern planters resented anything that got in the way of making money, which was the reason they came south in the first place.

But this is to get ahead of our story. At first, most of the newcomers were too flush with optimism at their prospects for easy riches and too confident in their abstract sense of justice to question for a moment the compatibility of their racial views with their free-labor faith. Nor did they think to question the compatibility of their own self-interest with the cause of moral progress. If there was one moral certitude that nearly all the newcomers shared, it was the free-soil conviction that "material and moral developments were but two sides of the same coin."[153] Yankee planters never doubted that they were true pioneers of free labor, evangelists of a more excellent way. Like the propagandists at home, they felt sure that their contributions to the economic well-being of the South would improve the condition of every class and race in the former Confederacy, expedite the progress of Reconstruction, and lay the foundation for true intersectional harmony. Had they not already given the cotton industry a significant impetus by showing the South that they were not afraid to invest their means in the experiment of black free labor? They thought so. The faith of Yankee planters was simple. Henry Lee Higginson put it tersely: "Northern men and money is [*sic*] needed. That is all."[154]

Northern planters often came south with a determination to introduce improved methods of husbandry. Prevailing opinion had it that "by applying the ways of the northern farmer to the southern plantations, much better results could be attained." The introduction of innovations, they thought, was some guarantee of large profits.[155] Many newcomers were not satisfied with the primitive agriculture that they believed characterized the cotton South. Some intended to practice deep plowing, to replace the heavy "slave hoe" with the lighter northern variety, and to experiment with the latest labor-saving machinery. There were even expectations that enterprising Yankees might one day invent a mechanical cotton picker. A few newcomers thought of diversifying southern agriculture and of trying to grow more cereal and garden crops, but most were too infatuated with cotton to do so.[156] Some of the large cotton-growing companies apparently attempted to rationalize the cotton-marketing system or at least to bypass the antebellum factors who had marketed the crop in the past. The United States Cotton Company had plans for "securing a share of the profit usually absorbed by the middle men who had hitherto moved the products of southern industry." Individual planters experimented more or less with the marketing of their own crops, but usually with little success.[157]

A few Yankees intended to reconstruct the South "on a more substantial basis than 'niggers and cotton.' "[158] They believed in developing "all the resources of these states." Albert T. Morgan and his brother had large ambitions for the Yazoo Delta in Mississippi. Former Union officers from Wisconsin, they believed that the South would rapidly fill up with thrifty immigrants now that slavery had been destroyed. The Morgans counted themselves fortunate in having the opportunity "to precede if [they] could not lead, this vast host, in the work of laying the foundations of this new empire by building canals, railroads, and other facilities for its development." They never did launch their projected railroad, but other Yankee planters had some success in diversifying their investments. A Union general and state senator from Ohio, Willard Warner, went from planting in Alabama to iron-manufacturing in Tennessee. His investments were extensive.[159] Other northern planters, moreover, had schemes for establishing national banks in their localities, each in the confidence that his new home was destined to be an "important point." James Waters and George Klapp wanted to establish such an institution in Natchez, Mississippi. Henry Thomas was sure that the venture would be of "great benefit to the people in Natchez, and to the country, besides offering . . . various chances of little 'specks,' in the shape of picking up sundry bales of cotton, and little acres of land at great bargains."[160] Langdon Williams vetoed the idea because he feared the country was heading for a general smashup under Republican rule. He was more confident that the main chance lay in setting up southern franchises for the horseshoe manufacturing company in which he was interested.[161] Levi Blossom, a prominent lawyer from Milwaukee who arrived in the area as a lessee in 1864, eventually did get around to establishing the Agricultural Bank of Natchez. However, with most Yankee planters the chartering of banks and the building of railroads were more of a vision than a reality. About the only economic diversification that any of them succeeded in promoting was the establishment of sawmills, gristmills, and stores on their plantations.[162]

There is another important fact about the Yankee planter movement that should not go unmentioned. Very few northern cotton growers intended to remain permanently in the former Confederacy. It made no difference whether they were abolitionists or transcendentalists, veterans addicted to the habit of command or city men fed up with the routine of the office. Practically everyone planned to return north sooner or later. Even those newcomers who aspired to the graces of rural gentility hoped to set themselves up back home before too much time had elapsed. George Benham, who wanted to become a southern planter in the grand style, was thinking of only a four-year residence, enough time to secure his "competency." [163] He was probably typical, although we should guard against exaggerating the transience of these men. Several northerners, such as the Morgans, considered making their future in the South, and still more wanted to wait and see. Alexander Winchell expected in 1863 that sometime soon the confiscated and abandoned lands that he and others were leasing from the federal government would be offered for sale. He therefore thought his chances were rather good for purchasing "a permanent foothold." His imagination sketched in the details: "And then there will be the reorganization of society—there must be public duties to perform and men to perform them and so on . . . who can penetrate the possibilities of the future?" he asked himself. No doubt many northern planters were trying to hedge their bets in the expectation that opportunities of a more permanent sort might one day open before them. [164]

Many of the newcomers, however, were consciously on their way to doing something else. General Francis P. Blair, Jr., was not really a Yankee, but he represents a viewpoint all too common among the emigrants to the cotton districts. His wealth nearly exhausted by the war, he formed a cotton-growing company in 1865 and sent his brother-in-law to manage a leased plantation in Louisiana. Blair said he was fed up with politics (he had been a Republican congressman from St. Louis, Missouri, before the war) and wanted to return to the life of a private citizen. The feeling was short-lived. By the beginning of 1866 he was hoping "to do well with the cotton plantation and have enough to indulge my own predilections in the next Presidential canvass." [165] Many northern planters, in fact, wanted to strike a vein in order to set themselves up at home in another line of business. One Massachusetts woman wrote of her friends in the South, "The best wish anyone can give them [is that they] will make their fortune and come home to New England to enjoy it." [166] And if the hope of an alternative career did not make the Yankee planter think of his planting experience as a short one, an aversion to southern culture did. "Living in the South is *not* living at the North by a great deal," explained one northerner who was considering cotton-growing. "It will be impossible for me to get accustomed to things, or rather the *lack* of things here." Not even General Adelbert Ames and his wife could find a way to fit the South into their long-range plans, even though he served as carpet-bagger U.S. senator and governor of Mississippi and bought a plantation there during Reconstruction. When Mrs. Ames reflected on the "baleful climate, the lack of goodwill and refinement in the people," the absence of all features of agreeable society, she thought that she and the general should buy or build property in Cuba when and if it was annexed by the federal government and "only visit or board in the 'Sunny South' " in the meanwhile. [167] To northerners, it seems, the South was not a place where civilized people would wish to spend their lives.

It was certainly the intention of the Waters family to return to New England to enjoy their fortune. The controlling aim of their plantation speculations was to reunite the family in Salem. "How we are all scattered and when shall we all come together in old Pleasant St?" they wondered. "Something ought to come out of such an outlay of 'enterprise' and effort." [168] They did not mean to liquidate their southern investments entirely but only make them more of a sideline. "If we can only get ahead and get hold of one or two places down here and put them in charge of competent managers," Clifford Waters wrote from Louisiana, "I think that we shall be able to spend most of our time in a civilized region and only come down here for three or four months of the year." [169] To be an absentee planter was the central aspiration of most Yankee cotton growers. And northerners who could afford it seem sooner or later to have regarded their plantations as places to visit, not to live. [170] Those missionaries at Port Royal who wanted the confiscated plantations distributed among the freedmen had no stronger argument against the scheme of the tax commissioners than the fact that the "gentlemen who have recently visited Port Royal about land are tempted there *alone* by present high prices of cotton. Their object seems to be, to make the greatest amount of money in the shortest possible time, to run the lands & laborers at the exhaustive point, & be off to spend their profits elsewhere." [171] Admittedly there is persuasive logic in arguing that the lure of a new frontier, such as the South appeared to be at the time, drew many northern immigrants to the region. The promoters, businessmen, and land speculators who transferred their enterprises to the former Confederacy were indeed "testimonies to the appeal and veracity of the frontier image." [172] But the Yankees who went into cotton-planting in these years seem to have regarded the South as an exotic land or a distant colony where men went to make an easy fortune in order to return home to live in comfort. Northerners were in the South "to suck some honey," but their hive was in the North. [173]

In all this there was something reminiscent of the absentee sugar planters from the British West Indies who lived in the metropolis and only invested in the colonies. "The slave plantation represented to them a distant enterprise in which to produce high profits," Eugene Genovese writes of these English absentees; "it could not and did not represent a way of life, a home, a community." [174] Northern newcomers to the South doubtless saw their own plantation investments in the same light. They seldom intended to make cotton-growing a way of life. The southern plantation to them was largely a dollars and cents question, and perhaps a place that one visited now and then to escape the severity of northern winters. If these new planters were young men of reduced means, or bankrupt housebrokers, or Union veterans without an opening in the North, they often entered planting with "an almost desperate determination to 'make or break.' " [175] And if they were older businessmen who had already made a fortune at home, they were looking to diversify their portfolios abroad. In neither case were they permanent settlers.

How would the old masters greet the new masters? Northern speculators were familiar figures in the Old South, but never before had they come in such numbers, let alone as liberators and conquerors. What would white southerners, in particular, make of them? The answer is tied to the question of how northerners acquired their southern land.

3 Southern Expectations

Any study of the Yankee planter movement must ask how northern men acquired their financial interests in plantations. The question has a bearing on the survival of the plantation system as well as on the persistence of the old planting class. It also has significance beyond the light it sheds on the economic history of the period. It touches on how the ex-slaveholders viewed their future, how they regarded northern immigration, and how they meant to treat the newcomers. For to ask how northerners got their lands is to ask why southerners sought northern men and capital to restore the plantation economy. By and large the old planting class was extremely accommodating to the Yankee mania for southern plantations. The reasons ranged from despair to hopefulness. If some natives feared that the northern influx posed a threat to the region's identity, many others believed that the South could not only absorb the new planters, but turn them to positive advantage. Former Confederates tried to make the best of a bad bargain.

Obviously not all southern plantations passed into northern hands through normal business channels. Government sales of abandoned and confiscated lands were substantial in the South Carolina Sea Islands. At the various Direct Tax sales here during and after the war, northerners purchased anywhere from forty-one thousand to forty-seven thousand acres of plantation lands, amounting to over one-half of the plantation land that the federal government auctioned off. Exactly how many northerners bought in is hard to say, because most of the land purchased by military personnel fell immediately into the hands of northern speculators.[1] Even so, government sales of confiscated plantations were of minor importance when viewed in the larger context. They were confined chiefly to the Port Royal area, although some plantations were sold off by the government in Virginia and North Carolina.[2] And because of the uncertainty of government titles, northern purchasers did not always consider these plantations good bargains and preferred to buy directly from the old owners.[3]

There is very little evidence, moreover, that any sizable number of Yankees acquired plantations at sheriffs' sales.[4] A few carpetbaggers may have obtained land in this fashion in the 1870s, after the Panic of 1873 caused widespread distress in the planting districts. Marshall H. Twitchell, the Republican boss of Red River Parish, Louisiana, increased his landholdings substantially by buying land forfeited for the nonpayment of taxes.[5] But during the period before

Radical rule acquisitions of this sort were rare. The homestead and stay laws that the Johnsonian legislatures enacted to exempt real property from foreclosure partially account for the infrequency of forced sales, but when northern creditors were involved, federal courts were not obliged to recognize this legislation.[6] Plantation land was selling at such a low rate anyway that there was little incentive to buy in at the sheriff's office and thus risk angering the dispossessed family's neighbors. In short, most Yankees acquired their plantations from the old proprietors, for the South in general was very receptive to northern investments after Appomattox.

"It is a great mistake to suppose that northern men and northern capital are not welcome here," one southern governor told John T. Trowbridge in the summer of 1865. "They are most heartily welcome; they are invited."[7] That this was a universal sentiment among white southerners at the time is open to question, but there can be no denying that a significant element in the late Confederacy ardently desired northern men, capital, and enterprise. The elected governors of Florida, Mississippi, and South Carolina blessed the idea of northern immigration and investment. One of them advertised his readiness "to welcome with open arms abolitionists and all others who aid in settling and developing the resources of the State." Governor Lewis Parsons even toured the North to invite men and money to Alabama.[8]

From throughout the South in the early postwar years came reports of a great wish "to see men of enterprise and means from the North and [East] to settle among us, and lead off in works of permanent utility."[9] This kind of talk, which began much earlier than most historians have realized, was not confined to such "New South" advocates as *DeBow's Review*.[10] Southern editorialists by the score announced that their region supported the idea. A paper in the Florida interior declared that "our citizens cheerfully welcome all good and true men, it matters not from what portion of our common [soil] they hail."[11] Southerners themselves were somewhat surprised at the turnabout in attitude toward northern men. "One can scarce conceive of the changed state of feeling here," wrote an Alabama planter who had sat out the war in Europe. "Instead of looking upon the northern people as enemies to be hated, they seem to greet them as welcome visitors. They are wanted here as merchants, as overseers, as planters—in any capacity they would seem to be acceptable."[12]

Many of the southern enthusiasts for northern men and capital had in view projects of an industrial and commercial nature. They wanted Yankee men and money in order to exploit the region's undeveloped resources, diversify its agriculture, and industrialize and urbanize the countryside.[13] James L. Orr, the provisional governor of South Carolina, never disguised the fact that he wanted to pattern his state after Massachusetts. One of James D. B. DeBow's lifelong ambitions, moreover, was to launch the South on a new departure, and after the war even such an unlikely convert as George Fitzhugh supported his program.[14] The cry for northern men, and indeed for all outside labor, even European and Chinese, also reflected a desire to replace the former slaves with imported labor. Some ex-slaveholders believed that the black race would die off without the protective care of kind masters; many others doubted that the freedmen would work without compulsion.

Nevertheless, many of the calls for northern men and money, at least in the Deep South, came from old planters who wanted help in getting back on their feet. The South in general had little choice after Appomattox but to seek outside capital, whether from the North or from abroad. Four years of war had greatly impoverished the region. One historian estimates that southern wealth in 1860, exclusive of slaves, "had shrunk in value at the end of the war by 43 per cent."[15] The conflict left visible scars in the planting districts. Many gin houses, dwellings, and farm tools were put to the torch and much livestock was stolen or butchered. Neglect usually finished off what the soldiers had left untouched. Practically one-third of the South's livestock and almost one-half of its agricultural machinery were destroyed during the war. Farm values decreased markedly during the war years, to a greater degree even than the decrease in cultivated area.[16]

To make matters worse, money and credit were in short supply. With the fall of the Confederacy came the collapse of the South's banking and credit facilities and the loss of much private capital that had been absorbed by Confederate bonds and securities. The fact that the South for many years following the surrender scarcely possessed a currency worthy of the name severely handicapped efforts to rebuild. Banking capital decreased from $61,000,000 in 1860 to $17,000,000 ten years later, while the volume of the region's currency declined from $51,000,000 to $15,000,000 in the same period. The obligation to assume part of the national war debt (the South's share has been minimally estimated at one billion dollars) and the hated federal tax on cotton scarcely helped matters. But probably the most formidable obstacle to economic recovery was the National Banking Act, which was passed during the war when the South had no voice in national councils. This legislation generally favored the East over the backcountry in the circulation of currency, and the former Confederacy was at the greatest disadvantage. The average per capita circulation of national currency in ten southern states in 1866 was only $1.70, as compared with a $33.30 average for New England and New York.[17] The realities of economic dislocation and a crippled credit system obviously obliged southerners to seek outside assistance, particularly from the North.

The old planters knew as much. All that they had left with which to begin anew was their land, and it was not only depressed in value but said to be roofed in with mortgages, the legacy of heavy investments in land and slaves during the flush 1850s. Ex-slaveholders with diversified portfolios, such as Pierce Butler, could liquidate outside investments in order to raise the cash for restoring their plantations to proper cultivation. Those old planters who had had the opportunity and foresight to salt away large stores of cotton during the war also possessed some means for financing a return to normal operations.[18] After the surrender, however, not many southern cotton growers were so favorably situated as the men who fell into these two categories. For most of the old elite an improvement in the situation seemed to depend on "northern capital getting down here," enabling them "to realize something for [their] residences as well as [their] plantations." The Johnsonian legislature in Mississippi reached the same conclusions. It did all it could to make Yankee investors feel at home. The spirit of hospitality broke out in South Carolina as well. The reasons were largely economic. The Charleston *Courier* advised, "the main thing at present is to dispose of lands to men who have the means of defraying the expenses of cultivation."[19]

With unerring instinct the old planting class and their allies had hit upon one of the most workable strategies for preserving the antebellum pattern of land tenure. There is no blinking the fact that the southern system of large-scale landholding owed its survival in large measure to the availability of northern speculative capital during and shortly after the war. To say this is not to minimize such important factors in the system's survival as the failure of the federal government to implement a program of land reform, the determination of the victor to keep the freedmen not only in the South but on the plantations, and the ability of the vanquished to improvise various financial and legal devices favorable to his own economic interests.[20] But it seems likely that in the complex process whereby the plantation order was rebuilt and transformed, northern investment decisions figured as significantly as federal policy and southern ingenuity. Yankee capital gave the southern landholding system a welcome reinforcement at a critical moment in its existence.

Some of this reinforcement arrived indirectly, by way of purchases of cotton that came to market in 1865, although a good portion of the $400,000,000 grossed in these transactions was eaten up in interest charges, processing and commission fees, and debt retirement. Other indirect help came in the form of loans to southern factors, merchants, and bankers, who were thereby enabled to make advances to hard-pressed planters.[21] But a great deal of the support was of a direct kind: the investments in plantation lands that countless northerners made during the period under consideration. Money from this source formed a large part of the funds that flowed into the plantation economy after emancipation.

One fact stands out very clearly: Southerners strained every nerve to encourage Yankee investments in the plantation economy. The classified sections of major northern dailies regularly featured advertisements from old planters seeking investors, partners, purchasers, and lessees.[22] Southern newspapers also brimmed with notices to catch the eye of the northern traveler.[23] If he happened to overlook the bargains in the local journals, there were plenty of planters around to acquaint him with attractive offers, once his sectional identity was learned. A Yankee planter in Georgia was solicited nearly every day "to send to [his] Northern friends offers of such and such valuable lands."[24] A former U.S. treasury agent in Alabama had twelve choice plantations placed in his hands within twenty-four hours of hanging up his realtor's shingle.[25]

When southerners did not send plantation propositions to northern brokers and capitalists, they frequently traveled north in person to seek investors.[26] Scarcely less conspicuous than the stream of pardon seekers calling daily at the White House was the current of ex-slaveholders visiting the financial centers of the North. New York City was overrun with importunate plantation owners. One scion of a Georgia Sea Island family visited Wall Street every morning to negotiate for " '*Greenbacks*,' to plaster them over the fields of the dead South to make them look green again."[27] Governor John A. Andrew and his associates were in almost daily consultation with southern planters in the fall of 1865; they were so overwhelmed with offers that it appeared to them as though "the whole South [was] to be sold." *DeBow's Review* was more conservative. It estimated that one-fourth of the South's agricultural property was up for sale.[28]

The Massachusetts governor's American Land Company and Agency certainly reflected the spirited market in southern lands. Within three months of its organization it was advertising for sale or lease upward of three million acres in plantations, and it had agents in South Carolina and Mississippi drumming up more business. Other northern-based land companies appeared to be doing just as well.[29] But southern land firms were not dragging their feet. The Southern Land Agency, with headquarters in Memphis and an office in Vicksburg, was doing a thriving business in the Mississippi Valley.[30] Better known and more extensive was the General Southern Land Agency, an outgrowth of a North Carolina land company founded in the summer of 1865 by J. M. Heck and Kemp P. Battle. Its managers confidently expected to list two million acres of land throughout the South and to attract 100,000 northern immigrants in 1866.[31]

Although the old planting class seems to have been united on the need for securing northern capital, it was divided about the manner in which it should be accepted. Was the proper policy to sell out, lease, or try the free-labor experiment with borrowed capital?[32] In some localities everyone was at sea. Hale County, Alabama, was in "such a disorganized condition that no one [knew] what to do, what he [could] do, what he should do," Henry Watson, Jr., discovered upon his return from Europe. His old friends daily asked him "what they should do about this & that, should they sell, should they rent, what is their property worth?" Watson had no ready answers, for he was as unsure about the future as they were. The confusion and uncertainty were doubtless unsettling, but there must have been some consolation in knowing that options were available.[33]

Probably the most popular alternative was to borrow northern money, and it is safe to assume that most northern investments in the plantation economy came in the form of loans. Ex-slaveholders who resolved to give black free labor a trial usually found it easy enough to obtain operating capital in the North. Of course there were some planters who had to sell out because they failed to raise fresh capital or hold off their creditors.[34] One ex-slaveholder complained that northern capitalists would give southern men a respectful audience but then would dispatch "an agent who would not 'divide the profits.' " It was his opinion that most southern planters seeking capital in New York returned home disappointed. Nevertheless, he managed to secure northern capital on good terms for his family's plantation in Georgia, and we should probably pay more attention to his experience than to his opinion.[35] Immediately after the war northern money seemed to be available to any southern planter who was willing to pay the premium. Prewar creditors usually greeted old southern customers warmly and made known their readiness to make arrangements for the settling of old debts and the lending of new capital. Cotton prices were at such heights in 1865 and 1866 that few creditors doubted that a fair season would yield more than enough to retire old accounts. If antebellum sources of credit had run dry, there were new wells to tap. Northern companies specializing in southern plantation investments seem to have sprung up overnight once hostilities ceased.

A few of the Yankee land companies also specialized in advancing capital to ex-slaveholders, and private investors were not in short supply.[36] Northern money seemed so abundant that southern entrepreneurs visiting the North to organize loan associations were confident that they could raise large sums "in a few days."[37] A group of planters and former Confederate officers from Tennessee and Georgia had great expectations for the brokerage firm they organized in New York City in the fall of 1865. Styled the American Cotton Planters' Association, the company bargained extensively with capitalists in the North and dispatched an agent to Europe with instructions to negotiate a loan not exceeding $60,000,000. The enterprise came to nothing, however.[38]

Yankees with capital to lend frequently traveled south to inspect the ground personally. Places like Charleston were crowded with them in the winter of 1865-66. They would quietly check into a hotel, interview a few planters, make an investment or two, and return home, all within a few days. "Many a planter is working his farm today by the aid of capital supplied by some gentleman at the North who was wise enough to act quietly and discreetly," wrote the Charleston *Courier.*[39]

Although northern credit was bountiful during presidential Reconstruction, the terms for its use were often stiff. Yankee investors commonly demanded, and got, a first mortgage on the plantation as security, a first lien on the crop, and interest payable either in cash or in a predetermined portion of the harvest. When the interest was in money the rates ranged from 10 to 25 percent per annum, with 15 percent being about average. When the interest was in crops, the lender usually received one-half of the net proceeds; but there were many variations, some involving a combination of both modes of payment, say, 10 percent interest *and* one-fourth of the crop.[40] Occasionally the southern borrower received a fee for management services, though when salaries were offered (varying between $1500 and $5000 a year), the planter normally took a cut in his share of the proceeds—one-third instead of one-half. Some northern investors asked for only one-third of the net proceeds but then demanded exclusive control over the marketing of the crop and an option to purchase the plantation within three years or some other specified period of time.[41] There were regional variations in the terms of credit. In the scramble for capital the large planters on the river-bottom lands of the lower Mississippi Valley seem to have had a decided edge over all competitors, probably because their soils were so productive and their plantations in such good repair. For a loan of $20,000 they sometimes received as much as $7000 in rent and management payments plus one-third of the crop, yet they did not have to mortgage their lands. At the other extreme (and probably more representative) were the terms advertised by the American Cotton Planters' Association. These combined the worst of all the possibilities: a mortgage on the plantation and its improvements, a first lien on the crop, 10 percent interest per annum, a one-fourth share of the net proceeds of the harvest, and a pledge to market the crop through the party or parties making the loan.[42] However they are viewed, these sharecropping agreements were entirely on the side of capital. Yet many southern planters were more than happy to accept them. In describing a typical northern loan, an editor in Mississippi conceded the harshness of its terms but nevertheless called it "the fairest proposition made to the planters by any body of men of which we have heard." At the very least, such offers freed ex-slaveholders of the necessity of sacrificing their plantations.[43]

This may have been true, but some old planters bridled at the stiff conditions of northern loans, especially the "ruinous mortgage upon the planting lands."[44] An ex-slaveholder in the South Carolina low country preferred to sell one of his places rather than "go into these extortionate bargains for cultivating it." He reasoned that the proceeds from its sale would enable his family to "avoid the same kind of arrangements for [their] other property." The Louisiana man who sold George Benham his place did just that. With the sale money he bought up the outstanding notes on his other plantations at below par, "thus making up in discount" what he lost by selling some of his land at depressed prices.[45]

The idea of selling part of one's land in order to raise the capital with which to work the remainder seems to have been a popular one among some large planters. Southern land agents and editorialists occasionally urged it as the proper policy in the circumstances.[46] The plan made sense, particularly if there were any question in the planter's mind as to whether he would be able to procure enough labor to work all of his lands. Without adequate resources one could not afford to be overextended. As one planter explained the situation confronting his family, "We must, on the same principle that induced the famous English Farmer *Mechi*, to sell one of *two excellent Farms* in order to improve the *remaining one*—sell some of our land & give our whole attention to the rest."[47]

Other plantation sellers, however, were less hopeful of adjusting to the new scheme of things than were the large planters or ex-slaveholders who borrowed northern capital. Some wished to sell out and quit planting entirely. Old Confederates who thought it "impossible for any gentleman to live in this country" talked of emigrating to another slaveholding country, such as Brazil, or moving to Mexico, the Northwest, or New York City.[48] Others might enter trade. For those who considered leaving the country the desire to escape "Yankee rule" was strong.[49] Some feared high war taxes; others believed that the federal authorities meant to confiscate the estates of large landowners and leading Confederates. During the summer of 1865 it was not clear whether even pardoned Confederates could regain lands affected by the Direct Tax laws or General William T. Sherman's Field Order Number 15, which had given the freedmen possessory title to a strip of land along the south Atlantic coast.[50]

The major motive of those who wished to sell out, whether they left the country or not, was "to get away from the free negro." Most of the southern sellers lacked confidence in black free labor and were not inclined to experiment with it; the more timorous feared black domination and Negro suffrage.[51] "The majority of our citizens have come to the conclusion that the negroes will not work on the plantations in a manner that will pay for the necessary investment of capital," an editor in northern Florida wrote.[52] An Ohio man planting in Mississippi thought that the largest class of sellers were those who felt "unable to satisfactorily control their labor."[53] This current of pessimism ran deep. To men accustomed to complete control over their workers, the prospect of persuading ex-slaves to labor without compulsion was not very inviting. Few believed that the freedmen would respond to the incentives of classical economics.[54] Those who gave free labor an early trial found the result dispiriting. Managing free blacks is "not only very laborious, requiring constant vigilance & the exercise of tact & firmness both, but it is irksome," one Georgia planter wrote. "I do not think I could stand another twelvemonth overseeing freedmen, even with the prospect of realizing $5,000.00 nett [*sic*]."[55] Others questioned whether the profits were there. If land values were depressed now, some reasoned, where would they be after the present labor experiment failed? Better to sell while the northern demand for plantations was great, a few counseled, than to run the risk of seeing land values driven down to even more ruinous levels once the free-labor system collapsed.[56] Cynicism about the freedmen went beyond economics. The desertion of faithful retainers and the unexpected growth of independence among the fieldhands struck directly at the ex-slaveholder's image of himself as a kind patriarch who enjoyed the affection of his black family. Some old planters found it too painful to have anything more to do with such faithless, inscrutable people.[57]

Emigration from the South was generally frowned on. It meant cutting loose from lifelong associations and abandoning the region in the hour of its greatest trial. But even if one stayed at home, selling out entirely was not considered sound policy either. The land panic that swept through some areas caused alarm: "Owners of real estate are sacrificing broad acres to strangers and parting with their birthright for a mess—a small mess—of greenbacks," a newspaper in Augusta, Georgia, warned.[58] The South might indeed recover some of its war losses by selling its lands at a low price, but few old planters wanted that kind of prosperity, or had a desire to abandon the only occupation they knew anything about.[59] Some of this opposition to plantation sales had a distinct anti-northern animus. "Johnson has gone and sold his plantation to a Yankee," Whitelaw Reid overheard one local man exclaim to another. "Is it possible? . . . Why I thought Johnson was a better citizen than that."[60] In some localities public sentiment was strongly against land sales to northerners. Planters in northern Alabama had reportedly leagued together to prevent selling plantations to the "damned Yankees." A South Carolinian told a northern reporter that selling to Yankees was impossible: "*State pride forbade it.*"[61]

Plantation sales seemed all the more objectionable for being unnecessary. Unless the planter was desperate to quit the country, renting out one's plantation for a season or two was more sensible than selling at depressed prices. A former Confederate official thought the planters were crazy even to consider putting their rich lands on the market at the current prices. "First you lost your slaves," he lectured a group of them, "and now you propose to give away your plantations! . . . Lands that are worth sixty and eighty dollars an acre, you're selling for ten and twelve. Why, you can rent them for half of that."[62] He was close to the mark, for leasing seemed a fairer proposition than borrowing northern capital. Some rental contracts called for a division of the crop, especially after the 1866 and 1867 seasons, when northern demand had abated considerably; but most leases specified a cash payment, normally one-half down and the balance at the end of the year. In 1866 planting lands in Alabama commanded $3 to $5 an acre while $5 to $8 was the asking price in Mississippi; along the Mississippi River some plantations went for as high as $22 an acre, though the majority were in the $10 to $15 range. A few owners even rented out their plantations in return for having them repaired and restocked. Most contracts, however, obliged the lessee to stock the place himself. The bulk of the leases ran for a year and some were for as long as three years.[63]

In truth, a few of these agreements were simply another way of borrowing northern money. William Henry Trescot leased his plantation on Barnwell Island, South Carolina, to the wealthy diplomat Henry Shelton Sanford for three years at an annual rent of $1,000 and 10 percent of the profits. But Trescot continued to manage the place in the same manner as "when he planted the Island himself." This agreement differed significantly from the conditions attached to northern loans in that Trescot did not have to mortgage his lands.[64] An attractive feature of leasing was that the owner might get his plantation restored to proper cultivation without accepting yet another lien on property that might already be heavily mortgaged.

"I think that you will find your lands a very available recourse after a little while," a Georgia planter told a cousin who was thinking of moving to Latin America. "The proper plan will be to lease them out & live upon the money & not to undertake to plant them yourselves under a new system."[65] Apparently, many southern planters recognized the logic in the argument, for by the beginning of 1866 plantation leasing had become a policy some ex-slaveholders found hard to resist. "I had decided to work my plantation on my own account," another Georgia planter wrote, because he believed it was "the true policy of landowners in that section—the best way to preserve the value of our remaining property." But leasing had taken hold in his neighborhood, and since many friends "whose business is planting determine to lease their places, I must try to do so too."[66] Renting plantations to northerners seems to have been most prevalent in Alabama, Mississippi, and Louisiana, but it was also a common practice elsewhere in the Deep South. At the time Whitelaw Reid visited central Alabama, northerners were going into leasing in a big way. In the canebrake region the planters were usually new men who had rented their land.[67] Along the Mississippi, especially above Natchez, Yankees "were generally renting. There was only here and there an instance where they had purchased." Plantation advertisements in the Natchez *Democrat* seldom solicited buyers, but prospective lessees had a lengthy list of choice estates from which to choose.[68]

Even some freedmen found the leasing system to their liking. A few contracted with Yankees to rent plantations for them in return for a share of the crop. It was the only way they could get around the white opposition to selling or renting lands to blacks.[69]

In fact, there is little doubt that the selling of plantations to northerners had taken a back seat to leasing by the end of 1865. This does not imply that northern purchasers were insignificant. Although most Yankee planters in Florida were lessees,[70] many appear to have bought their places, and some of the better-known northern planters elsewhere were buyers—men such as George Benham, Charles Stearns, Henry Lee Higginson, and Edward Philbrick. Yet by all accounts most newcomers leased rather than bought places. Indeed, it is fair to say that the leasing of plantations to Yankees, and to other southerners for that matter, partly explains why the expected large turnover in southern cotton lands did not materialize, at least immediately after the war.[71] Northern men and money helped not only to shore up the plantation system, but to rescue the old planting class as well. Jefferson Davis had predicted the outcome from his prison cell in Fortress Monroe: "The land will not pass to any great extent from its former proprietors. They will lease it for a few years to men with capital, and then resume working it themselves, or sell portions of it with the same object, not materially decreasing their own possessions."[72]

Yankees who had hoped that southern plantations would pass permanently into northern hands were naturally disappointed at the spread of leasing. A temporary northern presence was not considered the best means of remaking the South in the image of the conqueror. Critics of leasing tended to blame the decline in land sales on Andrew Johnson's liberal southern policy. The pardon of leading Confederates and the restoration of their lands, some believed, allayed apprehensions of confiscation and thereby removed somewhat the incentive to unload plantations.[73] But it seems unlikely that decisions in Washington had much to do with the growing popularity of leasing as opposed to selling.

For one thing, the widespread practice of renting plantations reflected adjustments in the market for lands. The great rush for cotton plantations in the winter of 1865 and 1866 had driven up prices beyond the means of many would-be purchasers. Whitelaw Reid estimated that during this period "the price of lands through the South, either for lease or sale, advanced fully fifty percent." Along the St. Johns River in Florida, for example, where northerners had settled heavily, land prices rose by one-third. Some who had been tempted south by good bargains "took northern exchange, and went home again." But many decided to lease instead, even though rents had skyrocketed.[74]

Moreover, quite a few northerners preferred to rent rather than to buy. Those who anticipated a short residence and a quick killing, as many did, must have considered leasing a good way to hedge against losses. Also, Yankees who believed that large landholdings were on the way out probably saw little advantage in a permanent investment, unless they had philanthropical plans for the freedmen, which few had. Some of the biggest investors in cotton plantations certainly found leasing to their liking. Senator William Sprague's company rented its thirteen plantations along the Mississippi. The United States Mutual Protection Company, one of the many corporations that had sprung up during and after the war, also leased many valuable plantations in northern and central Mississippi.[75] Practically the entire federal command staff in Alabama went into leasing in a big way. General John McArthur, General William Wood, and his brother, General Charles Wood, and assorted colonels and majors, some of them Confederate, were "arranging for pretty heavy operations." Their plan was to lease a number of small plantations, usually five each, and hire competent overseers to manage them. Whitelaw Reid thought it "a splendid opening for careless men to lose money."[76] Though not an absentee, Reid was a high roller himself. Together with Francis J. Herron, a former Union general who also became a commission merchant in New Orleans, he leased three large plantations in Concordia Parish, Louisiana, in 1866 and 1867, and later acquired an interest in Alabama planting lands.[77]

Yet the real explanation of the popularity of leasing lies with the old planters themselves. They recognized the advantages of renting instead of selling long before Andrew Johnson assumed the presidency. Almost as soon as some planting districts fell under federal occupation the natives began to lease their places to newcomers. By February 1865 planters in northern Alabama were renting plantations to ex-Union officers.[78] The practice had already become popular in the Mississippi Valley, particularly around Natchez and Vicksburg, the year before. By a conservative estimate, over a quarter of the plantations rented under the supervision of the Treasury Department, were leased directly from their owners.[79] Military regulations almost compelled them to lease, because planters of "doubted loyalty" were required to take on a loyal partner, who was usually a northerner.[80] But what began as a matter of military necessity became the adopted policy of even Unionist planters. The reasons were not exclusively financial. Many southern planters who were disaffected with the new order of things reasoned that a northern lessee might be very useful in view of the labor readjustments that lay ahead.

The great planters of Natchez, Mississippi, illustrate the trend. Men such as Stephen Duncan, Alfred V. Davis, Levin R. Marshall, and William J. Minor, whose diversified portfolios and large landed interests set them apart from the ordinary slaveholding planter, were angry at "the great secession blunder" and stayed at home when the federal armies arrived in 1863.[81] Stephen Duncan, at least, was not unmindful of the huge profits to be made from wartime cotton, and he appears to have invested in United States 5-20 bonds during the war.[82] These men quickly signed the oath of allegiance, though one of their Yankee lessees thought their Unionism was "half pretense, to save their property."[83]

Not only did they save their lands, but they realized some ready cash as well. They were more fortunate than the lesser planters from the outlying areas, who, during the war, could often get no better terms than a sharecropping arrangement. But practically all of the Natchez nabobs leased their plantations at good prices in 1864 and 1865, chiefly to northerners.[84] Alfred V. Davis got $5,000 for the rent of his Good Hope plantation in Concordia Parish, Louisiana, in each of those years. Stephen Duncan asked $15,000 for the lease of one of his plantations in 1864. He informed one Union general that a "*reliable* man, who would take *a valuable* plantation, with *everything* on it, labor included, . . . can be accommodated, on application to Yours very truly."[85] Whether he got his price is not recorded, but he probably found a lessee. Northerners who could afford the rent preferred plantations controlled by the Natchez elite. These places were generally in good repair and safely situated. The owners were also believed to have some influence with the Confederate guerrillas.[86]

The last consideration was not a small worry in a territory where the guerrillas were thick and the federal authorities less than sympathetic to northern planters. After reports began to circulate that General William T. Sherman opposed having his troops used for the protection of government lessees, several northern plantation prospectors immediately grasped the advantage of coming to terms with one of the numerous "semi-loyal" owners who claimed that for a few thousand dollars, payable in advance, they could secure the goodwill of the guerrillas. Even Yankee lessees who had already taken out leases with the government saw nothing wrong with signing a contract with the owner or his agent as well, upon the latter's pledge "to do all in their power to have us unmolested." It was a point in the lessees' favor if they could manage without relying on the assistance of federal troops, who found fun and profit in depredating northern plantations on the rare occasions when they did patrol the outlying areas.[87] Still, buying protection was a gamble. Southerners who advertised their influence with the marauders were promising more than they could deliver. Confederate scouts often preferred to strike their own bargains with the Yankees, intimidating the lessees into agreements to furnish them with contraband articles from Vicksburg and Natchez in exchange for immunity from their raids. Or they simply broke up the operations of the northerners, sometimes out of anger at the owners for collaborating with the enemy. Most of the Yankee planters in the twilight zone between Confederate lines and the immediate vicinity of Union garrisons were forced by guerrilla raids to abandon their plantations midway through the season. At least one-third of the plantations that had been leased in 1864 were later abandoned for this reason.[88]

Some old planters did have considerable influence with the guerrillas and they were not averse to exercising it. A major planter from the Vicksburg area who had fled to Texas at the arrival of the Union armies knew that he had to resort to unorthodox methods when he discovered on his return home that his property, as well as that of his neighbors, had fallen into the hands of the Association for Mutual Protection, the syndicate of northern lessees in which Alexander Winchell and his colleagues at the University of Michigan had a large interest. The southerner claimed he was the authorized agent for his neighbors who were seeking refuge in Texas. But from the standpoint of business leverage his legal authority in the matter did not serve him nearly so effectively as did his apparent control of an irregular guerrilla band composed of deserters from both armies and a few of his neighbors' sons. After three or four crippling raids on the operations of the association, one of which resulted in the death of Winchell's brother, Winchell and his associates "yielded to necessity" and came to "terms with the very rebel upon whom we charged most of our disasters." In July 1864 the lessees agreed to evacuate the 20,000 acres under their control and to permit the southerner to finish cultivating the cotton and take responsibility for its marketing, in return for one-half of the proceeds.[89] Thus did Winchell's cotton-planting experience come to an early end. He despaired of receiving satisfaction from Union officials in Vicksburg, or at least from the provost marshal there, who seemed to be on poker-playing terms with some of the raiders.[90] In this business of fleecing the Yankee lessees, Union officials and Confederate guerrillas often had a great deal in common. What the latter did not secure by means of direct action, the former skimmed off in the form of fees charged for processing red tape.

But shaking down the newcomers was chiefly a sport of lesser planters in the lower Mississippi Valley. The Natchez elite probably took little part in the game. They owned better than table stakes and preferred to be dealt into the action available at Union headquarters. Lorenzo Thomas, the adjutant general of the U.S. Army, received their best hospitality. He had become acquainted with them while stationed there before the war, and his return to Natchez in 1863 to recruit black troops scarcely lessened his welcome among the old elite.[91] Thomas was happy *"to see his old friends and talk of days gone by."* He was also very obliging. He released William J. Minor's plantations from government leasing and announced his readiness to do anything he could "to help out his old friends."[92] Presumably this meant opening doors at the Quartermaster's Department and cutting red tape, as he had done for his son and his friends, who had first crack at the most eligibly located plantations that the Natchez elite could offer. Thomas W. Knox was not the only northern prospector who was disappointed to find "that the best plantations in the vicinity had been taken by the friends of Adjutant-General Thomas, and were gone past our securing."[93]

Thomas was also very sympathetic to the political aspirations of his old friends. When Stephen Duncan and Levin R. Marshall told him in the fall of 1863 that they and their associates were anxious for Mississippi to "resume her proper position in the Union," Thomas advised them to "elect members to Congress, and let them go to Washington, and claim their seats." They naturally gave his plan their most cordial approval and warmest support, and in fact went him one better by suggesting that a military governor be appointed to supervise the canvass, proposing for the position one of their own, Judge William L. Sharkey, who later served as the state's provisional governor under Andrew Johnson. Thomas recommended the plan to his immediate superior, Edwin M. Stanton, the secretary of war, but nothing came of it, possibly because Judge Sharkey desired "the undercurrent of Unionism to show itself more decisively before any action should be had."[94] Meanwhile Thomas worked assiduously to see that the regulations concerning the management of the freedmen did not assume a shape that would unduly inconvenience the old elite. He had sold himself on the idea that the system of free labor should approximate as nearly as possible the usages of slavery, since the latter represented "the results of experience"; and he later recommended scrapping the Freedmen's Bureau.[95] The general was as steadfast and loyal a friend as the Natchez elite could have hoped for in these turbulent times.

The leading men of Natchez knew this and continued to seek Thomas's assistance after the war. In the fall of 1865 Levin Marshall, John Minor, and Elijah Smith were staying at Thomas's Washington home. All were "anxious for Father to go down river and take a plantation," his son wrote; "his influence there would be such as to create a friendly feeling towards him on all sides." Thomas's friendliness with Andrew Johnson was already well known. Alfred V. Davis rented his Pittsfield plantation to the general in 1866.[96] Although Marshall apparently lost out in the bidding for Thomas, he got Frank P. Blair, Jr., another conservative and influential Union general, to lease his Cabin Teele plantation after the war.[97]

The Natchez elite had more than financial and political reasons for renting their plantations to well-placed northerners. Leasing was particularly appealing to the Duncans and Minors because it spared them the headaches of managing black wage earners. The old planters soon discovered that no matter how many friends they had at headquarters they still had to manage their plantations in accordance with the labor regulations that originated in the Department of the Gulf. Even if it had been permissible to plant in the old way the fieldhands would have forced adjustments. Some slaveholders behind Confederate lines had to pay wages in order to keep their plantations operating.[98]

The Natchez elite were no happier with the first results of the free-labor experiment than were the majority of ex-slaveholders. Stephen Duncan, Jr., complained of the "*Machiavellian* diplomacy" now required to manage the hands. Payday was unbearable. "I have just paid off the negroes & a more unpleasant, disgusting business I have never attended to," he wrote to his father.

The trouble was that the blacks were reluctant to accept Duncan's terms for the coming year and "tried very hard to make their own terms & wished to exact a great many things that I could not allow."[99] In time the Natchez planters came to recognize the economic feasibility of the new system, but they never became accustomed to the change in attitude of their former slaves. William J. Minor conceded that "we may do, in a pecuniary sense, as well as ever. But the satisfaction of planting on a well regulated plantation is gone."[100]

The answer seemed to be to withdraw from the field for a while. If it was a "perfect *dogs* [sic] life" to govern the freedmen, then perhaps it was better to "let them that freed the negroes work with them." The fieldhands appeared to have more confidence in the newcomers' paying them wages, so why not allow the Yankees to try their hands at the business?[101] "Authorize me to rent," Stephen Minor implored his father, "and I will take in a partner who has and will continue to have influence over the hands (and in other places)." Many lesser planters in the area had apparently arrived at the same policy. When Thomas W. Knox and his associate were scouting for a plantation to lease in 1864 they found quite a few semi-loyal planters who were eager to get "some Northern man to manage the niggers."[102] This conservative policy of assured income and minimal irritation had obvious advantages, but the Natchez elite seem to have enjoyed them the most. Not long after the surrender "these old fellows" were living out "their ease at the New York Hotel," one of their northern lessees complained, and they expected, "without investing any capital or running any risk, to make as much money out of their plantations as they had ever made in old times from a cotton crop."[103] He failed to add that they were also being spared the headache of breaking in the new labor system.

The practice of using Yankee lessees to secure good income and to discipline the freedmen may have originated with the Natchez planters, but it was not peculiar to them. Wade Hampton III quickly saw the merits of the arrangement when he visited Mississippi after the war to tend to his plantation properties there. Government lessees had operated five of them during the conflict and Hampton saw no reason to change management now. "It will be a good thing for my negroes to have Yankees so near them," he explained to his sister, "and this will be sure to make them more contented."[104]

This kind of reasoning had also become widespread in Hampton's home state of South Carolina, especially in the low country. Some of the old planting class there concluded that the newcomers might have better luck with the freedmen than the former masters. "My views upon the subject have undergone a material change the past month," a former Confederate general wrote in the fall of 1865. "The negro will be made to work for the Yankee—whilst with our own people he will manifest a disinclination to be employed by us." Others along the seacoast of Georgia voiced similar sentiments. Armistead Burt had no doubt that the Yankees would manage the freedmen.[105]

Ex-slaveholders had some reason to feel as they did. Former slaves had gained possessory title to much of the planting land in the coastal areas of South Carolina and Georgia, and they were not willing to relinquish their homesteads and sign labor contracts with the old owners. The conflict created "many gaps in the agricultural system" of the low country "into which a Yankee might step," reported one northern correspondent on the scene. "Many of the plantations are therefore offered for rent at reasonable rates."[106] Some old planters decided that northerners should have the vexation of dispossessing the squatters. A few even preferred to let the new men worry about negotiating with the federal government for the restoration of their land. This gambit was not always successful. The Freedmen's Bureau refused to allow Floyd King's New York lessee to take possession of the family plantations on St. Simon's Island, Georgia, "on the ground that they were to be secured to the blacks."[107]

Admittedly, the land crisis confronting the low-country planters was unique. But former slaveholders deep in the interior had also concluded that Yankee managers might succeed with freedmen labor where natives could not. Indeed, the decision to lease plantations to newcomers probably derived as much from this sort of reasoning as it did from financial necessity.[108] John Dennett of the *Nation* attributed the eagerness "to secure northern men as lessees of plantations" to the growing conviction that Yankees enjoyed a privileged status with the ex-slaves. "These freedmen will work a heap better for a Yankee than they will for one of us," he frequently heard.[109] Within five years "the cotton-growing regions will be an utter waste," a young Alabamian told Whitelaw Reid, "unless you Yankees, who don't know anything about cotton growing come in, learn it, and get the niggers to work for you. They won't half work for us." Henry Watson, Jr., felt the same way. He confessed that "in all probability a man from the North might control them [the freedmen] better than their old masters." He decided to lease his plantation in Greene County, Alabama, in order to avoid "the necessity of being annoyed by freed negroes."[110]

Clearly many old planters had concluded that the free-labor experiment, at least during its early phases, was not worth the candle. Some expected "a fierce struggle between the whites & the blacks," though "eventually the blacks must come to order & work or perish." All the same, few white planters had a stomach for the contest.[111] Under the circumstances it was smart policy to leave the conflict to the liberators.

The decision was not always reached voluntarily. The keen competition for labor in the winter of 1865-66 sometimes forced the choice on local planters who initially had tried to plant on their own account. Northerners appeared to be having greater luck attracting hands. Some ex-slaveholders simply abandoned the field to the new men because it was easier to find lessees than plantation workers. "I could have hired a dozen Yankees [managers] for brother William for a third [of the crop]," one southerner wrote to his brother from New Orleans. Few labor seekers could write so glowingly of their prospects. Albert T. Morgan's landlord in Yazoo County, Mississippi, apparently determined to lease his place after he failed to induce his former slaves to return from the contraband camps they had fled to during the war.[112]

Old planters who determined to resume operations regardless of the hazards occasionally discovered that they were unable to operate alone. One expedient decided upon by ex-slaveholders who were having trouble finding labor was to form a partnership with a northern man. Several local planters in Carroll Parish, Louisiana, "reckoned it would be a good thing to get one of these Yankees for a 'pardner,' the niggers are so fond of 'em." They reasoned that they had the land and the knowledge of cotton cultivation, while "the Yankees [could] furnish the niggers and the money."[113] These "pardnerships" seem to have been fairly common in the early postwar years. They had sprung up in nearly every neighborhood and " 'peared to be working well." [114]

The difficulties that southern planters experienced in obtaining black labor also created a heavy demand for northern overseers. Even officers of the hated Negro regiments were solicited. In the spring of 1866 old planters overran the camps of United States Colored Troops looking for hands among the soon-to-be-discharged black soldiers. The northern officers knew an opportunity when they saw one. "Fact is," one of them told a group of local planters, "you had better make your bargains with us than with the niggers. We control 'em; and we don't mean to take 'em to anybody's plantation without being paid for it." The officers asked high prices, which ranged from $2,000 to $6,000 a year or a considerable share of the crop, simply for supplying laborers, "preserving order on the plantations and retaining the confidence of the negro." [115] Many ex-slaveholders were happy to come to terms. One captain in the Ninety-sixth United States Colored Infantry received $2,000 annually merely for standing at the gate and issuing instructions to his former soldiers as they left for the fields. He was not hired "as manager or for [*his*] services but for the sake of getting the hands," who would only hire on if their commander told them to. [116] A few northern planters had to strike a bargain with these laborbrokers in blue. George Benham agreed to give one Union colonel $3,500, the use of his sawmill, fifty acres of plantation land, and a $1,500 annual salary for the use of some of his men. Benham was not so fortunate as General Lorenzo Thomas, who sent his son to recruit laborers among the soldiers he had enlisted two years earlier. [117]

Officers of the black troops were in great demand because of the direct control they exercised over their former soldiers. Yet some southern planters were so desperate to obtain labor and keep it that they regarded any set of federal shoulder straps as worth a high price. One Alabamian offered a Union captain from New York one-half the net proceeds from his plantation near Vicksburg, Mississippi, if the northerner found workers for the place. [118] A Louisiana planter offered another federal officer the same share of the crop plus $1,500 yearly if he would "show his person frequently about the plantation so that the darkies would believe that they had a Yankee employer." [119] This was an extravagant price for the services involved; possibly the old planter in this case feared any more Yankee influence with the freedmen than was necessary to keep the blacks on the plantation. Most southerners surely wanted more for their money. If the newcomer enjoyed such influence with the freedmen, let him use it regularly, though under southern guidance. Even those white southerners who objected to Yankees' planting on their own account considered the use of northern overseers acceptable. One large planter from the South Carolina low country refused to take his family on a visit to Beaufort—"the town is not fit for a white lady to stay in," he complained. "Yankees and negroes are all the rage." Nonetheless, he hired two Yankees who had planted at Port Royal to manage his plantation on the coast. [120]

Not every white southerner was happy with the movement of northerners into his neighborhood. Some smaller planters and many nonslaveholders, especially in the planting districts, were said to be bitterly opposed to Yankees. The denizens of saloons could be counted on for trouble, some reports had it, and the women bore an undying hatred for everything northern.[121] There was a group among the old elite that also opposed northern immigration in any form. Some of them contended that "the South can, and ought to be entirely independent of the North"; if the South needed outside capital, Europe was the place to get it.[122] Bitter war memories were strong. Northern investments in the South could never be permitted, one ex-Confederate bristled when he was approached by the agent of a Yankee capitalist. "The atrocities and barbarities practiced by your army can never be forgotten by any true southern man."[123] The fear of economic dispossession, however, that lay behind much of the resistance to land sales was equally potent. Northerners "have but *one idea* here," a frightened southerner wrote from New York City, "and that is to possess the Southern lands."[124] Unless the state legislatures took steps to prevent it, "the speculators that were amongst us during the war, and the moneyed men of the North, will in a few years, own all the property of the South, and the rising generation go with[out] an education." The northern planter movement had awakened old southern fears of the predatory designs of northern capitalists.[125]

The opposition to seeing "the country fill up with northern men" derived also from southern contempt for northern social ethics.[126] The northern man was said to be a miser, destitute of real honor, and lacking in those qualities that marked one as a gentleman. Those whose hearts were with the old regime were understandably dismayed by the prospect that young southern manhood might be replaced by "strange faces (Yankees), cold and heartless creatures; plotting and striving for the Almighty *dollar*."[127] A few urged caution, lest the South be "overwhelmed, confounded and demoralized by an invasion of washing machines, cooking stoves, codfish, cold meats, pickled pork, poor cheese, and Yankee notions generally."[128] Stephen Mallory, the Confederate secretary of the navy, ridiculed the idea of intersectional fellowship. Northerners and southerners "can no more mingle harmoniously than can an African 'tom-tom,' & an Aeolian harp." The southerner was "superior in all respects—in heart, soul, mind, life & character."[129]

These apprehensions were the most extreme expression of a general edginess about the Yankee's assimilability. If some doubted whether northerners could ever adapt to southern ways, others questioned if they would. The northern people were said to be a race of missionaries who could not refrain from meddling in other people's business. "The Yankee comes to impose Yankee ideas, and Yankee habits," the celebrated Jubal Early warned the South Carolina Senate. "His egotism will impress itself as it has done in the Northwest." These fears increased as southerners reflected on the political future. Northern men were considered to be so irrepressible that they would use any means, including Negro suffrage, to advance their private interests and forward their mistaken philanthropy.[130] And what kind of foolish, impractical notions might they put into the heads of the freedmen? Would the Yankees resume playing the parts they were rumored to have played in all those slave insurrections before the war? Would they try to incite the ex-slaves to commit acts of bloodshed and rapine? The possibilities were too awful to contemplate. Community stability and long-standing customs were at stake, as well as the delicate equilibrium between the races. If southerners cherished their traditions, some counseled, then they ought to resist the temptation of Yankee money and influence and "struggle through."[131]

How widespread these sentiments were during presidential Reconstruction is not easy to determine. Many white southerners in their gloomier moods must have shuddered at the thought that northerners in unprecedented numbers had usurped their places on the plantations. Even the normally confident William Henry Trescot at one time resigned himself to the likelihood that "northern habits, [and] northern people must take our places."[132] Now and then one catches a glimpse of an uneasiness that was better left unvoiced. Men talked of suppressing their "southern feelings" and working with the invaders. Others were not sure that this was the proper policy. It was bad enough to have to "borrow from anybody, but to be under obligations to a Yankee!"[133] A South Carolinian cautiously advised, "I think it right to borrow it from them if we can." The Johnsonian legislatures reflected the division in the southern mind. They promptly repealed usury laws and enacted legislation that would attract northern men and money, but they also passed bills that protected the old planting class from economic dispossession.[134]

It would be wrong, however, to suppose that the gloomier counsels prevailed. The desperation with which many southerners sought out Yankees to control the blacks and help ease the transition to free labor suggests a massive collapse of morale and self-confidence. Still, appearances are deceptive. Few who cooperated with the northern planter movement ever doubted their ability to control it and even turn it to advantage. Granted, there were a few who were so much at sea about how to run a plantation with free labor that they "thought of watching the Yankees and imitating their policy."[135] But most old planters believed they were in command of the situation. Their tactics of encouraging northern penetration of the planting districts were only a temporary expedient. "Let us accept the system with the Yankees," an ex-Confederate advised, "& after it is fairly established we shall control it as a matter of course.... Expediency is our policy just now."[136] Once the initial shock of defeat and emancipation had passed, a sober opportunism had set in.

Southerners who cooperated with the northern planter movement may have admitted that Yankees could initially get more work out of the freedmen than the old masters could, but they were not about to concede that the newcomers were better judges of the black character or more capable, in the long run, of managing plantation labor. Northerners who hoped to succeed in the business, one southerner asserted, would have to "benefit by our knowledge of the negro character."[137] The favor that Yankees enjoyed with the freedmen was at best temporary, growing out of the former slaves' infatuation with their new freedom, it was believed. Once the liberator and the liberated took each other's measure there would be a "violent and wholesome" reaction.[138] A short exposure to northern management would bring the blacks to their senses and teach them that their former masters were "their best friends."[139] Perhaps the exposure was just the dose of medicine that the restless freedmen needed, it was thought. If nothing else, Yankee taskmasters might make the ex-slaves appreciate the virtues of the old paternalism and dispose them to return to the protection of the patriarchal order.

The southern conviction seems to have been just as strong that the newcomers would quickly lose "patience with the negroes." The calculating Yankee, many southerners were sure, had no idea of the obstacles in the way of managing the ex-slaves. [140] There would be foot-dragging and resistance every step of the way until the northerner became thoroughly disgusted with the black race. Southerners had already seen this reaction in those antebellum northern settlers who had earned reputations for being the hardest drivers of slaves. Despite northern pledges to secure the black man his rights, moreover, southerners knew that the Yankee, by and large, had no special love for the Afro-American. Southerners were well posted on northern racial practices and fully aware of the ambiguities in the victor's moral crusade. *DeBow's Review* said that the northern states shared the South's "aristocratic feeling and bearing" in regard to racial distinction, and in fact "mounted a league higher" when they embraced Know-Nothingism and nativism. [141] So confident was the journal that Yankee planters would grow exasperated with the freedmen that it argued "everything is to be gained by bringing northern white men into contact with the negro, and nothing lost." If the newcomer was already conservative on the race question, he would have "his convictions confirmed." If he was a black Republican, "the chances are that association with the life-long object of his mistaken sympathy will convert him to our side." The experience might even cause welcome repercussions in the North, creating there a climate of opinion more favorable to the South's racial policy. [142]

What *DeBow's Review* was in fact suggesting was that northern immigrants would rapidly become "Southern in their interests." Ex-slaveholders found it hard to imagine that many northerners would settle in the South who were not "well-disposed already towards us." [143] No one denied that northern missionaries, newspaper correspondents, and political agitators were potential menaces, but Yankee planters were thought to be cast in a different mold. These northerners, some natives said, would "hate the government, the 'nigger,' and the rad*ical* party, as much as they, in order to get along peaceably." This had always been the case "when Yankees came down here ' 'fore the wa'.' " [144]

In short, most white southerners who accepted the northern planter movement seem to have been sure that the postwar immigrants would follow faithfully in the path blazed for them by their prewar predecessors. Ex-slaveholders knew that antebellum settlers from the North had fallen in easily with the ways of their adopted homes. Nearly everyone could give examples of northerners who had settled in their neighborhoods before the war, had become "devoted to the institutions of the South, and in all cases made useful members of society." [145] It was no secret, North or South, that some of the most ardent defenders of southern rights were "northern men with southern principles." [146] These prewar immigrants had been as hotly in pursuit of the main chance as were the more recent northern immigrants. They had come south with "hardly a change of linen" and before long were among the richest men in their communities. [147] The South had easily absorbed the antebellum speculators, and there was no reason that it could not do likewise now. If anything, the avarice of the newcomer was some guarantee that he might be rendered harmless. It was common knowledge, after all, that the quickest way to a Yankee's heart was through his pocketbook. Neither politics nor philanthropy stood in the northerner's way when profit was at stake, argued Albert Gallatin Brown, the southern nationalist. "Where he sees the dollar, he will throw [meta]physics to the dogs." [148]

Such southern hopes were not simply wishful thinking. To be sure, the victors had not completely forsaken the idealism that had caused them to loose ancient bonds of servitude. But they were working at cross-purposes. At the very moment when Republicans in Congress were deliberating measures that would limit the power of the ex-slaveholders, northern investors were helping to rescue a land system that would limit the freedoms of the ex-slaves. Here was an obvious conflict between the impulse to nationalize markets and the commitment to nationalize freedom, and it was the first of many indications that freedom would henceforth have to run in channels favorable to the development of a community of interests between businessmen north and south. After the Yankee planter movement had gathered momentum, there would be no turning back to the idea that liberty for the freedmen was inseparable from their ownership of land. Who in Congress, save the most ardent friends of the ex-slaves, would any longer take an interest in dissolving a pattern of land tenure in which northern wealth now had such a large and immediate stake? It is not an exaggeration to say that Yankee investments in southern plantations had subtly changed the climate of northern reform opinion and had set definite limits to the scope of the Reconstruction program.

But what of the limitations that the situation imposed on the old planters? It remains to say that people who are trying to make the best of a bad bargain are not likely to view their situation objectively. The old planters did not foresee that the forces unleashed by war and emancipation would eventually compel them to resemble the hard-driving and calculating Yankees who were settling in their midst. Northerners may have helped to preserve one of the bases of the ex-slaveholders' class power—they may in fact have shown them the advantages of becoming a *rentier* class [149]—but the newcomers could neither restore the paternalistic nexus of the master-slave relationship nor rescue the old planters from the necessity of becoming an employer class. Nor could they conform in all essentials to what southerners considered the standards of neighborly behavior. In the industrial and racial changes that lay ahead, there would be many occasions for disagreement between the old and the new masters about what constituted acceptable conduct toward ex-slaves and proper bearing toward ex-slaveholders.

The idea that northern planters were safe and therefore should be greeted hospitably was more than a simple expression of expectation. It was also a definition of the limits of southern tolerance, of what kind of behavior was acceptable and what was not. The message was that Yankee planters were to mind their own business and not depart from the script as written by their antebellum predecessors.

4 *The First Encounter*

At the beginning of 1866 it would have been hard to predict how northern planters would get along with their white neighbors. It was not that no one had made up his mind about the question. Quite a few people by then had fixed opinions about the kind of reception Yankee settlers could expect when they ventured into the former Confederacy. But opinions were contradictory. Some people were certain that northerners would be considered pariahs, to be expelled at the South's earliest convenience; others were just as sure that most southerners, except for a few recalcitrants, would treat Yankees tolerantly, if not kindly. Northern immigrants in the South at the time could not always agree about the temper of their new neighbors. The very confidence with which most men of the period expressed opinions about southern conditions speaks volumes about the polarization of sentiment that had taken place within eight months of the surrender. A careful observer, however, would have paused before making strong judgments. General James C. Beecher, the brother of Harriet Stowe, was more circumspect in his opinions than most of his contemporaries. "Constant contact with the minutiae of this mixed life," he wrote to General E. V. Sumner from his headquarters in the South Carolina low country, "makes me suspicious of *generalizations,* and very careful of making them."[1]

His example has not been easy for historians to follow. Since most Yankee planters were in the South approximately from the fall of 1865 through 1867, it has been tempting to view their situation solely as an issue in presidential Reconstruction. What we historians have thought of Andrew Johnson's policy, southern conditions, and the wisdom of federal intervention in the South has had considerable bearing on our perceptions of intersectional fellowship. Just as contemporaries did, we have used evidence regarding southern attitudes toward northern immigrants either to justify or to condemn the president's mild program of Reconstruction.[2] If we have emphasized the variety of conditions in the South, it has only been to debunk Radical propaganda. If we have stressed the theme of "southern outrages" or admitted that "much was going on in the South which was hard to deny or ignore," it has been in order to call into question the wisdom of the presidential plan of Reconstruction.[3]

Treating the evidence in terms of exhibits in an adversary proceeding is certainly a legitimate way of dealing with relations between newcomers and natives. It is the procedure by which the participants themselves tried to make sense of contemporary reality. The North believed fully that the treatment that former Confederates accorded Yankee settlers was an important measure of the South's readiness to "accept the natural results of the war."[4] A large category of northern grievances against the South, after all, had centered on the alleged mistreatment of Yankee travelers in the slave states and on the seeming willingness of southerners to set at defiance constitutional provisions guaranteeing to the citizens of each state the rights enjoyed by the citizens of the several states.[5] The victor now wanted assurances that the triumph of his arms had broken the southern habit of proscribing Yankees. He desired proof that the South had been chastened in defeat to the point that it would greet its conquerors with the proper spirit of respect.[6] But the victor also had other than psychological reasons for wanting to see his emissaries treated hospitably. Running through nearly all the plans of Reconstruction that filled the national agenda in these years was the assumption that northern emigration was a desirable and indispensable agency in the process of remaking the South in the image of the North. One cannot read the debates between conservative and radical reconstructionists without being struck by the fact that they were often arguing about whether a mild or a severe political settlement was necessary in order to open the South to settlers from the North.[7] In these debates evidence regarding southern attitudes toward Yankees obviously carried great weight. Only let it be shown that southerners were either friendly or hostile to the recent northern immigrants, and a strong case could be made for relaxing or stiffening the requirements for letting the South back into the Union.

Clearly we cannot disregard the political and policy implications that were involved in the issue of intersectional fellowship during the early years of peace. Much of the evidence was aimed at answering this question: On what terms should the South be restored to national counsels? But we can and should guard against overemphasizing the partisan dimensions of the relationship between newcomers and natives. What might have been sufficient evidence in a case either for or against a certain line of policy could be misleading in relation to the overall quality of intersectional fraternity at this time. We can agree that southern conditions did justify a radical Reconstruction policy and still leave unsaid a great deal that is historically significant. There is yet another consideration to bear in mind—one that possibly overshadows all the rest. The confrontation between Yankee planters and southern whites during these years was not a political melodrama staged for the benefit of policymakers in Washington. It was an attempt at peacemaking in personal, concrete terms, with all of the ambiguities that encounters of this kind always possess.

This is neither to argue the futility of generalizations about intersectional relationships during presidential Reconstruction, nor to suggest that presidential policy had no impact whatsoever on the prospects for fraternity. It seems safe to say that white southerners were antagonistic toward northern immigrants, especially Yankee planters, and treated them courteously only if they did not defy local usage. Yet it is important to keep in mind that this antagonistic spirit had shades of meaning and degrees of application, that it affected northern planters in different ways and at different times, and that it had a variety of outcomes, at least until the disastrous planting season of 1867. For although the South's determination to compel conformity was usually clear-cut, the relationship between newcomers and natives was very fluid. It varied according to geography and was subject to abrupt changes in mood and behavior. Each party regarded the other with curiosity and suspicion, friendliness and hostility, and always with pious self-esteem. The situation had contradictory possibilities: at times the chances for fellowship seemed as strong as the potential for antagonism. It was a situation in which the parties had to get to know each other better before matters could become clearly defined.

In any event, there is something to be said for concentrating for the time being on the period when most northern planters went south, from the fall of 1865 through the spring and into the summer of 1866. This period did not really mark the first encounter between Yankee planters and white southerners: lessees and Unionist slaveholders had become acquainted in Mississippi and Louisiana nearly two years before the war ended (of which more later). But it was the time of greatest initial contact and it is helpful to ask whether the relationship got off to a good start. This was the time when Andrew Johnson's southern policy began to bear fruit, when the former Confederacy supposedly lost its earlier submissiveness and became defiant and intractable, and when the North began to conclude that white southerners were implacably hostile to everything northern. Were intersectional relations strained by these adverse pressures and was unfavorable northern opinion about southern conditions well informed? We need to clear the air of these questions, or at least put them in proper perspective. There is another reason for asking how northern planters hit it off with their new neighbors. The great volume of evidence bearing on the subject of northern safety falls largely during the period when most Yankee planters first came into contact with white southerners. Many of the popular northern travel accounts of conditions in the South were based on observations made chiefly in the winter of 1865-66, and it should be pointed out that the Joint Committee on Reconstruction gathered most of its testimony in January and February of 1866.[8] In many respects, then, the evidence merits a hard look at this first large-scale encounter.

There is no doubt that Andrew Johnson's Reconstruction policy changed the southern mood from what it was just after the surrender and changed it with definite consequences for the comfort of northern men in the South. Whitelaw Reid saw the change set in shortly after the president issued his first Amnesty Proclamation in May 1865. Johnson's actions seemed to give ex-Confederates hope for the future, Reid thought, and made them "suspect that they were not so helpless as they imagined."[9] This mood grew in strength as the Johnsonian governments readied their states for the full restoration of all political rights, until by the eve of the Thirty-ninth Congress, in December 1865, the southern temper was "buoyant and defiant."[10] When the young reporter reached New Orleans, in November 1865, he was sure he had not misread the signs. One ex-Confederate was blunt about the new order that some southerners now hoped to inaugurate. "When we get in," he told Reid, "we'll put an end to this impudent talk of you Yankees about regenerating the South by Northern immigration. We'll require you to spend ten years in the State before you can vote."[11]

That this was not idle talk could be seen in the enactment by the Georgia legislature of a two-year residency requirement for voting.[12] It could also be seen in the defiant tone of the southern people in general. The president's attempt to restore home rule quickly in the South was enough to waken slumbering resentments toward the conqueror among the white population. The elections for state and national office came at the wrong moment for a people with a highly developed sense of political rights and personal freedom. The stump-speaking of those campaigns brought out the worst in a certain kind of politician and encouraged a style of gasconading for which the southern people were famous. A habit of making sectional denunciations arose that never entirely disappeared.[13] This was the kind of thing men like Governor John Andrew had hoped to prevent. Only by diverting "into channels of economy, the streams of political feeling and solicitude," he believed, could southerners be prepared to return to the seats of power. But raising political issues in the South before the people had had a chance to settle into new patterns of free-labor industry appears to have reopened old wounds.[14]

Northerners had been cautioned that they might "hear much to displease them," but no amount of forewarning could have adequately prepared them for the invective they encountered. Southerners talked frequently of their rights, their wrongs, and their demands. But much more provoking was the constant "abuse of the North and of Northerners."[15] No insult seemed too indelicate. When southerners were not calling Abraham Lincoln a baboon and Ben Butler a beast, they were expatiating on why Charles Sumner and Thaddeus Stevens deserved hanging. After they had exhausted their contempt for Union war heroes, they would turn to stigmatizing all Yankees as mean cowards who lacked the principles of a pickpocket. Ex-Confederates admitted that they had been "whipped" and had no stomach for resuming the fight, but the concession was not always made with grace, and certainly not in a manner to give northerners much pleasure. A certain class of southerners was fond of saying that it had been "overpowered by hirelings."[16]

Most of the time this kind of talk was addressed to no one in particular, but it was hard for northerners to escape. There was a period when it seemed to be constantly in the air. Scarcely a barroom, hotel, or steamboat was free from it for long, and the street corners where the village rowdies gathered seemed to crackle forever with violent oaths against the scoundrels in Washington. If a northern man heard "nothing of it in the railroad car today," John Dennett reported, "tomorrow he may be shut in a stage with people who entertain him with nothing else." And the subject of sectional grievances sometimes had a psychological momentum all its own. The more southerners talked about their wrongs, the more bitter they became. Many northerners who were within earshot did not find such talk agreeable. George C. Benham would have preferred to work "in a boiler-foundry or stand alongside during minute-shooting, with a hundred-pound Parrotgun, as far as comfort [was] concerned."[17] The rhetoric of denunciation even made some Yankees wary of leaving their plantations "without an armed escort."[18] They were fearful that sectional rancor might be directed against them personally.

Occasionally it was. In the period of pre-Radical rule one need not have been a northern Republican politician in order to have experienced the ill will of the local people, although this would have helped.[19] In certain neighborhoods, Yankees who were hunting for plantations received a rude welcome.

"Looking for cotton farms are you," an angry southerner asked a northern traveler. "Damn you, you may buy them, but you shall never live on them."[20] Albert T. Morgan got much the same reception in late 1865 when he visited a town in northern Mississippi in search of a place. He was told that "no Yankee radical could ever come into that country, make a crop and get away with it." There were similar outbreaks of local hostility near Macon, Georgia. So fierce was opposition to northern planters in Stewart County that a southern planter was obliged to break a rental contract with two Union officers from Ohio. His neighbors warned him that the execution of his plans would result in his lessees being murdered and his own house being "burned over his head."[21]

Government lessees who survived the planting setbacks of the war years seem to have been singled out for special abuse. Like northern merchants who took over southern businesses in the absence of Confederate proprietors, they were particularly vulnerable to resentment for apparently having profited from the misfortunes of the South.[22] Even though it was understood that abandoned plantations would be restored once the present occupants had harvested their crops, a few owners would not wait until the cotton had been baled. One popular eviction method for the impatient was an appeal to civil authorities. Several Mississippi planters requested the provisional governor to restore their places. Others turned to the local courts, for sympathetic juries were not hard to find in these years.[23] Angry southerners did not spurn more direct methods of repossession. One government lessee in Louisiana, who in less than three years had made a sizable fortune from a number of plantations worked by two thousand freedmen, was given to understand that his future business plans should not include that state. A Massachusetts lessee of government plantations at Port Hudson, Louisiana, was in a similar situation. The reduction of the federal garrison made his neighbors restless, he reported, and they "plainly intimate that I would not be able to make a crop and . . . that my mill would not stand. I shall lose all I have."[24]

Whether these threats were ever carried out was not reported, but it would not be surprising if they were. Even northern planters who came south after the war had to contend with more than just menacing language. There were reports of assassinations (about which details are sketchy or unreliable) and cases of assault.[25] In Gainesville, Florida, for example, the local press applauded a mob that attacked the former provost marshal and commander of the black garrison when he returned to the area to engage in planting. The incident seems to have been an eruption of purely personal feeling, a reprisal for an alleged insult to the wife of a prominent citizen. But the fact that the sheriff and the judge and clerk of the Probate Court led the assault reflected unfavorably on the policy of home rule.[26]

More typical than the assaults on persons were depredations on property. Disruptions of northern plantations were not uncommon in this period. Several Yankee planters saw their laborers harassed, their property put to the torch, and their livestock stolen. Two Massachusetts men in north central Florida had their fences set on fire and a herd of cattle turned into their fields shortly after their arrival. A New Yorker leasing some of Wade Hampton's Mississippi plantations received the close attention of marauders. Another northern lessee in Mississippi lost two horses, in addition to having his gin house burned.[27] The list of depredations on northern plantations could go on indefinitely. It would not be accurate to say that this vandalism was commonplace, but neither would it be correct to make light of it. It seems to support the worst indictments of the president's policy of relaxing the war grip.

Much of the antagonism between northern planters and white natives grew out of the spirited competition for plantation labor. At the beginning of 1866 (the first full planting season after the surrender), planters who intended to resume planting on their own had to scramble to resupply their places with fieldhands. War-related causes had decreased the laboring population somewhat. Also, the black diaspora in the first flush of freedom and the determination of many black women to set up housekeeping aggravated the shortage. In Alabama and Georgia and in the interior of South Carolina, the situation was acute. The prospect of cheap land on the seacoast and higher wages in the West drained off labor, or so the old planters thought.[28] Complaints of labor-stealing were common, and northerners who ventured into the area in search of hands often had a rough time of it. One Yankee from Mississippi awarded "the palm to the Georgians, as the meanest and most despicable class of people it was ever my misfortune to meet." He managed to secure a few laborers, but only after suffering gross insults from the whites, who had told the freedmen that the Yankees meant to sell them into Cuban slavery.[29]

Conditions were no better in the Mississippi interior, and in some respects they were worse. Even the correspondent of the conservative New York *Herald* considered the area "just about the hardest case on record."[30] Labor seekers from the backcountry had to overcome a reputation for racial vindictiveness when they bargained for the services of the freedmen who congregated in the camps and towns along the Mississippi River; the ex-slaves here distrusted the honey-coated offers of desperate ex-slaveholders from the interior. Many native planters gave up the effort and threw in with a northern man in order to exploit his supposed advantage with the freedmen—and perhaps to gain a secret revenge on the ex-slaves. It was believed that the Yankees would make black people regret ever having forgotten who their best friends were. But there were also old planters who wanted revenge on the northern interlopers as well. One former Union officer who planted on the Black River realized that being in head-to-head competition with his neighbors would not be pleasant for him. They were all of "the old set; mad at him as a northerner, and mad at the negroes as freedmen."[31]

In Yazoo County, for instance, the ex-slaves were warned that if they did not go to work for their former owners, they had better not live within forty miles, or else they would be killed.[32] Albert T. Morgan quickly learned the community's feelings on this matter. On the streets of Yazoo City an old citizen demanded of the freedmen with whom Morgan was negotiating, "What er you all doing y'here? You nigros better go back where you b'long, and quit running after these y'here d—n Yankees." If the freedmen missed his point, Morgan did not. Henceforth, he determined to seek his labor in the contraband camps near Vicksburg, where he was not so well known.[33]

Some planters from Ohio ran afoul of public opinion in Yazoo County. An armed band of twenty men visited their place and warned the ex-slaves "that they should not work for Yankees," and if they did, the vigilantes swore "they would kill them, shoot them at night, and in the field when at work, burn up their houses, steal or kill their mules," and generally make life miserable for them. The southern seller of the plantation, who had not completed negotiations with the parties from Ohio, wanted federal troops to intervene because he feared that "some who claim to be the militia are engaged in this lawlessness." His fears were probably justified. Yazoo was one of those counties where vigilantes who wanted Yankees out of their neighborhood seem to have operated with impunity.[34]

Feeling was also none too good when southerners competed with each other for scarce plantation labor. It was a disagreeable business, this sudden necessity of having to bargain for the services of people who but a short time before were at one's beck and call, and it required one of the most difficult psychological adjustments that former slaveholders were called on to make. Cherished notions of racial domination were upset; many friendships were strained or broken. The old planting class tried to combine to restrict the labor competition, but the vigilance of the conqueror and the greed and individualism of the ex-slaveholders themselves frustrated the effort. So, in their bitterness and confusion, the old planters occasionally fell to lashing out at each other.[35] Louisianians who looked for hands in Georgia or South Carolina were no more welcome than were northern men on the same mission. And a Mississippian who ventured into a neighboring county to fill his gangs was just as likely as a Yankee to be threatened with mob violence.[36]

Still, the old planters seem to have lashed out with particular vehemence at the northerners in their midst. The psychology at work involved more than mere resentment of the Yankee's supposed advantages with the ex-slaves. As 1865 drew to a close and the competition for labor grew in intensity, a fear of violence and race war began to push to the surface of southern minds already agitated by political uncertainties in Washington. The reluctance of the freedmen to make contracts for the 1866 season encouraged rumors to the effect that the ex-slaves were planning to rise during the 1865 Christmas season in order to slaughter their former owners and seize their lands if the federal government failed to give them forty acres and a mule. The ensuing panic bore a strong resemblance to the slave insurrection scares of antebellum times, not only in its style of summary justice but also in its tendency to blame Yankee agitators (among others) for stirring up a people believed to be otherwise devoted and childlike. In the confusion and uncertainty that characterized the first year of peace, when the ex-slaves refused to sign contracts and to play traditional roles, it was understandable that some southerners fell into old habits and imagined evil designs in their Yankee competitors.[37] It would not be the last time that northerners were scapegoats for the racial instability that southerners saw all around them.

One fact is striking: though one seldom hears of southern men having their workers stampeded by "mischievous boys," the experience was familiar to several northern men.[38] The case of two New Yorkers planting in Clarke County, Mississippi, deep in the interior, illustrates the problem that Yankees sometimes faced. An armed band destroyed $600 worth of their property in early 1866 and would have done greater damage but for "the determined action of the negroes," some of whom were wounded. The raiders returned a few days later to bother the freedmen in the fields, and the marauders managed to elude capture not only because it was easy for them to escape into Alabama, but also because the feeling of the county was "too largely in sympathy with the offenders."[39] Even worse was the uncooperative attitude of the local district attorney. He had followed legal forms, impaneling a grand jury that indicted the vigilantes, but this was seemingly an empty gesture. He did not consult with the northern victims, who he believed were looking for "the stimulus (so palatable to Yankee cupidity) of an Executive reward."[40]

This kind of anti-Yankee sentiment colored the general lawlessness that convulsed the South shortly after the war. All that historians have said about the danger of mistaking southern lawlessness for southern disloyalty is certainly well taken.[41] Local planters suffered fully as much from the breakdown of law and order as did the newcomers. The marauders and "Texas scouts," who seemed to find Mississippi a congenial territory, seldom chose their victims on the basis of sectional identity. They vandalized plantations according to the ease with which they could be plundered and called themselves Yankees or Rebels to suit their convenience. Everyone was fair game. Yet northern planters were often regarded as objects of "legitimate plunder in this respect."[42]

The desperadoes realized that in some localities anti-Yankee sentiment was a force in their favor. The horse thieves who were convicted of murdering three southern planters in Yazoo County and who then begged leniency on the ground that they thought the victims were Yankees knew the popular pulse. Even though it was "notoriously true" in the neighborhood that the murdered men were "as true and gallant soldiers for the Confederacy as ever went to battle," the maneuver met with some success. Enough of the local citizenry was aroused to persuade the governor to stay the execution of the convicted men.[43] It seems that only the wife of one of the murder victims recognized the cruel irony of the situation. "When men once yield to the temptation of vice and crime," she lamented, "they know no distinction between friend & foe—all must alike suffer."[44] But this was a price that quite a few southerners—or at least Yazooans—appear to have been willing to pay.

On the whole, then, critics of presidential policy had some reason for their complaints. The invitation to southerners to take matters into their own hands did give rise to a sectional animus that belied all the editorial effusions that Yankees were welcome and could expect considerate treatment. Radicals did not need to manufacture stories about southern outrages in order to convince themselves that northern men who engaged in cotton-planting "must be prepared to expect obstructions of any kind that a jealous and envious malignity can suggest."[45] There was enough popular malice and official indifference to give the accusation substance and ample evidence that Andrew Johnson's courtship of the South had emboldened the malcontents among the southern people. Thus, it is altogether understandable that some Yankee planters feared not only for their property but also for their lives, that others felt that if they did not leave the region soon they might kill someone or be killed themselves, and that still others returned north as staunch Radicals of the Sumner variety.[46] A political associate of Senator John Sherman of Ohio may have been typical of those northerners who abandoned their plans to enter into business in the South. A short visit to the former Confederacy convinced him "that the South is at present no place for a northern man who has any respect for himself." "Loyalty is below par," he wrote Sherman, "and treachery commands a premium."[47]

What effect all this had on northern public opinion is a well-known story. It required only another year of southern "outrages" and the bloody riots in Memphis and New Orleans in the spring and summer of 1866 to convince moderate and conservative Republicans and northern business interests that the presidential policy of leniency and immediate restoration would have to give way to a more radical solution to the southern problem. The hardening of northern sentiment had more than a little to do with the fear that southern hostility was keeping northern men and capital out of the former Confederacy. Many Yankees had frankly begun to wonder whether the regenerative agency of northern emigration would ever be given anything like full scope in the absence of a sterner Reconstruction program. Already a pall had fallen on the Yankee planter movement or at least on certain organized expressions of it. As early as March 1866 Governor John A. Andrew began to wind up the affairs of his American Land Company and Agency, and he closed its books for good in February of the following year. In the fall of 1865 Andrew had been so impressed with the goodwill and moderation of the southern men of wealth and position with whom he was consulting that he had favored a Reconstruction policy that relied on the cooperation of the former Confederates. But six months of adverse publicity had caused his faith to desert him. The governor was not alone in concluding that the policy of early home rule had put the South "in no state of mind fit for cooperation with us in assuming the direction of government and managing for its future."[48]

This verdict against the South rested on reasonable grounds of evidence. Former Confederates had not fully satisfied the requirement that they greet Yankee travelers and settlers in that spirit of contrition and cordiality that the victor believed was his due. Instead, the conquered were recalcitrant, defiant, abusive, and anything but neighborly. The defensive nationalism of the South, in which distrust and contempt of Yankees had always played a large part, seems hardly to have been diminished by the experiences of defeat, emancipation, and military occupation.

Yet there is a danger of overemphasizing this hostility to Yankees, as fierce as it sometimes was. The malice and resentment only tells us something, not everything, about the place of Yankees in popular esteem. In many respects the hostility was simply a variation on a theme, or more accurately, perhaps, a line of counterpoint that by itself could only hint at the richness of the complete score. The cacophony of anger and war hatred was heard mainly in the interior areas of the Deep South, away from the major thoroughfares, and even in these neighborhoods it was not always maintained at the same intensity, but instead rose and fell according to a variety of circumstances. Through the fall of 1865 and into the summer of 1866, in fact, southern conditions were never so bad that most northern settlers could not live with them. If some Yankee planters were packing up to leave, many more intended to stay. Henry Lee Higginson was hardly disturbed by the crescendo of bitterness that rose from the South in the late fall of 1865. He thought that his new neighbors in Bryan County, Georgia, were as friendly as he had any right to expect. "I do not mean that these people love us," he admitted; "they cannot & ought not as yet, & I don't love them: but we all (Georgians I mean) are pretty civil, & get along very well." An Ohio man planting in Alabama had not been in the area long enough to form a definite opinion, but he was cautiously optimistic: "Like the climate & hope to like the people & country."[49]

It is possible that the novelty of southern life and the dazzling prospects of quick cotton fortunes made the dangers of arson, bushwhacking, and miasmatic fever seem worth the risk. Everyone agreed that the South was the place for a young man with grit to make some money.[50] Even so, something more than love of adventure and the calculation of profit must account for the sense of relative well-being among so many northern planters at this time. There was much about southern conditions that inspired confidence.

In truth, some southern leaders of public opinion were alarmed at the ugly sectional feeling that the president's policy seems to have aroused, and they did their best to calm the troubled waters. They had harsh words for the "few thoughtless persons amongst us, who do and say things calculated to keep alive the embers of discord and strife between the sections"; and they gave voice to fears that the malcontents might justify the indefinite continuation of military rule and goad the Radicals in Washington into pushing their schemes with renewed zeal.[51] They even heaped reproach on southerners who made a point of ostracizing northern immigrants. A hotel operator in New Orleans who refused the patronage of Yankees, a weekly paper in Vicksburg argued, was "clinching the chains that have been binding us, and he deserves the contempt and detestation of every honorable southern man."[52] If faithfulness to southern traditions of generous hospitality did not warrant overcoming old prejudices toward Yankee settlers, then expediency did. "Let us endeavor to sift the wheat from the chaff," the Selma *Daily Messenger* urged its readers, and not drive away the better class of northern immigrants, particularly men who invested in cotton plantations. Such a policy would only invite "the low flung and ignoble" from the free states to "take advantage of their own meanness to undermine the fortunes of our people."[53]

The feeling that southerners should repress indiscriminate hatred for Yankee settlers seems to have originated chiefly in the conviction that the true road to recovery lay not in politics but in economic endeavor. The duty of the southern people, it was often argued, was to put business before politics and work hard to make the South great in all things economic. In a sense this was but a variation on the old southern nationalist argument that the South could not be truly independent until she was able to compete with the North industrially. But the former Confederacy's anomalous political situation gave the doctrine new relevance. What sense did it make to agitate political issues so long as the region's fate rested with policymakers in Washington? "Away with your maudlin politics," a Georgia editor thundered, "in which, do what you will, we are but puppets in the end."[54] The refusal of Congress to seat the South's representatives demonstrated the truth of his remarks rather clearly. Early advocates of the "New South Creed" believed all along that an economic departure was a sure defense against the intrigues of Radical marplots. One of the J. D. B. DeBow's correspondents advised, "Let us have roads and a great future awaits us in spite of

Radicalism . . . it may be best not to show too much overweaning anxiety . . . for representation." [55] Even southerners who pined for an approximation of the old order recognized the futility of too much political agitation. "If it is understood that our plantations are being worked to advantage," the Charleston *Courier* reasoned, "our [northern] friends will say 'let well enough alone.' " [56] Of course, few argued that southerners should be completely indifferent to their political interests, and few could totally disregard the political debates in Washington. But several ex-Confederates warned of the danger of being consumed by the Reconstruction controversy.

To a people faced with the need to repair the devastation of war and secure the means for supporting their families, this advice to put business before politics made obvious sense. And they seem to have followed it instinctively, regardless of any appreciation they may have had of its political ramifications. By all accounts the southern people in these years were preoccupied with their own business affairs rather than with events in Washington. With them the importance of rescuing their sectional honor was less a felt need than that of rescuing their plantations from four years of neglect. Stories that have survived of once proud and wealthy masters and mistresses having to do work that four years earlier they would have considered unthinkable are not just the syrup of the "Lost Cause" myth. [57] The economic condition of the southern people compelled a close concern with private affairs. News of the crop, of the weather, or of the movement of the cotton market in Liverpool commanded more attention than reports of how the South's case stood with national authorities. As much as the northern men who poured south during and after the war, southerners were swept up by visions of immense fortunes to be made from one good cotton crop at prevailing prices. At least they were bending most of their energies toward moneymaking. [58]

In fact, it was this mania for money, as George Benham remembered, that seemed to mellow "the sentiment toward us newcomers." This was not the first time in the history of the sectional crisis that a shared interest in pursuing the main chance had led the lions to lie down with the lambs; nor would it be the last. [59] The desire for quick riches appears to have brought out the Americanism in southerners and to have caused their thoughts to move in the direction of reconciliation and reunion.

Most of all, the economic preoccupations of the southern people killed their appetite for endless political talk. By February 1866 northern planters were noticing a decided improvement in the attitude of their new neighbors. [60] The waters of sectional abusiveness receded almost as quickly as they had risen. The debates in Washington over the political status of the former Confederacy could still cause the rivers of southern bitterness to overflow their banks, but only for short periods of time.

Andrew Johnson's policy had simply failed to harden the southern mood into an implacable hatred of northern immigrants. Clearly, it did not lead large numbers of local whites to renege on their promises of considerate treatment of settlers from the free states. Many southerners still found it quite natural to greet northern planters warmly. The ex-Confederate officer who welcomed George Benham and his associates to Carroll Parish, Louisiana, was markedly friendly. "Make yourself perfectly at home, gents, perfectly at home," he told the immigrants. "Lots of new men coming into the country. That's what we want: the more the merrier. Plenty o' land here; plenty o' niggers. Yankee capital, and Yankee enterprise is all we want." Introductions to leading citizens were cordial. "I noticed the expression of each new face as we were presented," Benham recalled, "and was unable to see anything that looked like hostility."[61]

Benham's experience was not unique. The James brothers found the people of Alachua County, Florida, hospitable and helpful. A future carpetbag senator from Alabama said that he and his planting partner had received only "the kindest treatment and *heartiest encouragement* from all our neighbors." And his partner had been alone on the plantation and beyond the immediate reach of U.S. troops.[62] Numerous were the reports from Yankee planters throughout the Deep South of having been put under special obligations for kind services. Many old inhabitants assisted the newcomers in the selection of plantations, advised them freely about the methods of cotton agriculture, and in some cases even helped them in "the hiring of hands." A northern man in Georgia was very fortunate in his choice of a neighborhood. During his first year the local people frequently spent their Sundays going over his plantation with him to show him what to do.[63]

Sometimes the cordial reception was insincere. Whitelaw Reid believed a few natives "were very willing to forego manifestations of Rebel spite for the sake of furthering their chances of a good bargain." The ink had scarcely dried on some contracts before friendliness cooled noticeably. George Benham and his associates soon felt like "so many fat geese tied in the market, and every passing southerner was at liberty to pluck a feather from us." He thought the whites had a habit of giving wrong and costly advice in order to make a few extra dollars from the newcomers.[64] Getting a good trade out of the Yankees was certainly a popular policy. Some southerners neglected no opportunity for "recovering the worth of all negroes from the Yanks."[65]

More often than not this southern hospitality seems to have been genuine. Usually it lasted well beyond the signing of a business agreement. Throughout the winter and spring of 1866, in fact, something of an *entente cordiale* prevailed between local whites and even northern planters who later became pariahs in their new homes.[66] There was a surprising degree of social intercourse, even more than ardent advocates of northern immigration had imagined possible. A northern investor in Louisiana cotton lands, who had lived in New Orleans since the war, received a cordial reception whenever he visited the plantations in which he had an interest. The planters brought out their best wines and gave the man a grand tour of the country.[67] Albert T. Morgan and his brother were treated no less graciously by their landlord, Colonel J. J. U. Black, who insisted that they stay in his home until their quarters on the plantation were ready for occupancy. The Morgans were often honored guests at the dinner table.[68] Similarly, a South Carolinian who put up a planter from New York refused to allow his visitor to pay board. And it was not uncommon to find northerners and southerners sharing households when they worked plantations jointly.[69]

This hospitality toward northern men often went further than many southern households were willing to go. The instinct to keep Yankees at arm's length was strong and pervasive. Many years would have to pass before southern women would suffer gladly the presence of the conqueror in their drawing rooms. Some northern planters would find the southern people cool and reserved, sometimes rude, and would discover that the only intercourse open to them was the "Arab hospitality" of a few of the former nonslaveholding whites in the community. Even Yankees who had no reason to complain of their treatment at the hands of the old inhabitants realized that local society was not theirs to enjoy. Moreover, the bitterness of the "stay-at-homes," as those who did not serve in the military were often called, was said to know no bounds. And then there were the "mischievous boys" and the young hotspurs of the old aristocracy who neither forgave nor forgot and swore loudly that they would "show the Northern interlopers . . . the way home," the veins in their necks swelling all the while. They always seemed to be contriving ways to make life unpleasant for the newcomers, and they had to be watched and guarded against.[70]

Standing in contrast to such malice was the cordiality of important groups in the local community, and their friendship often made all the difference. It was surely a point in a newcomer's favor that former Confederate officers seldom bore a sectional grudge. They were known to enjoy swapping war stories with their counterparts from the North. But in truth nothing worked more to a northern man's advantage than to have the friendship of leading citizens, men of such social standing that they could hold in check the ill-feeling of the malcontents. A native innkeeper told Sidney Andrews that "any Northern man would get along well enough if 't was knowed that he was befriended by the best men in his neighborhood."[71] Colonel J. J. U. Black made it a point to introduce Albert T. Morgan to Yazoo City's substantial citizens. "Well, By G-d sir," the Colonel exclaimed in his characteristic manner, "he's a Yankee but a gentleman and my guest, by G-d sir." This open friendliness had a telling effect on the way Yazooans regarded the Morgans.[72]

As expansive as this hospitality could sometimes be, it usually had conditions attached. The expectation that northern planters would quickly become southern in thought and feeling was in many respects a requirement that they must become so. The newcomers were on probation, actually "on an experimental trial," and the consideration accorded them was at times as guarded as it was sincere.[73] The conviviality of Colonel Black was grounded in the conviction that Albert T. Morgan would eventually "become one of us."[74]

Yet not even the colonel or others like him could be entirely sure that the immigrants would measure up to expectations. If some of the better men of the community were conciliatory, they were also nervous, and for good reason.[75] Despite their inexperience, the amateur cotton growers were brashly self-confident and gave some indication that they meant to shake things up. J. D. B. DeBow described a group of them near Decatur, Alabama:

They have note-books and guide books and exchange information. They make close and nice calculations of cost, results, and profits, and have all the details set down in their pocket-books. They cipher out vast results. . . . They laugh to scorn the experiences of the old planters. They regard them as old fogies. Cotton can be cultivated on new rules and with Northern machinery. There are to be cultivators and buggy ploughs and cotton-pickers and cotton-thrashers and all that sort of thing.

"Well, all things are to become new perhaps," DeBow allowed, "but it might be upon the safe side to hasten a little slowly."[76]

Old planters usually agreed. They generally made great sport of the new plows, cotton planters, cotton cultivators, hay cutters, sewing machines, and india-rubber boots that the newcomers brought with them. It irritated them to be told, however obliquely, that accustomed ways of doing things, the fruit of long experience, were outmoded, old-fashioned, and had to give way to the superior ideas of the North.[77] In time southerners would gain satisfaction in seeing northern plantations go to seed, despite their having been "cultivated according to the latest and most improved Yankee plan of raising corn and cotton." And the newcomers in turn would regret ever having been so heedless of native advice regarding innovations.[78]

This, however, was still in the future, and at the time no one was sure what the northerners' zealousness meant. A few southern editors were not bothered by it, at least not those who believed that "in agricultural pursuits we must take lessons from our northern neighbors."[79] This was more than others could concede. Their open-mindedness came from knowing that the new man "will find out his mistake."[80]

Maybe these "Yankees" can find something better than the Calhoun plow, they say, or the old way of planting and cultivating cotton, but they reckon not; they reckon they will get tired enough of these new-fangled instruments. They reckon they knew pretty well how to raise cotton " 'fore the wa' "; maybe not, but from the crops they raised they think they did, and they reckon the Yankees will think so themselves 'fore the season is over.[81]

They reckoned, too, that the Yankees would become certified southerners in all essentials before much time elapsed. Yet they craved reassurance, some better passport to fellowship than the mere fact that the northerner had seen fit to invest his means among them. To an expectant community, any straw in the wind gave comfort. Men from the Northwest often got a special benefit of the doubt. "Yo're not a Yankee, yo're a Western man," Colonel Black corrected A. T. Morgan, perhaps recalling a regional alliance that had failed but might yet be revived.[82] Philadelphians also received some allowances, possibly because their city had once been a favorite residence of many wealthy slaveholders. Northerners usually allayed early apprehensions when they hired the services of southern overseers, as most did. This was some indication, however small, that they did not intend to cut themselves off from the influence of local whites.[83]

Anxious southerners did not have to wait long for concrete expressions of immigrant goodwill. The northern planting community was also expectantly watchful and eager to please. The new arrivals keenly felt the pressure to make themselves acceptable to their new neighbors. They had been told on numerous occasions that if they expected agreeable social intercourse they should mind their own business and avoid giving needless insult to the southern people.[84] They seldom felt that this was asking too much or bordered on an ultimatum. They reasoned that they had come south to build up the region, not to destroy or humiliate it—they never tired of reminding their hosts of the fact—and from the treatment they had received already, they were sure that further acquaintance and more recruits from the North would melt away such suspicions and prejudices as still remained.[85]

A number of northerners went to great lengths to placate southerners. Throughout the region in the winter and spring of 1865-66 there were many Yankees who were "loud in praise of the people of the South."[86] They spoke respectfully of the Confederate Lost Cause, defended the South's determination to give office to men who had stood by their section, and denounced the leading Radicals in the North as "the only disloyalists left."[87] Their contempt for radical Republicans was occasionally prompted by economic self-interest. A tax of three cents per pound that the federal government had imposed on southern cotton earmarked for the export market angered the newcomers no less than it did the natives. Large numbers of northern planters in Alabama hastened to make known their displeasure with Congress for laying plans to add another two cents to a tariff that was already upsetting rosy predictions of huge profits.[88] Their mood may have resembled that of some of their counterparts in Florida. A newspaper editor in Gainesville said that the cotton tax was making Yankee planters of his acquaintance

> feel what we have felt and become accustomed to long since, that is, oppression. Some have been honest enough to confess that they came here radicals, but have declared war against that party forever. The delicate touch which their pockets have received have [*sic*] converted them.[89]

Here was support for the prediction that greed would sooner or later lead the recent arrivals to accept the southern view of things.

Many northerners who advertised their southern principles were not acting out of sincere conviction. Drummers for commercial houses in the North outdid all competitors in the art of flattery, for they knew what was needed to reopen old lines of trade. Yankee merchants and hotelkeepers who adorned the walls of their establishments with portraits of Confederate heroes also grasped the business truth that the customer is always right. Yet Yankee planters could sometimes be just as complimentary and fawning.[90]

Some Yankees could not wait for a decent interval to pass before proclaiming their southern antecedents. A northern storekeeper and planter in Port Gibson, Mississippi, said he was from Natchez (where he had spent some time the year before). "I am as good Confed[erate] as Eney [*sic*] of them," he boasted to his partner in the North.[91] Eben Loomis of Massachusetts also found it useful to disguise his origins. On the way to Florida he told his southern traveling companions that he was "last from N[ew] York City, but recently *from Virginia*. It don't always do to tell the *whole* truth."[92] Frequently Yankees who checked into southern hotels announced that they were from one of the border states they had passed through on their journey south. One northerner who claimed a Missouri residence swore the gambit worked splendidly.[93]

Usually it was fear of making enemies that caused many Yankees to conceal their identities.[94] But the desire for agreeable social relations was an added temptation to be less than frank about one's origins. Not long after his arrival in north-central Florida, a New York man was swept up in the social life of the community, mixing freely with former Confederate soldiers and attending choir practice and soirées at the homes of leading citizens, none of whom suspected he was a Yankee. He decided the truth made little difference, "for as long as a man proves himself to be a gentleman it matters not whether he be grey or blue."[95]

Southerners were seldom fooled by this dissembling. The Yankee who said he was a South Carolinian from Port Royal deceived no one; everybody knew the background of the white population on the Sea Islands after the war. But the natives required few clues to guess a northern identity: a style of dress, a certain bearing, and a twanging loquaciousness were sufficient giveaways.[96] And they did not care for deliberate deception. The New Yorker who at first found his social life in northern Florida unusually agreeable was soon reminded of the treachery of snap judgments. Within two months of his arrival it was said about town that he had boasted of killing "many a reb," though he claimed he had said no such thing. Once the "*whole* truth" got out, he had to conclude that "Northern people are not *welcome* here and are treated with cool politeness."[97]

The New Yorker failed to realize that northern immigrants hardly had to hide their origins in order to get along. Nothing pleased southerners so much as those newcomers who frankly admitted they had been "black Republicans" before and during the war but now had little faith in the capacities of the freedmen and no sympathy whatever for the idea of black suffrage.[98] Newcomers of this sort were generally pronounced "splendid fellows," for their candor on the race question was just the kind of reassurance that uneasy southerners desired most.[99] It indicated a heartfelt and ingenuous readiness to fall in with the region's folkways, and it reinforced the conviction that recent arrivals from the North were really no different from the Yankees who had come south before the war. Southerners saved their best consideration for northern planters who scorned schemes to uplift black people. "As Mr. Sexton does not believe in the progression of the negro," an Alabama paper said of a Chicago native, "he will find no difficulty in his communion with his new neighbors." [100]

Just how common northern doughfaces were in these years is hard to estimate. George Benham believed they were only a handful; Whitelaw Reid complained that the spirit of "Northern flunkeyism," as he styled it, "was manifest everywhere." In Florida it was said that "half the northern men, as fast as it serves their interest to do so, side with the secesh." [101] It may have been so. Even Yankee planters who were determined not to break faith with their principles usually found it expedient to give concrete assurances of goodwill. Albert Morgan, whom no one can accuse of sycophancy, agreed to head a delegation of old inhabitants that called on the military authorities in Vicksburg for assistance in suppressing an anticipated Negro insurrection. Even though it was against his better judgment, Morgan readily cooperated with his neighbor's attempt to lift their movement above suspicions of purely sectional feelings. He was "anxious to be well thought of by the people of Yazoo." [102]

This natural desire to be "well thought of" led some northerners to cooperate with ex-Confederates in matters of federal patronage. Willard Warner apparently strengthened the friendly feeling for him and his planting partner by his determined efforts to have a southern man confirmed as the postmaster of Montgomery, Alabama. [103] The young James brothers likewise found the mail service a convenient way to prove their good intentions to the people of Alachua County, Florida. They succeeded in having a post office established in Gordon, and in gratitude, the citizens of neighboring Waldo elected Garth James postmaster. He returned the favor by giving all the postal business to the local storekeeper. [104]

A few newcomers even tried to assist natives who had lost their federal appointments because of test-oath restrictions. In Darlington, South Carolina, the retiring federal revenue assessor persuaded his Yankee replacement to give him the chief clerkship, "which still gives me the control of the office." [105] The Internal Revenue collector in Greenville, South Carolina, also recognized that a certain kind of carpetbaggery had its uses. He wanted the northern son-in-law of a local resident to be named his successor. It would be an arrangement to everyone's advantage. If the Yankee received the appointment, he planned to give the outgoing collector "all the appeals and legal part of the office, and share his compensation" with the southern man, and to favor his southern father-in-law with the head clerkship. [106]

Of course northerners who attempted to secure federal appointments in disregard of local sentiment were sometimes scorned, or worse, and most Yankees had the good sense to consult the feelings of their neighbors. [107] But so long as northerners of good character (and preferably southern affiliations) were willing to defer to southern guidance, they were more acceptable to ex-Confederates than natives who had taken the oath. Allowing southerners who had opposed the Confederacy to fill political office cut against the grain and weakened the effort to present the North with a united front. [108] Unlike southern Unionists, whom white conservatives universally despised and treated nearly as badly as the freedmen, northern men were a special case. Sympathetic Yankee officeholders, who, some natives believed, had influence with the Johnson administration, could be used to signify an absence of sectional prejudice. [109] Southerners prided themselves on their friendly feelings for northern settlers, and by their own lights they had reason for self-congratulation. The attorney-general of Alabama was being honest when he told his counterpart in Massachusetts, "I have not known a period within ten years in which Northern men would have been treated with more respect than now." [110]

On the whole, then, relations between Yankee planters and white southerners were not entirely acrimonious during the time when they were making each other's acquaintance. It may even be fair to say that relations were generally harmonious, despite the dissonances occasioned by presidential policy. The example of courtesy set by the leading men in the community was something of a restraint on those southerners who could not abide the Yankee presence. Between many northern planters and a certain class of old inhabitants there was a surprising amount of social mixing and a generous disposition to help each other out—a sort of cautious maneuvering to reassure one another that no harm was meant and that therefore each should try to make the best of things in the expectation that the relationship would one day be on a more solid footing.

A sour note sometimes crept in. Just when southerners seemed to be settling down into economic pursuits, a presidential confrontation with Congress would reawaken their resentments and encourage them to "show how much they are injured & how they are suffering." [111] At these times the most considerate southern host was apt to break out in a torrent of abuse against the national government. But no insult was intended to his northern guests. At best, it was taken for granted that the newcomers shared the quarrels of the South and thus would not take exception to any expressions of futile anger, an assumption that quite a few northerners found it convenient to humor.[112] At worst, it was a half-conscious effort to determine the true feelings of northern neighbors, for southerners could not easily shake the gnawing fear that perhaps they might be misjudging the character of these postwar immigrants. Thus, a violent epithet against the Union was likely to be followed by quick apologies and an anxious look to determine the Yankee's reaction. If it was polite silence, as would be the case for quite a while with men like Albert Morgan, who had no enthusiasm for completely shedding his identity and who could see "no good likely to result from contending with them," suspicions were only bound to deepen.[113] Nevertheless, southerners, too, were unwilling to push the issue. Their sectional abusiveness was always more of "a pastime than a steady purpose." The fact is that neither party talked much politics.[114] Neither wanted to do so as long as the prospects of large fortunes appeared so promising.

Still, this relationship was a good deal more fragile than either newcomer or native cared to admit. Mutual greed could mitigate hostility but not subdue it entirely. Always just below the surface lay social and ideological antagonisms of the sort that could easily be inflamed by competing assumptions of superiority and mutual disappointments of expectations. It was foolish of southerners to expect all the new arrivals to renounce their ideals so soon after the triumph of northern arms. And it was reckless of northerners to suppose that the old inhabitants could easily be induced to surrender some of their most cherished notions. If one thing united the gracious hosts and the hotspurs, it was a determination not to put up with alien influences in their communities. The only thing dividing them was that the gracious hosts had consulted past experience and had concluded that there was no peril in according the Yankees "that degree of confidence which will enable us to determine what their real merits are."[115] The danger was that in certain localities, and with regard to certain Yankees, further acquaintance might lead to mutual alienation, while "minding one's own business" might only darken suspicions. And if business prospects ever worsened and political clouds became threatening, the atmosphere of goodwill and mutual forbearance might suddenly vanish.

5 *"The New Dispensation"*

No justification for the northern planter movement was more popular than the argument that the ex-slaves required humane and intelligent supervision such as only Yankees could give them. It was often argued that if the freedmen were ever to rise from the condition of slavery, northern men would have to help them. Old slaveholders lacked faith in the black free-labor experiment and were unfitted for it by temperament and training. But Yankees who went south in these years to plant cotton were of a different background and a different mind. They were sure they could work the freedmen to the mutual advantage of employer and employee, and they meant to prove it. Some of the newcomers were committed to helping the ex-slaves become independent farmers; still more wanted to teach them proper Christianity and the mysteries of the primer; but most of all, the majority of the newcomers wanted to acquaint the freedmen with the values of bourgeois society: regularity, punctuality, sobriety, and frugality. Above all else, northern planters wanted to make the ex-slave a good worker. Their prospects for gain partly depended on it. How much useful industrial training the freedmen received is difficult to say. One thing is certain: the ex-slaves did learn about Yankee greed and about the ways in which the marketplace would now impinge on their lives. This was "the new dispensation."[1]

Confidence in the ability of the ex-slaves to adjust to free labor was not universal among northerners interested in cotton-planting. A few questioned whether the freedmen would work and passed up opportunities to buy or rent plantations. "*No money* can be made by planting cotton with negro labor in my opinion, *on a large scale*," Edward Atkinson's cotton agent wrote to his father. "It may do as a philanthropical measure, but as a profitable investment, you had better keep on building houses on Beacon Street."[2] There was an interest in using white labor, and northerners who had the means seem to have been especially attracted to the idea of adapting foreign immigrants to the work of cotton-raising. William Sprague's company sent out a crew of one hundred Germans to its plantations along the Mississippi River and later added some Dutch, Danish, and Swiss hands. The experiment had mixed results. Higher wages in New Orleans continually caused many of them to run off, and the remainder proved difficult to please. J. Floyd King, one of Sprague's plantation superintendents, estimated that the immigrants ate at least "one third to one half more than the negro, and do not accomplish more than two thirds as much work." King believed there was one positive aspect. When the immigrants were put to work among the freedmen there seemed to be a good effect on both black and white, from the standpoint of productivity.[3]

George Benham's attempt to work northern white hands did not score even this small success. Not only were they without farming experience, but they were rebellious, intractable, and fond of loafing. They rose late, forever complained about the food, and annoyed everyone with their nightly parties. They refused to do hard work, insisting that it belonged to the blacks, and performed sloppily such jobs as they could be persuaded to undertake. Benham was not at all upset when they deserted after the first payday. Nor were the black workers, who resented the special treatment that the white hands received. The black cook hailed their departure. It was the first squad of white hands she ever served, and she hoped it was the last. "I was done used-up wid mindin' dat dey shouldn't dash out de grub, and no mistake."[4]

Benham's experiment with northern black labor was nothing to write home about either. He was confident that "a short time under their sunny southern sky would make them as much the Sambo as ever."[5] But the first day of plowing was one he preferred to forget. His black Yankees were not experienced farmhands. He recounted:

> Now they had the plow down, now the plow had them down, their mules plunged off on all sorts of tangents, hame-strings flew right and left, three or four plow-beams snapped square in two, in what seemed to be the frantic effort of these novices to get down into China. . . . There was no medium with them, it was either the speed of the wind or a sudden halt—this just as the plow spun on the surface or buried itself to the hilt, so to speak, in the earth.[6]

Benham called a halt to the confusion after about three hours. Except for the furrows plowed by his two experienced farmers, "the piece of ground looked as if it might have been the arena of a bullfight, or the rooting-place of a drove of hogs." One-quarter of his plows needed repairs at the blacksmith shop, and the mules and hands both were some time recovering from the workout. Benham henceforth sought hands from among discharged black soldiers.[7]

These abortive attempts to use imported labor in the cotton fields simply underscored the indispensability of the freedmen. The newcomers learned what the natives were to bear in upon them repeatedly throughout the remainder of the nineteenth century: the South could hardly do without the labor of ex-slaves in raising her major staples. Immigrants from whatever source were poor substitutes for freedman labor. The advantages that they had did not offset the problems of desertion, discontent, language barriers, and inexperience.[8] If the South were ever to regain her preeminence in cotton production, she would have to rely on the labor of people who had traditionally grown the staple.

The majority of northern planters accepted this truth and were more than willing to try the experiment of black free labor. Fortunate for them that they were, for they had to turn to someone to compensate for their lack of cotton-growing experience. Very few northern planters had extensive knowledge of agriculture and none was familiar with raising cotton, let alone managing a plantation. Their duties were myriad and unfamiliar. "I have to be master, father, judge, jury, justice of the peace, storekeeper and head man in general," Eben Loomis explained to his sister. "Our whole mode of life here is so totally new and different from old habits that I hardly know how to begin to describe it," James Waters wrote. "We are a little community by ourselves on the plantations."[9]

Managing this community posed special problems, particularly of an agricultural nature. One had to be knowledgeable about how to raise and gather a cotton crop. From the selection of seed to the picking and ginning of cotton, the entire operation required care and intelligence. And there was nothing comparable to the vexations of keeping one's crops clear of weeds, as many newcomers painfully discovered.[10] Most of all, an understanding of plantation field labor was necessary. It may be stretching a point to compare southern plantations with the northern factory system, but it is true that many historians and free-soil critics alike have greatly underestimated the efficiency of the agricultural routine under slavery. The planter had to be a good judge of abilities in order properly to assign laborers to the various field gangs, and these gangs had to be carefully synchronized and paced if the work were to proceed smoothly. There was a constant battle to stay one step ahead of the elements. All the phases of preparing a crop were on a schedule imposed by the vagaries of the growing season.[11] In the best of circumstances it was hard to achieve the proper timing and discipline; after emancipation, as we shall see, it required even greater tact and skill. There were other requirements as well. A successful cotton planter, according to a southerner who had studied the matter carefully, "must have cotton-planting sense. He must have sound common sense, good perceptive faculties, strong animal energy, indomitable perseverance, good governing faculties, and an all-conquering will."[12] Obviously, northern planters had their work cut out for them.

Most newcomers were sensible enough to seek help. They often hired southern overseers, though it was not always a simple matter to find one who knew his business, laid off the bottle, and got along with the hands.[13] Yankees also placed great reliance on the black drivers, for the field gangs required "a man of a good deal of authority and energy to make them do their duty—especially during the hoeing season." These drivers had to be chosen carefully, for an overbearing personality sometimes caused a mutiny in the fields.[14] A few northerners even used black foremen exclusively. A planter from Massachusetts got his agricultural training "chiefly from the negroes on the plantation—a Yale graduate at the feet of ex-slaves." It was a situation familiar to "Gideon's Band" at Port Royal.[15]

Northern men did not consider their lack of planting experience a grave handicap. They were sure that an understanding of how men made other men work without compulsion would overcome whatever deficiencies they had in practical knowledge. The idea that Yankees would be singularly successful at plantation enterprise rested by and large on the proposition that "it will be much easier for them to learn the simple business of raising cotton than for the old planters to learn how to manage and get work out of the negroes as free laborers."[16] Confidence in the ability of ex-slaveholders to adjust to the new realities was not very strong; the instincts of generations would not disappear overnight. But Yankees knew from personal experience what free labor meant, understood "the workings of its machinery," and were "not disturbed by the irregularities connected with it, which seem utterly inadmissible to the Southerners."[17] The newcomers were not averse to paying wages and would even pay by the day, week, or month, as circumstances required. They did not expect to exercise despotic control over their laborers, had no use for "groveling subjects," and were perfectly willing to recognize gradations in performance and ability. They also realized that they must be ever ready to acknowledge and reward faithful industry, just as they had to be prepared to rebuke and discourage backsliding. Their motto was "a fair day's wages and a fair day's work."[18]

The industrial ideas of northern planters, of course, came straight from the world of laissez faire capitalism as described by the Manchester school of economic thought. "The only incentive to faithful labor is self-interest," it was believed.[19] The choice facing all men was either the misery brought on by idleness or the comfort gained by honest toil. The freedmen must either work or starve, and work steadily and faithfully, or else they would be replaced with more reliable hands. "Necessity of getting a living," John Murray Forbes wrote, "is a great secret of providing for sheep, negroes, and humans generally." The only coercion called for was the threat of discharge or docked pay; the driver's lash as an impetus to labor was as unnecessary as it was inhumane.[20] The economic world of the Yankee planters was a self-regulating one, governed by natural laws, and the labor of ex-slaves had "to come into the market like everything else, subject to the supply and demand."[21] Wages in a capitalist economy found their own level as free agents bargained for goods and services. Yet the laws of the marketplace were not so inexorable as to be incapable of infringement. The South during slavery had defied them for generations and seemed yet determined to restore the discredited institution, or something close to it. But in the hands of humane and dedicated men, it was thought the free-labor system would work with clockwork efficiency and determined impartiality.[22]

At its best, the free-labor philosophy conceded the freedman the right to "determine the value of his own labor and [to] be left to take the responsibilities of his own existence and well being, as well as that of his family."[23] At its worst, it held that the ex-slave must henceforth "root, hog, or die," and some northerners were indifferent about the outcome.[24] Edward Atkinson, the chief spokesman for the free-labor point of view, left little room for sentimentality in his theories. "If they are to die out from incapacity, so be it," he wrote of the freedmen. "Better they should die as inferior men than live as high class animals." This attitude was at considerable variance with the softer side of the southern doctrine of racial paternalism, which held that "inferior men" should be protected in their infirmity and not forced to take their chances in a competitive race for which their native endowments supposedly did not equip them. But the theoreticians of laissez faire capitalism, on occasion, assigned greater importance to the competitive race itself than to the fate of its contestants. Atkinson philosophized that death was "only an accident in the midst of life or at the beginning of it," and meant very little in the larger perspective. However, freedom was "essential to the development even of inferior men."[25] Naturally, he frowned on gratuitous philanthropy and warned often of the danger of high wages to black initiative. Nothing should be done that would make the freedmen conclude that they could supply their wants with a minimum of effort. Atkinson and his generation believed in the therapy of hard times. The worst disservice that one could do to the ex-slaves was to give them free land. It would encourage them in "idleness and improvidence."[26]

But Atkinson did not rule out the idea of black landownership. He was the most articulate exponent of the proposition that the plantation system was bound to yield sooner or later to small freeholds through natural processes.[27] Several northern planters, in fact, believed that small farms were the wave of the southern future, and they were more than happy to roll with the tide. Henry Lee Higginson, who told his hands not to expect forty acres and a mule at Christmas time, impressing upon them that other laborers would be put "into their houses if they do not work for us," nevertheless thought that the desire to own a farm "indicates the foundation of an excellent agricultural population." He did not discourage this ambition.[28] The idea was that "the possession of sufficient land elevates and dignifies a peasantry."[29]

There were several private enterprise attempts to provide the freedmen with their own farms. When it became clear that the federal government did not intend to confiscate and redistribute the large estates of the South, abolitionist-minded entrepreneurs thought that business companies might be able to promote a measure of black landownership. Governor John A. Andrew, who saw no incompatibility between northern-owned plantations and southern black farms, attempted to get his American Land Company and Agency into the business of buying plantations and reselling them to the landless poor, lending them as well the necessary seed capital with which to get started. His project ran up against the opposition of his advisers (Atkinson thought the scheme would do the freedmen "more harm than good"), and the unwillingness of the southern legislatures to sanction such a venture. Moreover, corporations chartered in one state could not own land in another state without the latter's permission.[30] Other land-reform business projects met with more success. The American Missionary Association (AMA) and the American Freedmen's Union Commission both invested in plantations in order to divide them eventually among the ex-slaves. Several agricultural villages sprang up as a result of the AMA's efforts.[31]

Northern planters themselves sometimes took steps to help the freedmen obtain land. Despite his commitment to the large-scale organization of labor, Edward S. Philbrick, in 1865, sold some of his land to freedmen for one-half the price he asked of white men. The action failed to appease his critics, who noted that the price he quoted the blacks was still much higher than what he had paid for the land originally.[32] Another Port Royaler, Frederic A. Eustis, who supported the Sea Islands experiment despite his prewar residency, "wouldn't sell any land to a white man except the overseer's yard and ten acres," apparently feeling that the bulk of his plantation should go to the people on the place.[33]

A few Yankees adopted the plan of share-renting their land to the freedmen as a means of helping them to become independent farmers. The idea that tenantry was one rung on the agricultural ladder leading toward farm ownership had had many adherents in the North before the war, and even Garrisonians on occasion had advised slaveholders to abolish slavery and work their land on shares with their former slaves.[34] Henry W. Warren, a teacher from Massachusetts, encouraged the hands on his Mississippi plantation to be frugal with their share of the crop proceeds. Once they had saved enough to buy a mule and a few farming tools, he contracted to sell them some land. By the 1870s the former slaves "were cultivating nearly the whole of the 'old plantation,' either as their own property or under contract of purchase." Strongly committed to making the ex-slaves freeholders, Charles Stearns also resorted to share-renting land to his hands when he discovered that only a few of them could afford to purchase individual plots. He was lucky to have succeeded this far. Only some heavy borrowing and the timely aid of Boston abolitionists prevented his Georgia plantation "from falling into the hands of the rebels, which would have frustrated our project of dividing it among the blacks." Even these methods bore an incomplete harvest. Stearns eventually sold his place to a colony of religious enthusiasts and teachers from Massachusetts.[35]

Yankee planters as a rule did not make a habit of trying to help the freedman acquire a freehold. Their lack of energy in this direction had partly to do with the northern conviction that the ex-slaves had to undergo a period of tutelage before they could strike out on their own. Estimates of the duration of the transition to independence varied somewhat, but there seemed to be a loose consensus that "it will take a long time to educate the negroes up to that point where they must depend entirely upon themselves."[36] Back of much of the radical rhetoric concerning equal rights and equal opportunity lay the conservative assumption that even under the most favorable conditions, black people as a group would never become anything more than a permanent servant class. All that many Republicans wanted to do for the freedmen was to give them a fair chance to find their own natural level somewhere near the bottom of the social scale.[37]

On one thing many northerners did seem to agree: the experiment with black freeholds on the south Atlantic coast had proved the failure that had been predicted all along. The freedman farms at Port Royal and in the coastal settlements set aside for black occupancy by General William T. Sherman's Field Order 15 usually suffered in comparison with Yankee-operated plantations. A correspondent for the Boston *Daily Advertiser* had "grave reasons for believing that the laborers on the plantation directed by Northern men were doing a larger amount of work per head than those in the freedmen's settlements."[38] The trouble was that although the experiment had proven the ex-slave's capacity for self-support, it had also shown that he was more interested in subsisting on his garden crops, fishing, and hunting than in raising cotton. Edward Philbrick had come to the conclusion that "the amount of cotton planted will always be a pretty sure index of the state of industry of the people." But the freedmen had discovered that they could do quite well by marketing their game and vegetables to the soldiers' camps.[39] The newcomers felt that the ex-slaves should instead be bending all their energies toward producing for the market. It cut against the northern grain that seemingly "the freedmen does [*sic*] no more work than will suffice for his immediate wants and occupies his time in travelling from one place to another."[40]

Yankee planters generally felt that the former slaves needed improvement in a number of areas. Their agricultural habits were thought to be slovenly and careless, their sense of responsibility imperfectly developed, and their morals stunted and deformed. It was the judgment of one government lessee that the freedmen would never be able to "thrive by themselves" until they were thoroughly "systematized." Most of all, the ex-slaves had to be taught that freedom did not mean "to do just as they please."[41] A frequent complaint heard in these years was that the freedmen "have no idea of *real* sensible freedom and fancy the word means license complete and unrestrained."[42] What they needed, of course, was to be hired out "to a set of tight-fisted Yankee farmers, who would be just toward them, taking nothing and giving nothing for nothing, and without a spark of sentiment in them."[43] But Yankee businessmen and lawyers posing as farmers would do just as well.

Northern planters intended to make the freedmen more reliable workers by inculcating in them the bourgeois ethic of sobriety, responsibility, and above all else, steady industry. There would be no toleration of slipshod and hurried work, or of malingering and tardiness. The former slaves were to work with the regularity that has since come to be identified with the modern factory system, but that at that early date was associated only with steadiness and constant application. They would have to learn that freedom was not an opportunity to overindulge their supposed instincts for a more relaxed pace of life. "Negroes need to be taught," wrote Whitelaw Reid, "that liberty means, not idleness, but merely work for themselves instead of work for others; and that, in any event, it means always work." A northern planter in the Sea Islands was more blunt. He told his hands that "being free means harder work than they had ever done before, or starvation."[44] A chance to support oneself and one's family by less than back-breaking work was apparently not among the blessings that freedom conferred.

Whether northern men could be successful in imposing an industrial discipline on the plantation system remained to be seen. The slaveholders had tried to do it, but with only limited success. They found it hard to reduce to an unvarying routine a branch of industry that by its very nature moved in fits and starts according to the cycles of the seasons and the fluctuations of the weather. They also knew the dangers of trying to drive labor at too hard a pace once the oppressive heat and humidity of the southern summer had set in. Still, the great obstacle in the way of making cotton plantations into "factories in the field" was the work ethic of the slaves themselves. Tied to the natural rhythms of agriculture and reinforced by an African sense of time, the slave work ethic placed a high premium on the communitarian value of labor and on the social value of leisure. The slaves spurned the idea of routinized work, though they were not averse to hard work, and they considered time as something that was passed, not consumed. It reduced to the fact that because they were slaves, they could not be made to give their labor in any other than a grudging way. The social system in which they had grown up held out to them few of the material and psychological incentives that historically have been instrumental in inducing laboring people to internalize the values of industrial life. The slaves' ideas of work derived from the needs of an oppressed people to resist dehumanization. As Eugene Genovese explains it, "The black ethic represented at once a defense against an enforced system of economic exploitation and an autonomous assertion of values generally associated with preindustrial people."[45] The slaveholders had prevailed only to the extent that they had made their plantations profitable in a capitalist economy, but no further. Could Yankee planters succeed at establishing a factory-like regimen on the plantations even in the absence of the traditional restraints and coercions? They thought so. They felt sure that their system of incentives, of rewards and punishments, of moral and educational training, would change the psychology of the former slaves in ways that naked force and paternalistic deception never could.

But the northern men's confidence that they could succeed with the freedmen where others had failed derived only partly from their faith in the efficacy of the free-labor system. They knew it helped to have natural laws on one's side: They were certain that the freedmen would come around once they saw "that work or starvation is before them." But their self-assurance came also from their determination not to be caught in the contradiction that had plagued the old slaveholding class, which had been in the embarrassing position of preaching efficiency while practicing the aristocratic graces.[46] Not only would the new men exhort their laborers to practice industrial efficiency, they would show them how. One of the greatest shortcomings of the cotton system under slavery, it was believed, had been the lack of close attention to small details. Black people would have been much more reliable workers had their masters not relied so heavily on overseers and had instead given their estates the "personal supervision" that distinguished the practices of all successful managers. One should not take any man's word that a job had been done well. A good free-labor planter "ought to ride over the fields every day and make himself master of every part of the field—and direct attention to any part that may need it," wrote the Boston merchant who financed Eben Loomis's plantation.[47] Land reform critics of the government plantation leasing system in the Mississippi Valley had no stronger argument against its monopolistic tendencies than the fact that "lessees of more than one plantation are unable to give their personal supervision and so employ the old overseers whom the former masters had employed." Northern small farmers would be better employers for the freedmen simply because of the personal interest they would take in their work. Whitelaw Reid was sure that "with a capital of a few thousand dollars, and a personal supervision of his work, a Northern farmer, devoting himself to cotton growing, may count with safety on a net profit of fifty percent."[48] But Yankee planters were also confident that they could bring a new style of management to plantation affairs, even though they had to rely on a class of foremen that had been thoroughly discredited. "I should believe that a Southern overseer would be useful in various ways," Henry Lee Higginson wrote, "but we must oversee & *boss* our own job."[49]

To Higginson and his partners this meant rolling up shirt sleeves and pitching in. Like many other northern planters, he believed that the freedmen would work well "if some one would show them how."[50] "Bye and bye when they see us plough and chop and hoe, and drive mules and clean horses as well as show them the use of unknown tools like scythes," he felt, "they will feel still more persuaded to do their whole duty."[51] Even newcomers with aspirations to the aristocratic graces did not find personal supervision a chore to be avoided. George Benham also thought that the freedmen were like a "plastic mass" only needing intelligent guidance and good examples. These he supplied by working in the fields with the hands, "now taking the lead with the plow gang, now assisting in logging, and now knocking down the weeds before the plows, all the time performing the duties and drudgery of a day-laborer." Charles Stearns's aim was "to establish a model farm, or self-supporting industrial school; where all that related to man's external welfare should be taught and practiced, as well as those things that concerned his moral and intellectual progress." He made it a point to work alongside his farmhands at least part of the time.[52] Another industrial-school enterprise was the Georgia plantation financed by Boston philanthropists and managed by William and Ellen Craft, the ex-fugitive slaves. Freedmen received instruction in the latest agricultural methods from northern farmers during part of the day and applied their knowledge in the field for the remainder of their work shift. Even northern wives got into the act, for they were often as determined to establish order in the house as their husbands were to maintain efficiency in the fields.[53]

This kind of personal supervision was not entirely unfamiliar to countless small slaveholders, and even a few large planters had on occasion tried to set an industrious example, at least for their overseers. But some of the Yankees brought a reformatory zeal to the practice that doubtless would have shocked the racial and paternalistic sensibilities of the southern gentry. Even so, the freedmen seemed to respond well to it. Higginson thought that industrious examples removed somewhat "the feeling of caste." The people on Stearns's place said it felt good "to be treated like a man, and to feel that we have no master."[54] Even Higginson's overseer got into the spirit of the thing and began to whitewash his own house, after seeing his employer's example.[55] There was a danger of overdoing it, however, for the ex-slaves had absorbed from their former masters certain notions of what usages were appropriate to a gentleman, and one might lose the respect of his hands if he rushed precipitately into these matters. The thoughtful missionaries at Port Royal grappled for some time with the problem of how to introduce "democratic manners" into their relations with the people. Some northerners believed they knew the solution: See to it that the "tone is dignified and perfectly earnest," Edward E. Hale advised a plantation superintendent at Port Royal. "Do not make the negroes think that they have fallen into the hands of a under-toned set of men."[56]

Yankees also had fixed notions about the proper way to govern black people. Charles Stearns came south with the conviction that "kindness was more potent than force" in controlling men, and he resolved to manage his hands strictly by "moral means." The young James brothers also were dedicated to proving the effectiveness of fair treatment as a way of handling laborers.[57] It would be wrong to maintain that theirs was the common standard, but it is enough to point out that even such Negrophobes as James Waters and George Klapp believed that the ex-slaves deserved something better than the mere outlawing of the driver's lash. They pledged to their workers to avoid "roughness & *peremptory* tones" when addressing them.[58] One northerner spelled out in some detail how he thought the freedmen should be governed. After witnessing an extended skirmish between a southern mistress and her domestic servant, he told the lady that she should "never speak a cross word to them except when unavoidable, encourage them to do right, and give them credit when they did so."

"Speak to them seldom," he admonished her, "and make them understand at such times that she meant what was said."[59]

Naturally, not all Yankee planters took their responsibilities so seriously. The absentee planters, who some thought were not insignificant in numbers, simply left the business of labor management to southern overseers in much the same way as had their antebellum counterparts. So, too, did a few government lessees in the Mississippi Valley, where the danger from guerrillas was constant. On plantations worked jointly by northern and southern men, the former often assumed charge of the financial end of the plantation operation, leaving labor management to the more experienced partner.[60] And there was always the northerner who discovered that plantation duties were not the novelty he had hoped for. Clifford Waters made a self-discovery on his plantation in Louisiana. "I like authority in the abstract," he confessed, "but practically I am afraid I am disposed to shirk." He never looked forward to being left with the general management of the place. It was very disagreeable. " 'Do that which you hate' Emerson says & I think I am doing it pretty decidedly."[61] But Clifford may have been untypical. His brother James was more self-reliant, and although he had his doubts about the character of the freedmen, he felt that "by right management, & constant discipline, they can be improved, & the *men* can be made to work & behave well."[62] He enjoyed the challenge, and his probably was the more representative attitude. The Yankees, in the main, relished their role as pioneers of free labor on this newest frontier of American labor relations.

So much for the reformist spirit and élan of the new masters. What of their institutional innovations and departures? How did their system of labor differ from that of the old masters?

Any treatment of this subject must begin with the planter-missionaries at Port Royal. They were far ahead of their contemporaries in encouraging the freedmen in habits of initiative. "Strike the fetters off at a blow and let them jump, or lie down" was how one of them explained the missionaries' approach to labor management. "I let them go ahead very much as they choose," Charles P. Ware wrote. "I make regulations for the good of all, as in the matter of carts, oxen, etc., but the minutiae I do not meddle with, except as a matter of curiosity and acquirement of knowledge."[63] Their system of labor reflected their point of view. While still a plantation superintendent for the government, Edward S. Philbrick had abandoned gang labor and substituted for it a modified version of the task system of labor organization common to the rice districts of the Georgia and South Carolina low country. He assigned each worker or his family as much cotton land as they thought they could work and paid them "for each unit of work performed upon it—so much for planting, so much for hoeing, and, later, so much per pound for picking." The wages were low, however. He also gave them garden plots from which they were expected to supply most of their own provisions. The system worked better than Philbrick had imagined possible. He had adopted it because of the people's resistance to being driven any longer in gangs, and because of an insufficient number of white foremen to give the gang system the supervision he felt it required. In the rice fields during slavery the task system tended to stimulate speedier labor, but with Philbrick's modifications, the hands seemed to work with even greater celerity. By midday they had often finished their tasks and were at work in their gardens or filling up the day as they saw fit. Inasmuch as preindustrial people are naturally task-oriented and prefer to "attend upon what is an observed necessity," Philbrick had hit upon a strategy of labor organization that even today is considered by social engineers as the most effective way of introducing preindustrial cultures to the habits of industrial life. He was rewarded amply for his ingenuity. Philbrick consistently made decent profits, netting in 1863 alone $80,000. It would seem that the freed people were responsive to the incentives of personal initiative, and that they could manage quite well with a minimum of supervision. But the tendency of black Port Royalers to emphasize market-gardening over cotton-growing, as we have seen, strengthened somewhat Philbrick's conviction that the ex-slaves still need guidance and good examples.[64]

Whether or not Philbrick's personal example had an effect on the freedmen, his task system with variations seems to have found favor with many Yankee planters in the general vicinity. Before long several northerners within the orbit of Port Royal appeared to be using his methods. After the first strike on his plantation for higher wages, Henry Lee Higginson visited the Sea Islands to get acquainted with the task system, and he seems to have eventually adopted many of its essentials. It is doubtful whether many of Philbrick's emulators went so far as one lessee at Port Royal, who said "that all he had to do was to ride over his plantation once in two days, and to spend with each gang of laborers about five minutes, long enough to give directions and to inspect the work going on." Philbrick and his associates liked to keep a closer watch on things than this, and for this reason some who adopted his system eventually changed it and made it hardly distinguishable from the task system that slaveholding cotton growers sometimes employed: labor was by the task, but the hands received neither their own acreage nor task rates.[65]

As minor as they might seem, Philbrick's innovations in the plantation work routine appear to have been the only major change that Yankee planters saw fit to make during these years. Such changes were by no means practiced extensively. Most newcomers had too much capital at stake and too little experience in plantation management to feel comfortable with a major departure from proven usage. Some northerners thought they were overhauling the old order in a significant way, but their reforms were actually more illusive than real. Often they were simply normal procedures dressed in a pleasing name. Charles Stearns applied his "cooperative principle" in a familiar fashion. His idea of an "equitable distribution" of the profits between capital and labor seemed to envision first a form of share wages and then tenantry, hardly startling innovations for the period; even these changes were not hurriedly adopted. Stearns eventually concluded that "although co-operation is the grand remedy for the ills complained of by working-men, yet the freedmen are not sufficiently advanced, intellectually, or morally, to render its adoption among them, a practicable thing." He had in mind the unwillingness of the more ambitious workers to be paid at the same rate as the shirkers. Those who were needed most in a cooperative enterprise "preferred working for themselves," or choosing for themselves the people with whom they would cooperate.[66] High ideals were not the only thing northern planters eventually abandoned. A commitment to personal supervision also seems to have gone by the board before long. When the sharecrop tenantry system was finally established, it met no appreciable resistance from those northern planters who still remained in the South. Their readiness to adopt it had more to do with economic and personal considerations than with the aim of helping the freedmen become landowners. Like their southern counterparts, the new men, too, were often all too glad to be relieved of the problems of managing plantation labor.[67]

Tenantry, however, was in the future. The contract labor system that originated in the Department of the Gulf under Generals Benjamin F. Butler and Nathaniel P. Banks established the legal order under which plantation routine would be organized in the early years of freedom. The contract system also had continuity with the past, many of its leading features having been recommended by the slaveholders themselves. The need to do something with the thousands of slaves who had fled to federal lines during the war prompted these racially-conservative generals to compromise with representatives of the old order. Congressional law prohibited officers of the federal government from returning fugitive slaves to their masters, yet "loyal" owners, who were exempted from the provisions of the Emancipation Proclamation, had a legal right to reclaim their property. What were Union commanders to do when "it was simply impossible to distinguish between freedmen and slave?" The obvious answer was to return black people to the plantations in such a way as to skirt the question of slavery. The early contract labor systems in the Department of the Gulf either expressly conceded the right of slave ownership or waived the question entirely. The conservatism of the compromise did not trouble Generals Butler and Banks, whose first priority was to help President Lincoln win the loyalty of southern whites by restoring the plantation economy.[68]

Possibly it is these compromises with slavery that help explain some of the harsh features of the wartime contract labor system. In a few respects the system represented a wholesale infringement of the rights of free labor: for example, by fixing wages it denied a laborer the right to bargain as a free agent with his employers; by obligating a laborer to contract for a year, it seriously restricted his freedom of movement and his freedom to change employers. The entire apparatus was really a system of vagrancy laws that left black people with the choice of working on the plantations or laboring on the public works. And it was even bolstered by such familiar methods of slave control as the pass system and patrols (led by U.S. provost marshals), even though corporal punishment was forbidden or delegated to military authorities. In March 1864 General Lorenzo Thomas "for the sake of uniformity" established the system in the Mississippi Valley.[69] There were modifications of the program over the years. The objectionable pass and patrol system was eventually abandoned, and the contract labor program as it was administered by the Freedmen's Bureau after the war was in general a marked improvement over its predecessor. The Bureau apparently derived its reforms from General Rufus Saxton's methods of supervising labor contracts on the Sea Islands. He recognized the right of laborers to bargain freely with employers, even if he claimed the authority of final approval. As a referee of labor contracts, the Freedmen's Bureau did good service by preventing gross impositions on the ex-slaves. But it could not entirely transcend the tainted origins of the system it was mandated to administer. Although conceived by radical abolitionists to protect and advance the rights of the newly liberated, the Freedmen's Bureau eventually became an arm of presidential Reconstruction, and its agents often enforced vagrancy laws in the manner of wartime federal authorities.[70]

It was from this contract labor system that Yankee planters by and large derived the essentials of their own labor programs. Not surprisingly, most of the plantation work went forward under the old gang labor system, with the substitution of wages for the driver's whip. Hands were assigned to plow gangs, hoe gangs, and trash gangs, for example, and each crew was directed by a black driver, under the general supervision of the overseer or the planter, as the case might be. Ten hours of labor, or from sunup to sundown, was the normal workday, with a short breakfast in the field and a one- or two-hour lunch break at the workers' quarters. These work schedules fluctuated with the seasons, shortening during the off-months in the winter and lengthening during picking season. Saturday afternoon and Sunday customarily belonged to the hands, although many Yankees considered the shortened Saturday as a "relic of slavery" and tried with limited success to make their laborers work the full day. Most northern day laborers and craftsmen at the time worked ten hours a day, six days a week, when they could find full employment. Christmas was an appointed holiday, as was the Fourth of July, one small sign that conditions had changed.[71]

As a general rule, northern planters paid cash wages. Contract regulations permitted wage payments in a share of the crop. Such payments were low when fixed by the government and noticeably higher once the freedmen received the right to bargain with the planter. A few planters paid their workers in shares (not to be confused with share-renting), but Yankees seemed to prefer cash payments, partly because they obviated complicated settlements at the end of the year.[72] However, the freedmen's wishes in this matter may have been decisive. Usually they wanted cash wages because they did not like to wait for their money until the end of the year.[73] The pay scale varied temporally and geographically. It never exceeded $10 a month in wartime Louisiana and Mississippi, and this figure does not allow for deductions for clothing and medical care. There was an improvement after the war, when the military relaxed its control. Because of the heavy demand for labor in the area, first-class hands received anywhere from $12 to $18 a month and sometimes more. In Alabama, Georgia, and South Carolina the rates were somewhat lower; labor shortages in Florida tended to drive wages upward. Of course women, children, and the elderly everywhere received smaller wages, the rate depending on whether they were second- or third-class hands.[74]

As was the custom of the South, northern planters usually supplied their farm hands with weekly rations, consisting normally of a peck or two of meal, a few pounds of pork, and a pint of molasses. In cases where garden plots were assigned, it was not uncommon to make the hands responsible for their own provisions, as was the case on the South Carolina Sea Islands. Wartime regulations in the Mississippi Valley prohibited lessees from commuting the cost of rations, which was a lucky thing for the workers since the allotting of garden plots was only encouraged, not enforced. After the war northerners who paid their laborers above the going rates also made the people supply themselves, thus taking back with one hand what they gave with the other.[75] The idea of supporting the aged, in addition to having to hire the young, usually outraged the business principles of the new men, though Whitelaw Reid thought that "in the main, their feelings get the better of their business habits."[76] This was not always the case. Military authorities in the West had their hands full with the number of old and disabled plantation people whom lessees had turned off their places. Wartime contracts finally stipulated that planters were responsible for the care of the sick and disabled. Still, it went against the grain. The birth of two baby girls on William Waters's place at Port Royal was not an occasion for rejoicing. "This catastrophy [*sic*] will deprive me of 4-1/2 acres of Sea Island [cotton land] and obliged me to give her [the mother] 3/4 of an acre of corn land to support them." Whatever elements of paternalism persisted in the northern way of planting, support for nonproductive hands was not among them.[77]

The usual practice everywhere was to withhold at least part of the laborer's pay until the end of the season. Initial contract-labor regulations recommended that workers not be paid at all until the crop was harvested. Black people resisted this provision with all of the devices available to them, and later regulations stipulated partial payments during the season.[78] As it finally happened, northern planters generally paid their hands one-half of their wages monthly, reserving the remainder until year's end. Rare were the Yankees who paid in full, either daily or whenever the people asked for it. Henry Lee Higginson and his partners tried paying in full in order to secure the people's confidence; so did some experimental lessees in Mississippi, who paid daily wages of a dollar and got good results. Eben Loomis was not so fortunate with the practice, for his hands ran off in the middle of the season because of rough treatment from the overseer. It was fear of just this sort of eventuality that made Yankees stick to the common method of withholding one-half of the monthly wage. They were as anxious as southerners to guarantee that they had enough hands to see them through the season. No amount of talk about teaching the freed people the sanctity of contracts or about providing them with a compulsory savings plan could disguise the coercive aspects of the withholding practice.[79]

The new planters also employed incentives, most frequently during the picking season. The hands might be assigned a quota and given a bonus when they exceeded it. The promise of extra holidays, more molasses, and more money was the usual reward, but northerners soon discovered that a shot of whiskey or a plug of tobacco also had its uses.[80] Just as common as incentives, however, was a schedule of fines. Usually deducted from pay, they were normally levied for absenteeism, feigned sickness, and thievery, and sometimes for abuse of livestock and equipment, swearing, "insolence," and wife-beating. Again, the whole scheme of fining laborers for misconduct originated with the contract labor system, although individual Yankee planters appear to have been very resourceful in making elaborations.[81]

On the whole the labor system of the newcomers was not a major departure from the ways of the past, let alone from the usage of the surrounding community. A few northern planters simply adopted the labor contracts the old owners had signed with their ex-slaves at the end of the war. Even the contracts Yankees drew up on their own occasionally bore a disturbing resemblance to the requirements that the old order had been accustomed to exacting. James Waters and George Klapp demanded "courteous bearing & language" from their hands.[82] A former Freedmen's Bureau agent planting in the South Carolina Sea Islands required his workers "to conduct themselves honestly, civilly and respectfully towards E. M. Stoeber."[83] The habits of the old regime died hard, even under northern management.

The newcomers adopted another southern practice that indicates their priorities. Practically all of them were overextended in cotton. "The fact is," wrote George Benham, who had wanted to make his plantation self-sufficient, "all our energies were bent in the direction of cotton."[84] The tendency was most pronounced in the Mississippi Valley during the war. A great deal of cotton went to waste because the lure of vast profits often tempted lessees to plant more ground than they could care for. There was not much improvement after the war. It chagrined those southerners who called for greater agricultural diversification that an arrival from the North "straitaway [*sic*] contracts cotton on the brain and down he goes."[85] To the stock argument that Yankee immigration would guide the South away from its one-crop dependency, a Louisiana man replied that "Northern lessees of Southern plantations have this year shown the worst examples in this respect." The natives at least raised some corn, he noted, but the newcomers, "not caring what becomes of the place or the negroes another year, have raised little or none, and the consequence will be very great suffering." A few Yankees raised garden crops for the local market, but this was a sideline like their sawmills.[86] On balance, Willie Lee Rose's criticism of the cotton fever of the Port Royal missionaries applies with equal force to the thousands of Yankee planters throughout the South in these years: "In their complete devotion to King Cotton, the planter-missionaries were as loyal as ever the former slavemasters had been. This was the largest blind spot in the thinking of the Atkinson free-labor school."[87]

There was one innovation that northern planters helped to advertise, if not introduce: the plantation store. It would be foolish to argue that plantation stores would never have emerged after the war except as Yankees introduced them. The institution grew naturally in a one-crop, plantation economy that was pinched for credit and forced to devise new ways to retain control of the laboring population. The old elite had to adjust to storekeeping in order to survive in the new order. But it is safe to say that a higher percentage of northern than southern men had merchandising establishments on their places, at least during the early phases of labor readjustment. Practically all Yankee planters had taken up "counter jumping," as some styled it, and in several instances they seem to have pioneered the practice in their neighborhoods.[88] Ex-slaveholders were sometimes reluctant to rush into a business that in the past had seemed slightly unrespectable. And if the old master was averse to dickering with his former slaves over wages, he was not always eager to trade with them in candy and breastpins. Northerners had no such scruples.

Willie Lee Rose is certainly correct in warning us against viewing the projects of some northern planters as the conspiratorial beginnings of a later economic imperialism that rendered the South a tributary to the North. The plantation store was actually considered a reform measure at the time. Two arguments were advanced in its behalf. One stressed the theme of increasing the "civilized wants" of the ex-slaves. This argument, often phrased in terms of how emancipation would considerably enlarge the southern market for northern manufactures, generally reflected the sincere desire of abolitionists to improve the living standards of the freedmen. But running through this argument—though it sometimes requires reading between the lines to see it—was the assumption that the former slaves would become more industrious in proportion as they became "more ambitious to have the comforts and luxuries of life."[89] The plantation store, in other words, would be the dispenser of the material rewards that would make the freedmen appreciate the values of steady industry.

The second argument for plantation stores probably counted more heavily with a certain group of reformers. It too had the aim of changing the psychology of the freedmen, emphasizing the importance of enlarging the personal freedom of the former slaves in order to make them more responsible for their own lives. This argument appealed strongly to Edward Philbrick, who disdained the practice of granting privileges to laborers. He welcomed the idea of obliging the freedmen to subsist on their own garden crops and wanted to make them buy everything that they might need for daily existence, including their tools. This practice, he believed, would tend to draw out their independent instincts.[90] The men who wanted to reform the Civil War contract labor system in the West also wanted to move in the direction of granting "the freedman's right to intervene in his own affairs."[91] About the only good thing they saw in the present program was the three-dollar commutation for clothing, which theoretically gave the laborer the right to clothe himself (but in practice was used to reduce still further his pitiably low wages). The reformers advocated making the hands responsible for their own food and clothing, and the labor regulations that the Treasury Department tried to impose at various times during the war incorporated their recommendations, with the stipulation that goods be sold for no more than a 15 percent markup. This provision of the new system alarmed General Nathaniel P. Banks because he saw in it the outlines of future debt peonage. It was a remarkable insight for a man who had hitherto thought only of getting the contrabands back on the plantations. Eventually the Treasury regulations were annulled, and so, too, was the provision requiring the laborers to feed themselves. But the suggested change in the matter of clothing remained, and apparently without a ceiling on profits except in the Department of the Gulf.[92] If all northern planters had operated nonprofit stores as did Edward Philbrick, the government's laxity of controls would not have been a serious oversight. But Philbrick was an exceptional man.[93]

Some northerners probably went into planting simply as a way of entering merchandising. It was said in South Carolina, for example, that the only way outsiders could profit from storekeeping was "in connection with a large plantation system." "Negroes who have money are excellent customers to such traders as cater to their prevalent barbaric tastes." However that may have been, other Yankees became shopkeepers almost by inadvertence.[94] James Waters initially had little interest in opening a store on his plantation. On the eve of his first trip downriver to New Orleans, in early 1864, his hands deluged him with "the most unlimited orders for all sorts of things." Two wanted a black dress and a winter cloak, others wanted a barrel of oranges apiece, and many came forward with similar orders, "which, of course, I cannot humour them in to any extent."[95] Apparently, the awakening of consumer appetites in his labor force gave him second thoughts. He returned from New Orleans with a fair stock of fabrics.

Any doubts that Waters may have had about his speculation were dispelled on the first day of business. After the hands received the first pay of their lives, they made a "grand charge" on the jerry-built store of Waters and Klapp, and in three minutes it was jammed.

> The first thing they spied was the calico,—that having the brightest colours and being the least useful of anything to them; and immediately, about four young wenches were clutching & pulling the unfolded end, each clamourous for the first dress—'gib me ten yahds' 'gib two dollahs wuth' etc. from all directions. I presided over the dry-goods at first, & Gill over the shoes,—but all struck for the calico first, and we both went at it. I wielded the yard stick in the most approved counter jumping style, and tossed out the pieces at the most rapid rate—receiving the money on the spot. The women jammed about the table so, that our elbows hit them in the face, and the yard stick hardly had room to work. We kept it up until dark, and then closed the doors, with the announcement that we would open again the next morning.[96]

Sunday's business was no less spirited. All the calico disappeared, as did the yellow handkerchiefs, and the cottons were in a fair way of doing the same. This was the first chance that Waters and Klapp had had for taking the blacks unaware, and it kept them "on the broad grin half the time." Waters thought it was "the most droll & grotesque display" in his memory, "better than any comedy I ever saw."[97]

Though these first transactions with the plantation people had comic aspects, they had a profitable side as well. Money piled up "like ice cream" in the large tin pan that served as cash register. Sales exceeded the payroll by $170, Waters discovered to his surprise. He thought a lot of money "must have been stowed away in these shabby old cabins, where doubtless there is a good deal more."[98] By the time Waters and Klapp restocked their shelves a month later, the demand from the quarters had scarcely abated. While the monthly payroll only came to $200, store receipts were in excess of $900, doubtless savings accumulated from the sale of poultry, fish, game, and garden vegetables over the years.[99] Waters and Klapp had learned a lesson in postemancipation economics that they never forgot. They went on to maintain a store on every plantation they leased during their stay in the South.[100]

Waters and Klapp apparently operated strictly on a cash basis. This was also the practice of many other northern planters and the approved method of the New York *Tribune*. "He who proposes to work a plantation by free labor," it advised, "should fill up a small store with Flour, Meal, Bacon, Tea, Coffee, serviceable Fabrics, and whatever else is most needed by his laborers, provide himself with a moderate supply of Greenbacks, and then say, 'I want labor; I will pay so much per day for it; your money will be ready at Sundown, and the Store will open at that hour.' "[101] A few newcomers did operate on the *Tribune* plan of daily cash payments and nightly store sales, but where the payment was daily it was usually in tickets that could be exchanged at the store. Credit was also extremely popular and may have been the dominant practice. It would be advanced against either the freedmen's half-pay customarily reserved until year's end or his share of the crop, as the case might be.[102]

Built into the system of plantation stores was the opportunity for unlimited abuse. The ex-slave's ignorance of cash transactions allowed for some sharp practices.[103] The occasional privilege that a few slaves had enjoyed to market fowl and vegetables in the neighborhood afforded them some idea of the meaning of money but gave them little real knowledge of the operation of a general store. Rare was the master like Joseph Davis, the Confederate president's brother, who had allowed his remarkable slave, Benjamin Montgomery, to run a store on the plantation.[104] Ever since the people could remember, the master had issued clothing yearly and rations daily or weekly, and if some of the hands thought that the Yankee's store was simply a more generous continuation of the usual ways, they may be forgiven. The people on Thomas Knox's plantation had difficulty understanding why the clothes he brought back from New Orleans were charged to their accounts and not distributed as gifts, as had been the custom in times past.[105] And few plantation hands, we may suppose, grasped the legerdemain by which the new men drew up their payrolls—the deductions for lost days, the fines for misconduct, and the credit at the store. Whitelaw Reid described the puzzlement of one hand when he received his first cash wages ever. The freedman "took the money as if it were fragile glass, and must be handled very carefully or it would be broken, and went off very much with the air one always imagines, the man must have worn who drew the elephant in a raffle."[106]

This unfamiliarity with the cash nexus was not easily overcome. If freedmen assisted each other in the field or in their gardens, repayment was in kind, not money. Husbands and wives did not always share their wages. And in the plantation stores the ex-slaves sometimes insisted on receiving change after each purchase before placing another order. "These are very strange people, these darkies," wrote a cultivated New Englander who took her own understanding of accounts for granted.[107] Most of all, the freedmen attached more importance to tangible possessions than to their monetary equivalents. It irritated Yankees that black people asked the highest prices for whatever one wanted to buy from them, and were "perfectly indifferent wither [sic] you buy it or not." But the consumption habits of the former slaves more than compensated for their tightfistedness in this respect. Whatever they take a fancy to, William Waters discovered, "they will have it, if they have the money to pay for it regardless of cost."[108] With time the freedmen learned the mysteries of the marketplace, but in these plantation stores they seemed always one step behind the Yankees.

Naturally, the temptation to take advantage of the ignorance of former slaves was strong. To men bent on making a fortune in a hurry, it was almost irresistible. Half of the lessees in the Mississippi Valley admitted that their store profits ranged from 15 to 25 percent, and there were some lessees whose markups were nearly 200 percent over the wholesale price. James Yeatman told of seeing shoes selling for $2.50 that could be bought in St. Louis for $1 a pair and of calicoes that were over triple the retail price at which they sold elsewhere.[109] Yet, even assuming that most northern planters kept their profit margins within reasonable bounds, the tendency everywhere was to carry the expensive rather than the cheap line and to stock goods whose value to an agricultural peasantry was at best questionable. The propriety of selling seven-dollar fancy boots might be debated (shoes were a valued item), but the merchandising of five-dollar garters and expensive meerschaum pipes would seem inexcusable from a strictly humanitarian, though not a business, point of view. All sorts of baubles, trinkets, and gewgaws lined the shelves, too, for the newcomers understood and exploited the people's penchant for dressing up on holidays. Even worn clothing had its uses. A northern planter in Florida sold "everything in the shape of old clothes" that he could spare, including a six-year-old coat at twice its original cost. Near the top of any list of fast-moving items were tobacco and whiskey, the latter of which, in some establishments, "was always watered down at least one-fourth, and the 'fine' was kept up by a liberal introduction of red pepper pods."[110] One may be forgiven comparisons with the sharp practices of colonial traders the world over.

Yankee planters did not see their methods in this light. They tended to blame the victims for their own victimization. One lessee advised some hands who grumbled at the amount their wages had been reduced by store credit not to throw away their money on "fish, and candy, and rings, and breast pins, and fine hats." "If you will have them, we'll sell them to you," he continued, "but you had better not buy so freely."[111] This attitude was slightly disingenuous because the freedmen were sometimes captive customers whose tastes were largely shaped by what the planter thought would move off his shelves. The people generally preferred to do their shopping on the plantation, but if they wanted to take their business elsewhere, they might run up against unwritten understandings that the planter had an "exclusive right to sell to the hands on the plantation whatever they will buy."[112] These understandings violated the precepts of the New York *Tribune* plan of storekeeping, and they were hard to enforce at Port Royal, where many hands had moved off the plantations onto their own land. Competition between independent storekeepers on the South Carolina Sea Islands after the war was rather keen. All the same, northern men, and southerners too, tried to enforce their "exclusive right" and ran off itinerant peddlers who tried to cut into their trade. One reason for maintaining a plantation store in the first place, Lorenzo Thomas explained, was to prevent the laborers from having "to go off for what they want."[113]

As attractive as the idea of social control was, the ruling consideration in the new men's calculations was mostly monetary. Many of them soon discovered that their store trade was an excellent way to meet a payroll and cut costs. A choice selection of goods usually made it unnecessary to have a great deal of cash on hand at the end of the month.[114] The scheme of paying with tickets was one method of avoiding cash payments. But some Yankees dispensed with cash payments altogether and paid strictly in goods. Clifford Waters estimated that this way of operating saved 20 percent of the cost of labor.[115]

For the freedmen the results were predictable. They usually had little to show in the way of savings for a season's work. Some of them went deeply into debt at the planter's store. On one northern-operated plantation in Louisiana after the war, the laborers' debts at the store ran anywhere from $0.04 to more than $12; one freedman family earned $184 for the season, but its store account stood at $190.[116] The extent of the laborers' indebtedness sometimes had to be concealed, for there was a "danger of them running off if they knew how deep they had got into us."[117] By all accounts, government lessees in the West during the war abused their opportunities the most. One man earned $80,000 and never paid his laborers a cent. The paternalistic sensibilities of Floyd King were outraged at witnessing the final settlement on a Yankee plantation. "The accounts and pay list had been standing for three months, it was at the end of the Year, and not one man received more than four dollars—mostly they were paid 10-15-20 & 30 cents!"[118] The abuses of the new system caused some who had hailed the coming of the store to regret their initial enthusiasm. "My opinions with reference to Negroes purchasing their own supplies have been completely changed by the observations made in these places," wrote one government agent. "The employers should be required to furnish all needed supplies at cost, on plantation, letting their only profit from the laborer be his labor."[119] But it was too late. The system of plantation stores had already begun to develop into the supply merchant establishment that lay at the basis of the postemancipation cotton economy.

Indeed, it was relatively easy for northern men who stayed around for any length of time to slide into the role of furnishing merchant. What their planting experience had taught them, evidently, was that store profits were "something to fall back upon in case of failure." The fact that share-renting was pleasanter because it required "less urging and driving" was certainly a point in its favor, but the economic advantages of being primarily a merchant and secondarily a landlord seem to have outweighed the disadvantages.[120] Since the blacks began farming "on their own account," one northerner wrote, they consumed "on a much larger scale than formerly which makes the business of supplying them as lucrative if not more so than planting or renting."[121] He was referring to the fact that the freedmen now required not only their food and clothing, but also all of the tools and supplies necessary to raising a crop. After Clifford Waters shifted his operations to the South Carolina Sea Islands, he discovered this same truth. His plantation store consistently yielded good profits, and by the close of Reconstruction he was operating two stores and renting out most of his land.[122]

What made Waters's storekeeping operations especially profitable were his speculations on the freedmen's cotton. Buying seed cotton from black tenants increased one's store profits considerably; one could almost double one's money by reselling the cotton to a house in Charleston, say, though reselling became less possible as long-staple cotton prices fell steadily during Reconstruction.[123] These speculations were popular in the Port Royal area during the period. "As every white man who does not raise cotton is buying up all the seed cotton they can get hold of," Frederic A. Eustis's northern manager informed him, "I think you cannot do better than to let me buy some for you."[124]

If the planter had a gin, his profits from cotton-buying were naturally better. But, again, conducting one's speculations through a store was best of all. As Clifford Waters explained it, "We pay always cash for cotton but if we have a good stock of goods the negroes will turn right around & spend the money in the store, giving us a double profit." In Columbia County, Florida, Ambrose Hart and his partner, on the other hand, simply paid for the cotton from their tenants with store goods. They expected profits of 100 percent.[125]

Of course Yankees were certainly not unique in maintaining plantation stores, let alone in becoming shrewd furnishing merchants. The practice caught on quickly among southern planters who doubtless would have discovered the advantages of shopkeeping had Yankees never set foot on their plantations.[126] Merchandising was the wave of the future in the cotton districts after the war. No planter could hope to survive in the New South unless he became a shopkeeper himself or worked out a general accommodation with one of the local merchants. For the one who controlled credit stood a good chance of controlling the crop as well, not to mention controlling the tenant farmers who raised it. The merchandising practices of northerners were in this sense but a variant of a more general social and economic development that was taking place in the South in these years.

But the northern presence did have an effect on the pace and speed of this development. After all, the newcomers showed the way, or at least planted the idea. Distributed in the thousands throughout the cotton districts of the lower South during early Reconstruction, Yankee planters were among the first to recognize the possibilities in the plantation store, and they had an undeniable knack for making it work. As much as southerners hated to admit it, they were watching the recent arrivals and hoping to profit from their example. In the depressed conditions of the postwar South, when economic survival itself seemed to hang by a thin thread, new techniques for making money (and for controlling the productive process) assumed a vast importance in the eyes of the old inhabitants, and so did the innovations of the men who southerners generally believed had "always made more money among us than we did ourselves."[127]

Maybe what the Yankees actually helped to popularize more than anything else was the philosophy of "close calculation" that typified the outlook of most newcomers in these years. It was a point of view that looked for the main chance at every turn, even if it meant cutting fish poles, curing moss, buying illicit cotton during the war, or turning a fast dollar by recruiting southern soldiers to substitute for the affluent in the North.[128] There was even money to be made from writing letters for the freedmen. William Waters entertained the idea of "putting out a shingle and offering my services to carry on nigger correspondence," but the going rate of five cents a letter was not attractive enough to draw him into the business.[129] The profit motive, of course, was not always so naked. Among the idealists in the Yankee planter movement, there was an effort to keep in mind the good work they were trying to do for the freedmen. Henry Lee Higginson admonished his wife not to concern herself about the growing plantation expenses. "Please remember that one great reason for our coming here was the work of great importance to be done for these blacks. Money is less valuable than time and thought and labor, which you have given and will give freely ... DO NOT FRET ABOUT ACCOUNTS!!!!"[130] But the speculative spirit colored even acts of benevolence. Profit with duty was how George Benham described the Fourth of July celebration he staged for his hands. Not only did the approaching holiday spur the hands to greater exertions in the fields, but it also caused a run on his store in order to prepare for the gala event. "Thus, in a very small way," he explained, the celebration was "a speculation."[131]

Possibly the interest of the newcomers in educating the freedmen redeems somewhat the greedier aspects of their enterprises.[132] Plantation schools were fairly popular among northern men. There was a certain poetic justice in converting the old plantation jail into a schoolhouse,[133] and even Yankees whose racism was strong could grant the importance of overcoming generations of illiteracy. Of course these schools were also pulpits from which might be preached the bourgeois gospel of hard work and moral probity. But this was a larger purpose. Plantation schools were seldom reduced to a narrow financial proposition.

As always seemed the case where the treatment of the freedmen was concerned, Port Royal was far ahead of the rest of the field in its commitment to black education. The first northern planters on the islands originally came as teachers, and most plantations had at least one instructor on the premises. Northern benevolent associations footed the bill, and after the War Department assumed control of the plantations and responsibility for the superintendent's salaries, more funds were freed for educational work.[134]

The placing of the Port Royal experiment on a private enterprise footing did not appreciably weaken the school system. The new military governor, General Rufus Saxton, was friendly to black education, as were the tax commissioners, who used the proceeds from the lease of plantations to pay teachers and maintain schools, in accordance with President Lincoln's instructions of September 16, 1863. The commissioners leased at least one-third of the school farms in 1864 to "well qualified men" whose only obligation in the way of rent was to keep up "good schools."[135] Some of the planter-missionaries who bought in at the tax sales took steps to guarantee that the educational program would not languish. Edward Philbrick saw to it that schools continued on the places he purchased, even after he leased them to later arrivals from the North. A few private owners went so far as to put provisions in their leases requiring lessees to maintain a schoolhouse and furnish living quarters to one or two teachers.[136] Plantation schools had become a tradition in the Port Royal area, sanctioned and enforced by the government on the one hand, supported and respected by much of the white population on the other.

Conditions were very different in the western theater, at least during the Civil War. Officials in the Department of the Gulf and the Mississippi Valley, it is true, promulgated measures for educating children under twelve years of age. Military commanders established school districts, appointed superintendents of education, and levied school taxes, occasionally on the cotton crop, to pay the expenses of operation. Yet only in the vicinity of towns and cities and contraband camps did any significant number of black people receive schooling. The exhortations of the authorities to lessees to educate the freedmen scarcely moved government lessees in the rural districts. There was too much of a speculative element in the West during the war. Men who wanted to make a quick killing were not the sort to place unnecessary burdens on their pocketbooks. Nor were northerners who had made their peace with the guerrillas—and many had—likely to adopt measures that might jeopardize that truce. Similarly, to planters who felt that the guerrilla scares had already seriously interfered with work on the crop, the idea of sacrificing more time for philanthropy was not very appealing. Under the circumstances, it required resolute action on the part of the authorities to make most northern men do their duty, and this action was not forthcoming. The immensity of the territory handicapped their efforts at enforcement; the attitude of responsible officials, with the exception of John Eaton and the men around him, was discouraging. What sense did it make for authorities to stress the importance of black education when the chief lord of leasing himself, General Lorenzo Thomas, had not bothered to encourage his own son to establish a school on his plantation? It should cause no surprise that one inspector of leased plantations in the area of Natchez and Vicksburg in 1864 could not find "that any general effort has been made for the enlightenment of the people in any direction." [137]

There seems to have been an improvement after the war. In 1866 the Thomas family set up a school on their plantation for the first time. Many postwar arrivals here and elsewhere in the lower South expressed an interest in educating their employees. Northerners such as Albert Morgan, George Benham, Garth and Robertson James, Charles Stearns, and Henry Lee Higginson, to name only a few, all ran schools on their plantations. Morgan contributed lumber and manpower to erect a schoolhouse in Yazoo City, Mississippi. [138] Of course, one might raise the objection that most of these men at one time or another had been touched by abolitionist influences, which is true. But even such Negro-phobes as James Waters and George Klapp found it no great imposition to set up a school on their place after the war. [139] This much can be said of plantation schools: they were not nearly as popular with the newcomers as plantation stores, but they were popular.

There were certain incentives that made the maintenance of a plantation school attractive. Northern benevolent associations paid the salaries of teachers sent out under their auspices and usually supplied textbooks and school materials, while the Freedmen's Bureau often furnished rations and transportation. For northerners who had connections, it was not hard to avail themselves of these arrangements. [140] Running a plantation school sometimes provided extra income to the planter. The fees occasionally charged to students could amount to a decent monthly income for the northern man or his wife, if they happened to be the ones giving instruction. Clifford Waters discovered that the income from his school was about all that he and his brother could depend on at the end of 1866, a particularly bad planting season. [141]

But for most newcomers who set up schools on their places, money was secondary to the good that could be done. Several northerners were unusually generous with their time and money, where education was concerned. The James brothers and their associates at Gordon apparently hired their own teacher, furnished him living quarters, and erected a schoolhouse. Another Yankee, whose accounts with the freedmen otherwise seemed shady, did as much. [142] Charles Stearns and the Higginsons gave freely of their time, holding classes at night, during lunchbreak, or whenever time could be made available. Stearns even set up a school-lunch program, which was very popular with the young students. A Yankee overseer for a southern planter, who happened to be "in favor of having the colored people taught," kept a night school for adults, while his wife taught the children during the day. [143]

Teaching the freedmen pretty much had its own rewards. All of the schools flourished in the beginning, for the ex-slaves were avid pupils. Only two persons on Stearns's plantation failed to show an interest in education. Most freedmen sensed that the written word had powers that could secure them more firmly in their newly-won liberties. Spelling books and reading primers were immensely popular in the quarters. The simple threat to take away schoolbooks was occasionally an effective disciplinary measure. Nearly everyone agreed that black children were "intelligent and teachable and seem to learn about as fast as white children." [144]

The strong interest of the freed people in education gave much gratification. The classroom was about the only place where the ex-slaves appeared to listen attentively to the homilies on hard work, reliability, honesty, and the need for obedience. Charles Stearns was "well satisfied with the result of my labors, at the close of the first summer. The hands had done well, as far as I could see. They had generally obeyed my orders, had worked tolerably well, and had shown a commendable interest in moral and religious teaching," he wrote. [145] His satisfaction was not to last. He learned that the freedmen had definite notions about the meaning of their status and were quite resourceful in enforcing them. He also learned that attempts to impose industrial efficiency and northern habits on the former slaves gave more headaches than he had bargained for. His was the experience of countless other northerners who tried to grow cotton in these years.

6 *"Negro on the Brain"*

Northern planters went South with an ingenuous faith. "Making money there is a simple question of being able to make the darkies work,"[1] they believed, and few of them doubted their ability to do that. But it did not take long for the new men to discover, with some bitterness and much disillusionment, that managing recently freed slaves was not the easy job that they had imagined. It demanded great tact and skill merely to avoid a reputation for injustice among the freedmen; and it required something more, a great deal more in fact, to make the ex-slaves conform to the Yankee's notion of what constituted an "efficient" agricultural laborer. For black people had ideas of their own about the meaning of freedom—or, at the very least, they intended to define their new status for themselves. They were not about to be driven by any man, whatever his origins, and they felt that if emancipation meant anything, it had to result in more material advantages, a relaxed plantation discipline, and most of all, greater personal and cultural autonomy. The truth is, northern men were no better equipped than southern men to deal with the changing realities in the freedmen's quarters. In some respects, they had more handicaps to overcome. If the old planters could not easily reconcile themselves to black free labor, the new planters found it hard to become accustomed to the work rhythms and folkways of the freedmen. It was something of a rude awakening for them to learn that northern training and temperament were not, after all, great qualifications for cotton-growing.

There is some truth in the frequently made assertions that the ex-slaves preferred northern to southern employers shortly after emancipation. It was understandable that black people, or at least some of them, regarded Yankees as liberators and would engage with them more eagerly "'cause dey freed 'em."[2] The widespread flight following Appomattox was in many respects an attempt by the freedmen to "improve their condition by leaving unsatisfactory employers," as one recent student tells us. Physical mobility was the most effective leverage the ex-slaves possessed in the new postbellum labor market. And what could be more natural than for disgruntled fieldhands to turn to employers who came from a region that had just loosed their ancient bonds? George Benham's cook, Aunt Clara, expressed a point of view that, while not common, had its adherents. The Fourth of July was "'pendence day," she told the people in the freedmen's quarters, "and we darkies hab to celebrate it, caze ob de 'pendence we put in de white folks up Norf who freed us."[3]

All the same, it is something less than gratitude to the liberators that explains the freedmen's general preference for the northern planter. Their greater readiness to hire on with him appears to have been mostly a matter of economic calculation. Former slaves "seemed to know a Yankee intuitively," wrote a northern planter in Mississippi. The newcomer's overbrimming confidence and his new machinery telegraphed his origins, as did the manner in which the old master class favored him with attractive bargains and conciliating kindness. "Of course the negroes see all that & do not respect them any more for it," Henry Lee Higginson thought. Some ex-slaves had singular standards by which to gauge prosperity. Clifford and James Waters were told by some fieldhands in Louisiana, "You so rich bof you genlmen dat de money comes out you cheeks. You skin rich."[4] Whether many freedman reasoned that a rosy countenance indicated wealth is perhaps doubtful, but they did sense that northerners were well-heeled or at least had the ability to meet a payroll. And it was far from clear to them whether their former masters had any money at all, let alone the disposition to pay. Why continue working for an old owner who likely was without capital, lacked faith in the system that was about to be inaugurated, and blamed his misfortunes on his former slaves, when a Yankee newcomer was available who had both the faith and the ability to pay? Some freedmen apparently concluded that "they'd rather work for ten dollars, and be sure of their pay, than for twenty-five dollars, and be cheated out of it."[5] This confidence in the northerner's ability and willingness to meet his obligations was often misplaced. But black people knew how to rectify their errors. The black soldiers at Natchez, Mississippi, who "sent a delegation around to the several plantations to see how the hands were treated" before choosing employers, had learned enough about the Yankee lessee class to grasp the advantages of being discriminating.[6] To the extent, then, that the freedmen based their employment preferences on the limited facts available to them, they acted as any sensible people would have done in their circumstances. They were moved not by unlimited devotion to the new men, but by economic calculation. They learned the requirements of marketplace economics rather quickly.

But it is dangerous to claim too much. The freedmen could not easily overcome generations of distrust for a white skin. A healthy skepticism of the intentions of the dominant race had helped black people survive the perils of chattel slavery. After emancipation they still suspected "everyone a little or much." Henry Lee Higginson even had difficulty in persuading his hands to sign a contract. They feared that if they bound themselves to work for a year, they would "be slaves at the end of that time." Charles Stearns had a similar problem, which he brought on himself by adopting the old planter's labor contract. Such a transaction struck the freedmen as too much like past usage, "when masters often sold land and slaves together." He later learned that the hands were no fonder of being rented out with the land.[7] A Yankee planter in Louisiana thought he was getting a bargain when a southern labor agent supplied him with some labor. But, again, the deal put the black people in mind of "the old order of things."[8] Patient reasoning was required to bring them to agree to a contract; a belligerent tone got one nowhere. As one aged ex-slave explained it,

"Musn't talk dat way wen you hire nigger. Must talk mighty soft to 'em."[9] Black people were not about to drop their guard even with the liberators, and they looked continually for tangible assurances of goodwill before they placed confidence in any man.

Thus, gaining the trust of the freedmen took quite a while. Some small gesture of personal recognition, a remembering of a name or even an inquiry after health, could carry a new man a long way in his relationship with his hands. Albert Morgan said that his considerate manner of addressing the ex-slaves stood in such contrast to the imperious language of the old masters that he gained a lot in esteem with them.[10] Usually, however, a few months of regular pay were required before the freedmen began to let down their defenses. Edward Philbrick had recognized this truth earlier even than the men who made federal policy. One of the greatest handicaps to the governmental operation of plantations during the war had been the tardiness of the payroll, and he welcomed the sale of plantations for the reason that it gave him a chance to test his free-labor ideas under more favorable circumstances.[11] William Waters also learned quickly that he could "do nothing with the negroes unless I pay them promptly to the day." The slightest delay in settling with the hands would meet the strongest resistance from the freedmen's quarters and could result in a strike of the entire force.[12] But not even regularity of pay could always allay distrust. A northern man might congratulate himself on gaining the freedmen's confidence, only to discover halfway through the season that he had been taken in by the people's friendly manner. The habits of generations were too deeply ingrained to yield easily.

A few northern planters lost the freedmen's confidence before they had a chance to win it. Yankees who attempted to get a foothold in the coastal area of South Carolina and Georgia that General Sherman had set aside for black occupancy received a different reception from what they expected. The federal government had reneged on its promise of free land to the ex-slaves, and under President Johnson's directives and the Freedmen's Bureau's supervision, the plantations on which thousands of black people had recently staked out claims were gradually restored to their old owners. The freedmen were bitterly disappointed, and for good reason. They had been doing quite well cultivating on their own account, and in some of the settlements they had even established their own civil governments, "with Constitution and laws, for the regulation of their entire affairs, with all the different departments of Schools, Churches, building roads and other improvements." Their anger was understandable when they were told that they must either contract with the old owners or evacuate the property. They were not willing to do either, in any case. Nor did they intend to extend open arms to the men who the ex-slaveholders believed would bring them to terms.[13]

It seems that the black homesteaders were inclined to interpret literally a clause in Sherman's original order forbidding whites to enter the territory without proper authorization.[14] A party of Pennsylvanians who landed on Johns Island to look over some plantation property for which they were negotiating met with rough treatment. Although they had obtained the state Bureau commissioner's permission to make the trip, the freedmen arrested them anyway as soon as they put ashore and then marched them twelve miles across the island to see the resident Bureau agent. Before the journey ended, the interlopers' escort had grown to one hundred and fifty armed and angry people, full of threats to kill any "cussed white man who cum on Jim or Jon for take he property." The agent quickly freed the prisoners, though not without grumbling from the people.[15]

The affair on Johns Island may have been the most spectacular instance of black resistance to dispossession, but it was not an isolated incident. Throughout the area of Sherman's land grants came reports that the freedmen were arming themselves and vowing not to give up their lands.[16] General James C. Beecher, Harriet Beecher Stowe's brother, had his hands full trying to discipline the blacks in his jurisdiction. Before arresting the ringleaders in the Johns Island affair, he prohibited a black meeting on Wadmelaw Island, South Carolina, that aimed at preventing white trespassing. The people on nearby Edisto Island were just as restless. They appointed a commissioner to represent their case before authorities and declared they were "at liberty to hold meetings when and where they pleased."[17] In some cases, Beecher cut rations in order to restore order; at other times, he used troops to place Yankees in possession of their leased plantations. Beecher also dismissed a civilian Bureau agent who he said was "largely instrumental in instructing the freed people to acts of stupid violence."[18]

Military authorities in Georgia faced similar problems. General Davis Tillson, the Freedmen's Bureau commissioner, had to resort to strong measures to install some northern planters upon the coast. St. Catherines and Sapelo Islands were his largest headache. Tunis G. Campbell, a northern-born black, had received authority to organize self-government among his charges, and he had thrown himself into the work with commendable zeal. His headquarters was known as the "Republic of St. Catherines" and boasted of a bicameral legislature. He had done good work. One citizen of the republic later testified that Campbell "told the colored people how to behave and how to live peaceably *among themselves.*" Campbell perhaps did his job too well, given the political realities at military headquarters. He raised a standing army and placed armed pickets around the coast to prevent an invasion of white men. This move brought him to the attention of the authorities.[19]

General Tillson dismissed Campbell early in 1866, for reasons that are not entirely clear. But they probably had something to do with the complaints of Yankee planters who had been trying to find a lodgment on the islands under Campbell's regency. At any rate, the two northerners whom Tillson placed on Sapelo Island pretty much had their own way. One freedman who witnessed the transition later claimed that the Yankees stole "everything the colored man made, and . . . this stealing and outrage was done by the direction of Gen'l Tilson [sic]."[20] The commissioner was nearly as obliging to the two newcomers who succeeded Campbell on St. Catherines Island. He consolidated the freedmen's land grants that he did recognize at one end of the island, in order to allow the northerners to work an unbroken unit of land.[21] By May of 1866 most of the Georgia Sea Islands were "under the control of northern men." General Tillson got high marks for quietly helping Yankees "to get a foothold on the Coast." Already New Englanders were envisioning the day when "it will become the fashion to take a winter trip to St. Simon's for a deer hunt, rather than a summer tour to the Adirondacks or Moosehead Lake."[22] It was rather a sad ending for an interesting experiment. The freedmen drew the appropriate conclusion. As one ex-slaveholder in the low country observed, "They find the Yankee only a speculator and they have no confidence *in* anyone."[23]

As every close student of Reconstruction knows, northerners at Port Royal had discovered two years earlier how the freedmen could react to the breaking of promises. The failure of the federal government to carry out its preemption scheme, which would have applied the western homesteading principle to the tax lands on the islands, had a predictable effect on the ex-slaves. The blacks "had all set their minds on owning for themselves and swore they'd never work for a white man."[24] On some plantations bought or leased by Yankees in the winter of 1863-64, the people simply refused "to have anything to do with the new proprietors." With the help of friendly military authorities, they forced a commission merchant from Albany, New York, to relinquish the leases he had acquired to thirteen plantations.[25] The freedmen's anger even recoiled against their old friends. Edward Philbrick now had trouble asserting his right to land that a year earlier his workers had been glad he had bought. A few freedmen informed him that they would work the land for themselves, even though he had already dismissed one gang for similar tactics a short while before. On the Cherry Hill place, the hands coolly told Philbrick and William Waters, his new lessee, that "the plantation belonged to them by right, that they were born & brought up on the land, that their masters had run away and left them in possession of the land, and no white man, except their old master, had a right to take the land from them." From this point onward, as Willie Lee Rose tells us, things were never the same again on the South Carolina Sea Islands.[26]

The freedmen did not have to be told that in an agricultural republic there was no surer guarantee of independence than the ownership of land. An ex-slave in the Mississippi Valley put the case clearly: "What's de use of being free if you don't own land enough to be buried in? Might juss as well stay slave all you' days."[27] The instincts of black people after emancipation were in the direction of greater independence and more autonomy for themselves and their families, and the newcomers would have to reckon with this fact of life continually. If the freedmen could not possess land of their own, they would at least see to it that the conditions of their existence conformed to their ideas of how the plantation should now function. And they meant to have a say in what those new realities would be.

Northern planters with ambitions for reforming plantation agriculture were usually among the first to learn of the spirit in the freedmen's quarters. The hands generally resisted efforts to modify their work routine unless it involved abandoning the gang system altogether. They were tenacious in sticking to old ways of doing things, Harriet Beecher Stowe thought, "even when one would have thought another course easier and wiser." She had no luck in trying to change their diet. Charles Stearns's remonstrances against eating pork (he disliked the smell of hogs about the place) were received coldly by the people. He could not persuade them to accept a double ration of beans and rice in its stead.[28] Attempts to introduce new machinery were also expensive failures. The loss or destruction of valuable equipment dampened the reform ardor. Before long, some Yankees were concluding that the lighter and cheaper agricultural utensils of the old order had certain advantages that they had never seen before. This resistance of the hands to change commonly evoked complaints of "negro conservatism," of an unreasonable commitment to "old ideas, old customs, old ways of performing labor, and especially old sins." The charge was probably correct, for laboring people the world over have an instinctive affection for order and predictability.[29] Even so, something else was involved in the freedmen's reluctance to embrace such changes in routine. Not even the survival of the old slavery-bred habit of rebelliousness can account for their reluctance to accept change. What the ex-slaves seemed to be saying was that reform initiatives of this kind should properly originate in the quarters, not in the Big House. Henry Lee Higginson came close to the heart of the matter: "*Now* they cannot be induced to talk, to ask questions. They will listen but not heed much from a white man."[30] The freedmen had too much else on their minds to be bothered with the advice of even well-intentioned friends.

The main question for the great mass of ex-slaves in the early days of freedom was how to carve out more living space for themselves while working for white men under conditions that bore too strong a resemblance to the slave past. Gang labor and constant supervision was not their idea of the condition of free men and women, and they had not abandoned their desire for land, which was so strong as eventually to compel the old planting class to compromise its opposition to land rentals to blacks. In the meantime, however, what could black people do to enlarge the sphere of their independence? They were not always sure of the answer, but they sensed that it lay in the direction of more pay, more food, shorter hours, and a general relaxation of the old plantation discipline.

One thing that Edward Philbrick's fieldhands had concluded was that if they could not have their own land, they would have to be paid well for working his plantation, "a great deal more than they were last year." On some places he leased to newcomers, the freedmen clamored for a dollar task. He refused their demands, but he had to raise the rates somewhat.[31] The circumstances of his problem with the hands were admittedly unique, for the land question was in the air in the South Carolina Sea Islands as it was nowhere else in the South. But the demand for more money was constantly heard throughout the region in these years. Whitelaw Reid averred that "nothing seemed more characteristic of the negroes than their constant desire to screw a little higher wages" out of the northern proprietor. The memory of these increasing demands had stuck with Charles Morse long after he left the South for other parts.[32] It was a common complaint among newcomers that the freedmen were never satisfied with their pay. Yankees soon came to regard payday with growing dread and the year-end settlement as a "formidable task" to be quickly put behind them. The hands seldom received their wages without challenging the planter's accounts. "Always several of them grumble and complain & are impudent and sometimes even have cried (the women only) because they thought they had not been paid enough," wrote James Waters of paydays on his first plantation in Louisiana.[33] Black discontent with wages seldom went over well with men who had a high opinion of their own generosity. "As for the niggers, they are niggers still," thundered one Yankee cotton grower. By his own lights he had paid them well, and "yet there was quite a fuss till I was done. . . . I never mean to give them the least thing over their due, it would be throwing away kindness."[34]

The freedmen saw things differently. As one of them explained to Whitelaw Reid, "Wen man got plenty, & he wont do nuffin but hole poe man down to skin of bargain, well I do no wat to say 'bout dat man. Mus take second look at him."[35] And many freedmen were doing just that. It did not take them long to realize that the northern man was inclined by and large to place a monetary value on everything, including their time. The habit he had of dividing up the work month into discrete units of money-time in order to get his full dollar value drove home this truth as nothing else could. The ex-slaves responded in kind. Some who contracted with a planter for a definite job were prompt in demanding overtime payments when their tasks obliged them to work on the weekends. One freedman in Louisiana, who was hired to feed the mules, did not like having to do his chore with greater frequency as the season progressed. When obliged to feed the mules on Sunday, "straightway Morton presented his claim for extra pay for this extra duty."[36] On the South Carolina Sea Islands, the hands expected additional pay even if the workday lasted only fifteen minutes longer than the stipulated schedule. "If he goes to the house for an axe he's to be paid extra for it," one planter complained. "It's well enough to pay a man for all he does, but who can carry on a farm in such a way as that?"[37]

If freedom taught the slaves to think more highly of their time, it also made them alert to any discrimination in the matter of pay. When Thomas Knox told a black midwife that she no longer had to split with the planter the ten dollars she had customarily received for attending white ladies in the neighborhood, she sought to press her advantage:

Didn't you say the black people are free?
Yes.
White people are free too, ain't they?
Yes.
Then why shouldn't you pay me ten dollars every time I tend upon the black folks upon the plantation?

It was a good question, and Knox could not answer it satisfactorily. He told her that black people had not "attained all the privileges that pertained to the whites," and that she must continue to offer her services freely to the plantation.[38] She was doubtless unconvinced.

But the freedmen's demands for better pay were not always so easily put off. The ex-slaves caught on quickly to the advantages of collective action. Strikes were not uncommon as the day for signing new contracts approached. On more than one occasion Edward Philbrick had to placate holdouts before he could make preparations for putting in the new crop. One could almost tell a strike was coming on when the hands began "complaining and plotting among themselves at a great rate."[39] Entire neighborhoods might be infected with a contagion of militancy. At the beginning of 1865, in the Port Royal area, there was "an understanding among the negroes on all the plantations that they will not work at last year's rates." Similar preparations were under way in the Mississippi Valley at the same time. "There has been a good deal of meeting on different plantations. All of Morrison's hands, and Packard's also, I hear," George Klapp reported on the affairs of his northern neighbors. This was an anxious moment for most newcomers, for usually some concession had to be made, if it was only the granting of garden plots or permission to grow cotton.[40] The freedmen were ever alert to opportunities for advancing their interests.

Ex-slaves were not always at a good advantage in their negotiations with the Yankees. Unfamiliarity with cash transactions was still a handicap. A crew of hands on George Benham's plantation talked themselves out of some extra money. They dickered when he asked them to cut some wood for seventy-five cents a cord. He told them to name their own price, and after consulting among themselves, they said they could not cut the lumber for less than ten dollars for twenty-five cords of wood. Benham readily came to terms; their figure was well below his original offer. "I know'd de boss'd come to our price," he overheard one of them tell another "with a knowing wink." Benham was sure he had taught the assertive freedmen a good lesson in practical economics, but he overlooked the fact that the money lost was probably secondary to the experience gained from bargaining with their employer. In these early days of freedom, black people were trying to test the limits of their collective strength, and though they had lost the first skirmish, they might yet win future engagements. Even small victories had their pleasures. "Want more molasses," one freedman demanded of Whitelaw Reid. He was surprised when Reid gave in: "Whoop didn't take much talk to git dat."[41]

If the freedmen were prepared to bargain and strike for better pay, they were also no less interested in enlarging and improving their diet. They could be just as captious about the amount and quality of their rations as they could be about their wages.[42] Like all working people, they enjoyed eating well and resented the continued practice of doling out rations according to the old formula. Any rule of distribution that made no allowance for disparities in the size of appetites or the needs of various families struck the ex-slaves as unfair. "Sah, I tell you de trufe, I don't git enuff to eat. Matter enuff, dat is, for a man as works hard all day long," a first-rate plowman told a northern planter. The new men seldom honored these requests, for they feared that recognizing special distinctions might undam a flood of similar demands.[43] So the freedmen continued to enlarge their pantries in a way that they had sometimes done in the past. They simply helped themselves. They broke into smokehouses and corncribs with regularity, until it reached the point, on most northern plantations, that everything pertaining to food was kept under lock and key. They were no respecters of the white man's garden either. A Yankee neighbor of Charles Stearns complained that the freedmen "would keep their meetings up until midnight, and then adjourn to my water-melon patch."[44] Nor were the northerner's livestock and poultry excepted from the general pilfering. William Waters put his finger on a problem common to many Yankee planters: "You can't keep poultry or pigs on your own account, for the negroes will be sure to steal them from you & if you hire a person to watch them, they will cost more than they are worth." George Benham tried to raise farm animals on his place, but he gave up for these reasons.[45] The pantry in the Big House was scarcely any safer; the house servants seemed to steal just as much as the fieldhands. The way it looked to many northerners was that the freedmen were all *"natural thieves."*[46]

"Stealing is no name for this trying vice," Stearns declared. "It is wholesale robbery of everything in their power to help themselves to, except articles of whose value they are ignorant."[47] It is true that the ex-slaves did not restrict their thievery to food. They occasionally walked off with garments, paddles, iron, and a host of other objects that they would sell if they could not use.

Thefts of cotton also posed special problems, and that is why most Yankee planters resisted black demands to grow the staple in their own gardens. Something of an epidemic of cotton-stealing broke out at Port Royal in 1865 and 1866. It was tempting for some black landowners who worked the white man's land to mix his cotton with their own, or to sell it to the numerous sharpers who hung around the islands during these years. Special safeguards had to be devised to curb the pilfering, but they were not entirely successful. "The truth is," William Waters confessed, "that with all our vigilance, the niggers will steal, & we may congratulate ourselves if they do not get the Lion's share."[48]

But food accounted for most of the thefts, by a large margin. George Benham never suffered so much as a minor burglary in his house, even though he was in the habit of leaving it unlocked and unattended, something he would never have done in the North. And his experience was probably typical.[49] The reasons the freedmen stole chiefly food were not hard to find. They would divulge their motives freely if caught in the act. One group of culprits explained that "they were poor, and they had to have a living and the people did not give them enough to live off of and they intended to have it in that way." Husbands and fathers might point to their religious duty to provide adequately for their families. They took seriously the biblical maxim that "he that provideth not for his own household, has denied the faith, and is worse than an infidel." They had gone to great lengths during slavery to supplement the family diet, often using their free time to hunt and fish in order to fill up the dinner table.[50] Stealing was not ruled out, for as Thomas Knox discovered, it was not easy to convince slaves that "the use of one piece of property for the benefit of another piece, belonging to the same person, was a serious offense."[51] Of course the practice of stealing after the war was sometimes merely the unconscious reflex of old habits. The reaction of one domestic whom William Waters caught pilfering the potato barrel was familiar to the old regime. She "coolly replied that she did not *take* many & that she herself only wanted a few to roast."[52] But most black people, after emancipation, probably reasoned the thing out. They knew their legal status had changed, but they were not sure that the conditions of their life were so different as to warrant discarding old habits. They would even acknowledge that thievery was wrong as a general rule, but things being what they were, stealing was still "one of those sins no man could live without committing."[53]

Some northern planters had the largeness of vision to recognize the origins of stealing in slavery. "The tendency of slavery," Benham averred, "was to educate a race of petty thieves."[54] But an intellectual grasp of the problem nonetheless failed to instill equanimity in the newcomers. Nor did understanding make it easier to control. It was not just that the freedmen were skillful and cunning thieves (which they were), but that they would inevitably close ranks when the planter tried to discover the culprit. "No earthly motive will ever induce them to betray one another," Charles Stearns learned to his disgust. One of the most demoralizing things about sitting on the Port Royal Plantation Commission, which had been established to curb stealing, was this black solidarity against white accusers.[55]

Still, northern men tried hard to stamp out thievery. They would lecture and scold until they were blue in the face. Monetary fines or a loss of rations were common ways of punishing thieves, even though the government often prohibited the withholding of rations for any reason.[56] James Waters and George Klapp set up a "High Court of Pains & Penalties" on their Good Hope plantation. The court was unique, inasmuch as it handled freedmen's offenses against freedmen and succeeded in lessening somewhat the blacks' reluctance to break ranks. One of the more obvious hypocrisies of the newcomers had been their laxity in prosecuting thievery, save when it affected their own interests. The court of Waters and Klapp did try to do justice to those hands who suffered thefts of cotton during the picking season, but it may have defeated its own purposes in the process. Although the employers customarily required the guilty parties to make full restitution to their victims, they also seem to have awarded themselves the major share of the damages: the forfeiture of all pay on the day of the offense, and sometimes for every previous day. On occasion Waters and Klapp fined every fieldhand a certain amount of cotton if the culprit was not produced.[57] The overall success of the court was apparently not great, for the thefts appear to have continued unabated. The tribunal evidently lacked the impersonal majesty of civil institutions and could hardly disguise the class interests that lay behind it. About all that most northern planters could do regarding stealing was to suffer through, though it did "require the patience and purse of a Job to stand it."[58]

If the freedmen relied on old habits to enlarge and improve their diets, they also turned to familiar ways when they tried to gain more free time and relax the work routine. Northern complaints of shirking and laziness have a distinct antebellum ring to them. To the newcomers the ex-slaves seemed slow and stupid, wanting in methodical habits, and unreliable when any responsibility was given to them. "Put one at some task by himself," Whitelaw Reid averred, "and there was every probability that he would go to sleep or go fishing."[59] Black people, it was said, could not be made to do a full day's work, and Yankee planters counted themselves fortunate when the hands did "a 'middling fair' share of labor." The freedmen worked indifferently, were careless with their tools, and on any given day might leave the fields early or not show up at all.[60] This seemed to be the overall judgment of the great majority of northern planters. It is admittedly risky to place undue reliance on the impressions of people whose racial attitudes poorly qualified them to make sound judgments on these matters.[61] But the evidence is too massive, from both northerners and southerners, to prevent concluding that the freedmen did not work the plantations as hard as they had under slavery. This was how the ex-slaves intended it, and the new man might find his crops in the weeds if he failed to stay on top of his business. The freedmen were often as interested in enlarging their free time as they were in increasing their material incomes, which is not an unusual ordering of priorities among people who have not yet assimilated the inner compulsions of modern economic man.[62]

The freedmen did not rely solely on the techniques from their slave past to increase their leisure time. They also quickly discovered that freedom had opened up possibilities not available before. The more efficient hands were no longer willing to bear the larger share of the work load if the planter was not prepared to recognize degrees of competence among the laborers. The dividing of workers into first-class and second-class hands and so on was too gross a distinction. Charles Stearns's "cooperative principle" sank on just this failure to see that the better workers resented being paid at the same rates as the loafers. George Benham also learned that the good hands were loath to head to the fields so long as the laggards held back in the quarters. "We's ready to go out ef' so-and-so will go," they replied to Benham's orders to get to it, "but we don't want to be de onlyest ones to go to de field."[63] The ex-slaves could also use one new freedom in order to gain another. Before he put a stop to it, Stearns's hands claimed the privilege of carrying their guns to the field in order to shoot game that crossed their furrows. The practice retarded work considerably, but the fieldhands maintained that any reversal of policy "was a great encroachment upon their rights as freemen."[64]

In few circumstances could the freedmen be made to labor under unfavorable conditions. Benham confronted what may have been a typical problem when he tried to persuade his hands to work in the rain in order to clear some choked-up ditches. He told the laborers that the cotton was sick (it was in the weeds) and that they were its doctors and had a "religious duty" to cure the patient. They thought his reasoning silly. They replied that "dey was free, and dey wouldn't work in de mud and de water for nobody."[65] The ex-slaves placed a high value on whatever free time the planters gave them, and they were not about to sacrifice it even if work had fallen behind schedule for one reason or another. Vainly did the new men implore the hands to work a full day on Saturday to make up for lost time: "but it was 'in de contrac' '—no work on Saturday."[66]

The way the ex-slaves saw it, the only religious duty they had was to increase their leisure time. Stearns said that whenever "they deemed it necessary for their physical welfare that they should enjoy a holiday, they *took* that holiday, however different might be our opinion on the subject." Not even the promise of two holidays in the future could dissuade them once they had made up their minds. The interesting thing about these unauthorized work stoppages was that usually on the night before, "the larger part of the disobedient crowd might have been found at their prayer meeting, shouting and singing the Praises of God."[67] It would seem that the black religious sensibility could be the cutting edge of this determination to relax the old discipline.

But lively prayer meetings were not nearly as disruptive of plantation routine as protracted funerals. If a death occurred on a Wednesday, for instance, religious exercises might consume all of the next day and night, while the funeral itself took place on Friday. What was maddening to the northerners was that the freedmen in an entire neighborhood helped bury the dead on various plantations, "which of course increased the number of holidays," much to the disgust of the newcomers.[68] Even more irritating was the ex-slaves' custom of "preaching a funeral" more than once. A Yankee planter in Florida gave this description of one such service:

> It seems there had been no deaths, weddings or other opportunity to give vent to their deep religious feelings (?) for the past two months. So as to have a pretext for getting together and having a big time they collected to re-preach a funeral service over a poor little child that died, was buried, prayed for and preached over two months ago. They commenced about Sundown last night and kept it up without intermission until 10 o'clock this morning when they concluded that they would all hold up a little while to take the Lord's Supper. They then resumed the funeral again and are at it yet . . . and will be until about daylight tomorrow.[69]

Although this protracted service fell on the weekend, plantation work still suffered, for it was always a "struggle to tone up again" for the new week. One plantation superintendent at Port Royal "complained that a religious revival could break up two weeks' work in the cotton field, and he did not approve."[70]

Slaveholders had never been keen about sacrificing part of the workweek to accommodate black funerals; they generally insisted that they be held at night. The new men shared their sentiment, but seemingly there was little they could do to enforce their wishes. The freedmen went ahead and held their religious meetings anyway. Black people attached special importance to funerals, which, as Eugene Genovese tells us, "figured prominently as a religious ritual, a social event, and an expression of community."[71] That funerals and prayer meetings could also serve to create more free time for the freedmen was fine, too; perhaps they even intended it this way. The laborers on Charles Stearns's plantation, who occasionally dropped what they were doing in the field to sing a spiritual, doubtless sensed that something more was involved than the outpouring of religious sentiment.[72] Enlarged opportunities for spiritual expression and increased secular freedom seemed interwoven in their minds.

Black women appear to have been especially assertive in seeking more free time. A complaint heard frequently in the early postemancipation period was that the freedwomen by and large wanted to leave the fields and keep house exclusively. "Most of the field labor is now generally performed by men, the women regarding it as the duty of their husbands to support them in idleness," an Alabama editor complained. No doubt he overstated the case and completely misread the motive, but there were enough instances of women withdrawing from plantation labor to evoke general comment. At the very least, black women sought and gained shorter working hours, evidently with the approval of their husbands. It is not surprising, moreover, that the freedwomen should have tried to create more time for themselves, considering the importance they and their spouses attached to family life.[73] Slavery was a severe hardship for black mothers. Not only were they required to perform heavy fieldwork (northerners often marveled at the strength and endurance of women fieldhands)[74] but they had to maintain a house and care for their families as well. The general practice of keeping a mess for the entire plantation community lightened their burdens only slightly. After chopping out cotton all day, there was scarcely sufficient time, not to mention energy, for discharging their domestic responsibilities.[75]

The determination of black women to set up house could lead to sharp conflict with the Yankee planting class. Run-ins were prevalent in the Mississippi Valley during the war. The establishment of free labor there was no boon for the women. Enlistment of black soldiers had depleted most of the plantations of first-class male hands, leaving the burden of fieldwork on the aged, the unfit, and the women. Efforts by federal officials to guarantee lessees an adequate number of male hands failed to redress the sexual imbalance on the plantations. In the Skipwith's Landing district alone, only slightly more than a quarter of the workers could be considered first-class laborers. Around Natchez, Mississippi, well over 50 percent of the hands were women. On the plantation of James Waters and George Klapp nearly 85 percent of the force were women.[76]

Waters and Klapp had their problems. After one year's planting experience it was their judgment that "fifty men are better than one hundred & fifty women as a rule, & cost of course far less."[77] The women, especially the young women, they thought, were the worst loafers on the place; it was nearly impossible to secure from them "the *regular* performance of their duty, which they are disposed to shirk like children." Their favorite strategy was feigned sickness, and from all appearances this was a widespread problem in the area at the time. To combat it, many Yankees adopted the practice of daily issuing the hands different-colored tickets in order to designate whether the freedmen had worked a full or partial day.[78] But this method of time-budgeting escaped the attention of Waters and Klapp. As the season progressed on their plantation, the workweek of the women gradually shrank because of one medical complication or another. By the end of July only one-third of them were turning out regularly for the Friday shift. Klapp finally staged "a sort of coup d'état," cutting off rations right and left, "very much to . . . the surprise and disgust of everyone." "I tell you there were some long faces around," he reported to his partner. The coup worked well, for the women returned to the fields the following week.[79] There was little else they could do if they expected to feed their families. But the freedwomen did not give in easily to pressures from the planters. Women hands seem to have been among the most militant fighters for their rights among the ex-slaves.[80]

If some northern planters complained of discontent on payday, burglaries of the smokehouse, shirking, and malingering, other Yankees told a different story. Albert Morgan recollected that "the best of feelings existed between the laborers and ourselves." Apparently there was no trouble on Tokeba, his plantation in Yazoo County, Mississippi, not even a minor slowdown in the fields. "Altogether it *was* just smoking on Tokeba." Another northern planter a few counties away claimed that "the negroes on our plantation were industrious and efficient and we had little reason to complain of them in this regard."[81] Ridgeley C. Powers, the future carpetbagger lieutenant-governor of Mississippi, explained what it was about the freedmen that gave him satisfaction: "They are easily satisfied, have few wants, are easily controlled, and have wonderful capacity for enduring labor."[82] Two ex-officers planting in Alabama said they had "never employed so docile, industrious, and good humored a set of people in all our experience." And a northerner planting in Georgia testified that he had trouble only with one fieldhand out of a total work force of nearly a hundred.[83] Clearly, not every Yankee planter had difficulties with his labor.

Why this should have been is not easy to explain. It may have been because of the planter's liberal-mindedness or his selective memory. Northern opinions of black diligence usually improved during the harvest, which usually galvanized the communitarian work spirit of the freedmen. They worked most energetically at cotton-picking time. On occasion they might even ridicule as a "no-account fellow" any picker who fell too far behind the general pace.[84] Yankees who employed former black soldiers, moreover, generally expressed satisfaction with this contingent of their labor force. Even Clifford Waters had to admit that black veterans had "learned the difference between real discipline & the mere freaks of arbitrary control. They all seemed desirous of working & are respectful and prompt."[85] But it would seem, too, that the perspective of the observer could influence his opinion considerably. Henry Crydenwise, a New York officer who became an overseer to his black troops, had worked on a farm all of his life and was therefore familiar with the rhythms of agricultural labor. He was impressed with what he saw. "To see us plough almost as much in one day as you plough each year, while at the same time a half dozen other kinds of work are going on is quite a sight," he wrote. He never believed that the freedmen had an aversion to hard work.[86]

The real cause of conflict between the newcomers and the freedmen was not hard work but steady work. The ex-slaves were capable of great exertions at critical moments of the growing season, and if given their own land, they could shame the northern man by the fruits of their industry. On Charles Stearns's plantation the freedman who worked fifteen acres of land on his own account obtained almost three times as much cotton as Stearns did from thirty acres "worked by several hands on shares." The black man's cotton was not in the weeds as Stearns's was and was altogether cleaner and healthier than anything the northern man had been able to cultivate hitherto.[87] The freedmen had often said that they could manage alone, if only given a chance. "They kin do it, sir," Edward Philbrick's hands advised; "don't you worry yourself, sir; they kin find herself [sic], sir." But what rankled the newcomer was that the ex-slaves had their own notions about when to do it. Why should they go to cut firewood, they asked, "until it was needed to burn?"[88] They saw no sense in finding something to do just for the sake of keeping busy. There was a time for everything—for leisure as well as work—and work, after all, was regulated pretty much by the cycles of the growing season. Besides, they had been driven too long to abide it any further. What was the use of being free, one hand asked a northern planter in Georgia, "if he had to work harder than when he was a slave?"[89] The Yankee work regimen was not the entertainment the freedmen thought they had been invited to. Their ambition after emancipation was to develop more fully a work ethic that was more human and natural than the regimentation that old masters desired to preserve and new masters wanted to increase. Already stories were starting to circulate about "an unaccountable prejudice among the colored people [against hiring] themselves to Northern people."[90] One ex-slave who found employment in the North doubtless spoke for many of his brothers and sisters who stayed home: "I didn't lak de Yankees. Dey wanted you to wuk *all de time*, and dat's sumpin I hadn't been brung up to do."[91]

Nor had black people been exposed to the fastidious standards the newcomers liked to impose. Nowhere were the two work ethics in sharper conflict than in the household. Stearns said that "the one grand and everlasting source of misery to every Yankee resident of the South, must be the entire and overwhelming destruction of all of his ideas of *order in the house*." It was a familiar complaint. Before long many Yankees had concluded that good cooks and housekeepers were rare, and that most domestic servants were "singularly worthless" and overpaid. Whitelaw Reid wrote that his "house was filled with negro servants who do nothing, & others who show them how."[92] A woman missionary at Port Royal tried to be "very philosophical, and ignore dirt and regularity," but she admitted "it would be easier to keep house in a small country house at home and do my own work (minus the washing) and live better than we do here."[93]

The problem was that northern people were too demanding to suit the views of black domestics, who had already come to an unwritten understanding with the previous occupants of the Big House. Harriet Beecher Stowe's ambition, for instance, was to produce a class of "well-trained servants—who could respect their positions and take pride in service." "The whole South would thank us," she thought. Someone should have cautioned her against easy results. It was the opinion of one southerner, Mary Boykin Chesnut, that "book-making which leads you to a round of visits among crowned heads is an easier way to be a saint than martyrdom down here, doing unpleasant duty among the Negroes."[94] Mrs. Stowe might have nodded in agreement after learning that the ex-slaves had had their fill of certain kinds of guidance and instruction. Though fancying herself an expert on household industry, she frankly had a hard time trying to convert a woman fieldhand into an efficient domestic. Minnah, as she was called, was "kinky" and argumentative, did her chores indifferently, and sometimes deserted her work in order to feed her calves. Mrs. Stowe and the other white ladies on her son's plantation were soon "used up and exhausted with the strain" of attempting to get Minnah to do what they considered passable work. Minnah was fed up herself with the hounding of the white women. She returned to the fields enthusiastically, shouting to the gang, "I was born, I was raised, I was fairly begot, in de fields; and I don't want none o' your housework."[95]

Charles Stearns and his wife had more difficulty with Margaret, their black cook. Margaret had worked in white kitchens for most of her adult life, and she was frankly "jealous of her honor, her rights and prerogatives." She told Mrs. Stearns, "Ise want no white woman to trouble me."[96] Mrs. Stearns could not take a hint. She was always after Margaret to keep things in their place, clean up on Sunday, and improve her cooking. "Dese ere white folks the most 'ticular ones me ever seed; dey beats old missus all hollow," she would mutter audibly. "I shant stay wid 'em long."[97] Stearns's northern partner once even stood over Margaret with a watch to make sure she cooked the eggs for the proper length of time. She was disgusted: "Dem Yankees is a darn sight meaner than de old rebs; it's no use to try to suit 'em."[98] Margaret gave up trying and prevailed in the end. Mrs. Stearns, who was not "an extravagant lover of the colored race," fled north after only a month of "unmitigated warfare" against domestic disorder and Margaret's obstinacy.[99] Henry Lee Higginson's wife was ready to do the same. "The more I see of them," she wrote of the blacks, "the more inscrutable do they become, and the less do I like them." The feeling was apparently mutual. The housemaids quit after one season under her roof. [100]

The northern style of methodical habits and regular industry, in short, hardly helped the newcomers to enjoy great success at the business of working the freedmen. This style may even have handicapped them. Frances Butler Leigh, the daughter of Fanny Kemble and Pierce Butler, could not understand why her Yankee neighbor felt that the freedmen were working poorly; she thought they were doing fairly well, all things considered.[101] Her statement probably says more about differences in sectional perspective than in comparative productivity, for it would seem that the tradition of paternalistic racism gave the old slaveholders at least the advantage of equanimity. They had long since conceded defeat in the matter of trying to regularize the work habits of their slaves, and, making a virtue of necessity, they had invoked Scripture and pseudoethnology to prove to their satisfaction that differences in complexion rather than in condition were the reasons that black slaves could not be made to work like white freemen. This was to confuse the racial nature with the class nature of slavery, and to attribute to race habits and predilections that had their origins in class. It was an understandable fallacy for a slaveholding culture in the American setting. No other ideological rationale except one based on race could suit the felt needs of a master class that had to come to terms with the democratic political forms, religious sentiments, and free labor institutions of the larger white community, North and South. To be sure, the racialist fallacy created a special set of problems for the old master class during the transition from slavery to freedom. It made the ex-slaveholders apt to view their labor difficulties in strictly racial terms and caused them to be extraordinarily sensitive about matters of racial etiquette to which the northern immigrants were largely indifferent. Nothing outraged and dispirited the old masters so much as the disintegration of habits of racial deference and obedience on the part of their former chattel.

But, as has been mentioned, the ideology of paternalistic racism did give the former slaveholders the advantage of equanimity over the newcomers—or perhaps we should call the advantage fatalism. If for no other reason than to preserve their peace of mind, former masters had learned to indulge a certain amount of shirking and obstinacy on the part of their black workers, and they were therefore prepared somewhat for the general breakdown of plantation discipline. Their racialist ideology had warned them to expect as much, even if it prevented them from comprehending the complex human aspirations that were fermenting in the black community in these years. The paternalistic myth that black people were children who needed parental supervision and indulgence had imbued the old planters with an aptitude for forbearance and patience in the face of the "small things," as Frederick Law Olmsted characterized the petty infractions of plantation discipline and decorum that he witnessed during his travels in the antebellum South. [102] Forbearance, in short, was one of the psychological manifestations of the compromise that slaveowners had been constrained to make with a labor force that was determined to resist the dehumanization of compulsory regimentation. Of course an indulgent temperament did not enable the ex-slaveholders to reimpose anything resembling the old plantation discipline. Nothing short of physical force could have accomplished that end. But the spirit of forbearance does seem to have given them a capacity for enduring provocations that drove the new men to distraction. A northern planter in Georgia saw this truth clearly, though he could not quite understand the reasons for it. When asked if southern men had more antipathy toward blacks than northern men, he answered,

> No, sir; and in some cases I do not think they have as much. I have seen cases where they were very forbearing, where I hardly could be so. That probably grows out of their loose and slack way of doing business, whereas a northern man would complain of it, brought up as he has been to do business strictly. I know it has been so repeatedly on our farm, and where I could hardly stand it . . . Southern men bear with the delinquency of negroes more than . . . northern men would. [103]

Yankees, then, were too thoroughly imbued with the bourgeois ethic to have developed an indifference to the "small things." And they seem to have quickly sensed as much. "If there is any better school in which to practice the glorious lesson of patience," Stearns wrote, "I should like to know of its whereabouts." [104] The newcomers were not only losing patience with the freedmen, but beginning to question the fundamentals of their bourgeois faith. After less than a year of managing the ex-slaves, a Port Royal missionary wondered whether "our style of development—that of regular, persistent industry—" was not so radically different from that of the former slaves as to challenge "the wisdom of attempting to yoke the two styles together." And toward the end of their careers in the Sea Islands, the first invaders were sure that northern men would "not have the patience to get along with the negroes." [105]

The problem was, as the Yankees saw it, that the freedmen seemed to have a mind and a will peculiarly their own. The ex-slaves were shrewd in matters affecting their self-interest, the newcomers admitted, but their wits seemed far ahead of their morals. [106] How should they be handled? That was the question that puzzled northern men increasingly. Too much leniency, it was thought, and one ran the risk of spoiling them. Once they were given approval, Yankees believed, they immediately relaxed their efforts. Nor would it do to show the ex-slaves too much kindness. The new men generally thought that the freedmen were naturally ungrateful. Had black people not grumbled about their good wages, pilfered pantries when they had been well fed, and resisted every step of the way the efforts of their well-intentioned superiors to instruct them in agricultural and industrial efficiency? No, kindness was not the answer. And yet reproof did not seem to be the remedy either, for it "never wilts them down, and discourages them as it does other mortals." [107] "It is no use to get out of temper with them," William Waters averred, "but I assure you, my patience is sorely tryed [*sic*] every hour of the day." [108] What was one to do?

About the only strategy most northerners felt was still available to them was to step up their driving of the hands. For some northern planters this simply meant an intensification of established practice, "put[ting] on the spurs," to use James Waters's frank language. [109] Benham gave up trying to set an industrious example and instead took to riding among his hands, "encouraging a little, scolding a good deal, and pushing everywhere." A Yankee in one of the Georgia Sea Islands, who was exasperated by the freedmen's short working day, was soon going "from house to house to drive them out to work." He then sat "under a tree in the field to see they don't run away." Northern overseers could be hard on the hands. Some were so harsh in their treatment that new and old planters alike had to fire them before the season was over.[110] It was just as well to get rid of them, for some Yankees learned that the antebellum overseer class had good qualifications for speeding up work. A southern foreman who was itching to get at the freedmen was delighted when his northern employer told him "to get the last drop of sweat and the last pound of cotton out of my niggers." He believed that if anybody could do it, he could. The overseer had no trouble in combining the Yankee's cash incentives with the technique of "humbuggin' a nigger." He staged a cotton-picking race for the hands, with cash rewards in order to find out "the extent of what each man could pick." "Then I required that of him every day, or I docked his wages."[111] It is doubtful whether many newcomers carried their speedup to these lengths, but it does seem evident that Negro-driving picked up usually midway through the season.[112] Large investments were on the line.

Yet there were definite limits to labor-driving in the postemancipation period. The freedmen were outspoken in their determination not to be pushed any longer. "Yas, free we is," one of them told a newcomer, "and us ant gwine to git down to *ye*, any more than to them ar rebs."[113] They meant what they said and had the resources to resist.

The freedmen at Port Royal were perhaps best situated to withstand the impositions of hard-driving northerners. The original missionaries to the islands had done their work well, even though some of them later regretted it. James Waters recognized the difference immediately when he visited the area. "Everything is the reverse of Louisiana," he wrote. "The air, water, land, woods, niggers, speech, mode of working, & *quality* of workmen. The blacks are petted babies here; in La., disciplined soldiers."[114] The truth was that the freedmen at Port Royal had considerable control over the amount of time they spent working white plantations. On the one hand, the small plots of land that most of them bought or rented (and on which they eventually erected houses) were sufficient to supply their own needs. On the other hand, the task system gave them some decision-making power over how much work they would do for the white man. William Waters wrote that the task arrangement put him "in a very awkward position, as the negroes decide how many tasks they will work, putting you entirely at their mercy." "I have negroes enough on this plantation to plant 75 acres," he complained, "& yet, all I can prevail on them to take is about 56 acres with the promise that they will do something more when they finish what they have already taken."[115] Another Port Royaler was in the same predicament. "He had hardly a single worker out of all his fifty-six who hadn't more land under cultivation for himself than for his employer."[116] The freedmen considered six hours a day long enough to work the white man's cotton, and if the planter pushed them beyond that, they considered him a hard master who wished to impose upon them.[117] Economic distress could overcome the ex-slaves' reluctance to work long hours on the plantation, as when the failure of their cotton crops in 1866 obliged them to feed themselves with what they could earn from working for the whites. But cajolery and threats were never sufficient. The freedmen at Port Royal were as close to being their own bosses as was possible in the early years of liberation. "You have no idea how independent these negroes are," William Waters wrote to his son. [118]

Freedmen in the interior seldom enjoyed the advantages available to their brothers and sisters at Port Royal. They had to devise other methods to get their way, some of which were old standbys. The easiest response to hard driving was simply to run away, as many apparently did. Almost forty hands deserted Eben Loomis's plantation en masse at the height of the hoeing season because of hard treatment by his overseer from Vermont. Loomis lost almost one hundred acres of cotton to weeds as a result. The fact that the Massachusetts man paid his hands in full each month partly explains why so many laborers deserted him at once. But the pay-withholding provision in most contracts does not seem to have seriously inhibited runaways. Waters and Klapp kept fairly busy trying to retrieve hands who skipped out midway in the season. [119]

On occasion the freedmen tried to shame the newcomers into better treatment. Too much northern faultfinding or discipline could draw from the freedmen invidious comparisons with their late masters. More than once the hands on Stearns's place denounced his attempts to enforce the contract as "the acme of oppression, as worse than the 'rebs' served them." [120] In a sense, this was the ex-slaves' way of telling the northerner that old plantation usage had to be respected, that "Master Frederic does this and that" differently. [121] Even during slavery, black people had customarily transformed privileges into rights that they would not sacrifice gladly, and the appeal to precedent was an attempt to preserve past gains. Edward Philbrick might have been gratified to know that his former hands held him in higher esteem than they did the Yankee who replaced him. [122]

These tactics probably got the freedmen nowhere, but there were other avenues of redress open to them. An appeal to higher authority was a popular one. The old practice of taking grievances with overseers directly to the planter was occasionally exercised, but the ex-slaves discovered that there were now authorities above the planter upon whom they could call. Some freedmen tried to be as familiar with the contract as their employer was, and were ready, when charged with a violation, to accuse him of not having read all of its provisions. They would also ask the Freedmen's Bureau or various military officials to intercede on their behalf. A group of Philbrick's hands once sent a remonstrance to President Lincoln complaining of their employer's "oppression." [123]

Some freedmen sought assistance from outside the normal chain of command. When Waters and Klapp hired an ex-Confederate soldier to stand armed guard over the mule pen and gin house, the hands immediately concluded that "the man had the gun to make them work in the fields." They reported their fears to a local detachment of black troops, who took matters into their own hands. Led by their white commander, they galloped through Waters and Klapp's fields slashing up the cotton with their sabres and shouting to the workers, "What are you such fools as to work this way, for these lessees wont pay you anything." The troopers also demanded a free meal from the overseer's wife, but she refused. "Much if not most of the trouble with our hands," James

Waters declared, "has been attributable to these black rascals in US uniform."[124] He failed to add that it was the hands who had invited the soldiers in to begin with.

The freedmen also fell back on their own resources. There were signs of individual rebelliousness: one freedwoman threw a "deadly missile" at her employer's head; another tried to stir up a mutiny when the planter threatened to draw and quarter her. In wartime Mississippi a former slave woman whom a government lessee had turned off his place "threatened to burn some of the cabins, and bring the rebels in upon us."[125] Cursing overseers was not uncommon, nor were threats against their lives. There was always the defiant hand who would say "he wasn't afraid of the overseer nor of no other d——d white man arrestin' him."[126] Occasionally the angry ones came in groups. When Stearns's overseer caught some of the workers stealing and said he meant to turn them in, they told him that "I was there to tend to your [Stearns's] buisiness [*sic*] and not to theirs and if I did tell they would all help to kill me." The overseer ran off rather than test their word.[127]

Group resistance was most effective, especially if it occurred under good leadership. On Waters and Klapp's Good Hope plantation, for example, the head of the plow gang was a "secret enemy" who incited the people to "all kinds of insubordination & indolence." The trouble involved his central role in the general opposition to working longer than the time stipulated in the contract. The freedmen considered the time necessary for eating breakfast and going to the field part of the normal work day; Waters and Klapp did not. The driver took matters into his own hands. He deliberately blew the morning horn an hour late and refused, point-blank, subsequent orders to sound it at the old time. He explained that "he would not ask them [the hands] to work over ten hours & they had been working eleven, etc." The planters succeeded finally in getting the gangs to the fields at the old hour, but the driver continued the resistance along other lines. The plow gang was not in the fields two hours before it stampeded the blacksmith's shop with demands that its plows be sharpened, and when this stratagem was used up, the driver took to complaining loudly, "so there was a general rumpus." The overseer tried to reason with him, "but he would not stop to hear & went through the field loudly grumbling." The hands followed their leader's example. Waters and Klapp resolved to get rid of the driver, but never succeeded.[128]

The people on Good Hope plantation also seemed to appreciate the importance of solidarity. They were in the habit of frightening off workers whom Waters and Klapp brought in from the outside. "No outsiders could live on dis place," one freedwoman declared; "dey had a field full of 'em once & dey had to leave."[129] This determination of the people to maintain their supremacy reflected in part the clannishness that one missionary in the South Carolina Sea Islands said was a strong characteristic of the ex-slaves.[130] But it also expressed the freedmen's sound instincts for closing ranks in the face of common adversity. They would no more tolerate scabs than they would defectors to the white men. This solidarity, as we have seen, crystallized as soon as the planter tried to collect evidence against a suspected thief. Strikes could bring it on as well. During one walkout on a northern-owned plantation a few hands wanted to return to work, but they explained that "dere was no use in deir wuckin' by demselves, cause de rest'd say they was a turnin' gin deir own color an' a sidin' wid de wite folks."[131] No sin was greater in the eyes of the freedmen than "going back on their color."[132]

The persistent intransigence of the ex-slaves soon began to affect the newcomers in an unexpected way. By 1867 an English correspondent traveling in the South reported finding a large number of northerners who had "a strong sense of the inferiority of the negro, and of the necessity of his being coerced into obedience and industry." He was probably not exaggerating, for after one or two seasons of free labor, cotton-growing Yankees seem to have been falling away in droves from the standards of their faith.[133] A few had even grown nostalgic for the discredited methods of the old order. James Waters had strong ideas about how to govern that class of freedmen that gave him most of his headaches. He thought that "many negro *women require* whipping."[134] His father was no sexist. "The lazy rascals can only be made to attend to their work by the whip of the negro driver," he thundered, "& all I wish is that I had the authority to put one in commission."[135] Government lessees in the Mississippi Valley did not permit the lack of authorization to get in their way. Quite a few freedmen complained of kicking and bodily blows of one sort or another at the hands of the planters. In the Department of the Gulf it was apparently no different. Superintendent of Free Labor Thomas Conway condemned those northerners who were "as ready to whip the freedmen, provided it will bring them gain, as they are to condemn the same conduct on the part of the man who formerly owned the freedmen."[136] Even the normally well disposed William C. Gannett at Port Royal once knocked down an ex-slave who he thought was misbehaving. George Benham never laid on blows, but he was not above chaining up runaways in a public place on the plantation in order to make an example of them. On the whole, the newcomers had lost all patience with the freedmen and only wished that "every Radical abolitionist at the North was compelled to carry on a cotton plantation."[137]

But even radical abolitionists had undergone a change of heart by this time. The Garrisonian Charles Stearns said that his ideas regarding the "superiority of moral means over brute force" were "put to immediate flight." His fieldhands were so *"aggravatingly provoking"* [Stearns's italics] that he no longer wondered at the southerners's "insane treatment of these laborers."[138] His advice concerning the governance of the freedmen sounded suspiciously like old spinach:

> My opinion, after a long and thorough trial, is, that a mixture of moral and physical means is necessary in governing them; the moving spring of which in all cases, should be overpowering *love*. Sometimes a fond parent punishes a refractory child severely. This he does, with love in his heart, and unfeigned sorrow at the sad necessity for his treatment, arising from the obstinacy of his child. He will not strike the child in the heat of passion; but calmly reason with it, and as a last resort, inflict bodily pain upon the offending little one.
>
> Precisely so must it be with the Southerners, in their treatment of the blacks. The first step on their part is to love them. The next to reason with them; and as a last resort to punish them perhaps severely. I am free to

confess that moral means alone, will not effectually control the unruly blacks. Their natures are too low at present to understand these motives. [139]

Stearns had not completely retraced the steps backward to the beliefs of the old regime. He felt that individuals should not arrogate the power of corporal punishment unto themselves; "the *law* can only do this [apply corporal punishment] effectually and fairly." [140]

As a last resort, most Yankee planters did turn to outside authorities for assistance in disciplining their hands. Military officials proved to be the best allies. During the war Army provost marshals took their duties as labor disciplinarians seriously, one student of the Department of the Gulf tells us, and, indeed, they "more closely resembled the ante-bellum patrol captain than an agent of the liberating army." The examples he gives of their sadism toward the plantation people painfully bear him out. The hands knew of the military's reputation and invariably chose the punishment offered by the planter whenever the alternative was to be turned over to the local provost marshal. [141] But garrison troops after the war did not forsake the tradition of their predecessors. To be dispatched to discipline the freedmen "was a favorite duty of the men," and the soldiers engaged in the work with great enthusiasm, occasionally murdering a hand in their overeagerness to follow the advice of the planters. Well, this was wrong and carrying the thing too far, but something had to be done short of "sending the nigger to heaven." "I think a large majority of us finally believed with them [the planters] that a little 'show of authority' would benefit the crop," a veteran of garrison duty in South Carolina remembered. [142]

Corporal punishment, however, was probably not administered that frequently, for the simple reason that the freedmen would no longer stand for it. [143] It did not matter a great deal to the planters, because military officials had other powers in reserve that were nearly as effective. The wartime system in the Mississippi Valley and at Port Royal of restricting free movement between plantations to pass-holders gave the newcomers some control of their labor force, as did occasional threats of military conscription. But it was the willingness of the military officials to come directly to the aid of the planter that proved most persuasive. Waters and Klapp seem to have been always calling on the local provost marshal to arrest and return runaways or remove and jail recalcitrants. Davis Bend, Mississippi, appears to have been a popular dumping ground for the latter. [144] The provost marshal was also a regular fellow. When he once received a complaint about Waters and Klapp's hard treatment of the hands, he quietly dropped the entire matter after a mutual army friend vouched for the character of the two lessees. The freedmen were not consulted. [145]

Freedmen's Bureau agents were often no less obliging to the planters. A southern overseer on a northern man's plantation in Louisiana could see no difference between the new officer in the district and "the old provost marshal, last year." "You just tell him exactly what you want done, and he'll be very apt to do just about that thing." [146] Charles Stearns had no experience for comparison, but he never doubted the usefulness of the Bureau. He wondered whether he could ever have managed his hands successfully but for this power in reserve. Not only did the agent return runaways, but he sometimes stood over them until their work was finished. George Benham appealed to the Bureau to retrieve deserters and punish malcontents, and other Yankees were just as likely to turn to the agents when they wanted a hand jailed or some labor performed.[147] Even civilian courts had their uses. A justice of the peace in Alabama declared that "three-fourths if not nine-tenths of the cases which came before him were brought by Yankees against negroes for violating contracts."[148] But Freedmen's Bureau agents, and the provost marshals before them, were more flexible instruments of coercion. In times of labor scarcity, such as generally prevailed during early Reconstruction, it was more important, from the planter's point of view, to have runaways returned than jailed. Confinement was the limit of civilian authority.[149]

Few northern planters had ever imagined before their arrival in the South that labor problems could reach such a magnitude as to necessitate outside assistance. The newcomers had appreciated the prudence of labor contracts that required newly emancipated slaves to hire on for a year and wait for the balance of their wages until the end of the season. Yet hardly anyone seemed to expect that coercion might be used in more naked and ugly forms. This was not in the free-labor script that Yankees had written for the plantation economy. The North, it would appear, had seriously misread the mood and desires of the black plantation community after emancipation. The northern planter saw this truth not just in the ex-slaves' determination to relax the old labor discipline, but also in the many ways that they indicated their resolution to assert the integrity of their private lives: in their readiness to mutiny or commit assault if the newcomer intervened in their marital disputes without an invitation; in their resentment of whites who snooped around in their cabins with officious advice about good housekeeping; in their quickness to walk out on a Yankee's Sunday sermon, sometimes in platoons, when he touched upon the sinfulness of stealing; and in the way their prayer meetings suddenly fell silent as soon as a white face appeared in the door.[150]

Perhaps nothing better illustrates the spirit of the black community after slavery than the general preference of the ex-slaves at Port Royal to live "in an area restricted to Negroes entirely."[151] It would seem that emancipation had awakened a strong separatist impulse at the time when the country was about to enter a period of progressive race relations. It should surprise no one. Having by stealth and genius created a folk culture that was expressively rich and essentially communitarian, the freedmen simply felt no burning need to sacrifice in freedom what had served them so well in slavery. They welcomed the opportunities emancipation occasioned to secure their families from outside interference, to set up their own churches, to institutionalize (insofar as they could) the habits of mutuality developed in bondage, and to give freer scope to rhythms of labor and leisure they had no reason to be ashamed of. Indeed, the labor readjustments they were forcing upon the South were likely but one aspect of larger cultural changes they hoped to bring about. The ex-slaves by and large were manipulating the market for their own purposes. They might have been in the market, but they were not of it.

In the changes they envisioned for themselves the freedmen would not eschew the cooperation of well-intentioned whites, but they wanted very much to work out their destinies for themselves. They had had enough of people who believed they were better judges of where the shoe pinched than the wearer himself.

Despite every indication that the freedmen had the will and resourcefulness to strike out on their own, northern planters by and large felt that black people needed further guidance and supervision.[152] The former slaves had not responded to free-labor incentives in the way they were supposed to. They occasionally used marketplace means to achieve nonmarket ends—or at least noneconomic ends—and they felt no compunction about resorting to stratagems learned in slavery, whenever it served their purposes. The frustrations of managing them usually caused the new men to come down with a case of what Willie Lee Rose has described as the "Plantation Bitters."[153] It was a form of disillusionment with the freedmen that was brought on by the realization that a Yankee temperament and training did not guarantee the quick fortunes and easy successes that had been fondly anticipated, a mood, for example, that led one planter to feel "like reading the riot act" instead of the Declaration of Independence at the Fourth of July celebrations that were coming to be a fixed holiday on northern-managed plantations.[154]

The planter-missionaries at Port Royal were certainly not immune to the frustration and disappointment that seemed to affect all northern cotton growers sooner or later. After a few years of managing the ex-slaves the enthusiasm and commitment with which they began their crusade had given way to peevishness and pessimism. Men and women who had entertained the idea of making their life's work among the contraband, Rose tells us, were now complaining often of "the freedman's agricultural and social failings, with a significant emphasis on his ingratitude and faithlessness."[155] Even Edward Philbrick had come to doubt whether "the present generation of negroes will ever work as they were formerly obliged to," and he concluded that "the race will not produce as much cotton this generation as they did five years ago."[156] If Philbrick had modified somewhat his cheap-cotton-through-free-labor thesis, other abolitionists on the islands had changed even more dramatically. "If a second Flood could come, and sweep off the whole race of blacks that now occupy this island, and it could be settled by intelligent farmers from N. England, what a garden it might be made and what a blessing it would be," a missionary on St. Helena Island told William Waters. As the years wore on, more and more Yankees began toying with the idea of displacing the freedmen with imported labor.[157]

Northern idealists elsewhere in the Deep South also lost faith, or at least changed the standards by which they judged their enterprises. Garth James, who at one time had considered it "a great privelege [sic] to lead these people right," by his fourth year in the South was congratulating himself on never having had "before so little trouble with my niggers, nor my crops as clean." Less than midway into their second planting season the Higginsons wrote that the freedmen looked more promising "at a distance than near to."[158] Whitelaw Reid shared their disillusionment, even though he had no serious complaints about the ex-slaves' productivity. It was the freedmen's desire to preserve certain aspects of the old paternalism that distressed him. He described this scene to an abolitionist woman friend in the North, an incident when a squad of his hands approached him after a day in the fields:

> Nigger, nigger, nigger, nigger, nigger. One, two, three, five of them. Asking about spelling books, of course, you say. Or moral pocket handkerchiefs. Or the right of suffrage. Bless you, innocent child! All they wanted was "Please Missah Reid, we's done wuck might' ha'd today, a choppin you' grass outen de cotton & we's mighty ti'ed, an' please suh, give us—a drink o' wiskey."

"I have now about 300 of these beings under my control," Reid continued. "They work well; but life among them is a fearful thing for one's rose-colored ideas. The present generation is bad material to develop. We shall do better with the next."[159]

Charles Stearns was no less pessimistic than Reid about the immediate prospects for the freedmen's elevation. Alarmed at finding his own "children undergoing a rapid transformation from white to black children," an apprehension familiar enough to the previous occupants of the Big House, he advocated establishing boarding schools, "where the children will be kept from home contamination for a few years, until good principles have taken root in their minds, and then send them out to influence others."[160]

Although they had revised their timetables, at least the idealists had not abandoned hope for the freedman altogether. The same cannot be said for the general run of northern planters. They indulged in the very Negrophobia that they initially thought was irrelevant in the economic sphere. If the freedman would not maximize his employers's profits in the expected manner, they reasoned, then the explanation must lie with race. The practice of belittling the humanity of laborers who resisted the industrial discipline had its precedents in the antebellum South and its parallels in the postbellum North.[161] But northern planters took to it with almost unexampled vigor. Having no tradition of paternalistic racism to fall back on, only frustrated expectations, they showed a capacity for racial spite that might have drawn blushes even from southern defenders of African slavery. To many newcomers, no slur or racial epithet seemed too crude where the freedmen were concerned. Black people were said to be sullen and stupid, worthless and filthy, lazy and thieving, and naturally depraved.[162] Some northerners even came to favor the idea of slavery, and not just its methods. These men were not simply the James Waterses and George Klapps, whose original proclivities for bondage merely grew stronger, but included some antislavery men as well. One Union general who said he had "fought four years to make the nigger free" was now "willing to fight the remainder of his life-time to put him back into slavery again."[163] A northern man at Port Royal agreed that working the freedmen could effect an amazing transformation of outlook. "It only requires a visit to these islands," he wrote in *DeBow's Review,* "to make a thorough pro-slavery man of the rankest Abolitionists."[164] This, essentially, was the same message that defenders of the peculiar institution had sent north for years, and it bears out the truth that racism originates as much in class frustrations as in anything else.

The racial hatefulness at times threatened to consume some of the newcomers. "I have written so much about negroes," William Waters confessed to his son, "that I am afraid you will think that I have got negro on the brain."[165] A Yankee planter in Florida knew the feeling of impotent rage and thought he had found an antidote:

> The "rascality," . . . duplicity, lying, thievishness, *total* depravity, vulgarity, lazyness, meaness, brutality, devilishness, hellishness and moral infamy of these cow killing and hog stealing wretches as a class *as they are here at the South* is simply and positively beyond the power of any pen, however gifted, to describe. I must say in all candor that I never in all my life have been so thoroughly disgusted, through and through, with anything before as I am with the negro character. The worst type of a drunkard is not to be compared to it. I also feel the need of some church privileges. I consider it is time I was identified with the church.[166]

But more Yankee planters escaped their frustrations by quitting cotton-growing than by seeking spiritual fortification. Charles Stearns had made his peace with God before he came South—was in fact receiving visions from the Lord with impressive regularity—and still could not see his experiment through. After four years at the business he decided that he could "never cultivate a farm successfully with the blacks as laborers." He continued, "Nothing can be done without incessant and minute supervision of them, such as I am not able to give them."[167] Another Yankee planting in Georgia came to the same conclusion. "I became satisfied that as years went by the negro could be depended on less and less," he told a congressional committee, "and the result is that I have sold out my farm." There were apparently many other newcomers who had sold out for the same reason.[168] The admission of failure was difficult for a Yankee to make, and it was not done without a certain amount of regret and self-doubt. Before two seasons were out, the Higginsons left their plantation "with a sense of utter failure." "Failure to do any good," Ida Agassiz Higginson confessed, "except the little I have done in school. Failure to manage the blacks well and quietly as servants; but I have learnt a great deal, and I suppose if I keep that in view, and remember it and also the errors, to avoid them in future, it will not be time lost, at least not personally."[169] There was some consolation in trying to put a brave face on the collapse of one's high hopes.

Yet it was not disillusionment with the freedmen that caused most northern men to give up cotton-planting. The more impersonal factors of overflows, drought, armyworms, and falling cotton prices were the major reasons that so many Yankees left the South earlier than they had planned. It was business failure, and not the failure of their idealism or of their managerial skills, that ruined the new men, by and large, and with serious consequences for their relations with the old slaveholders. For it was the peculiar dilemma of the northern planter that he could seldom remain on good terms simultaneously with both races of the southern people. How he got along with one element in the community often affected how he fared with the other.

7 *A Question of Business*

It was inevitable that bad feeling arose between northern planters and southern whites. Their relationship was never entirely stable, nor was it free of mutual suspicion. It got off on a good foot mainly because both parties refused to allow old antagonisms to disturb their devotion to moneymaking. They were too preoccupied with acquiring fortunes or recovering losses to have much appetite for the quarrels of the past. Obviously, a few poor planting seasons could dissolve the atmosphere of goodwill. The crop failures of 1866 and 1867 did nothing to improve the feeling between natives and newcomers. Nor did the enactment of the congressional plan of Reconstruction in the spring of 1867 increase fraternal regard. The granting of suffrage to the freedmen raised southern resentments against the conqueror to a new level of bitterness, and this at a time when the expectation of easy riches no longer served to keep the ill will in check.

Strains in the relationship could be seen developing before political and economic setbacks ruptured it completely. Each party's expectation that the other would shed its prejudices as a matter of course was a dangerous assumption. Southerners in particular may have taken too much for granted in thinking that the new men would readily fall in with the ways of the country. For the postemancipation immigration of northerners to the cotton districts was much less selective than the antebellum movements of people from the free states. It included settlers who would never have considered a southern residence so long as slavery existed, as well as men and women who were only convinced the more by the triumph of Union arms that the northern way of life represented all that was progressive and high-minded and therefore worthy of extension.

It is not surprising that many northern planters came to the South with a large measure of contempt for its people and its culture. They were thoroughly familiar with the free-soil critique of the region, if they had not already boned up on such prewar authorities as Frederick Law Olmsted and Fanny Kemble. In the eyes of the newcomers the South was crude and backward and its inhabitants were "ignorant, rude and lawless."[1] James Waters thought they were "damned benighted people!" after a search of the local stores failed to turn up any soft crackers. "They do not even *know* what is meant by the term, unless it is 'hard-tack,' " he complained. The entire population, in fact, seemed "sunk in barbarism," and did "nothing but drink, hunt & gamble, with very few exceptions."[2] A northerner in Alachua County, Florida, averred that Gainesville was a "community of drunkards."[3] The florid language of the natives had a certain shock value, too. A Yankee described one type that he thought was fairly numerous: "a blustering, square shouldered, hard fisted, fast talking, rum drinking young man of some 35 years who swears almost every other word he utters whether in the presence of ladies or not, and keeping about two-thirds intoxicated during the evening."[4] The impulsive southern temper was also alarming, especially when it was expressed in outrages against the freedmen. Clifford Waters believed that the South was a "nation of 'bullies.' " "The fact is," George Benham remarked, "there is no reason about these people." He attributed southern emotionalism to the effects of a semitropical sun, which made the blood run "warmly through the veins." "What is in the heart is instantly in the brain."[5]

Much of the South's religion also came in for some harsh words. Unless the newcomer was of an evangelistic leaning or from the "Burnt Over" district of New York, he generally had little use for the emotional vitality that typified the region's major denominations, whether white or black. The bourgeois northerner was uncomfortable in the presence of the gospel vigorously delivered and was shocked at the sabbath-breaking and rough-hewn devotional practices of some of the faithful. "Why they chewed tobacco all church time making the room resound with their expectorations. And when sitting down some of them would have their feet fully as high up as their heads on one arm," one northerner wrote in amazement.[6]

Yankees reserved special contempt for the nonslaveholding whites, with some important exceptions. The Unionists were usually admired for their rugged independence and wartime valor, and in counties where the Unionists predominated, the northern man seems to have experienced little ill will.[7] Still, the poor whites, as they were found in the planting districts, were scarcely the sort to evoke compliments from the newcomers. Lanky, sallow-complexioned, and dressed in patched butternut, the nonslaveholders were said to embody many of the vices that northern planters found objectionable in southern life. To Yankees this class of native whites seemed especially addicted to strong drink, coarse language, and violent behavior. If the local village was the scene of nightly murders, northerners were pretty sure who was committing them.[8]

The nonslaveholders might have derived some small consolation from learning that the new men did not hold them entirely at fault for such shortcomings. It was often said among the recent arrivals that the lower classes simply exhibited on "another scale the habits, & modes of life of their (so-called) superiors."[9] If the region suffered from illiteracy the reasons were not hard to find. Southern men of cultivation sometimes went for weeks "without picking up a newspaper!"[10] Natchez, Mississippi, that gem of antebellum splendor, was in actuality (as seen by the northern newcomers) a "perfectly dead community (mentally speaking)."[11] And if the old planters boasted any library at all, their literature "was quite ancient" and lacked "such advanced thinkers as Gerrit Smith, Garrison, Phillips, Sumner, Lowell, or Whittier, or even Seward or Emerson."[12] As for the palatial estates, they were considered to be the sorriest looking mansions that ever graced a country; few of the residences excelled second- or third-class dwellings in the North. On the whole, newcomers in the Deep South derived much pleasure from believing that the native white population from top to bottom was "ignorant, depraved and licenscious [*sic*] ."[13] These discoveries flattered their sectional vanity.

What struck the new men most forcibly, however, was the apparent indolence of southern society. They agreed in the main with what proponents of the northern emigration crusade had been arguing for years: the South was lazy. "If there is one word more applicable than another to the whole of Southern life," Charles Stearns observed, "it is that expressive Yankee term, *shiftlessness*."[14] Slothfulness and inefficiency were thought to be deeply embedded in the entire social fabric, particularly in the agricultural system, which "was excessively lavish and excessively faulty." George Benham maintained that the old planters were spendthrifts and poor business managers.[15] Again, the northerners thought that the freedmen and the poor whites simply reflected the bad habits of their betters. The ex-slaveholders, "damn them, . . . have never worked for a living & they don't mean to." [16] Northerners generally conceded that this "shiftlessness" was the natural consequence of a social system that had degraded honest labor and frustrated upward mobility. But some thought that the lack of enterprise might be owing to the relative ease with which one could eke out a livelihood in a country where living was cheap and resources bountiful.[17] However it was explained, the apparent want of industry offended the newcomers' bourgeois ethic. They were astonished to discover people who did not appear to care "whether they are rich or poor."[18]

Of course, northerners tended to forget that much of the South had only recently been carved out of a frontier to which a long and devastating war had nearly returned it. They also seem to have been blind to the reality around them. White southerners by and large did care about their economic condition in these years and were working hard to improve it. At least the ex-slaveholders and nonslaveholders were, and so were the freedmen in their own way. In fact, nothing excited more general comment shortly after Appomattox than the ease with which the South's young men showed themselves "to be as able in the cotton field as they were on the field of battle."[19] Some of the older heads were no less determined. Having fallen deeply into debt, the wealthy planter Thomas Dabney did not let his seventy years keep him from breaking new ground. "He had never performed manual labor," his daughter tells us, but after the war he "applied himself to learn to hoe as a means of supplying his family with vegetables." He even tried to "learn to plough, but he could not do it."[20] He was exceptional only in his heroic determination. Many other ex-slaveholders were making an adjustment. "Once I knew no thoughts for the future except those respecting high cultivation, promotion in the world, and pleasant society," Floyd King of the Georgia Sea Islands wrote in the summer of 1865, "but now it is far different; I accept the situation with cheerful courage, however." Senator William Sprague was fortunate to have so conscientious a manager as King for his Mississippi plantation investments. The Georgian saved Hoyt, Sprague & Company from more than one financial embarrassment.[21]

Still, one wonders how far this departure from old ways actually went. At issue, after all, is not whether ex-slaveholders labored hard after Appomattox but whether they completely forsook the style of living for which they were justly famous. The suspicion is that they did not. The habits of generations seldom yield easily, even when a society's central institution is overturned. Historically, the South has not shown a strong compulsion to save, as witnessed by a rate of capital accumulation among all of its income groups that has been noticeably lower than the national average.[22] There is some basis in fact for the many observations about the southern penchant for conspicuous consumption, and probably for the equally well-known legend of southern sociability. Why this has been so is far from being a settled issue. But whether the antebellum planter was basically an agrarian capitalist with some aristocratic tendencies or a "pre-bourgeois" seigneur with an incidental capacity for surviving in the capitalist marketplace, he seems to have had the ability to enjoy himself. The southern elite generally cherished values that went against the northern grain. Perhaps William A. Percy, one of their descendants, explains it best: "Their distinguishing characteristic probably is that their hearts are set, not on the virtues which make surviving possible, but on those which make it worthwhile."[23]

The old planting class, then, had an outlook regarding work different from that of the newcomers. Like their slaves—or maybe because of them and the limits they set on their own exploitation—they did not hold to a "time is money" philosophy, although they did want to make money. A northern teacher who resided in Yazoo County, Mississippi, right before the war saw this clearly. He was struck by the easygoing hospitality he met with in the unpretentious houses where he stayed. Clocks and almanacs were rare items in the planters' homes, he observed. "The word, haste, is not in a Southron's vocabulary." Instead, there was a measured pace about life in these parts and a readiness among the inhabitants to indulge their sociable instincts when they could find the time. If a passerby happened upon a group of planters talking on the verandah and he was known to one of them, he was politely introduced to the rest of the party and expected to stay and chat awhile, unless he had an important errand. Liquor flowed rather freely. Many of the planters kept "various wines and choice drinks."[24] Naturally, this northern man could not have been describing the neighborhood during the height of cotton-picking season. But it is safe to assume that these antebellum graces did not entirely disappear in the ashes of defeat and Reconstruction, though the choice wines may have dwindled appreciably. The southern people were indeed working hard after the surrender, with the possible exception of some of those planters who leased their places to northerners. Yet they doubtless retained some of their notions of what made survival worth while. Otherwise there is no accounting for the frequent northern condemnations of the drinking, hunting, and gambling that the new men saw around them.

Northern planters, in other words, had fastened onto the less attractive side of what C. Vann Woodward has called the Janus-faced "Leisure-Laziness myth" that has typified descriptions of southern character over the years.[25] It should surprise no one that the newcomers did so, since they seem to have thrived on hard work. Even a southerner who adjured his compatriots to roll up their shirt-sleeves and applauded them for following his advice, recognized that the recent arrivals went about their jobs in great earnestness. "Our 'Northern brethren' also, as far as capacity for labor is concerned, appear to be doing nobly. They tug and toil, and pour out their sweat in copious streams over their small cotton and big grass, and demonstrate their physical manhood in a most satisfactory manner."[26]

What is more, Yankee planters appear to have enjoyed keeping busy and welcomed the challenge of new duties. Henry Crydenwise's overseer duties kept him fairly busy, but by his own admission he was "best contented & most happy when my time is occupied." The astronomer Eben Loomis also put in a long day's work, yet he went to bed at night "with a sigh of satisfaction."[27] "The fact is," Garth James wrote to his exacting father, "No man has begun life, until he has systematized his duties." The James brothers found hard work in an agricultural setting just the sort of outlet their nervous temperaments required. "The familiarity which one acquires from working constantly with Nature and even reproducing her manifold and different problems," Garth explained, "opens one's eyes very sensibly to important truths." His older brother William was frankly envious. "How our life glides away in levity and mirth while you are mingling the sweat of your brow and your tears with the cotton-yielding mother-earth," he wrote to Garth from Massachusetts.[28] Young transcendentalists responded energetically to the new life of arduous toil and responsibility. Henry Lee Higginson and his comrades appeared to enjoy their plantation duties considerably, as did young Clifford Waters, at least for a while.[29] Of course not every Yankee threw himself into his work as enthusiastically as Higginson and Waters. Some newcomers were content to leave the plantation business in the hands of their southern partners, who did not always like this arrangement. One Mississippian complained that he had to attend to the plantation himself, "as my *Yankee* friends does [sic] not know anything about it & do not try to learn much as long as they have me." They wanted him "to run a large place for them" the following season, but he was leaning against the idea.[30] Even so, most northern planters seemed to have had a real passion for keeping busy. It was almost a therapeutic thing with some of them. George Benham, for one, believed that the pursuit of wealth tended to soften the spirit, as opposed to wealth itself, which could harden its possessor.[31]

Albert T. Morgan also subscribed to this philosophy. He thought that "fully as much comfort, even pleasure, could be extracted from the getting of money as from the thing itself, and with much greater profit to the head and heart if pursued with a right motive."[32] Morgan was an eager beaver whose plantation hummed with activity. He seldom found time for ordinary pleasures. A few black prostitutes who drifted out to his place in search of trade found him and his partners poor customers. "My! Yo' Yankees nebber will hab no fun, t'well yo' own dis yar whole blessed worl'!" they told them. "Yo' alwus so mighty busy an' peart." Morgan's aloofness had nothing to do with his racial preferences. He married a black woman while he was in Mississippi, even though he discountenanced "social equality."[33] He simply could not spare the time for carnal diversions.

As much as this enthusiasm for work was part of their temperament, it was also somewhat of a conscious effort not to fall in with the ways of a culture they despised. The large variety of new agricultural gadgets that northerners brought with them was the most obvious expression of their determination to remain distinctive. But this spirit had more subtle manifestations as well. George

Benham carried his intention to be different to the point of ignoring the old planter's precaution of riding in the fields with an umbrella. The northerner thought carrying an umbrella was an "effeminate habit." This flouting of regional customs could raise eyebrows in the neighborhood. For there was the ever-present pressure to conform, or as Benham unsympathetically put it, "to drink whiskey as often as the natives do, to take hand at poker, and, above all, to carry a pistol, under penalty of being branded a coward."[34]

There was the matter of drinking, for example. Several of the newcomers abjured the habit altogether, either on principle or because they did not like the southern brand of whiskey; like everything southern it, too, suffered in comparison with its northern counterpart. Not even the doctor's repeated admonition that a dram of bourbon in the morning was a medical necessity in a malarial climate could sway the abstinent northerner.[35] Troubles with white natives on this score usually began with the overseer. This class was apparently one of heavy drinkers, judging from the complaints of northern men. It seems that some new planters were forever averting near-catastrophes brought on by drunken overseers.[36] Curbing the overseer's drinking habit was never easy and it was sometimes dangerous. Garth James discovered that his overseer's inebriation

> was worse from the fact, that a white underling in this country, when one has occasion to reprimand him[,] assumes invariably the attitude of the high-toned injured innocent and hints and talks of pistols and the like. All one can do is to answer in the same, and to keep as stiff an upper lip as is consitence [*sic*] with one's liking of bowie-knives and revolvers.

James had learned quickly how to deal with it for the offended overseer apologized and promised not to drink while in his employ.[37]

But the trouble was that the teetotaling Yankee could not escape the temptations of alcohol no matter where he went. "You can't go anywhere to transact any business without being invited to take a drink," Clifford Waters complained. He described one encounter in a country store in Louisiana.

> Sitting around the store were three of the *ladies*? of Waterproof... & several genuine butternuts, long, lanky, yellow & dirty, all drinking whiskey while a barrel of the same stood in the corner & nearby a plentiful supply of tumblers. Imagine such a sight in our own country towns.

Waters naturally declined the hospitality of the company. He did not like "the habit even in gentlemen," and of course he would not stoop to place himself "on a par with these low devils."[38]

It was one thing to snub the cordiality of the village idlers and quite another to decline an invitation from one of the old planters. Sidney Andrews tells of a narrow brush with serious injury that resulted from his adamant refusal to join two prominent Georgians in a drink. The ex-Confederate colonel of the pair retrieved his pistol and stormed back to the hotel, demanding, "Now show me the man who won't drink with me!" The proprietor succeeded in averting a showdown, much to Andrew's good fortune.[39] Admittedly, this was an unusual case, partly because of the colonel's condition (he was many sheets to the wind) and partly because of the desperate methods of the aggrieved party. But refusing to have a drink with the local citizens "evoked at least a broad stare from the bystanders, if it did not actually give offense."[40]

At first Albert Morgan's unwillingness to have a "social drink" stunned his landlord, Colonel Black, who probably did not feel any more comfortable at his wife's appreciation of Morgan's abstinence. "Oh! he's all right," Black would explain to his companions. "He'll get out of that befoah he's been with me a six month."[41] But Morgan did not give in, and Black doubtless questioned whether his lessee would indeed "become one of us" on the appointed schedule. An equally grave offense was Morgan's failure to invite passing neighbors to stop in to have a drink. He and his partners did not have the "leisure for entertaining them . . . [because] we were busy." As Morgan himself realized, "This was a violation of one of the ways of the country, but it was business."[42]

The strains that conflicting outlooks on leisure and labor placed on the relations between natives and newcomers, however, were minor in comparison to the bad feeling that arose whenever a northerner violated the racial customs of the neighborhood. As usual, disagreements first developed with the overseers, who did not share the racial optimism of many of the new men. When the southern foremen were not snickering at their employer's susceptibility to the blandishments of the hands, they were fomenting trouble among the freedmen or swearing never to "give in to the new-fangled notions again." Sometimes the only alternative left to the Yankee was to discharge the overseer and try to do better the next time.[43]

But it was the surrounding white population who really made life difficult for such Yankees as defied accepted racial usage. The old planting class were too uncertain of the future to relax for one minute their scrutiny of the newcomer's conduct toward the freedmen. They were still very much in a frame of mind to blame racial instability on outside agitators, especially Yankees. Any minor departure from local custom could invite charges of being too "familiar" with the ex-slaves. Neither doing manual labor with one's fieldhands nor drinking from the "same gourd his 'nigger' used" was likely to win many friends for the Yankee.[44] Innovations were sometimes condemned as "certain to disorganize the labor of the country."[45] It says something about differences in sectional priorities that whereas the new masters were discomfited by the industrial disorder occasioned by emancipation, the old masters were more bothered by the racial disorder brought about by the same change.

Native ill will on this score did not always arise suddenly. Again, the experience of Morgan is instructive. A believer in democratic manners, Morgan made his landlord edgy by his habit of addressing the freed people as Mister and Missus and allowing them in turn to call him "Colonel" instead of the more deferential "Master." Colonel Black and his friends were sure that Morgan was setting a bad example. The heart of the problem, however, seemed to be that the ex-slaves were more independent in Morgan's presence and appeared to like him.[46] It was doubtless true, as Willie Lee Rose has perceptively observed, that one of "the greatest afflictions the Southern whites felt was the gnawing sense of having been supplanted in their relations to the black race."[47] Just as troubling to them was the apprehension that the Yankees were encouraging the freedmen to talk about their old masters and their experiences in slavery. There was usually substance to these fears.[48] Although the old planters had persuaded themselves that the newcomers and the freedmen would eventually part on bad terms, small changes in the script raised misgivings about the overall direction of the performance.

But there was no precipitous rush to ring down the curtain. The natives resorted to giving hints first. Black often reminded Morgan that no one understood the black man's character as well as his former master, and that the lessee should bear that fact in mind if he wanted to remain "popular with 'our people.' "[49] Advice sometimes came by way of example. Black seems to have made it a point to emphasize the old etiquette when addressing the freedmen in Morgan's presence. " 'Here you boy!' or 'Hi! boy,' " he would call out in language familiar to the Big House, in order to warn Morgan "not to be nice in [his] manner of addressing the freed people"—in short, to tell him that he "should fall in with the ways of the country."[50]

This sort of low-keyed counsel lasted about six months. By then Black concluded that the situation demanded a showdown. Associates in Yazoo had grown more uneasy with Morgan's continuing conduct, and even Black's own servants had recently become a little "saucy". One had the audacity to call him "Colonel" when she brought him his toddy.[51] And Black had never quite gotten over his resentment of Morgan's success at retrieving his former slaves from a contraband camp along the Mississippi River. "Without intending to do so," Morgan realized, "I had mortally wounded him in his pride and 'wronged' his family."[52] Black was somewhat more sensitive on this matter than most men were in his circumstances. He finally cornered Morgan on the streets of Yazoo City, reviewed the history of his lessee's relations with the freedmen, and demanded that Morgan issue a card denying the rumor that he had declared black women to be as good as white women. He explained that a public disavowal was necessary to vindicate the honor of the Black family, and "to allay the apprehensions of ouah people." The colonel had laid his cards on the table. "Why sir! must we surrender our cherished theories and dearest interests to please a handful of Yankee immigrants, by G-d, sir-r?" he demanded.[53]

Morgan was not the sort to cave in to these pressures. He refused to issue the card and finally broke his self-imposed silence. He told Black that he had the right to direct his laborers as he saw fit and said that he did not consider his manner with the freedmen "revolutionary, nor even thought of it in that light." These remarks failed to appease. "Well, by G-d, sir; as you make yo'r bed yo' must lie," Black thundered. "I took yo' for a *gentleman*; yo' are only a *scalawag*." As Morgan passed up the street "the group of men by the store uttered deep groans," in a sort of offstage chorus of assent.[54]

Morgan and his brother shrugged off the run-in with the colonel. Though no longer invited to the Black house for supper, the Morgans reasoned that their landlord did not represent the true sentiment of the community. [55] They were mistaken. Their attempts to educate the freedmen placed them beyond the pale of "good society" in Yazoo County. When they donated lumber and carpenters to a project to erect a schoolhouse for black people in Yazoo City, the opposition from the whites was so fierce that a detachment of federal troops had to be called in to protect the enterprise. That the Morgans should have been the cause of the town's occupation was bitterly resented, even though the old inhabitants had managed to charm the commanding officer into accepting their version of the trouble: the Morgans were stirring up bad race feeling by being too friendly with the freedmen. Local outrage with the Morgans peaked after they converted the plantation stockade into a schoolhouse and brought in their sister and her friend to teach the blacks. The natives thought it was scandalous, not to mention incendiary, to subject white ladies to such disagreeable tasks.[56]

Yankee "schoolmarms," as they were called, were never very popular in the South during Reconstruction. They usually encountered ostracism and worse in their contacts with the white population.[57] Northerners who established plantation schools generally fared no better. "This thing of 'book-larnin' 'mong the niggers' is generally hooted at," George Benham discovered. It was sometimes tolerated if conducted under a southern roof or by a southern teacher, but black education was frowned upon when it was conducted under exclusively northern auspices. Confederate guerrillas murdered at least one government lessee in the Mississippi Valley partly because of his educational enterprises for the plantation hands.[58] Charles Stearns suffered much grief simply because of his Sabbath school. Anonymous letters arrived warning him to end his efforts and occasionally his neighbors dropped by to monitor his classes. Gangs of men also prowled about the plantation. A few local whites approved his methods, but they were a minority. Most seemed alarmed when their own hands drifted over to Stearns's plantation to attend classes. "Some of the planters threatened very seriously those who attended, in one case with death," Stearns testified.[59] His neighbors feared that Stearns was a "political emissary from the North, come to instil into the minds of the blacks false notions of political and social equality."[60]

Indeed, any activity by northern planters that might be construed as a threat to the racial order aroused antagonism. Even Fourth of July celebrations on Yankee places were said to smack too much of social equality. It was one thing to treat one's hands to a picnic and quite another to read them the Declaration of Independence.[61] Not surprisingly, attempts to sell land to the freedmen met with bitter opposition. A prominent feature of most Black Codes was prohibitions against the renting or selling of land to the ex-slaves, and northerners discovered the strength of this sentiment whenever they tried to defy it. Members of an Ohio family in Louisiana were driven out of the state when they attempted to make the freedmen landowners, though eventually some of the leading citizens of the community invited them to return. One of the reasons John Andrew's American Land Company ceased its efforts to sell land to the freedmen was the apprehension that anyone who tried to do so "would be murdered."[62] It would appear that when northern planters showed they had independent notions concerning the governance of the freedmen, their honeymoon with white southerners was over.

The divorce proceedings were anything but amicable. Once the white population concluded that certain Yankee planters were alien forces who would not yield to the custom of their adopted homes, the ostracism of them was complete, relentless, and implacable. No longer could the newcomers look to the friendship of the leading citizens as a passport to fellowship with the larger community. The "despotism of public opinion" was now so strong that even natives who were not ill-disposed toward them could only keep up their friendship by stealth. "It was as if we were so many criminals, of whose acquaintance one should be ashamed," George Benham explained.[63] Albert

Morgan was singled out for special abuse. Around Yazoo City he was hailed as "Polecat" Morgan (a sobriquet that stuck) and was made to "walk in the streets with the niggers." He claimed that the natives regularly insulted all Yankee planters in the county.[64] Veils dropped, skirts lifted (only slightly), and faces turned away whenever a northern pariah made an appearance in town. This "offensive war of sentiment" was sometimes unnerving. "Did you notice what an ugly eye that Yankee has in his head?" one southerner asked another as Benham passed them on the street. On reaching home Benham went directly to the mirror to see if there was any truth in the remark.[65]

Yankees who experienced this ostracism felt not only unwanted, but unsafe. "I am here like Daniel in the lion's den," Stearns wrote to a friend back home; he believed that affairs in Georgia were about as bad as they had been in Kansas during "border ruffian times." He carried weapons whenever he ventured from the plantation, kept a breach-loading rifle handy, and slept with a pistol under his pillow. Morgan eschewed similar precautions, even though he was convinced that a conspiracy existed to drive all northern men out of Yazoo County; some of his Yankee neighbors always went about armed. Benham and his associates also believed that they were "as much in the enemy's country as were our soldiers during the war—the difference being that we were here unprotected and almost alone, while our soldiers had the army with them."[66] None of these men ever warmed to the idea of an early removal of the U.S. Army. They were positive that their safety depended on its presence.

They were also sure that their personal security ultimately depended on the triumph of congressional Republican policy over that of President Andrew Johnson. Newcomers who were inconvenienced by white natives often blamed their troubles on the White House. "Whenever the government wavered, and under the lead of that traitor, Andrew Johnson, attempted to re-instate the rebels in their former places, then did we tremble from fear," Stearns wrote characteristically.[67] It was natural that northerners should have felt this way. Their difficulties with new neighbors seem to have surfaced at about the time the National Union movement was gaining momentum. This attempt by President Johnson to unite conservatives of both parties and sections for a decisive showdown against radical Republicans in the northern congressional elections of 1866 aroused the South almost as much as had the southern elections the preceding fall. Few hints from Johnson and his allies were required to convince former Confederates that "not only were they being injured, but absolutely persecuted." The sectional bitterness that had more or less lain dormant for the past eight months now broke loose with renewed force. For a northern immigrant it was as uncomfortable as ever. "We have felt it keenly here," wrote Garth James in the fall of 1866 concerning the darkening of the southern mood, "and have been forced at times to hold our breath, and look at facts and take warning."[68]

Benham and his friends in Carroll Parish, Louisiana, felt the change most palpably. As he remembered, the elections of 1866 in the North were a time "when our neighbors seemed to think that everyone must take sides." "Andy Johnson's come to our rescue," a visiting neighbor told them. "We've all got to take sides for or agin the policy. We must know who our friends are, and who our enemies are."[69] Benham stuck to the practice he had always followed regarding political discussions, maintaining that he had no interest in politics and had come South only for personal gain. But this excuse was no longer sound currency in the neighborhood. A band of southerners who dropped by his plantation a short while later were in no mood for noncommittal responses. "This's the South's fight," they told the Yankees, "and everybody in the South's got to take an interest, or git out."[70] After the election southern neighbors made Benham and company feel their anger and frustration at the disappointing outcome. If, as many natives must have asked themselves at the time, the South had miscalculated so badly as to the real sentiments of the northern voting majority, then had it also mistaken the true character of the new planters from the North?[71]

But, as always, this political controversy was an evanescent thing, gone as quickly as it came. Southerners had no more stomach for prolonged debate now than they had during the fall of 1865, and organizers who tried to drum up support for the Johnsonian movement scarcely made headway against public apathy and private selfishness.[72] Momentary political spite only precipitated a reaction that had been brewing against some newcomers for quite a while; the elements of combustion had been brought together for other reasons. Differences in temperament and habits, in cultural values, actually, seem to have been the basis for many of the divisions that occurred between natives and newcomers during the period of presidential Reconstruction.

That differing cultural values should have caused bad feeling seems somewhat ironic, for there was much about the new man's situation that was driving him inexorably toward an identity of interest and sentiment with his white neighbors. Being in a traditional southern occupation (though one that was admittedly undergoing change) and in the midst of southern people, the northern man was bound to lose some of his peculiarities sooner or later and be made to see why it was that cotton-planting had been not a business proposition merely, but a way of life. Even a man like Morgan was susceptible to the influence of his surroundings. "Fact is," his brother warned him, "you're imbibing altogether too many of the ways of this country for your own good." He added, "You not only talk like a Southerner—you are beginning to look and act like one."[73]

Morgan's transformation was apparent only after he had been in the South for about five years. But other newcomers began to change much earlier than this, occasionally for reasons of necessity. Some northern planters responded to provocations and insults in ways familiar to the old order. The Union general with whom Benham teamed up once struck a southern man with his glove because of his belligerent language and returned home to oil his revolvers in expectation of the customary challenge. "I am living in a country where the code of honor is in vogue, and although I abominate the practice of dueling, yet I am in Rome and must do as Rome does," he explained. The challenge never came, but nonetheless he won "considerable *eclat* among those of the neighborhood who were constantly boasting that they recognized the code of honor."[74]

But usually the changes came about much more subtly. The seclusion of plantation life was somewhat foreign to the experience of most northern men, who had known only urban life or closely-knit rural villages. One of the greatest deprivations of southern existence, from their point of view, was the absence of cultural activities such as town life in the North made available. They missed the sort of society that was found in lyceums, temperance clubs, and debating societies, and they could not comprehend how culture and grace could possibly come from this isolated and dispersed way of living.[75] After a while they suffered from an acute loneliness that trailed off into boredom, and they were burdened in ways that some men are who have time on their hands that they know not how to fill. The irregularity of the growing season was something they were not entirely prepared for, accustomed as they were to the steady pace of commercial life. The novelty of their surroundings relieved the tedium somewhat, but not for long. There were too many lonely evenings on the plantation when the only thing that broke the silence was an occasional unearthly chant from a distant black cabin.[76]

It was not just the sounds and seclusion of the southern plantation that required getting used to; the vicissitudes of bringing in a crop obliged some of the most painful adjustments. To sensibilities accustomed to predictability in matters of business, the vagaries attending the growing of cotton came as a surprise. There was a host of natural causes, ranging from insects to inclement weather, that could destroy a half-year's work, and there was nothing one could humanly do to prevent the destruction. These things could deflate self-confidence, especially the youthful kind. Shortly before he entered planting, Garth James had "a superstitious belief in my power of not failing," he wrote, but by the beginning of his second planting season he felt otherwise. Clifford Waters, too, soon began to doubt his own capacities. "I am seeing more & more clearly everyday that I have no creative power & there seems to be no probability that I ever shall in this world."[77] It usually took only one unfavorable season to make young transcendentalists question whether planting was really the therapy they had imagined it to be. In place of self-confidence came a kind of fatalism that people in agricultural life customarily assume, a feeling that it was prudent not to live too far in the future. Garth James described his new consciousness to his mother: "My determination has been . . . not to think ahead at all, and not to fret, but to meet difficulties only as they come and to get over them and to forget them, as soon as possible."[78] What else was he to do?

He might have followed the example of the astronomer Eben Loomis, who immediately indulged his love for the outdoor life. No ascetic compulsiveness kept him from taking advantage of Florida's climate and countryside. Rising at five in the morning, he started the hands to work, often going to the field to show them what was to be done, and then returned to the Big House "to smoke the pipe of peace and contentment." There might follow, during the day, a ride through the fields to see how work was progressing, for he did not like "to walk in ploughed land." Often there were diversions: drinking in the sunshine and sounds of the languorous Florida climate, picking bunches of jessamine, and long rides to the seashore.[79] These activities could transport him into rapture whenever he gave his horse free rein. "Gods! how the rushing air smote me in the face at her first dash . . . [I]n her dizzying speed I seemed to be flying through the air on noiseless wings," he recounted. Such experiences made him understand "the Bedouin's love for his horse and his desert life."[80] But they also set back the work on his plantation. Loomis was not a very successful cotton planter.

It was easy for Loomis to slip into the habits of antebellum leisure, but others seem to have been driven to them out of resignation. The discovery that reforming zeal was a luckless enterprise on a southern plantation caused some adjustments. Charles Stearns soon gave up his determination "to set everything to rights." He explained, "It is of no use to war with these angry elements of carelessness and stupidity, and you soon become metamorphosed into a careless, ease-loving Southerner. Why this difference exists, I know not."[81]

Stearns might have found an explanation for his growing fatalism in the need to rely on the labor of ex-slaves. If there was one thing above all others that changed the newcomers, it was their inescapable dependence upon people whom they believed they should have been able to control but could not. The transformation in the immigrant consciousness could be seen in the vituperation and spitefulness, in the so-called "plantation bitters" that were ubiquitous in plantation life. It could also be seen in the galling feeling that came from having to live among these "despised others," from being obliged to make one's residence in what was in fact a black community. "Think of these holy New Englanders forced to have a Negro village walk through their houses whenever they see fit," Mary Boykin Chesnut wrote. She knew it would not be easy for northern people to enjoy for long the company of the ex-slaves. "No one who has not tried it, can imagine the deficiency in one's life thus occasioned," Charles Stearns wrote. "We saw faces it is true, but they were not those bearing the stamp of a well-trained intellect."[82] Even the thoughtful missionaries at Port Royal, who derived large satisfaction from working with the freedmen, had to admit that "they are not exactly companions for us." Their successors on the islands were elated when most of the ex-slaves dismantled their cabins and moved them off the plantation.[83] Not even the occasional pleasures of playing the patriarch remained to offset the disappointments. Some northerners tried it at first,[84] but the freedmen were no longer acting their parts. The sense of isolation was all the stronger because the new men often had "no one to see, or to do anything for you, but ignorant, stupid blacks."[85] A Yankee planter in Florida for a stretch of several months "suffered more or less from an indescribable feeling of lonesomeness like unto imprisonment" and "wanted to be out in the world where I could once more see a locomotive and a steamboat." He attributed this feeling more to the fact of "being surrounded by a hundred or more debased negroes than anything else."[86]

Of course debasement, like beauty, is in the eyes of the beholder, who in this case was middle class to the marrow. To discover that the freedmen, like other premodern people, were less than enthusiastic about the industrial ethic and preferred the work rhythms of a different economy was unsettling enough. But to learn that the ex-slaves not only cherished but wished to liberate from ancient restraints a community and culture painfully created during slavery was more than the newcomers could endure, especially when they too had to live in that community and make their peace with it. The experience of the thing nearly drove them to despair and at the very least caused many of them to seek comfort and meaning in the racism that at one period they considered irrelevant to the enterprises they were about to launch. Indeed, that racism would result from close contact and utter dependence was exactly the reaction that old planters had predicted all along.

But probably the reaction did not happen fast enough to suit most ex-slaveholders, and this is what caused the problems—at least in the interior. For it was only in the interior of the former Confederacy that northern planters suffered serious ill will from the native whites. Morgan and Benham and Stearns and all the rest who complained of white hostility were generally isolated in communities of strong southern feeling, cut off by and large from intercourse with people of their own kind. It was the general feeling of the time that "the further you go from main routes, the more hostile you find the inhabitants."[87]

One main thoroughfare where intersectional relations were particularly good was along the lower Mississippi River. One could travel from Vicksburg to Natchez without experiencing "the slightest difficulty from any hostility of the inhabitants." Practically all observers were agreed on this point, especially Yankees who were scouting for places to buy or rent.[88] Reports of northern journalists that the South was an inhospitable habitat from which Yankees would likely flee if the military withdrew never failed to scandalize the Vicksburg (Mississippi) *Weekly Herald*. "We say there are no such indications here," it editorialized. "There are many United States officers who have settled in our midst. We see them everyday pursuing the even tenor of their way, and exhibiting none of the signs of running away."[89] This was not simply sectional propaganda. Farther down the river at Port Gibson, Mississippi, a meeting to organize a militia company late in 1865 "passed off very agreeably, Yankee and Reb., 'so-called,' vieing with each other to promote the general welfare."[90]

Whitelaw Reid was in a good position to judge the mood in the area. He had spent a year on his Concordia Parish, Louisiana, plantation, had made frequent visits to neighboring Natchez, and had no complaints about his neighbors. "Your Wendell Phillips, . . . & some others are talking a great deal of nonsense about northern men not being able to walk the streets of New Orleans," he advised Anna E. Dickinson, his abolitionist friend. Reid's own neighbors, who included a one-armed ex-Confederate general, a former Confederate senator, and the author of a book on the divinity of slavery, knew him "as an abolitionist before the war, & a Radical since." Reid did not hide his opinions, but even so, he "never received one unpleasant word." His southern neighbors treated him "not only well, but with marked courtesy."[91] There was one unpleasant encounter with a former nonslaveholding white, "in patched butternut," who was heavily armed and full of fulminations against the war and black Republicans. "Why stranger, you don't mean that you voted for old Abe?" he asked Reid in astonishment. He continued, "Why by Godland, you're a blue-bellied abolitionist Yankee. Stranger if we had you up our way on the Black [River] we'd kill you." But the man quickly retracted his remarks, said he was "just jokin'," and declared that "we're the most hospitable people in the world." But "by Godland" he hated Yankees. "See here stranger I mean some kinds of Yankees."[92] Reid simply shrugged off the incident. He was not up on the Black River but on the Mississippi River, where social relations did not compel the new man to take seriously every outburst of gasconading to which he might be exposed.

Friendly relations between Yankee planters and the white population, from all indications, were quite well established long before Appomattox. Of course, the initial meeting was anything but cordial. The Natchez elite, who had chosen Union rather than risk their property for a secessionist cause they deplored, were perfectly willing to lease their plantations to the newcomers, but "the presence of such a crowd of 'Yankees' is hateful as poison to them," James Waters discovered, "and the loyal men cannot keep it from being seen." The old planters were "perfectly respectful" to their northern lessees and even tried to treat them well, but it went "against the grain." The contempt was mutual. Waters believed that the Natchez nabobs bore out "very well the impression I had formed of their ignorance and narrowness." He conceded they had "plenty of bravado and fume," but no real chivalry. "I should get sick of them very soon," he feared, "and would not like to settle here for over a year, unless the money came in very fast."[93]

But Waters underwent a quick change of heart. Before much time had elapsed he and George Klapp were making regular social visits to the home of their landlord, Alfred V. Davis, sharing whiskey and cigars with other prominent citizens of Natchez, and returning the hospitality whenever one of the old gentlemen or their sons dropped by the plantation to talk business and have a social drink. Waters and Klapp were not teetotalers, as were some of their compatriots. The two novice planters even got on well with their secessionist overseers.[94] By 1865 (they had decided to stay on for more than a year) they were boarding with a Natchez lady who was anxious to please. "I really am so fortunate in having such gentlemen in my house," she told her Yankee tenants, "but I feel . . . that I give you such a miserable return. . . . I do so want to make you both as happy as you can be away from yr. own home."[95] The consideration of the natives made James Waters feel unusually charitable. "There is more of the gentlemen in some of these men than I thought at first," he confessed, "but it is not of the highest kind of course."[96]

What helped to ease the entrance of Waters and Klapp into Natchez society was having some common ground for political discourse. They probably believed as much in social order and in African slavery as did their hosts. Liquor and conviviality flowed freely during good-natured discussions of how the goal of the war should never have been changed from a limited defense of the Union to a larger crusade for freedom. Waters agreed readily with Judge Winchester, one of Natchez's leading citizens, that Abraham Lincoln's emancipation policy would prolong the rebellion unnecessarily. The Salem man had no doubt that by liberating the slaves "we should simply concentrate the power & feeling of the South, strengthen & confirm wavering men, & turn good unionist [sic] into rebels." His southern neighbors could drink to that.[97]

If intersectional agreement about race, war, and politics opened the doors of Natchez's mansions to Waters and Klapp, their close acquaintance with General Lorenzo Thomas and his family guaranteed them that social intercourse would be unusually agreeable. The general had developed acquaintances here before the war and when he returned to organize the plantation leasing system and recruit black soldiers, he resumed seeing these acquaintances rather quickly. It will also be remembered that he made it a point to help out old friends in whatever way he could. The old planters of Natchez were not ingrates, for they not only knew something about New South business methods but Old South charm as well. Waters and Klapp basked in its glow. There were "official" excursions downriver to New Orleans aboard the *Rocket*, a military boat captained by one of the general's sons, with stops along the way to visit the stately mansions of the

Natchez elite. At Levin Marshall's sugar plantation the official party enjoyed the fine wines supplied by Samuel Davis, the brother of Waters's landlord. The following day sleek carriages brought them out to another gracious estate for a shellfish dinner embellished with vintage clarets and "the best champagne." At New Orleans there was more socializing and the French opera. Waters wrote, "If I had not plenty of business to attend to, I should be at no loss for amusement." "Still all these people live a most hopelessly superficial life," he told his brother, "and I should not want to keep it up long."[98] Even under the most tempting circumstances his bourgeois spirit did not succumb easily. Save for periodic apprehensions about guerrilla raids, he was hard pressed to remember that a war was being waged in the vicinity. And even the guerrillas were not always malicious. Waters thought they were "good-natured & reasonable, & generally only want your property & a drink."[99]

Waters and Klapp and the Thomas family enjoyed this Natchez hospitality for a good many years. The old planters of the area, as we have seen, liked having the general around, and he rented Alfred V. Davis's Pittsfield plantation in 1866. Waters and Klapp changed landlords that year, as they did every year, renting the Ravenswood estate from Don Antonio Yznaga del Talle, a Spanish nobleman who made his lessees feel at home.[100]

It would strain credulity, however, to imply that the social relations between the natives and the intruders were *always* on an even tenor. Sectional bigotry occasionally marred the good feeling. Although his Philadelphia antecedents caused the old inhabitants to assume that he was opposed to New England ideas, George Klapp took "particular pains to have it understood that he considers Massachusetts as the highest state & her ideas as the most advanced in the world."[101] What his hosts said in reply is not recorded, but they, too, could irritate their guests with expressions of regional pride. No group of southerners was more infected with the spirit of defiance that swept the South in the winter of 1865-66 than the Natchez elite. Even the Georgian Floyd King had to concede that "now that the negro are [sic] gone, and they have lost their credit, they are the most loud discontents in the land."[102] Their fuming especially put off Clifford Waters. "If the northerners suppose that the unexampled magnanimity which the Govt has shown to the South is appreciated or that any gratitude is felt for kindness shown to a vanquished enemy," he complained to his brother, "they are very much mistaken." He thought it would be "the greatest blessing to this country if the whole race of Southerners could be shipped to—well anywhere so that they could no longer curse this country with their presence." Clifford's attitudes were extreme, but even General Thomas was annoyed by the fervor of his southern friends.[103] Still, these things passed over, and life picked up where it had left off at the surrender, though not at the dizzying pace at which it had moved during the war. Although he did not believe in the ideal of the southern gentleman, George Klapp ended up marrying a southern woman and cast his fortunes permanently with a people whose social ideas he felt were far less advanced than those of New England.[104]

Admittedly, the experiences of Waters and Klapp were not typical of the relationships between northern planters and white southerners along the Mississippi River. Their association with the Thomas family allowed them to move in social circles that were closed to most newcomers. Yet there was a good deal of friendly feeling between the military and the old residents of Natchez and Vicksburg during the war, and one suspects that the northern lessees also participated in the intersectional amity.[105] In any event, northern planters felt no personal insecurity in these localities. No sense of lurking danger kept them from delivering large majorities to the gubernatorial candidacy of the southern Whig, Benjamin Humphreys, in the fall of 1865. And they were quite active politically in behalf of President Johnson's program of Reconstruction. It is some indication of the nature of intersectional relations in the area—or at least near Natchez—that Reconstruction fusion politics operated here according to the textbook. "There were peaceful relations and a well-understood political agreement," Pierce Butler tells us, "by which certain Federal offices were left to the Republicans, and local offices were left to the local people."[106]

The lower Mississippi River was not the only area of the Deep South where Yankee immigrants voted for southern conservatives during presidential Reconstruction. According to one local editor, many northerners in Florida had "affiliated with the late rebels, (so called) esteeming them now, since they have taken the oath of allegiance, to be good enough Union men to receive their votes and confidence."[107] He may have been talking about East Florida, where there was little evidence of discord between newcomers and natives. Harriet Beecher Stowe, whose son's plantation was on the St. Johns River, had no complaints about the conduct of her neighbors, although she admitted taking small part in local society. Eben Loomis and his partner, Frederick Bardwell, similarly experienced no discomfort from their neighbors in Duval County, Florida, along the east coast. Though they employed some of Bardwell's black former soldiers and operated a plantation school taught by a Yankee schoolmarm furnished by the Freedmen's Bureau, they were never interfered with in the slightest.[108] Farther up the coast, in Georgia, the toleration with which Henry Lee Higginson and his associates were initially received had not abated in the least. They were as friendly with the hands as a Yankee could be and also allowed white women to teach the freedmen. But these innovations evoked no signs of displeasure from their neighbors. At the end of 1866 Higginson could report having had no "shadow of trouble with any mortal," although, he added, the freedmen had to be treated carefully.[109] On St. Simon's Island social relations went beyond mere toleration. Pierce Butler and his daughter appear to have gotten along well with their Yankee neighbors. A Philadelphian who later managed one of the Butler plantations was an occasional dinner guest at the family home.[110]

By far the most pleasant locality for a northerner to be in during these years was the Port Royal area of South Carolina. It was a place that Yankees in the surrounding interior talked of moving to whenever rumors of troop withdrawals made them edgy.[111] A miniature northern community had sprung up on the islands since their invasion. Before two years had passed, Willie Lee Rose tells us, "the deepest associations of family-building with time and place were forming in the transplanted community."[112] The place was also becoming a winter resort for northern friends and relatives. And as the missionary ardor cooled and a different type of planter moved into the area, signs of social exclusiveness could be seen everywhere. Northerners who attended black churches began withdrawing to form their own congregations, and the new residents established a Planters Club to organize weekly sociables at the homes of members.[113]

The return of a few of the old white inhabitants after Appomattox caused some initial uneasiness. The Philadelphia schoolteacher, Laura Towne, whose idealism never soured, thought that the ex-Confederates were "crawlingly civil as yet, but will soon feel their oats." [114] The warm reception that the freedmen gave their owners made the newcomers uncomfortable. Memories of the freedmen's assertions that only their old masters could put them off the land were still fresh in mind. William Waters was not alone in mistaking the ex-slaves' affection for a few of their former owners for an indication that they would rather vote "with their old masters than with the Yankees." [115]

But it did not take long for amicable relations between northerners and southerners on the islands to develop. As for one longtime Beaufort resident with whom he held a conversation, William Waters saw him as "a most respectable gentlemen" whose opinion he would trust implicitly. [116] White southerners were likewise impressed with the civility and good manners of the northern interlopers. William Henry Trescot wrote glowingly of the hospitality of a young Bostonian who held government title to the plantation of one of Trescot's friends. The Massachusetts man was "very polite—there was nothing he could do that he did not do to make us comfortable." [117] Admittedly, lingering suspicions and resentments were too strong on both sides to permit the full blossoming of intersectional fellowship. But the northern community at Port Royal shortly following the surrender had reached a point in its development where it could be moved to commiserate with the tragic circumstances of the old elite. Some new men expressed their sympathy in a tangible way. One prewar resident recalled how a group of northerners donated the required amount of back taxes to save her family's house from falling under the auctioneer's hammer at the November 1866 Direct Tax sale. [118]

This emerging goodwill, which began well before the mutual revulsion against corrupt Reconstruction politics drove together whites of both sections, had a foundation in mutual self-interest. Many northerners who had already bought in at the Direct Tax sales seemed just as anxious as the old planters to put a halt to further government land sales. William Trescot, who acted as South Carolina's lobbyist in Washington during the early postwar years, was happy to discover that northern planters in the Sea Islands were "willing to act in concert" in an attempt to settle the confused land situation in the area and suspend the tax sales permanently. [119] A nagging uneasiness about the validity of their titles impelled these newcomers to look for some kind of *modus vivendi* that might avert possible eviction. They were also concerned about avoiding lengthy and bitter litigation lest it frighten off the investment capital needed to build the major metropolis that some northerners envisioned for the islands. And those Yankees who found it easier to make quick fortunes from land speculation than from cotton-growing had special reasons for wanting to see the tax sales ended, or at least their competition ruined. Cheap government lands were luring away their customers. [120]

But the major reason that many Yankees wanted the tax sales discontinued was the fact that the tax sales had made the management of plantation labor anything but easy. [121] Labor problems were a reason, too, for newcomers to the islands in these years to be civil to the old inhabitants. Practically every northerner in the area after the war was disenchanted with the freedmen, and none more so than the Yankees whom the tax sales had attracted South. There was "no hater of the Negro like these speculating planters," Laura Towne shrewdly observed.[122] It would not take too many years for them to come to accept even the most disreputable practices of their new home. "You would not wonder at the Ku Klux if you had to submit to such infernal injustice as we have [to], but only that there were not more of them," Clifford Waters wrote from his father's plantation in 1872.[123] As early as 1865, some Port Royal Yankees were taking the southern planter's view of political questions. They seem to have wished for an early end to military rule principally because it was in the hands of General Rufus Saxton, who always took care to see that the ex-slaves were not imposed upon or ejected from the plantations without proper cause. They were also critical of the Freedmen's Bureau, which struck many of them as "much too expensive a machine for the government to run merely to subserve political ends."[124] Nothing better illustrates the direction in which the Port Royal Yankee community was moving after the war than the fact that an ex-Confederate officer and "a regular John Brown Abolitionist" had united in a movement to organize local government in Beaufort under the old city charter well before radical Reconstruction commenced.[125]

But the spirit of sectional accommodation and cooperation was also flourishing in areas of the southern interior where northern planters had settled in compact colonies. It was often argued that "organized emigration," as this mode of settlement was called, was the only way that Yankees could emigrate to the South and not be tempted or coerced into making concessions to hostile public opinion.[126] The secretary of the American Land Company and Agency would advise no investment in southern plantations unless the investor could interest a prominent southerner in the enterprise or make arrangements to ally his property with that of several of his friends, so that they would be "within supporting distance of Each other [*sic*]." The method produced good results. One colony of about twenty northern planters who went to Mississippi under the company's auspices had gained "the moral control of an entire county" and were working their plantations free from any outside annoyance. The county in question may have been Madison, where a group of fourteen Yankee planters published an announcement in *DeBow's Review* proclaiming that "newcomers can feel as secure here as in any sparsely settled agricultural community of our Western States."[127]

The experience of the Gordon colony in Alachua County, Florida, furnishes another illustration of the point that where Yankees settled in groups, hostility from local whites was less pronounced—or at least appeared less threatening. Consisting of six Massachusetts men, including Garth Wilkinson James and his younger brother, Robertson, and Leonard G. Dennis, a future carpetbagger congressman, this colony of abolitionists experienced few inconveniences in one of the state's most prosecession counties. No repercussions followed from a legal battle that they helped to wage against one of the area's leading citizens, who had accused a freedman of stealing his pistol. A Gordon colonist served as counsel for the black defendant. The local jury, composed exclusively of local whites, could not agree on a verdict, and when the case was tried again in another locality, a similar outcome resulted. Garth James saw it as "a notable sign of the times."[128] Naturally, not all Alachuans welcomed the Yankee presence. "The people about us are wanting very much to sell out and get out of the way," Garth wrote to his father; "they feel our atmosphere and it depresses them." [129] And the heating up of the national political debate and the local mood made the newcomers slightly uneasy. But they were not seriously alarmed. They were confident that they could hold their own "to all eternity." "Our armory is good and we could arm some 30 or 40 negroes," Garth explained. [130] The need for such a precaution never arose. The Gordon colony had no trouble with white neighbors in the period of presidential Reconstruction.

Other colonies of Yankee planters in the southern interior fared just as well. In Noxubee County, Mississippi, the Ohio Settlement, headed by Ridgely C. Powers, who was soon to become the carpetbagger lieutenant governor, reported that their "treatment by the citizens here has been uniformly kind." [131] In Morgan County, Georgia, where forty to fifty northern families had settled, it was no different. One of their members had even been made a member of the State Agricultural Society. Colonies of northern planters in Alabama too had no complaint about their treatment and said as much when the opportunity presented itself. One settlement near Demopolis declared that they "had been uniformly treated with courtesy and respect by all classes of citizens during our entire residence here." Some months earlier a large number of them had attended a mass meeting held to endorse President Johnson's veto of the Freedmen's Bureau bill, with one of their number delivering the "most indignant speech against radicalism." [132] They obviously had not experienced harassment of the sort that is said to have made their counterparts elsewhere in the interior break out in a cold sweat whenever native whites organized a political meeting in behalf of the president's policy.

But these Yankee colonists by and large were only acting out on a smaller scale the drama being staged at Port Royal and other areas of the Deep South that had been heavily settled by northerners. It is one of the larger ironies of the northern emigration movement that predilections toward the southern point of view formed the quickest in those areas where Yankee immigrants were chiefly among their own kind. Along the lower Mississippi River and the South Atlantic seaboard the newcomers were so heavily concentrated that they could take their personal security for granted. At Port Royal it was the new men and not the old inhabitants who constituted the majority, "and better than all, there is already a strong skirmish line of Yankees spreading along the coast, with heavy reserves in the cities." [133] It was as though the freedom of not having to worry constantly about southern enmity had permitted these newcomers to indulge fully their spite toward the freedmen and to feel, therefore, a certain amount of sympathy for the white southerners' determination to keep the South a white man's country. A shared disdain for black people was the surest basis imaginable, in these years, on which to establish intersectional amity. And nowhere did the racism of northern planters flourish so luxuriantly as in those settlements where they felt relatively immune from hostile visitations, which is another way of saying that for the emotional reality of the planter's way of life fully to sink in required a certain amount of freedom from outside interference.

But northerners who were isolated in the interior, on the other hand, seldom felt entirely at liberty to give full rein to the racial resentment that had been building in them ever since their arrival. They did have to worry about the hostility of southern whites. They had heard enough veiled threats and ugly imprecations to make them shudder at any suggestion that they cooperate with the local people to push for an early end to military rule. They believed, as we have seen, that the safety of their persons and property required the presence of a standing army in the South. And as much as they may have been provoked on occasion by the interference of the Freedmen's Bureau in their affairs, they could no more view its termination calmly than could a homeowner stand idly by while his house went up in flames. Without the presence of the Freedmen's Bureau, one northerner explained, "planters would come to us and say, 'Here, you've got a nigger that belongs to us'; they would claim him, under State laws, and compel him to go and work for them. Not a first class laborer could we be sure of." [134] In fact, nothing caused an isolated northern planter to become broad-minded in his racial views more quickly than a run-in or two with ex-Confederates. All of the delinquencies of the freedmen would be forgiven as the newcomer reflected on the hurtful instruction they had received from their former owners. [135] And if these conflicts with the native whites happened repeatedly or assumed a threatening aspect, as was the rule in many parts of the interior, the Yankee newcomers quite understandably began to develop an alliance with their black hands. The freedmen seemed to be the only friends they had, aside from the Radicals in Congress, who were too far away to be of immediate service. As for the advice that they make a concession or two to the hostile public opinion all around them, the newcomers had tried to follow it and still had not allayed the apprehensions of the southern whites. What use was it, anyway, to try to appease the racial sentiments of a people who were pleased to call revolutionary those labor practices and social manners that appeared to the newcomers as the very embodiment of moderation?

It was, on the whole, not an unfamiliar scenario in the history of American race relations: southerners scapegoating northerners for the perceived racial instability in their neighborhoods; northerners replying in kind and blaming southerners for the awful state of labor conditions and morals in their community. And then both groups would swell with the sectional pride that the war had already inflated to an unhealthy degree, and one would begin to accuse the other of deficiencies in a moral code to which they both more or less subscribed. The charge of ingratitude would be answered with the accusation of hypocrisy, and so on through the entire litany of sectional recrimination. It was exactly this scenario that allowed Afro-Americans to make whatever gains they were able to make in the nineteenth century, the ironic scenario of white racists fighting with each other over questions of race. [136]

And what of the freedman, the man in the middle? Perhaps he understood the historical dynamic of the situation better than either the victor or the vanquished. The ex-slaves were running with the hare but hunting with the hound, as Mary Boykin Chesnut saw it, playing off northerners and southerners against one another whenever it served their interests, until forced to make a choice. "If I was in danger from the rebels," Charles Stearns wrote of his fieldhands, "they would rush to my protection, but that was because it was for their interest that I should live." [137] The freedmen were pragmatic, as usual. They knew that it was to their advantage to stand with those who had freed them rather than with those who had fought to keep them enslaved. And thus began the alliance—or rather *mésalliance*—that eventually developed into one wing of the southern Republican party.

It should be borne in mind that we are talking of general tendencies, not hard-and-fast social laws. The situation contained many crosscurrents. Several northern planters at places like Port Royal joined the Republican party and even developed into liberals on the racial issue, although every indication suggests that most carpetbaggers here—and in similar areas of the Deep South—were more conservative than not. And there were Yankee settlers who, despite their isolation in remote communities, were able to establish cordial relations with their southern neighbors. In this connection one thinks of the Union general William T. H. Brooks, who was so esteemed by the local whites near Huntsville, Alabama, that when he died in 1870 they marked his grave with "a Confederate emblem secured in concrete." That the general—and others like him—may have been a flunky of a transparent kind is possible, even likely, but there were other Yankees of similar circumstances and experience who were not. [138]

One fact seems clear: Partnerships between northerners and southerners were generally amicable, irrespective of locality. Men who entered into such arrangements were usually willing to accept each other for what they were. "We are of different politics, or rather sides," one southerner told a Yankee with whom he was trying to set up a partnership. "The question is whether you & I, though different . . . respect each other." [139]

Mutual respect, or at least forbearance, appears to have flourished at close quarters. A New Yorker who teamed up with a southern colonel, first in the lumber business and then in cotton-planting, hit it off well with his partner from the start. The southern man's wife was not so agreeable, and in the New Yorker's presence made constant "flings at the boorishness, stinginess, and vulgarness of the northern people at large." The Yankee "stood this for a week or two like Job," before taking up the defense of his region. Their sectional disagreement amused the colonel vastly, but it did not sour the spirit of the partnership in the slightest. Even the colonel's wife was not irreconcilable. She often cut the New Yorker's hair. [140] The experience of the Yankee overseer, Henry Crydenwise, was no less favorable. He and his wife lived with the southern family for whom he worked, and neither his school for blacks nor his readiness to defend the right of the hands to carry arms lessened the consideration with which his employer treated him. [141] He became involved with the religious life of the white community in his Mississippi home and earned not only the confidence of his hands but that of the local whites as well. When it was learned that he would not be staying with his present employer for another year, he had "numerous applications to engage with others in planting right here in this neighborhood." [142] Sectional prejudices were seldom so strong as to be invincible.

What is more, even when the anti-Yankee animus was at its implacable worst, things were rarely so bad as they appeared to northerners at the time. Although George Benham escaped one close brush with a drunken and murderous crowd of village toughs one night, few newcomers were actually physically molested. When liquor flowed freely, these types always seemed ready to harass an innocent bystander, regardless of his sectional identity. [143] Yet what was really inexplicable about this sectional hostility was the abruptness with which it could reverse itself on occasion. Benham and his associates had for a neighbor one of the most "unreconstructed rebels" that this passionate period afforded. She gleefully refused to do small favors for the nearby northerners, declaring that "arsenic is good diet for Yankees!" But the medical aid that her northern neighbors furnished during her husband's critical illness seems to have mellowed her bitterness marvelously. [144] In the same way, Charles Stearns's own personal misfortune called forth unexpected sympathy from his heretofore hostile neighbors. He could scarcely comprehend the kindness of his old enemies after his wife's death. "The Southern character so conflicts itself," he confessed, "that it is hard to understand it properly. At one moment, breathing out the most intense hatred towards all Northerners; at another, extraordinarily zealous in attempts to benefit either one of these very Northerners, or some of their own acquaintances." [145] Personal peacemaking sometimes has ironies not found in official diplomacy.

If intersectional relations during most of presidential Reconstruction were generally amicable and even somewhat elastic in areas where the feeling toward newcomers was less than cordial, the situation became brittle when business prospects worsened. The willingness of natives and immigrants to pocket their differences had derived in part from the faith that by so doing they might pocket something more tangible. Everyone was trying to make a quick killing, "striving for a common goal," as George Benham explained, "which is to be reached, if at all, by a journey along a common road. There is a kindred interest, and therefore a kindred feeling naturally springs up." [146] But a succession of crop failures disappointed expectations of easy fortunes and seems to have dissolved the goodwill that still existed between northern planters and their southern neighbors.

The sum of it was that cotton-growing in the period from 1863 through 1867 was not the cornucopia that had been anticipated. Certain speculators may have made large profits from the high-priced staple, but the majority of Yankees who raised it did not. [147] It was a rare individual, like Edward Philbrick, who netted handsome returns from his investment. Whitelaw Reid tells of one government lessee who arrived in the Mississippi Valley in 1864 worth less than $100 and within two years had gained title to a plantation that was valued before the war at $200,000. [148] James Waters and George Klapp did well in 1864, their first planting season, netting over $23,000 for the concern. They considered themselves fortunate that year, however. "Others who have gone into the business heavily are ruined, & I doubt whether any of these places in this part of the state will pay half of their expenses. Many will not pay a quarter," James Waters wrote. [149] He did not exaggerate. Guerrilla raids set back the planting operations of many northern lessees, whose greed for extensive tracts made them particularly vulnerable to disruptions of this sort. "All the efforts made the past year to raise cotton on the vacated plantation, by the New England pattent [sic] improved plan, have resulted in disaster to all concerned," remarked one observer. [150]

Indeed, misfortune visited Waters and Klapp the following year. They barely cleared expenses in 1865, and the subsequent two seasons left them deeply in the red. Theirs was the common experience, for the early postemancipation years presented planters from both sections with formidable problems. If scarce labor and defective seed handicapped the general effort to return to full-scale cotton production, a host of natural disasters defeated the attempt altogether. Heavy rains in the spring retarded plantation work considerably. Planters in Louisiana and Mississippi paid dearly for the wartime neglect and destruction of the levee system. Along the Mississippi River and lesser tributaries, overflows necessitated replanting the entire crop.[151] Too much rain in the spring, moreover, was likely to be followed by too little rain in the summer. And just when picking season was about to commence, regiments of army worms invaded the cotton fields stripping the stalks of most of their foliage. Every year between 1864 and 1867 this melancholy scenario was reenacted, with few variations, throughout the Deep South, and every year experienced planters swore they had never seen such a poor season for cotton as the one that had just ended.[152] The newcomers had no standard for comparison, but they sensed that things could not be much worse. "It would seem that since the commencement of the rebellion," one Port Royaler lamented, "the elements, worms, & all the forces of nature had conspired against the intruders of the southern soil."[153] Henry Lee Higginson would not have disagreed. "I fear that many men experimenting at the South this year have had bad luck & will go home disheartened," he wrote from Georgia at the end of 1866. Hoyt, Sprague & Company liquidated its plantation investments after only a year of operations, and many lesser northern cultivators did the same.[154]

The real disaster came in 1867, when the bottom fell out of the cotton market. Hitherto, the high price of cotton had kept losses within tolerable limits and kept alive the possibility of quick killings from black free labor.[155] Even some of the most luckless lessees during the war were sure they could recover their losses—and then some—if only given another chance. Losing streaks seldom discourage gamblers who still have a stake to play with, and in 1865 and 1866 credit was still generous.[156] But the fall of cotton prices to a low of fourteen cents a pound in 1867 was a grave blow to men who discovered that incidental expenses were greater than they had counted on. The cost of operating a plantation in the early postemancipation period was perhaps double what it had been in 1860, and at the very minimum it was a good deal higher than anyone had expected. In 1867 selling one's cotton did not even pay the expense of raising it.[157]

This combination of setbacks ruined nearly every Yankee who grew cotton in the South in these years. The planting business was "an occupation that proved disastrous," one newcomer remembered. "I have lost heavily & do not suppose any of the officers will come out even in this vicinity," wrote another, a former Union major in Florida. "For my part, I have lost two years time and all of my capital," added a Union officer who had planted near Jacksonville.[158] The financial losses ran into the thousands of dollars. Henry Lee Higginson and his partners alone lost $65,000 after two years of cotton-planting. After the same amount of time Frank Blair, Jr., owed his creditors $26,000. The Morgans figured their losses at $50,000. George Benham & Company dropped over $100,000.[159] Everyone was more or less cleaned out. "Almost *every man*, northern or southern, planting here, is *ruined*," James Waters wrote from Natchez at the end of 1867.[160] It was an embittering experience. One disappointed Yankee planter summed up the feeling of most of his comrades: "What a d——d piece of business the whole thing is!" [161]

But the widespread crop failures of the early postwar period embittered the old planting class more than anyone else. They had counted heavily on restoring their fortunes from one or two good cotton seasons; yet financially they were worse off now than immediately following the war. In 1867 there was simply no market for cotton land. The South Carolina Sea Islands were something of a bellwether. In 1867 the Direct Tax commissioners continually had to adjourn their land auctions *sine die* for lack of bidders. [162] Nor was there any prospect of borrowing northern money. One southern planter who went to New York City to secure capital discovered that investors were unwilling to trust their money beyond their immediate neighborhoods. *DeBow's Review* spoke "by the card when we say, that not one in fifty of the contracts or loans of last season have been renewed, and certainly not one per cent of the new applications for capital has been successful." [163] Even northern capital that had already been promised to the old planting class was no longer very flush. A Vicksburg native had to be satisfied with $10,000 for the $25,000 that was still owed to him for a thousand-acre place he had sold a short while earlier. Yankee lessees proved less reliable. Many of them begged for reductions in rent, and if their losses were too heavy (and sometimes when they were not), they simply ran off. Absconding was a habit several of them had acquired during the war. [164] James Waters was grateful for a thousand-dollar loan from his cousin in 1868, for it enabled him to leave the South "with flag nailed to the mast, while almost every other poor devil who has tried his fortune in that country has gone away with his colors in the dust—their latest impressions being generally sheriff's sales or unpaid niggers & so forth." Floyd King was glad to see them go. He stated, "It looks like just retribution on most of them who are heading away to the North again, having lost all their ill gotten gains obtained during the war thro' speculation and by pilferings." [165]

Desperation gripped the South after the crop failures of the early postwar years. Southern courts and sheriffs kept busy issuing writs of attachment and writs of replevin as creditors and debtors struggled to salvage something from the general wreckage. So grave was the threat of massive forced sales in the spring and summer of 1867 that the military commanders in Mississippi and South Carolina temporarily suspended all proceedings for the collection of debts. [166] The scramble to save one's bacon aroused many antagonisms, especially of the sectional kind. Northerners and southerners never liked each other's business ethics in the first place. Natives sometimes found the Yankees "a hard set to deal with." Newcomers, on the other hand, thought southerners were too loose in their business practices and unwisely committed to substituting personal honor for formal contracts. A suggestion that a business agreement be put in writing could draw the retort, "my word is as good as my bond." [167] So long as times were palmy, differences in commercial outlook were easily brushed aside, but under depression conditions they became aggravated. Albert T. Morgan had no idea that a simple request to a Yazoo native to pay his lumber bill at the earliest convenience would cause resentment. "What in the hell do you mean, you Yankee s—— of a b——?" the southern man thundered. "By G—d, sir, I'll have you to bear in mind that I pay my debts; I'm a gentleman, by G—d, sir, and if you don't know it, I'll teach you how to conduct yourself toward one, d——n you." The lesson came in the form of blows well laid on. It was the first time Morgan had been physically assaulted in his new locality.[168]

The hard times brought to the surface a lot of suppressed sectional feeling. One southern landlord in Georgia who was angry about his lessee's plantation school had the northern man arrested for failure to repay a loan of some corn, and when that issue was resolved, he had him jailed again for a delay in paying the rent.[169] But even intersectional relationships that one would have thought were impervious to rupture came apart abruptly under the financial strain. Alfred Davis's friendship for General Lorenzo Thomas and family, for one, apparently stopped at the bank-vault door. When the Thomases fled north after army worms destroyed their crop in the summer of 1867, Davis attached all of their property on the plantation, personal effects included. "If Davis has *lately* seized on what little is left," Lorenzo Thomas averred, "I hope the money will make him drunk enough to bring on appoplexy [*sic*]." The case was eventually settled out of court, but the bad feeling on both sides endured.[170] James Waters and George Klapp hoped that their Spanish landlord, Don Antonio Yznaga, would not hold them accountable for the crop failure on his plantation. Waters wrote that Yznaga had tried "to gouge us out of the last cent we had & a good deal more too, which he will never get—damn him." "The rank is but the guinea's stamp," George Klapp observed acidly. It took three years to reach a settlement.[171]

Even partnerships, those most durable of all intersectional relationships, dissolved rather easily. A Freedmen's Bureau agent in Louisiana "was killed in a fight which grew out of a business partnership, and in the trial that followed the jury rendered a verdict of justifiable homicide."[172] This was admittedly an extreme case. A Yankee planter in Wilcox County, Alabama, in a more typical example, was alarmed when his southern partner signed over to his brother-in-law the deed for one-half of the plantation for one hundred dollars. "The object of course was to defraud myself & others out of our just dues," the northern man wrote. He was sure his safety lay "in the protection which I sincerely trust the Mil. authorities may give me."[173] Northern planters did not always favor civil litigation to recover debts, especially in the South.[174]

There may have been good grounds for northern misgivings about the impartiality of the southern legal system in matters of this kind. A few southern lawyers were not above representing both parties to a suit, advising the Yankee to bide his time while pressing the southerner's case vigorously. Sheriffs could be quite frank in declaring that "we don't go by Yankee law here, thank God."[175] Albert Morgan and his brother came out the losers when Morgan's landlord succeeded in transforming a local judicial proceeding into a struggle between "our people" and the "damn Yankees." After worms devoured the Morgans' 1867 crop, Colonel Black attached all of the Morgans' property in order to guarantee not only the last installment of that year's rent, but the entire rent for 1868 as well. He suspected his tenants were planning to flee their debts, a reasonable fear considering the widespread departure of northern lessees at the time. An appeal to the local commanding general won the Morgans a short reprieve, but no more. Despite the suspension of the debt proceedings, their property was sold for virtually nothing at a sheriff's sale, and they were unable to bid on it because none of their friends back home was willing to risk any more money in Mississippi. "Every Northern planter was either in the same dilemma as ourselves," Albert Morgan wrote, "or had already gone down, and had left the country, or was about to do so." [176] Morgan overstated the situation somewhat. Amicable settlements of business affairs were a possibility. And some southern lawyers and judges tried hard to secure justice for the new men. Even so, the sentiment in the community generally favored the old planters, even in disputes involving only a few bales of cotton. [177]

The hardening of southern feeling toward northern planters had other causes as well. The crop failures could not have come at a worse time. At the end of 1867 white natives faced not only continued economic hardship but a political reorganization such as they swore they would never accept. Only months earlier Congress had enacted a Military Reconstruction bill that enfranchised former slaves and disfranchised a significant number of former slaveholders, and the machinery of this political program was just then being put into operation. It was a calamitous turn of events from the white southerner's point of view. Onto his burden of economic ruin had been heaped the humiliation of sharing political power with his former slaves. He was sore, confused, frightened, and angry that he had no recourse left but to accommodate at last the will of the conqueror. He was also very much in a mood for searching out scapegoats. And to make matters worse, no longer did the dream of easy riches act to restrain the political bitterness and keep the stream of sectional resentments within navigable channels. George Benham always believed that the South's hatred of northerners and the freedmen might have abated had there been anything like a good crop in 1866, or 1867 for that matter. [178] The tendency of the South at this time to blame all its misfortunes on the teachings of the newcomers would seem to bear him out.

We should guard against stretching a good point too far. The fact is that the congressional plan of Reconstruction had intensified sectional bitterness to a level that not even prosperity would have been able fully to dispel. The rise of political carpetbaggery stirred deep emotions and reawakened the old fear that Yankee incendiaries would foment discontent among the black population. Throughout the period of radical Reconstruction the South would continue to maintain that northern immigrants would receive a friendly welcome if only they minded their own business and refrained from meddling in Republican politics. But the political realities of the period were such that white southerners could no longer hide their suspicions of outsiders who came among them. More than at any time since before the war, northern newcomers had "to show some further passport to the goodwill and suffrages of their fellow citizens, than the mere locality of birth." [179]

Yet from the longer view of Reconstruction history, it was true that the collapse of economic dreams had killed the prospects for intersectional harmony. Admittedly, the relationship between northerners and southerners contained many crosscurrents and varied according to time and place and individual idiosyncrasies. But one fact is clear. If a blowup between Congress and the president could sour intersectional harmony, and if antipathies of culture and memories of war, not to mention disagreements over racial usage, could destroy neighborly feeling, especially in isolated areas of intense southern feeling, a shared interest in the main chance could cause natives and newcomers alike to forget their differences and to get on with the business of making money. Nothing promoted goodwill between northerners and southerners during the period of presidential Reconstruction so much as the mutual drive for self-enrichment. Nothing dissipated that goodwill so much as the economic disappointments of 1866 and 1867. For a brief period following Appomattox something of a rehearsal for redemption and reconciliation was being staged. Things would not improve again between victor and vanquished until businessmen in both sections concluded that the time had arrived to liquidate political Reconstruction and to bend all their energies toward getting rich from the South's resources. The result was the restoration of southern home rule and the sectional settlement that goes by the name of the Compromise of 1877.[180]

Epilogue
"The Best I Can Do"

The crop failures of 1866-67 had other fateful consequences besides embittering intersectional relations. The agricultural depression of the early postwar period effectively ended the northern planter movement. Occasionally a man of means went south after 1867 in search of a cotton plantation, but the current of immigration had by this time clearly reversed itself. George Benham estimated that "nine-tenths of the newcomers" abandoned the field after their early planting disappointments. He may have been stretching the point, but not by much. Once it became clear that cotton-growing was not a "short road to wealth," there was nothing to keep most of the new men in the South. "Large amounts of money can be made here, if one will give enough for it," Eben Loomis still believed. "But the country is only half-civilized at best and I do not feel like trying to make a home in such a country."[1] Nor did many other northern planters consider putting down permanent roots in the former Confederacy. They had generally come south to secure an investment that would set them up in grand style back home. So, with the failure of their dreams, most Yankees drifted back to the free states—but not always in discouragement, because for some of them "the mere certainty . . . [of] going North is next to ecstasy." In 1867 Loomis returned to his position in the Nautical Almanac Office in Cambridge, though he did not like it as well as he did before his "taste of liberty in Florida."[2]

The heaviest losses in the ranks of northern planters occurred among the lessees. Having the smallest material stake in the South, they were the first to leave. By the fall of 1867 General Lorenzo Thomas was back in Washington, and early the following year he resumed his position as adjutant-general of the U.S. Army. He was also appointed secretary of war *ad interim* in an abortive attempt by President Johnson to oust Edwin M. Stanton from the cabinet, but he never succeeded in gaining possession of the office. His son, Henry Thomas, found work in the adjutant-general's office, too, but only as a clerk. "It is a position I should never [have] chose[n]," he confessed, "but we poor devils have to grab at anything."[3] General Frank Blair, Jr., on the other hand, did hook a position he had been angling for, the vice-presidential nomination on the 1868 Democratic ticket. But this fish got away. After his planting failures in Louisiana, Blair was "forced to seek political positions with salaries attached in order to gain a livelihood for his large family."[4]

A few lessees even dared to expand their operations after initial setbacks. In

151

1867 Whitelaw Reid bought an interest in a plantation in Alabama, "and at the end of two years he found himself not a loser indeed, but a gainer only in business experience that strengthened his already pronounced and self-dependent executive abilities."[5] These abilities were soon given full scope when Reid became managing editor of the New York *Tribune* in 1869 and editor-in-chief in 1872. He later served as ambassador to France and Great Britain and became in all ways a Republican stalwart. He was more fortunate than Alexander Winchell, who returned south to teach at Vanderbilt University many years after the guerrillas had cleaned him out in Louisiana. His subsequent visit was also unpleasant for him. When he ventured to question the biblical theory of the age of the world, he was "stripped of his office, and sent home to his native Michigan with the Tennessee Methodist Conference's denunciation of himself as an emissary of 'scientific atheism' and 'untamed Speculation' ringing in his ears."[6]

But most lessees neither stayed in the South nor returned there after cotton-growing failures. They were in different circumstances than were purchasers of plantations. "Those of us who had bought land were chained to the situation," explained George Benham.[7] The northern purchasers often ended up just as land-poor as their southern neighbors, with real estate on their hands that neither produced a good income nor commanded an acceptable sales price. Henry Lee Higginson did succeed in cutting loose from his Georgia place in 1868, joining his father's banking firm in that year. He distinguished himself in business and became the sort of useful citizen who contributed to the arts and supported his college. Charles F. Morse, his partner, struggled on at the plantation until the end of 1870, finally leasing it at a nominal rent to a young northerner who "liked that kind of life." Morse later met with good fortune in the West, where he found ample opportunity to take charge of men as a manager with various railroad and stockyard companies owned by friends in Boston.[8]

Those newcomers who never returned north met with varying degrees of success. A few of them accumulated large holdings of land and married their sons and daughters into the local elite. George Benham was still in Carroll Parish, Louisiana, in 1880, having apparently acquired his "fine competence." By the mid-1870s he was said to be a prosperous man, who served as "a vestry man in the Providence (Lake) Church" and leaned toward "respectability, alias conservative Republicanism." Together with his brother, he was the dominant force in parish politics.[9]

In fact, a large number of northern cotton growers who remained in the South beyond 1867 entered Republican politics.[10] They often did so for the predictable reasons of profit and philanthropy. After losing their property to Colonel Black, Albert Morgan and his brother became carpetbaggers because they saw in the congressional plan of Reconstruction a "means for a restoration to ourselves" and an opportunity "to secure to the freed people the right to life, liberty and the pursuit of happiness."[11] During his political career in the South, Morgan appears to have kept these two aims in good harmony. Just how far other carpetbaggers succeeded at promoting benevolence through enlightened self-interest is another question. Many of them seem to have tried to make a living from politics. They held as many offices as they could at the same time, looked upon every scrap from the pork barrel as indispensable to their personal well-being, and committed many minor—and sometimes major—peculations. This behavior is understandable, even though it made for a great deal of factional disunity within the Republican party. Having failed to make a lot of money at planting, this class of carpetbaggers reasoned that they could at least make an acceptable amount at politicking. An associate of one of the officers in the United States Cotton Company explained why he was prepared to accept an appointment as county treasurer in South Carolina: "I imagine that you will be somewhat surprised at this course I have taken and wonder how I can content myself to live in this *blasted* country," he wrote to a New York friend in 1872. "My only answer is that I think it is . . . the best that I can do. Everything is objectionable except the salary of the office which will be at least $2000 a year."[12]

But carpetbaggers like Morgan—and there were many of his type—did try to keep in view the idealistic purposes of their political work. Morgan paid dearly for his commitment. After an assassination attempt by his political enemies, he was driven from Yazoo County in 1875 during the violent overthrow of Reconstruction known as the "Mississippi Plan." Through the efforts of black friends in Washington he secured a position in the Pension Office, and he later moved to Colorado to try his luck at mining. Although the remainder of his life was clouded by personal failure and family tragedy, Morgan held firmly to his ideals and even enlarged them to fit the realities of late nineteenth-century American life. He was friendly to Populism, contemptuous of imperialism, and hostile to monopoly capitalism. He finally placed his hope for mankind's redemption in a program of Christian socialism.[13]

Charles Stearn's own odyssey followed a parallel path, including a violent ejection from political office by an enraged mob of southern whites. By the 1880s he, too, had become an advocate of Christian socialism along the lines suggested by Edward Bellamy, and he had grandiose plans for settling large numbers of northern laborers and southern freedmen in an agricultural and manufacturing colony he envisioned for middle Tennessee. Despite his disappointments with the ex-slaves, Stearns never forsook his faith in their improvability.[14]

The Gordon colony's utopian vision had long since given way to worldly considerations. Some of its members returned home at the end of 1867; a few stayed on the premises and became Republican politicians; others shifted their operations to more favorable locations within the state. In 1868 the James brothers bought another plantation in Alachua County, but they never did escape from their speculation "whole," by which they meant unscathed. Repeated visitations from the army worms and the intermittent agricultural depression forced them to liquidate their planting investments in 1870.[15] Their last few years in Florida were anything but pleasant. The dispersal of the Gordon colonists and the involvement of a few of them in Republican politics caused the old inhabitants to make known their hostility in ways they had not done before. An armed band with murder on its mind prowled nightly around the plantation of one of the carpetbagger colonists. Garth James was "insulted grossly" on the streets of Gainesville one day and was told shortly afterwards by "one of the best friends I thought I had in the whole country . . . that hereafter I was his enemy"—all because of James's service with a black regiment. The incidents caused him to be "rebaptized" in his free labor faith, though they did not alter his political opinions, which had been "growing more conservative of late upon the subject of these detestable . . . Carpetbag governments."[16] After leaving Florida the two brothers moved to Milwaukee where they secured positions with the railroad. Garth died in his late thirties, never having enjoyed good health after he was wounded in the war, and Robertson, who had also suffered physically from military life, later returned with his family to Massachusetts and took up residence in Concord. Robertson could no more make his peace with the new industrial order than Albert Morgan and Charles Stearns could, and his exposure to its methods in Milwaukee filled him with self-contempt. He never did shake the transcendentalist habit of self-preoccupation. His novelist-brother Henry James said he was "an extraordinary instance of man's nature constituting his profession, his whole stock-in trade." Nervous and high-strung, Robertson turned to the Swedenborgianism of his upbringing in order to dispel his self-confessed "ignominy of drink and debauchery." He suffered from frequent bouts of depression.[17]

Frederick Stowe often went on binges of heavy drinking. Cotton-planting seems only to have worsened his alcoholism. The plantation failed to return any profits at all and put his mother several thousand dollars out of pocket. Mrs. Stowe later sent her son to work in her orange grove in Mandarin, Florida, but this experience was no cure, either, for his problem. Stowe came to a tragic end. He sailed for San Francisco in the early 1870s and after putting ashore was never seen or heard from again. "He was eventually presumed dead or shanghaied, unless he was living on in self-imposed exile under an assumed name."[18]

The Waters family and its collateral relatives also came to a sad end. Cousin George Klapp took his southern wife to Philadelphia at the end of 1867 only to find business dull, and he returned to Natchez the following year to make a living by subletting to the freedmen plantations he had leased from the owners. He slipped into an uncomfortable dependence on his southern in-laws, who appear to have enjoyed the reversal of roles.[19] James Waters, meanwhile, was selling portable railroads in Maryland and Delaware, while Clifford Waters joined his father in operating the family place in St. Helena Island, South Carolina, after the breakup of affairs in Louisiana. The fortunes of the House of Waters did not improve in the Palmetto state. Simply staying out of debt was a constant struggle, and it was usually accomplished only by calling on the assistance of a wealthy cousin in Salem. In 1881 Clifford finally quit the Sea Islands to engage in stock-raising in North Dakota, but this venture also came to grief and he lived out his life in California, "suffering the depression of conscious failure."[20] He felt he had "made the great mistake . . . in starting in life, of not having some definite plan or object in life, . . . of drifting about like a travelling tinker doing what Emerson so earnestly urges us to avoid, namely, *'job-work.'* "[21]

In fact, the exposures and anxieties of planting life apparently broke the health of every member of the family who pursued it. James Waters had gone blind by 1880 because of his privations in the Southwest, it was thought, and the rest of the family at that time seemed used up with the worry and care of the past fifteen years. Even the "family interest" notion came in for some sharp reappraisal. The elder William Waters's declaration from his deathbed that he "never cared for money" drew the murmuring complaint that "much might have been spared us this last thirty years had *Fr* cared a little more for it!"[22]

It was an unfair criticism of an unwarranted confession. The elder Waters had cared very much about moneymaking, or else he would never have become involved in the great speculative craze of the Civil War years.

If the northern planter movement was imbued with a missionary attitude toward the South, if it included individuals who entertained goodwill toward the freedmen, if the men who joined it were sometimes seeking a new way of life, it differed only in complexity of motive from the stampede of forty-niners to California or wildcatters to Texas. The movement was, in truth, one of the first indications after Appomattox that the South would be remade not in the image of the free-soil North of small-farming agriculture, but in the image of the Gilded Age North of commercial exploitation. This is perhaps not very surprising. At the time most Yankee planters were arriving in the South, the free states were already well on their way to becoming a part of modern industrial society. The northern newcomers had simply put the South on notice that in the changes that lay ahead it would have to assume an integral, if subordinate, role in the new national market order that developed after the Civil War.

Appendix

Methodology and Sources of Tables

The following tables are based on a sample of 524 northerners who grew cotton in the lower South roughly between 1862 and 1876. The number bears a respectable relationship to the upper and lower estimates of the Yankee planter population. On the one hand, it represents one out of every one hundred newcomers, if the number of northern cotton planters reached as high as fifty thousand; on the other hand, it stands for one-fortieth of the total, if the "universe" is closer to twenty thousand. The ratio is acceptable in either case and would only improve should the total population prove to be substantially less than I have surmised.

The sample's reliability, moreover, varies according to categories. It is on strong ground when it speaks to the origins of northern planters; it is somewhat less reliable about occupational backgrounds; and it is least useful regarding ages. Nor can the sample claim to be random. It is actually a catalogue of everyone who turned up in the course of extensive research, the details of which I will not go into here. Further relevant information can be found in the bibliographical essay. My remarks, therefore, will pertain chiefly to the various types of materials I used.

Primary and secondary literature yielded much useful information. Autobiographical writings, of course, were an indispensable source of data, as were the various state studies of the Reconstruction South. These are discussed at greater length in the bibliographical essay. Most of the information in the tables, however, came from strictly biographical materials. The nineteenth century abounded in biographical publications of every sort. I found state and local biographical collections and histories, city directories, and college alumni directories particularly useful. But the most valuable materials of this type were undoubtedly the voluminous histories of Union regiments that fought in the Civil War. Most regimental histories contain biographical sections, which usually appear in the back of the book but are sometimes interspersed in the text. I scanned all of the volumes available in Sterling Memorial Library at Yale University, which has a respectable collection (approximately four hundred volumes). Also useful were the reports of state adjutant generals. The seven-volume work, *Massachusetts Soldiers, Sailors, and Marines in the Civil War* (Norwood, Mass., 1933), is in a class by itself. This collection lists the ages and occupations of all Massachusetts veterans, by regiment and company where applicable, at the time of their enlistment. The *Biographical Directory of the*

American Congress, 1774-1961 yielded some unexpected finds. Several carpet-bag congressmen and senators had been cotton planters.

The personal letters of various northern cotton growers offered many clues about their authors and their authors' friends. Governmental records were of some help. The "Applications for Leasing Abandoned Plantations" in the Mississippi Valley (which form part of the Freedmen's Bureau papers) were somewhat disappointing. Unless correspondence accompanied the application, the material revealed little about the lessee. The Records for the Direct Tax Commission for South Carolina were more helpful, but here again one had to depend largely on incoming correspondence to find out something about northern lessees and purchasers. Item 80 of the "Port Royal Correspondence" provided a relatively complete biographical portrait of the Port Royal missionaries. Finally, the newspapers of the period were of inestimable value. Northern correspondents in the South usually missed few opportunities to mention any Yankee planters they encountered on their travels. I was occasionally lucky enough to learn more about these settlers from other sources.

This collective biography is by no means a random sample. By and large the sources from which it derives are slanted toward people who are admittedly exceptional. Only a select group of persons ever appears in published material in the first place, and fewer still are the numbers of those persons who leave behind memoirs and manuscript materials. Even regimental histories have their limitation: the biographies for officers are much more complete than those for enlisted men. Taken together, these might be major shortcomings but for the fact that this collective biography is at least not inconsistent with what we know about cotton-growing in this period. A man needed a fair amount of money and good connections in order to enter the planting business, and money and connections meant that he was probably just the kind of person who could have been a Union officer, or who might in later years have been written up in a local biographical collection. These tables also tend to confirm the impressions of northern travelers at the time. At any rate, I have tried to gather all the biographical information I could put my hands on. This involved painstaking rummaging through volumes that have been collecting dust since the time of Bull Run. A typical research experience might read thus: a newspaper in Selma, Alabama, mentioned that a Capt. Sexton of the Chicago Board of Trade regiment had leased a plantation in the neighborhood; I would then try to track him down in his regimental history, only to locate him eventually in an *Album of Genealogy* for Cook County, Illinois. With biographical data at such a premium, I welcomed every scrap of information that came my way, regardless of whether it strengthened my case or not.

A few words about the tables themselves. The "geographical origin" category refers only to the person's last place of residence before moving south, not to his birthplace.

The "college experience" columns merely signify college attendance. Some of my assumptions here should be noted. I have assumed that all physicians, engineers, and ministers were college-trained to some extent. Many might question this supposition, correctly pointing out that the entrance requirements for the professions in the mid-nineteenth century were not nearly so formalized as they later became in the early twentieth century. Though I may have erred on the side of generosity regarding the college experience of doctors, engineers, and ministers, I doubtless overlooked quite a few lawyers and businessmen who had attended college, but whose biographical histories were too sketchy to register this fact. The inclusions and omissions here probably balance each other out.

The "occupation background" categories are not nearly so refined as I would have liked. But the information by and large is too general to attempt a more specific categorization. Often the only thing that could be determined was that the planter had been a "businessman" of some sort. The business column, therefore, includes everyone from manufacturers, railroad promoters, and merchants to gristmill operators, office clerks, and haberdashers. When a man listed himself as a farmer-merchant, I included him with the agriculturalists in order to weight the evidence as much as possible in favor of an occupation that is surprisingly underrepresented. Journalists posed a problem. If a man was a reporter, I considered him a professional; if he had graduated to editor, I lumped him with the businessmen, on the theory, I suppose, that nineteenth-century newspaper owners were as fully occupied with increasing their subscribers and advertisers as they were with gathering the news. The other professionals include lawyers, doctors, ministers, teachers, statisticians, and politicians (when no other occupation was given). The Port Royal missionary sample, moreover, required special treatment. Many of the planter-missionaries were recent college graduates who had not yet entered an occupation. Because "students" struck me as too imprecise a category, I took the liberty of classifying recent college graduates according to the careers they were to adopt in later years. This practice was also followed for the few students who comprise part of the non-Port Royal category.

Table 1 Geographical Origins, by Region, of Northern Planters in States of the Lower South, 1862–1876

State	New England[a]		Mid-Atlantic[b]		Midwest[c]		Far West[d]		Total in Sample
	Total Number	%	Total Number	%	Total Number	%	Total Number	%	
Alabama	4	7.8	13	25.5	34	66.7	–	–	51
Florida	29	87.9	4	12.1	–	–	–	–	33
Georgia	15	55.6	9	33.3	–	–	3	11.1	27
Louisiana	28	27.5	19	18.6	55	53.9	–	–	102
Mississippi	23	26.4	15	17.2	48	55.2	1	1.1	87
South Carolina	75	57.3	51	38.9	5	3.8	–	–	131
Total	174	40.4	111	25.8	142	32.9	4	0.9	431

Source: See the discussion of methodology.
[a]Includes Maine, Vermont, New Hampshire, Massachusetts, Rhode Island, and Connecticut.
[b]Includes New York, New Jersey, Pennsylvania, and Delaware.
[c]Includes Ohio, Indiana, Illinois, Michigan, Wisconsin, Minnesota, Iowa, and Kansas.
[d]Includes all western states and territories.

Table 2 *Age and Education of Northern Planters in the States of the Lower South, 1862–1876*

| State | Age | | College Experience | |
	Mean Age[a]	Total in Sample	Total Number	%[b]
Alabama	32	28	16	29.1
Florida	30	23	9	21.4
Georgia	32	12	11	36.7
Louisiana	34	45	23	16.5
Mississippi	32	26	17	15.6
South Carolina	34	85	52	34.9
Total	33	219	128	24.4

Source: See the discussion of methodology.

[a]This figure has been computed for the age as of 1865 except in the case of the Port Royal Missionaries where 1862 has been taken as the base year.

[b]These percentages are functions of the respective state totals in the sample of 524 (see the final column of table 14).

Table 3 *Occupational Background of Northern Planters in States of the Lower South, 1862–1876*

State	Labor Total Number	%	Agriculture Total Number	%	Business Total Number	%	Professions Total Number	%	Total in Sample
Alabama	—	—	—	—	5	22.7	17	77.3	22
Florida	—	—	3	15	8	40.0	9	45.0	20
Georgia	—	—	—	—	9	52.9	8	47.1	17
Louisiana	—	—	1	1.5	42	64.6	22	33.8	65
Mississippi	—	—	2	6.1	9	27.3	22	66.7	33
South Carolina	5	5.2	7	7.2	27	27.8	58	59.8	97
Total	5	2	13	5.1	100	39.4	136	53.5	254

Source: See discussion of methodology.

Table 4 *Most Highly Represented Northern States, in Descending Order,*
1862–1876

State	Total Number	%[a]
Massachusetts	120	27.8
New York	84	19.5
Illinois	54	12.5
Ohio	43	10.0
Total	301	69.8

[a]These percentages are functions of the total number of planters whose
geographical origins have been determined: 431.

Table 5 *Geographical Origins, by Region, of Port Royal, South Carolina, Missionaries, 1862–1863*

Organizational Affiliation	New England		Mid-Atlantic		Midwest		Far West		Total in Sample
	Total Number	%	Total Number	%	Total Number	%	Total Number	%	
Education Commission	40	97.6	—	—	1	2.4	—	—	41
American Missionary Association	2	8	22	88	1	4	—	—	25
Total	42	63.6	22	33.3	2	3	—	—	66

Source: Records of the Direct Tax Commission for South Carolina, NA.

Table 6 *Age, Education, and Land Investments of Port Royal, South Carolina, Missionaries, 1862-1866*

Organizational Affiliation	Age		College Experience (as of 1862)		Direct Tax Sale Purchasers	
	Mean Age (as of 1862)	*Total in Age Sample*	*Total Number*	*%*	*Total Number*	*%*
Education Commission	31	36	26	63.4	17	41.5
American Missionary Association	38	23	9	36	2	8
Total	34	59	35	53	19	28.8

Source: See Table 5.

Table 7 Occupational Background[a] of Port Royal, South Carolina, Missionaries, 1862–1868

Organizational Affiliation	Labor		Agriculture		Business		Professions		Total in Sample
	Total Number	%	Total Number	%	Total Number	%	Total Number	%	
Education Commission	1	2.8	—	—	6	16.7	29	80.6	36
American Missionary Association	3	12.5	1	4.2	8	33.3	12	50	24
Total	4	6.7	1	1.7	14	23.3	41	68.3	60

Source: See Table 5.
[a] See discussion of methodology.

Table 8 *Geographical Origins, by Region, of Northern Planters with No Military Experience (Excluding Port Royal, South Carolina, Missionaries), 1863-1865*

State	New England		Mid-Atlantic		Midwest		Far West		Total in Sample
	Total Number	%	Total Number	%	Total Number	%	Total Number	%	
Louisiana	7	16.7	6	14.3	29	69	–	–	42
Mississippi	3	27.3	1	9.1	6	54.5	1	9.1	11
South Carolina	8	53.3	7	46.7	–	–	–	–	15
Total	18	26.5	14	20.6	35	51.5	1	1.5	68

Source: See discussion of methodology.

Table 9 *Age and Education of Northern Planters with No Military Experience (Excluding Port Royal, South Carolina, Missionaries), 1863–1865*

	Age		College Experience	
State	Mean Age	Total in Sample	Total Number	%[a]
Louisiana	40	9	6	9
Mississippi	32	5	1	5.9
South Carolina	43	6	4	18.2
Total	39	20	11	10.4

Source: See discussion of methodology.

[a]These percentages are functions of the respective state totals of northern civilian planters: Louisiana, 67; Mississippi, 17; South Carolina, 22.

Table 10 *Occupational Background of Northern Planters with No Military Experience (Excluding Port Royal, South Carolina, Missionaries), 1863–1865*

State	Labor		Agriculture		Business		Professions		Total in Sample
	Total Number	%	Total Number	%	Total Number	%	Total Number	%	
Louisiana	–	–	–	–	23	82.1	5	17.9	28
Mississippi	–	–	–	–	2	40	3	60	5
South Carolina	–	–	3	21.4	7	50	4	28.6	14
Total	–	–	3	6.4	32	68.1	12	25.5	47

Source: See discussion of methodology.

Table 11 *Geographical Origins, by Region, of Northern Planters with No Military Experience (Excluding Port Royal, South Carolina, Missionaries), 1863–1876*

State	New England		Mid-Atlantic		Midwest		Far West		Total in Sample
	Total Number	%	Total Number	%	Total Number	%	Total Number	%	
Alabama	2	25	1	12.5	5	62.5	–	–	8
Florida	14	77.8	4	22.2	–	–	–	–	18
Georgia	5	41.7	6	50	–	–	1	8.3	12
Louisiana	15	23.8	12	19	36	57.1	–	–	63
Mississippi	15	28.3	7	13.2	30	56.6	1	1.9	53
South Carolina	14	46.7	16	53.3	–	–	–	–	30
Total	65	35.3	46	25	71	38.6	2	1.1	184

Source: See discussion of methodology.

Table 12 *Age and Education of Northern Planters with No Military Experience (Excluding Port Royal, South Carolina, Missionaries), 1863-1876*

State	Age		College Experience		Total in Sample[a]
	Mean Age	Total in Sample	Total Number	%	
Alabama	30	2	1	9.1	11
Florida	36	9	3	12	25
Georgia	35	2	1	7.1	14
Louisiana	36	15	9	9.5	95
Mississippi	29	8	2	3.1	64
South Carolina	43	6	9	21.4	42
Total	35	42	25	10	251

Source: See discussion of methodology.

[a]This represents the total of all civilian northern planters in the sample.

171

Table 13 Occupational Background of Northern Planters with No Military Experience (Excluding Port Royal, South Carolina, Missionaries), 1863–1876

State	Labor		Agriculture		Business		Professions		Total in Sample
	Total Number	%	Total Number	%	Total Number	%	Total Number	%	
Alabama	—	—	—	—	—	—	2	100	2
Florida	—	—	2	20	4	40	4	40	10
Georgia	—	—	—	—	3	60	2	40	5
Louisiana	—	—	1	2.6	29	74.4	9	23.1	39
Mississippi	—	—	—	—	5	50	5	50	10
South Carolina	—	—	3	14.3	9	42.9	9	42.9	21
Total	—	—	6	6.9	50	57.5	31	35.6	87

Source: See discussion of methodology.

Table 14 *Percentage of Northern Planters of Civilian and Military Backgrounds, 1863–1876*

State	Civilian		Military		Total Sample
	Total Number	%	Total Number	%	
Alabama	11	20	44	80	55
Florida	25	59.5	17	40.5	42
Georgia	14	46.7	16	53.3	30
Louisiana	95	68.3	44	31.7	139
Mississippi	64	58.7	45	41.3	109
South Carolina	107	71.8	42	28.2	149
Total	316	60.3	208	39.7	524

Source: See discussion of methodology.

173

Table 15 Geographical Origins, by Region, of Northern Planters with Military Experience, 1862-1876

State	New England		Mid-Atlantic		Midwest		Far West		Total in Sample
	Total Number	%	Total Number	%	Total Number	%	Total Number	%	
Alabama	2	4.7	12	28	29	67.4	–	–	43
Florida	15	100	–	–	–	–	–	–	15
Georgia	10	66.7	3	20	–	–	2	13.3	15
Louisiana	13	33.3	7	18	19	48.7	–	–	39
Mississippi	8	23.5	8	23.5	18	52.9	–	–	34
South Carolina	19	54.3	13	37.1	3	8.6	–	–	35
Total	67	37	43	23.8	69	38.1	2	1.1	181

Source: See discussion of methodology.

Table 16 Age and Education of Northern Planters with Military Experience, 1862-1876

State	Age		College Experience		Total in Sample
	Mean Age	Total in Sample	Total Number	%	
Alabama	32	26	15	34.9	43
Florida	26	14	6	35.3	17
Georgia	31	10	10	62.5	16
Louisiana	33	30	14	31.8	44
Mississippi	33	18	15	33.3	45
South Carolina	31	20	8	19	42
Total	32	118	68	32.9	207

Source: See discussion of methodology.

175

Table 17 *Occupational Background of Northern Planters with Military Experience, 1862-1876*

State	Labor		Agriculture		Business		Professions		Total in Sample
	Total Number	%	Total Number	%	Total Number	%	Total Number	%	
Alabama	–	–	–	–	5	25	15	75	20
Florida	–	–	1	10	4	40	5	50	10
Georgia	–	–	–	–	6	50	6	50	12
Louisiana	–	–	–	–	13	50	13	50	26
Mississippi	–	–	2	8.7	4	17.4	17	73.9	23
South Carolina	1	6.3	3	18.8	4	25	8	50	16
Total	1	0.9	6	5.6	36	33.6	64	59.8	107

Source: See discussion of methodology.

Table 18 Rank and USCT Service of Northern Planters with Military Experience, 1863-1876

State	Officers[a]		Field-Grade Officers		USCT[b] Officers		Total Military Sample[c]
	Total Number	%	Total Number	%	Total Number	%	
Alabama	42	97.7	19	44.2	2	4.7	43
Florida	15	88.2	8	47.1	6	35.3	17
Georgia	10	62.5	8	50	1	6.3	16
Louisiana	35	79.5	18	40.1	6	13.6	44
Mississippi	38	84.4	23	51.1	1	2.2	45
South Carolina	36	85.7	7	16.7	8	19	42
Total	176	85	83	40.1	24	11.6	207

Source: See discussion of methodology.
[a] All officers, including the two sub-categories shown in the following columns. (Note that these sub-categories overlap.)
[b] United States Colored Troops.
[c] Officers and enlisted men.

Notes

Abbreviations

AA	Alabama State Department of History and Archives, Montgomery, Alabama
AGO	Adjutant General Office
BRFAL	Bureau of Refugees, Freedmen, and Abandoned Lands
CU	Cornell University Library
DU	Duke University Library
EU	Emory University Library
FU	University of Florida Library
GA	Georgia Department of Archives and History, Atlanta, Georgia
HU	Houghton Library, Harvard University
LC	Manuscripts Division, Library of Congress
LSU	Louisiana State Department of Archives and History, Baton Rouge, Louisiana
MA	Mississippi Department of Archives and History, Jackson, Mississippi
MHC	Michigan Historical Collection, University of Michigan
MHS	Massachusetts Historical Society, Boston, Massachusetts
MiHS	Minnesota Historical Society, St. Paul, Minnesota
NA	National Archives, Washington, D. C.
SCA	South Carolina Department of Archives, Columbia, South Carolina
SCL	South Caroliniana Library, University of South Carolina

SEC, NEEACo, KSHS	Southern Emigration Correspondence, New England Emigrant Aid Company, Kansas State Historical Society, respectively
SHC	Southern Historical Collection, University of North Carolina
SHSW	State Historical Society of Wisconsin, Madison, Wisconsin
YU	Yale Archives, Yale University

Preface

1. *Rehearsal for Reconstruction: The Port Royal Experiment* (New York, 1964).
2. Boston *Daily Advertiser*, Feb. 13, 1866; "Letter From Charleston," ibid., Apr. 12, 1866.
3. A. Warren Kelsey to Edward Atkinson, Nov. 16, 1865, Atkinson Papers, MHS.
4. *The South: A Tour of Its Battle Fields and Ruined Cities* (New York, 1969), p. 380; see also Whitelaw Reid, *After the War: A Tour of the Southern States, 1865-1866,* ed. C. Vann Woodward (New York, 1965), pp. 382, 405-06.
5. Trowbridge, *The South,* pp. 402 and 411; see also Reid, *After the War,* p. 291; A. W. Kelsey to E. Atkinson, Nov. 16, 1865, Atkinson Papers, MHS.
6. There are some state estimates based on the 1870 census of the increase in the northern-born population since 1860. Maurice M. Vance tells us that in Florida there was a net increase of 1,167 northern settlers over the ten-year period ("Northerners in Late Nineteenth Century Florida: Carpetbaggers or Settlers?" *Florida Historical Quarterly* 28 [July 1959]: 3). James Garner, apparently also utilizing the 1870 census, states that there were 1,610 persons living in Mississippi in 1870 "who had emigrated there from the Northern states since 1860" (*Reconstruction in Mississippi,* with an introduction by Richard N. Current [Baton Rouge, La., 1968], 414n). Neither Vance nor Garner makes any estimate as to how many of these newcomers were planters. I doubt that it would pay the effort to try to find out from the census.
7. Petition of Citizens of Alabama Remonstrating Against an Increase of the Tax on Cotton, June 1, 1866, Records of the U.S. Senate, RG 46, NA; see also Trowbridge, *The South,* p. 448.
8. William C. Harris, *Presidential Reconstruction in Mississippi* (Baton Rouge, La., 1967), p. 169; see also his footnote. Trowbridge, *The South,* p. 411.
9. E. Merton Coulter, *The South During Reconstruction, 1865-1877* (Baton Rouge, La., 1947), p. 205.
10. *The Northern Teacher in the South, 1862-1870* (New York, 1967), p. 35.
11. Richard N. Current, "Carpetbaggers Reconsidered," in David H. Pinkney and Theodore Ropp, eds., *A Festschrift for Frederick B. Artz* (Durham, N.C., 1964), pp. 144-50.
12. Trowbridge, *The South,* p.400. Northern capital does not seem to have penetrated the Louisiana sugar parishes to any great extent until after 1868 when the Civil War in Cuba interfered with sugar production on the island. But "At least half the planters after 1870 were either Northern men or were supported by Northern money." This is another story, however. (Roger Shugg, *Origins of Class Struggle in Louisiana* [Baton Rouge, La., 1968], p. 249; see also Richard J. Amundson, "Oakley Plantation: A Post-Civil War Venture in Louisiana Sugar," *Louisiana History* 9 [Winter 1968]:22).

Chapter 1

1. John A. Andrew to Frank E. Howe, Mar. 10, 1866, Andrew Papers, MHS; see also New York *Times,* June 18, 1865.
2. Boston *Daily Advertiser,* June 27, 1865.
3. The best studies of federal policy toward southern blacks during the Civil War are:

Bell I. Wiley, *Southern Negroes, 1861-1865* (New Haven, Ct., 1965); Louis S. Gerteis, *From Contraband to Freedman: Federal Policy Toward Southern Blacks, 1861-1865* (Westport, Ct., 1973); V. Jacque Voegeli, *Free But Not Equal: The Midwest and the Negro During the Civil War* (Chicago, 1967).

4. Wiley, *Southern Negroes*, pp. 175-95.

5. Willie Lee Rose, *Rehearsal for Reconstruction: The Port Royal Experiment* (New York, 1964), pp. 3-43. The quotation is on p. 33.

6. Voegeli, *Free But Not Equal*, p. 96; see also Gerteis, *From Contraband to Freedman*, pp. 119-22. On how the North backed and filled its way into the crusade for freedom, see C. Vann Woodward, *The Burden of Southern History*, rev. ed. (Baton Rouge, La., 1968), pp. 69-74.

7. Voegeli, *Free But Not Equal*, pp. 95-112. The quotations are on pp. 97 and 109. See also Gerteis, *From Contraband to Freedman*, pp. 122-23.

8. Lorenzo Thomas to Edward M. Stanton, Apr. 1, 1863, L. Thomas Letterbooks, AGO-Generals Papers, NA; Gerteis, *From Contraband to Freedman*, p. 123.

9. L. Thomas to E. M. Stanton, Apr. 1, 1863, L. Thomas Letterbooks, AGO-Generals Papers, NA.

10. Gerteis, *From Contraband to Freedman*, pp. 19-20; Rose, *Rehearsal*, pp. 203-04 and 213. For an excellent study of one of the better managed contraband camps, see Cam Walker, "Corinth: The Story of a Contraband Camp," *Civil War History* 20 (Mar. 1974): 5-22.

11. Sarah F. Hughes, ed., *Letters (Supplementary) of John Murray Forbes*, 3 vols. (Boston, 1905), vol. 2, pp. 171-72.

12. Lorenzo Thomas to E. M. Stanton, April 12 and 14, 1863, L. Thomas Letterbooks, AGO-Generals Papers, NA.

13. L. Thomas to E. M. Stanton, April 12, 1863, L. Thomas Letterbooks, AGO-Generals Papers, NA; Gerteis, *From Contraband to Freedman*, pp. 125-26; Wiley, *Southern Negroes*, pp. 185-86.

14. Voegeli, *Free But Not Equal*, p.106; C. Peter Ripley, *Slaves and Freedmen in Civil War Louisiana* (Baton Rouge, La., 1976), pp. 37-68.

15. Preliminary Report of the Direct Tax Commission for South Carolina, Jan. 1, 1863, in "Minutes," Records of the Direct Tax Commission for S. C., NA.

16. Rose, *Rehearsal*, pp. 199-216. The quotation is on p. 213.

17. Preliminary Report, Jan. 1, 1863; William H. Brisbane to Joseph J. Lewis, Feb. 2, 1864, Dec. 2, 1864, and Jan. 2, 1865, in "Minutes," Records of the Direct Tax Commission for S.C., NA.

18. American Land Company and Agency, Circular no. 2 (1866), p. 1, MHS.

19. Gerteis, *From Contraband to Freedman*, pp. 169-81.

20. Rose, *Rehearsal*, pp. 279.

21. New York *Times*, Feb. 26, 1865; see also New York *Tribune*, Jan. 30, 1865; and Boston *Daily Advertiser*, June 15, 1865.

22. New York *Herald*, Aug. 28, 1865; see also Philadelphia *Public Ledger*, Jan. 12, 1866; *Christian Register*, Sept. 16, 1865; John R. Dennett, *The South As It Is, 1865-1866*, ed. Henry M. Christman (New York, 1967), p. 270; A. Warren Kelsey to Edward Atkinson, Sept. 8, 1865, Atkinson Papers; Henry Lee Higginson to Horatio Woodman, Nov. 2, 1865, Woodman Papers, both in MHS.

23. Boston *Daily Advertiser*, Jan. 18, 1866; see also "Letters From the South," in ibid., July 31, Aug. 19, 1865; Boston *Daily Herald*, May 18, 1865; John T. Trowbridge, *The South: A Tour of Its Battle Fields and Ruined Cities* (New York, 1969), pp. 572-73; Whitelaw Reid, *After the War: A Tour of the Southern States, 1865-1866*, ed. C. Vann Woodward (New York, 1965), p. 151.

24. New York *Times*, June 18, 1865; see also *Christian Register*, Sept. 16, 1865; A. W. Kelsey to E. Atkinson, Aug. 12, 1865, Atkinson Papers, MHS; *Report of the Joint Committee on Reconstruction*, Apr. 30, 1866, 39 Cong., 1 sess., no. 30 (Ser. 1273), pt. 3, p. ₊4; George W. Smith, "Generative Forces of Union Propaganda: A Study in Civil War Pressure Groups" (Ph.D. diss., University of Wisconsin, 1939), pp. 462-63.

25. New York *Herald*, Aug. 28, 1865. Actually, this was an old remedy. For at least two decades prior to the firing on Fort Sumter northerners had talked up the idea of "redeeming" the South by colonizing it with Yankees. Interest in the subject was not

peculiar to any party, though admittedly the enthusiasm was keenest among Republicans. There were even a few ambitious but abortive attempts during the 1850s to plant colonies of northerners within the border slave states, and projects of a related kind were still being proposed well into the war years. All of this has an obvious bearing on the subject at hand and may be said to constitute the ideological backdrop to the northern planter movement. But the relationship between the prewar and postwar northern emigration movements is problematic. Yankee planters did not figure at all in these antebellum programs for redeeming the South. Advocates of northern colonization before the war thought of sending to the slave states only yeomen, mechanics, and the "middling" classes of free society. The aim was to abolish the plantation system and concentrate the population in and around agricultural and manufacturing villages, after the northern pattern. But this is a large subject that deserves separate consideration. See Eric Foner, *Free Soil, Free Labor, Free Men: The Ideology of the Republican Party Before the Civil War* (New York, 1970), p. 54; George Winston Smith, "Antebellum Attempts to 'Redeem' the Upper South," *Journal of Southern History* 11 (May 1945): 177-213; G. W. Smith, "Carpetbag Imperialism in Florida," *Florida Historical Quarterly* 27 (Oct. 1948): 99-156.

26. The quotation is in A. W. Kelsey to E. Atkinson, Aug. 18, 1865, Atkinson Papers; E. Atkinson to W. M. Neill, Feb. 19, 1866, Atkinson Letterbooks, MHS. See also John A. Andrew to F. P. Blair, Sr., Apr. 12, 1866, Andrew Papers, MHS; A. D. Gurney to Senator E. D. Morgan, June 1, 1866, Cotton Tax Petitions, Records of the U.S. Senate, NA; Edward Atkinson, *Cheap Cotton by Free Labor* (Boston, 1861), pp. 4-31; Thomas W. Conway, *Introduction of Capital and Men From the Northern States and From Europe, Into the Southern States of the Union* (New York, 1866), p. 11; *Commercial and Financial Chronicle*, Sept. 2, 23, 1865; New York *Tribune*, Aug. 29, 1865; and George Winston Smith, "Some Northern Wartime Attitudes Toward the Post-Civil War South," *Journal of Southern History* 10 (Aug. 1944): 261-62, 271.

27. Edward S. Tobey, *The Industry of the South: Its Immediate Organization Indispensable to the Financial Security of the Country* (Boston, 1865), pp. 7-15. For the debate between Boston and New York commercial interests about the wisdom of government-operated plantations, see George Ruby Woolfolk, *The Cotton Regency: The Northern Merchants and Reconstruction, 1865-1880* (New York, 1958), pp. 49-57.

28. John A. Andrew to F. P. Blair, Sr., Apr. 12, 1866, Andrew Papers, MHS. Among the company's subscribers were such free-labor enthusiasts as John Murray Forbes and George L. Stearns. Henry Greenleaf Pearson, *The Life of John A. Andrew*, 2 vols. (Boston, 1904), vol. 2, p. 267. For more details about this land agency, see my "The American Land Company and Agency: John A. Andrew and the Northernization of the South," *Civil War History* 21 (Dec. 1975): 293-308.

29. Rose, *Rehearsal*, pp. 272-96 and 308-09.

30. James E. Yeatman, *A Report on the Condition of the Freedmen of the Mississippi* (St. Louis, 1864), pp. 8-9; George W. Julian, "Homesteads for Soldiers on the Lands of Rebels," in his *Speeches on Political Questions* (New York, 1872), p. 224; John L. McCarthy, "Reconstruction Legislation and Voting Alignments in the House of Representatives, 1863-1869" (Ph.D. diss., Yale University, 1970), p. 59; John Syrett, "The Confiscation Acts: Efforts at Reconstruction During the Civil War" (Ph.D. diss., University of Wisconsin, 1971), pp. 51-52.

31. New York *Tribune*, May 24, 1865.

32. John A. Andrew to Francis C. Barlow, Jan. 20, 1866, Andrew Papers, MHS; see also "Free Labor as Missionary," *Christian Register* (Boston), Jan. 16, 1865.

33. For a couple of examples, see Reid, *After the War*, pp. 383 and 490; Trowbridge, *The South*, pp. 380-82; [George C. Benham], *A Year of Wreck* (New York, 1880), pp. 8-11; Smith, "Generative Forces," pp. 463-65.

34. James D. Waters to mother, Feb. 12, 1864, Box 12, folder 5, Waters Family Papers, Essex Inst.; see also Alexander Winchell to Zachariah Chandler, May 12, 1864, A. Winchell Papers, MHC. Many prospective lessees may have returned north, but enough stayed to rent the bulk of the abandoned plantations in the area. See "Plot of Vicksburg and Natchez Districts for Leasing Abandoned Plantations," MA; William C. Harris, *Presidential Reconstruction in Mississippi* (Baton Rouge, La., 1967), p. 21.

35. Boston *Daily Advertiser*, Jan. 15, 1866; see also [Benham], *A Year of Wreck*, pp. 37-38, 81; Reid, *After the War*, p. 382.

Chapter 2

1. See the appendix for a full discussion of the sample and the sources on which it is based.

2. Boston *Daily Advertiser*, Sept. 1, 1866.

3. Quoted in Willie Lee Rose, *Rehearsal for Reconstruction: The Port Royal Experiment* (New York, 1964), pp. 43-44.

4. Ibid., pp. 43-44, 48-49.

5. Elizabeth W. Pearson, ed., *Letters from Port Royal, 1862-1868* (New York, 1969), p. 177.

6. N. E. Carpenter to Amos A. Lawrence, Dec. 18, 1863, Lawrence Papers, MHS; Power of Attorney, Feb. 12, 1864, Reuben G. Holmes Papers, SCL.

7. Brig. Gen. Isaac F. Shepard to Commissioners of Leasing Plantations, Dec. 11, 1863, in "Applications for Leasing—In Competition" (entry 2384), BRFAL Records, NA. See also Uriah Raplee to Commissioners of Leasing, Nov. 2, 1863, in ibid.; Thomas W. Knox, *Camp-Fire and Cotton-Field: Southern Adventure in Time of War* (New York, 1865), p. 317; David H. Overy, Jr., *Wisconsin Carpetbaggers in Dixie* (Madison, Wis., 1961), p. 17; entry of Nov. 29, 1863, Alexander Winchell Diary, MHC; George Winston Smith, "Generative Forces of Union Propaganda: A Study in Civil War Pressure Groups" (Ph.D. diss., University of Wisconsin, 1939), pp. 463-65.

8. The quotations are in William D. Waters to Abigail Waters, Jan. 12, 1864, and Feb. 1864, Box 12, folder 1. See also S. D. Gilbert to James D. Waters, Nov. 10, 1863, Box 11, folder 7, Waters Family Papers, Essex Inst.

9. C. C. Drew to Clifford C. Waters, Oct. 30, 1864, Box 13, folder 2, in ibid.

10. William E. Wording to E. A. Rollins, Feb. 26, 1867, vol. 116, John Sherman Papers, LC. See also William H. Brisbane to E. A. Rollins, Jan. 26, 1867, and W. E. Wording to Thomas Harland, Mar. 25, 1867, Gen. Corr., Records of the Direct Tax Commission for S.C., NA.

11. Gen. M. H. Chrysler to Lewis Parsons, July 29, 1865, and Edward S. Welling to L. Parsons, Sept. 13, 1865, Gen. Corr., Gov.'s Corr., AA.; see also Ezra J. Warner, *Generals in Blue: Lives of the Union Commanders* (Baton Rouge, La., 1964), passim; Whitelaw Reid, *After the War: A Tour of the Southern States, 1865-1866*, ed. C. Vann Woodward (New York, 1965), p. 382.

12. John A. Wilder to Eben J. Loomis, Nov. 2, 1865 (for the quotation), and Dec. 29, 1865, Box 8, Todd Family Papers, YU.

13. Thomas Montgomery to mother, Jan. 16, 1866, Thomas Montgomery Papers, MiHS. See also T. Montgomery to parents, May 22, 1866; and T. Montgomery to James C. Montgomery, Dec. 5, 1866, in ibid.; also Edward M. Main, *The Story of the Marches, Battles, and Incidents of the Third U.S. Colored Cavalry* (New York, 1970), p. 55.

14. Report of Benjamin C. Truman, *Senate Executive Documents*, 39 Cong., 1 sess., II, no. 43 (Ser. 1238), p. 7.

15. William L. Burt to John A. Andrew, Nov. 10, 1865, Andrew Papers, MHS. See also New Orleans *Tribune*, Aug. 18, 1865; William C. Holbrook, *A Narrative . . . of the Seventh Regiment of Vermont Volunteers* (New York, 1882), p. 206; G. G. Benedict, *Vermont in the Civil War*, vol. 2 (Burlington, Vt., 1888), p. 77.

16. Truman Report, pp. 6-7. See also the biographical sections in Alfred Roe, *The Twenty-fourth Regiment of Massachusetts Volunteers* (Worcester, Mass., 1907); Virgil G. Way, *History of the Thirty-third Regiment of Illinois Veteran Volunteer Infantry* (Gibson City, Ill., 1902); and Petition of the Citizens of Alabama Against an Increase of the Tax on Cotton, June 1, 1866, Records of the U.S. Senate, RG46, NA.

17. Theodore Blegen, *Civil War Letters of Colonel Hans Christian Heg* (Northfield, Minn., 1936), p. 82; see also T. S. Ellsworth to Edward Atkinson, Dec. 19, 1863, Atkinson Papers, MHS.

18. Quoted in Peter F. Walker, *Vicksburg: A People at War, 1860-1865* (Chapel Hill, N.C., 1960), p. 215.

19. H. Brown, Jr., to J. P. Williston, Feb. 16, 1864, Atkinson Papers, MHS. One Wisconsin soldier in the area complained that "all his officers had 'ossified cotton on the brain.'" (Overy, *Wisconsin Carpetbaggers*, p. 12); Isaac Shoemaker Diary, May 6, 1864, p. 3, DU.

20. Horace S. Fulkerson, *A Civilian's Recollections of the War Between the States*, ed. P. L. Rainwater (Baton Rouge, La., 1939), pp. 172-73. See also James D. Waters to mother, Mar. 27, 1864, Box 12, folder 5, Waters Family Papers, Essex Inst.; George C. Harding, *The Miscellaneous Writings of George C. Harding* (Indianapolis, Ind., 1882); Brig. Gen. I. F. Shepard to Commissioners of Leasing, Dec. 11, 1863; and application of Calvin Shepard, Sept. 25, 1863, both in "Applications for Leasing Abandoned Plantations–In Competition" (entry 2384), BRFAL Records, NA.

21. James D. Waters to Edward S. Waters, Feb. 1, 1864, Box 4, folder 5, Waters Family Papers, Essex Inst.

22. Betty Dent Smith to James Garner, Oct. 5, 1899, Garner Papers, MA; L. Dent Report on Leasing Plantations, June 1, 1863, LSU. See also William H. Yeatman to L. Dent, Nov. 17, 1863; application of Daniel B. Staats, Dec. 2, 1863, and Mar. 16, 1865; application of M. M. Wheedon & Co., Feb. 29, 1864, all in "Applications for Lease of Abandoned Plantations" (entry 2383), BRFAL Records, NA. Staats was an agent and Wheedon was a clerk of the Leasing Commission. See also R. W. Lansing to E. M. Keyes, Dec. 16, 1863, Keyes Papers, SHSW.

23. James E. Yeatman, *Suggestions of a Plan of Organization for Freed Labor, and the Leasing of Plantations Along the Mississippi River, Under a Bureau or Commission to be Appointed by the Government* (St. Louis, 1864); Louis Gerteis, *From Contraband to Freedman: Federal Policy Toward Southern Blacks, 1861-1865* (Westport, Ct., 1973), p. 138.

24. Gen. O. O. Howard's circular of May 22, 1866, Boston *Daily Advertiser*, May 22, 1866. See also O. O. Howard to George Whipple, in Boston *Daily Advertiser*, May 15, 1866; O. O. Howard to President Andrew Johnson, Aug. 23, 1866, in Report of the Commissioner of the Bureau of Refugees, Freedmen, and Abandoned Lands, *House Executive Documents*, no. 1, 39 Cong., 1 sess. (Ser. 1285), p. 769.

25. Boston *Daily Advertiser*, Aug. 10, 1866. See also New York *Herald*, June 13, 1866; Howard A. White, *The Freedmen's Bureau in Louisiana* (Baton Rouge, La., 1970), p. 34.

26. Boston *Daily Advertiser*, July 25, 1866; June 15, 1867; *The Maine Bugle* (Oct. 1895), pp. 335-36; Warner, *Generals in Blue*, pp. 490-91, 506-07; Colonel Samuel Thomas, the Freedmen's Bureau chief in the area of Vicksburg, Mississippi, bought seed cotton from the freedmen cultivators at Davis Bend at seven cents a pound, which was "a loss to the producer of $50 to $60 on the bale." (Benjamin Montgomery to Joseph E. Davis, Oct. 14, 1865, J. E. Davis Papers, MA.)

27. New York *Herald*, May 14, 1866, and June 13, 1866.

28. Augusta (Ga.) *Daily Constitutionalist*, Dec. 27, 1865.

29. Gainesville (Fla.) *New Era*, July 20, 1866; J. F. B. Marshall to E. E. Hale, Feb. 9, 1867, SEC, NEEACo Papers, KSHS. Ely's operation had other shady features. When the colony disbanded, Ely never refunded the $10 per head fee he had charged the freedmen for transporting them to New Smyrna. (Jerrell H. Shofner, *Nor Is It Over Yet: Florida in the Era of Reconstruction, 1863-77* [Gainesville, Fla., 1974], pp. 71-72.)

30. New York *Herald*, May 8 and 12, 1866.

31. William S. McFeely, *Yankee Stepfather: General O. O. Howard and the Freedmen* (New Haven, Conn., 1968), pp. 250-53; New York *Herald*, May 8, 12, 22, 1866.

32. O. O. Howard to President A. Johnson, Aug. 23, 1866, Report of the Commissioner, *House Executive Documents*, no. 1, 39 Cong., 1 sess. (Ser. 1285), p. 769; see also Boston *Daily Advertiser*, May 22, 1866.

33. Boston *Daily Advertiser*, June 12, 1866.

34. Roger Shugg, *Origins of Class Struggle in Louisiana* (Baton Rouge, La., 1968), p. 264; Harriet Beecher Stowe, *Palmetto Leaves* (Boston, 1873), pp. 185-91; Samuel Johnson, *The Battle Cry of Freedom* (Lawrence, Kans., 1954), pp. 277, 280-84.

35. Charles Boynton to T. B. Forbush, Aug. 1, 1867, SEC, NEEACo Papers, KSHS. See also Fred A. Shannon, *The Farmer's Last Frontier: Agriculture, 1860-1897* (New York and Toronto, 1945), p. 36; Paul W. Gates, *Agriculture and the Civil War* (New York, 1965), pp. 129-247.

36. Clarence H. Danhof, "Farm-Making Costs and the 'Safety Valve': 1850-1860," *The Journal of Political Economy* 49 (June 1941): 317-59.

37. John T. Trowbridge, *The South: A Tour of Its Battle Fields and Ruined Cities*, with an introduction by Otto H. Olsen (New York, 1969), pp. 380-81; Reid, *After the War*, p.

490; [George C. Benham], *A Year of Wreck* (New York, 1880), pp. 8-9; American Land Company and Agency, Circular no. 2 [1866], MHS.

38. Eight hundred dollars was about the upper limit of capital possessed by those farmers and laborers who inquired into the New England Emigrant Aid Company's project to plant a colony in Florida. N. Barlow to T. B. Forbush, July 30, 1867; B. W. Blackinton to Forbush, May 5, 1867; G. W. Williams to Forbush, Apr. 22, 1867; Henry S. Adams to Forbush, Feb. 14, 1867; and C. N. Nute to Forbush, Jan. 1, 1867, SEC, NEEACo Papers, KSHS.

39. Some northern farmers apparently had "the intention of acquiring a practical knowledge of cotton culture, and next year of buying or hiring plantations to work for themselves." Boston *Daily Advertiser*, Dec. 9, 1865. See also Charles L. Lease to Gov. Benjamin G. Humphreys, Nov. 20, 1865, vol. 77, Gov.'s Corr., MA; Edward Barker to T. B. Forbush, Nov. 30, 1866, SEC, NEEACo Papers, KSHS; H. M. Crydenwise to parents, Apr. 3 [1866], Crydenwise Papers, DU.

40. Brig. Gen. I. F. Shepard to Commissioners for Leasing, Dec. 11, 1863, "Applications for Leasing Abandoned Plantations—In Competition" (entry 2384), BRFAL Records, NA. See also Hiram McCollam to Andrew McCollam, Feb. 23, 1867, McCollam Papers, SHC; J. C. B. Sargent to E. E. Hale, Dec. 3, 1866, and George H. Pierson to T. B. Forbush, Dec. 20, 1866, SEC, NEEACo Papers, KSHS.

41. John Murray Forbes to Edward Atkinson, Mar. 24, Aug. 24, 1865, Atkinson Papers, MHS.

42. A. Burwell to Commissioners of Abandoned Lands, Dec. 19, 1863, "Applications for Lease of Abandoned Plantations" (entry 2383), BRFAL Records, NA.

43. David H. Overy, Jr., *Wisconsin Carpetbaggers in Dixie* (Madison, Wis., 1961), pp. 14, 18-19, 36-37, 63. See also *The United States Biographical Dictionary and Portrait Gallery of Self-Made Men*, Wisconsin volume (Chicago, 1877), pp. 99-100.

44. William P. Irwin to the secretary of the treasury, Mar. 15, 1866, Gen. Corr.; "Minutes," entry of Mar. 25, 1864, both in Records of the Direct Tax Commission for S.C., NA; Gainesville *New Era,* Jan. 20, 1866; *Florida Union* (Jacksonville), July 21, 1866.

45. [Benham], *A Year of Wreck*, p. 38. See also application of S. A. Duke, Jan. 3, 1865, "Applications for the Lease of Abandoned Plantations" (entry 2383), BRFAL Records, NA; Floyd King to Lin [Caperton], Dec. 24, 1865, Series A, Thomas Butler King Papers, SHC.

46. *Trow's New York City Directory for 1866,* 79 (New York, 1866), pp. 469, 923; Thomas G. Belden and Marva R. Belden, *So Fell the Angels* (Boston, 1956), pp. 52-56; Rose, *Rehearsal*, pp. 19 and 143; Gov. William Sprague to S. P. Chase, Feb. 8, 1862, item 52, "Port Royal Correspondence," Records of the Fifth Special Treasury Agency, NA.

47. George E. Spencer to Grenville M. Dodge, Aug. 1, 1865, G. M. Dodge Papers, Iowa State Dept. of History.

48. Gainesville *New Era*, June 22, 1866; New York *Herald*, June 2, 1866; "United States Tax Sales, City of Fernandina-Nassau County-Florida, 1864-1865," in Samuel A. Swann Papers, FU.

49. J. Floyd King to Lin [Caperton], Dec. 24, 1865, Series A, Thomas Butler King Papers, SHC.

50. Harold F. Williamson, *Edward Atkinson: The Biography of an American Liberal, 1827-1905* (Boston, 1934), pp. 3, 11-12, 279-82; Charles P. Warner, *Representative Families of Northampton,* 1 (Northampton, Mass., 1917), pp. 81-84.

51. George W. Smith, "Some Northern Wartime Attitudes Toward the Post-Civil War South," *Journal of Southern History* 10 (Aug. 1944): 260-61.

52. Rose, *Rehearsal*, p. 215.

53. Circular of the Port Royal Cotton Company [c. 1865], Markham-Puffer Papers, CU; Army, Navy, or Marine Land Certificate, no. 158, Feb. 24, 1864, Records of the Direct Tax Commission for S.C., NA.

54. Subscription list, Sea Island Cotton Company, Dec. 24, 1864; Alfred Ely to C. C. Puffer, Nov. 6, 1865; Sea Island Cotton Company, circular to stockholders, Sept. 15, 1866; Ferreby to William Markham, Nov. 28, 1865, and undated letter, all in Markham-Puffer Papers, CU.

55. Quoted in Overy, *Wisconsin Carpetbaggers*, p. 18; Smith, "Generative Forces," p.

465; application of Wesley Ditts, Jan. 30, 1865; Wilson C. Lemert to C. A. Montross, Jan. 9, 1865, "Applications for Lease of Abandoned Plantations" (entry 2383), BRFAL Records, NA.

56. Alexander Winchell Diaries, entries of Dec. 3, 1863, Dec. 10, 1863, Dec. 26, 1863, Jan. 1, 1864, Apr. 30, 1864, and June 9, 1864; see also A. Winchell to J. E. Johnson, Dec. 5, 1863, also in the diaries, MHC.

57. A. Winchell to Zachariah Chandler, May 2, 1864, A. Winchell and Family Papers, MHC.; H. Brown, Jr., to J. P. Williston, Feb. 16, 1864, Atkinson Papers, MHS; A. Winchell Diary, entry of Nov. 15, 1864, MHC; Mark Boatner III, *Civil War Dictionary* (New York, 1959), p. 414. Combinations for mutual protection were not uncommon in the Mississippi Valley during the war. Occasionally, lessees hired scouts to protect them from the Confederate guerrillas, "each planter being assessed for the purpose 500 dollars for the season." (C. C. Drew to James D. Waters, Oct. 12, 1864, Box 11, folder 1, Waters Family Papers, Essex Inst.)

58. A. Winchell Diary, entry of May 14, 1864; see also Apr. 30, 1864, MHC.

59. H. Brown, Jr., to J. P. Williston, Feb. 16, 1864, Atkinson Papers, MHS. See also A. Winchell to C. A. Montross, Feb. 11, 1864 (two letters), "Applications for Lease of Abandoned Plantations" (entry 2383), BRFAL Records, NA. Also, A. Winchell to H. Brown, Jr., May 16, 1864, A. Winchell Letterbook; A. Winchell to Z. Chandler, May 2, 1864, A. Winchell and Family Papers; A. Winchell Diaries, entries of May 7, 1864, and June 4, 1864, all in MHC.

60. William Markham to Fairchild Andrews, Feb. 3, 1865; W. Markham to D. R. Maynard, Feb. 4, 1865, Markham-Puffer Papers, CU.

61. The quotation appears in Sea Island Cotton Company, circular to stockholders, Sept. 15, 1866; see also contract with Robert V. Richardson, May 1867; William J. Randolph to W. G. Markham, Jan. 25, 1867, Markham-Puffer Papers, CU.

62. Application of John Lynch & Co., Mar. 1, 1864, "Applications for Lease of Abandoned Plantations" (entry 2383), BRFAL Records, NA; Chicago *Tribune*, Aug. 14, 1866. For other examples of partnership arrangements see "Agreement Between D. D. Slauson, Sen. Partner, and W. H. Carroll, Jr. Partner," Jan. 1, 1867, D. D. Slauson Papers, LSU; Whitelaw Reid Diary, "1862," entry of Nov. 20, 1865, and F. J. Herron to [Thomas J.?] May, Feb. 17, 1866, Reid Papers, LC.

63. Chicago *Tribune*, Aug. 14, 1866; Garth W. James to Henry James, Sr., Mar. 27, 1866, G. W. and R. James Papers, in possession of Prof. William Childers, University of Florida; "Petition of George W. Colby and other Residents of Alabama Against the Increased Tax on Cotton," June 1, 1866, Records of the U.S. Senate, NA; William L. Burt to John A. Andrew, May 10, 1866, Andrew Papers, MHS.

64. D. D. Haskell to Gov. Lewis Parsons, Nov. 4, 1865, and Edward S. Welling to Gov. L. Parsons, Sept. 13, 1865; James M. Shute to Gov. Robert Patton, Feb. 10, 1866, Gov.'s Corr., A.A.; Main, *The Story of the Marches*, p. 55; A. S. Gurney to Sen. Edwin D. Morgan, June 1, 1866, Records of the U.S. Senate, NA. Cf. Paul E. Johnson, *A Shopkeeper's Millenium: Society and Revivals in Rochester, New York, 1815-1837* (New York, 1978), pp. 26-27.

65. Clifford C. Waters to E. S. Waters, Apr. 6, 1865, Box 4, folder 3; William D. Waters to E. S. Waters, Oct. 5, 1866, Box 4, folder 2, Waters Family Papers, Essex Inst.; General Power of Attorney, Mar. 27, 1871, Box "O," folder 1, Butler Family Papers; and Frances Butler to P. C. Hollis, Mar. 3, 1868, Box 24, folder 3, Wister Family Papers, both in the Hist. Soc. of Pa.; Adin Mann to C. A. Montross, Feb. 13, 1865, "Applications for Lease of Abandoned Plantations" (entry 2383), BRFAL Records, NA; *Report of the Joint Committee on Reconstruction*, 39 Cong., 1 sess. (Ser. 1273), 4, p. 140; Jimmy G. Shoalmire, "Carpetbagger Extraordinary; Marshall Harvey Twitchell, 1840-1905" (Ph.D. diss., Mississippi State University, 1969), p.96; Henry W. Warren, *Reminiscences of a Mississippi Carpetbagger* (Holden, Mass., 1914), p. 11; Albert T. Morgan, *Yazoo; Or, on the Picket Line of Freedom in the South* (Washington, D.C., 1884), p. 17. For family capitalism, see Johnson, *Shopkeeper's Millenium*, pp. 21-28; Bernard Farber, *Guardians of Virtue: Salem Families in 1800* (New York, 1972), pp. 75-96.

66. F. A. Redington to Gov. Lewis Parsons, Sept. 4, 1865, Gen. Corr., Gov.'s Corr., AA; A. Winchell to Z. Chandler, A. Winchell and Family Papers, MHC; [Benham], *A Year of Wreck*, pp. 16-17; Bliss Perry, *Life and Letters of Henry Lee Higginson* (Boston, 1921), p.

248; Charles F. Morse, *A Sketch of My Life* (Cambridge, Mass., 1927), p. 26; John Wilder to mother, June 8, 1865, Box 8, Todd Family Papers, YU; Henry M. Crydenwise to parents, Feb. 11, 1866, Crydenwise Papers, EU.

67. Sarah F. Hughes, ed., *Letters (Supplementary) of John Murray Forbes,* 3 vols. (Boston, 1905), vol. 2, pp. 48-49.

68. Morse, *A Sketch*, pp. 25-26. See also Edward Atkinson to Hugh McCulloch, Feb. 28, 1866, Atkinson Letterbooks, MHS; "Eben Jenks Loomis" [n.n., n.d.], Box 126; Mary Alden Wilder Expense Account Book, 1866-1876, Box 121; and Frederick W. Bardwell to Eben Loomis, Dec. 20, 1865, Box 44, all in Todd Family Papers, YU; Thomas C. Franklin to Thaddeus Stevens, Dec. 10, 1865, vol. 5, Stevens Papers, LC; Deming Jarves, Jr., to Hugh McCulloch, July 13, 1865, and Pliny Freeman to H. McCulloch, Feb. 6, 1866, Gen. Corr., Records of the Direct Tax Commission for S.C., NA; Hiram W. Lewis to James Garner, Jan. 18, 1900, Garner Papers, MA; *History of the 73rd Regiment of Illinois Volunteers* (1890), p. 539.

69. Forrest Wilson, *Crusader in Crinoline: The Life of Harriet Beecher Stowe* (Philadelphia, 1941), pp.. 498, 515.

70. J. Floyd King to Lin [Caperton], Jan. 1, 1866, Series A, Thomas Butler King Papers, SHC; John Lockwood to John Fox Potter, May 5, 1864, Potter Papers, SHSW; [Benham], *A Year of Wreck*, pp. 7-12; Warren, *Reminiscences*, p. 11; Reid, *After the War*, pp. 490-91; Trowbridge, *The South*, pp. 381-82.

71. [Benham], *A Year of Wreck*, p. 7.

72. Knox, *Camp-Fire*, p. 311.

73. A. Winchell to J. E. Johnson, Dec. 5, 1863, A. Winchell Diary, MHC. Some of these keen-eyed entrepreneurs were highly placed in the Lincoln administration and the Republican party, using their influence to make mouth-watering profits out of the various cotton rings in which they had an interest. (Ludwell Johnson, "Contraband Trade During the Last Year of the Civil War," *Mississippi Valley Historical Review* 49 [March 1963]: 635-52; idem, "Northern Profit and Profiteers: The Cotton Rings of 1864-1865," *Civil War History* 12 [June 1966]: 101-15.)

74. E. Wakeley to [D.K.?] Tenney, Feb. 28, 1864, Tenney Papers, SHSW.

75. Wesley C. Mitchell, "The Production and Consumption of Wealth," pp. 5-10; Reuben A. Kessel and Armen A. Alchian, "Real Wages in the North During the Civil War: Mitchell's Data Reinterpreted," pp. 11-30; Thomas C. Cochran, "Did the Civil War Retard Industrialization?," pp. 167-79; and Stephen Salsbury, "The Effect of the Civil War on American Industrial Development," pp. 180-87, all in Ralph Andreano, ed., *The Economic Impact of the Civil War* (Cambridge, Mass., 1967); J. G. Randall and David Donald, *The Civil War and Reconstruction* (Boston, 1961), pp. 481-86. Stanley Engerman questions the prevailing assumption that relative profits rose during the war. But he offers no substantial evidence to the contrary and is content to make the point that "it is possible that no shift to profits occurred during the wartime inflation." ("The Economic Impact of the Civil War," in Andreano, ed., *Economic Impact*, pp. 198-99, 200.)

76. N. Langdon William to James D. Waters, July 13, 1865, Box 13, folder 7, Waters Family Papers, Essex Inst.

77. N. L. Williams to the "Boys," Dec. 6, 1864, Box 13, folder 7; see also N. L. Williams to J. D. Waters, Mar. 1, 1865, Box 11, folder 7, Waters Family Papers, Essex Inst.

78. N. L. Williams to George G. Klapp, Mar. 27 [1865]; see also N. L. Williams to G. G. Klapp, Mar. 21, 1865; N. L. Williams to the "Boys," Apr. 20, 1865, all in Box 13, folder 7; N. L. Williams to J. D. Waters, Mar. 1, 1865, Box 11, folder 7, Waters Family Papers, Essex Inst.

79. N. L. Williams to J. D. Waters, Oct. 12, 1865, Box 11, folder 7, Waters Family Papers, Essex Inst.

80. Mitchell, "The Production and Consumption of Wealth," in Andreano, ed., *Economic Impact*, pp. 5-6; Eugene M. Lerner, "Investment Uncertainty during the Civil War—A Note on the McCormick Brothers," *Journal of Economic History* 16 (Mar. 1956): 35-38. After some initial reservations Amos A. Lawrence concluded that plantation investments were sound policy. "That land will never be worthless, whether South Carolina society be good or bad," he wrote to his nephew in Port Royal. (Quoted in Smith, "Some Northern Wartime Attitudes," p. 261.)

81. [C. C. Puffer to William Markham?] [c. early 1865], Markham-Puffer Papers, CU.

Wool prices more than doubled between 1861 and 1864, owing to the decline in the supply of cotton and the heavy demand for uniforms by the federal government. Wayne D. Rasmussen, "The Civil War: A Catalyst of Agricultural Revolution," in Andreano, ed., *Economic Impact*, p. 71.

82. Hadden & Harris to Gov. Lewis Parsons, July 27, 1865, Gen. Corr., Gov.'s Corr., AA. See also Edward O. Lord, *History of the Ninth Regiment New Hampshire Volunteers* (Concord, N.H., 1895), pp. 664-65.

83. H. W. Tenney to brother, Feb. 21 ("make a pile"), Mar. 23, 1864, Tenney Papers, SHSW; Gerart Hewitt to W. M. Smith, July 6, 1865, W. M. Smith Papers, DU ("the War would open up").

84. Gerart Hewitt to W. M. Smith, July 6, 1865, W. M. Smith Papers, DU; see also Mitchell, "Production and Consumption of Wealth," pp. 8-10; and Kessel and Alchian, "Real Wages in the North," pp. 11-30.

85. Noah R. Harlow to John A. Andrew, June 20, 1866, Andrew Papers, MHS; Adin Mann to C. A. Montross, Feb. 13, 1865, "Applications for Lease of Abandoned Plantations" (entry 2383), BRFAL Records, NA.

86. W. Reid to Richard Smith, Dec. 8, 1865, Reid Papers, LC. For similar complaints, see Alfred Gilmore to Gov. James L. Orr, Jan. 6, 1867, Gov. Orr Papers, SCA; and C. C. Parker to Gov. Lewis Parsons, July 25, 1865, Misc. Corr., Gov.'s Corr., AA.

87. A. Winchell to J. E. Johnson, Dec. 5, 1863, A. Winchell Diary, MHC.

88. A. Winchell Diaries, entries of Nov. 29, 1863, and Jan. 17, 1864, MHC; see also Warren, *Reminiscences,* p. 11; A. A. Hunt to John A. Andrew, Nov. 13, 1865, Andrew Papers, MHS.

89. Liabilities, however, were $90,000,000 less than in 1857. (Emerson D. Fite, *Social and Industrial Conditions in the North During the Civil War and Reconstruction* [New York, 1910], pp. 105-06; Randall and Donald, *The Civil War and Reconstruction,* pp. 480-81.)

90. Elbridge G. Dudley to Henry Seabrook, Dec. 8, 1865, James Butler Campbell Papers, SCL. See also E. L. Devereaux to James D. Waters, May 17, 1866, Box 11, folder 8, Waters Family Papers, Essex Inst.; U.S.A. Tax Sale Certificate, no. 35, Mar. 11, 1863; "Cash Sales Land Certificates," Book A, Mar. 17, 1864; and "Minutes," Dec. 3, 1866, p. 296, Records of the Direct Tax Commission for S.C., NA.

91. A. Burwell to Commissioners of Abandoned Plantations, Dec. 19, 1863, "Applications for Lease of Abandoned Plantations" (entry 2383), BRFAL Records, NA.

92. William D. Waters to Abigail Waters, Aug. 1828, Aug. 8, 1832, Mar. 16, 1833, Sept. 9, 1833, Box 12, folder 1; mayor of Salem to W. D. Waters, Sept. 22, 1858, Box 10, folder 2; scrapbook, Box 99; Abigail Waters to W. D. Waters, Apr. 10, 1864, and J. D. Waters to W. D. Waters, May 16, 1874, Box 10, folder 3; C. C. Waters to E. S. Waters, Aug. 29, 1865, Box 4, folder 3; W. D. Waters to A. Waters, Mar. 14, 1864, Box 12, folder 1, Waters Family Papers, Essex Inst.

93. J. D. Waters to E. S. Waters, Apr. 10, 1864, Box 4, folder 5; J. D. Waters to mother, Jan. 29, 1864, and Mar. 27, 1864, Box 12, folder 5. This acquaintance deepened into a closer relationship. Waters and Klapp on occasion shared households with the Thomases, who treated them as part of the family. James Waters handled some of Henry Thomas's business dealings in the South, and Henry advanced Waters and Klapp capital during the 1865 season. (James D. Waters to E. S. Waters, Mar. 15, 1865, Box 4, folder 5, Waters Family Papers, Essex Inst.)

94. J. D. Waters to W. D. Waters, May 16, 1864, Box 10, folder 3. See also J. D. Waters to mother, Mar. 27, 1864, Box 12, folder 5; Waters Family Papers, Essex Inst.; E. S. Waters to Henry F. Waters, Mar. 9, 1864, Box 8, ESW folder, H. F. Waters Papers, Essex Inst.

95. C. C. Waters to J. D. Waters, Dec. 20, 1864, Box 11, folder 2 (for the quotation); W. D. Waters to A. Waters, Feb. 22, 1864, Box 12, folder 1; J. D. Waters to E. S. Waters, Dec. 29, 1864, Box 4, folder 5; W. D. Waters, Sept. 24, 1866, Box 4, folder 2, Waters Family Papers, Essex Inst. Collateral branches of the Waters family also had plantation connections. After the war one cousin managed Pierce Butler's Georgia Sea Island plantation; another purchased two plantations at the first tax sale at Port Royal.

96. C. C. Waters to J. D. Waters, Dec. 20, 1864, Box 11, folder 2; J. D. Waters to W. D. Waters, Jan. 22, 1865, Box 10, folder 3; Waters Family Papers, Essex Inst.

97. J. D. Waters to H. F. Waters, Jan. 23, 1865, Box 8, JDW folder, H. F. Waters Papers;

C. C. Waters to E. S. Waters, Jan. 24, 1866, Box 4, folder 3, Waters Family Papers, Essex Inst.

98. Rendig Fels, *American Business Cycles, 1865-1897* (Chapel Hill, N.C., 1959), pp. 92-96; see also Randall and Donald, *Civil War and Reconstruction,* pp. 537-38.

99. Charles F. Morse to Ellen, June 18, 1865, C. F. Morse Papers, MHS; Warren, *Reminiscences,* pp. 95-96.

100. O. O. Howard to George Whipple, in Boston *Daily Advertiser,* May 15, 1866.

101. The respective quotations are in Thomas Montgomery to James C. Montgomery, Dec. 5, 1866, T. Montgomery Papers, MiHS; and Henry M. Crydenwise to parents, Sept. 18, 1865, Crydenwise Papers, EU. See also Charles W. Dustan to mother, Feb. 13, 1865, C. W. Dustan Papers, SHC. "I do not relish the idea of going back home again as a beggar which I shall almost be," one Union colonel wrote on the eve of his discharge. (John A. Wilder to Eben J. Loomis, Nov. 2, 1865, Box 8, Todd Family Papers, YU.)

102. C. F. Morse to Robert [Morse], June 4, 10, 22, 1865, C. F. Morse Papers, MHS; see also Morse, *A Sketch of my Life,* p. 25.

103. Perry, *Life and Letters,* pp. 232-36, 240-41, 245, 248.

104. Henry C. Thomas to J. D. Waters, July 24, 1865, Apr. 23, 1865, and Oct. 1, 1865, Box 11, folder 7, Waters Family Papers, Essex Inst.

105. Henry M. Crydenwise to parents, Feb. 11, 1866 (for the quotation), Sept. 18, 1865, and Nov. 11, 1866, Crydenwise Papers, EU. See also William L. Bliss to New England Emigrant Aid Company [summer of 1866], and A. Henry to T. B. Forbush, Jan. 13, 1868, SEC, NEEACo Papers, KSHS; Joseph Logsdon, "An Illinois Carpetbagger Looks at the Southern Negro," *Journal of the Illinois State Historical Society* 62 (Spring 1969): 55.

106. John A. Pettit to Gov. William L. Sharkey, July 27, 1865, vol. 70, Gov.'s Corr., MA; T. A. Post to Henry C. Warmoth, Mar. 9, 1865, H. C. Warmoth Papers, SHC; *War Letters, 1862-1865, of John Chipman Gray and John Codman Ropes* (Boston and New York, 1927), p. 503. "I am going South to see whether there is anything in which I can engage to make some money," a public official in Ohio wrote Senator John Sherman. "I am entirely out of practice as an atty and must get at something to keep together soul and body." (Joseph Geiger to John Sherman, Oct. 19, 1865, vol. 86, Sherman Papers, LC.)

107. The respective quotations are in John A. Wilder to Oliver Wendell Holmes, Dec. 11, 1866, Box 45; and J. A. Wilder to Eben Loomis, Nov. 2, 1865, Box 8, Todd Family Papers, YU. He eventually found work as a defense attorney for a Confederate prison official for whom he won an acquittal at a military trial. (Thomas R. Bright, "Yankees in Arms: The Civil War as a Personal Experience," *Civil War History* 19 [Sept. 1973]:215.)

108. John A. Wilder to mother, June 8, 1865, Todd Family Papers, YU; C. F. Morse to Robert [Morse], June 22, 1865, C. F. Morse Papers, MHS.

109. Albion W. Tourgee, *A Fool's Errand: A Novel of the South during Reconstruction* (New York, 1966), pp. 23 and 26. Tourgee's personal history after the war resembled that of his fictional character. After returning home in 1864 he had only indifferent success in a number of occupations—law, journalism, and teaching. He went south in the summer of 1865 to engage in planting, law, and the nursery business. (Otto H. Olsen, *A Carpetbagger's Crusade: The Life of Albion Winegar Tourgee* [Baltimore, 1965], pp. 26-28.)

110. The quotations are in A. Winchell Diaries, entries of Jan. 17, 1864, and Dec. 5, 1863, MHC; see also C. C. Waters to J. D. Waters, Nov. 16, 1864, and Dec. 20, 1864, Box 11, folder 2; H. F. Waters to J. D. Waters, Dec. 19, 1864, Box 11, folder 7, Waters Family Papers, Essex Inst.; T. D. Slauson to Daniel D. Slauson, Apr. 1, 1866, D. D. Slauson Papers, LSU. Southern opportunities had a way of boosting a man's self-confidence. Wrote one Union colonel who resolved to try his luck in the South: "I am getting terribly old, Mother dear, and Oh! *So* smart. I should not wonder if I found myself a millionaire even yet and I'm past 30." (Charles W. Dustan to mother, Mar, 7, 1865, C. W. Dustan Papers, SHC.)

111. [Benham], *A Year of Wreck,* p. 16.

112. Thomas C. Franklin to Thaddeus Stevens, Dec. 10, 1865, vol. 5, Stevens Papers, LC; Henry F. Waters to J. D. and C. C. Waters, June 21, 1867, Box 11, folder 8; C. C. Waters to J. D. Waters, Nov. 16, 1864, Box 11, folder 2, Waters Family Papers, Essex Inst.

113. Millicent Todd, *Eben Jenks Loomis* (Cambridge, Mass., 1913), pp. 3, 20.

114. Eben Loomis to wife, Apr. 28, 1866, Box 8, and Eben Loomis to Molly Loomis, Feb. 11, 1867, Box 9, Todd Family Papers, YU.

115. [Benham], *A Year of Wreck,* pp. 16-17.

116. William L. McMillen to Henry Clay Warmoth, Nov. 30, 1869, June 6, 1874, Warmoth Papers, SHC; Overy, *Wisconsin Carpetbaggers*, p. 10; Francis W. Binning, "Henry Clay Warmoth and Louisiana Reconstruction" (Ph.D. diss., University of North Carolina, 1969), p. 55.

117. G. G. Klapp to J. D. Waters, Mar. 21, 1868, Box 11, folder 8; see also Klapp to Waters, Oct. 8, 1865, Box 11, folder 7, Waters Family Papers, Essex Inst.; and William R. Taylor, *Cavalier and Yankee: The Old South and American National Character* (New York, 1961).

118. Alfred Gilmore to Gov. James L. Orr, Jan. 6, 1867. See also David O. Allen to Gov. Orr, Nov. 16, 1865; Henry Hubbard to Gov. Orr, Apr. 10, 1867, Gov. J. L. Orr Papers, all in SCA.

119. Clifford C. Waters to Joseph Linton Waters, Jan. 9, 1867, Box 27, Joseph Linton Waters folder, Waters Family Papers, Essex Inst.

120. The respective quotations are in Capt. G. B. Russell to John A. Andrew, Oct. 2, 1865, Andrew Papers, MHS; C. F. Morse to Robert Morse, June 10, 1865, C. F. Morse Papers, MHS. See also Thomas Montgomery to father, Apr. 4, 1866, T. Montgomery Papers, MiHS; Col. George E. Spencer to G. M. Dodge, May 25, 1865, G. M. Dodge Papers, Iowa St. Dept. of Hist.; H. M. Crydenwise to parents, Sept. 18, 1865, Crydenwise Papers, EU; Morse, *A Sketch*, p. 25; Perry, *Life and Letters*, p. 248.

121. H. M. Crydenwise to parents, Apr. 16, 1864, Crydenwise Papers, EU; Charles W. Dustan to mother [c. 1864], C. W. Dustan Papers, SHC.

122. Quoted in George M. Fredrickson, *The Inner Civil War: Northern Intellectuals and the Crisis of the Union* (New York, 1965), pp. 173-74.

123. Main, *The Story of the Marches*, p. 55. See also John A. Wilder to E. Loomis, Nov. 2, Dec. 29, 1865, and Jan. 4, 1866, Box 8, Todd Family Papers, YU. The attempt to make planting serve as a surrogate for military life was not always successful. A former Union captain planting cotton in South Carolina found that his mind kept reverting "to my old occupation, and I finally conclude that the military service is my sphere." (Capt. W. W. Sampson to Gov. James L. Orr, May 27, 1866, Gov. Orr Papers, SCA.)

124. Fredrickson, *Inner Civil War*, pp. 29-35, 72; Perry, *Life and Letters*, pp. 108 and 138.

125. Perry, *Life and Letters*, pp. 183-84.

126. Fredrickson, *Inner Civil War*, pp. 172-73; see also Perry, *Life and Letters*, pp. 232-35.

127. C. C. Waters to E. S. Waters, July 7, 1865, Box 4, folder 3; see also Clifford C. Waters Diary, July 5, 20, 1864, Box 2; C. C. Waters to E. S. Waters, Apr. 16, 1865, Box 4, folder 3, Waters Family Papers, Essex Inst.; J. D. Waters to H. F. Waters, June 30, 1863, Box 8, JDW folder, H. F. Waters Papers, Essex Inst.

128. C. C. Waters Diary, Oct. 3, 1864, Box 2; see also C. C. Waters to J. D. Waters, Nov. 11, 16, 1864, Box 11, folder 2, Waters Family Papers, Essex Inst.

129. C. C. Waters to J. D. Waters, Dec. 20, 1864, and Nov. 16, 1864, Box 11, folder 2; see also C. C. Waters Diary, July 17, 1864, and Oct. 3, 1864, Box 2, Waters Family Papers, Essex Inst.

130. C. C. Waters to J. D. Waters, Apr. 12, 1864, and Nov. 16, 1864, Box 11, folder 2, Waters Family Papers, Essex Inst.

131. J. D. Waters to H. F. Waters, Apr. 1863, Box 8, JDW folder, H. F. Waters Papers, Essex Inst.

132. Hughes, ed., *Letters (Supplementary)*, 2, pp. 48-49.

133. Rose, *Rehearsal*, pp. 38, 48, 213-14.

134. Williamson, *Edward Atkinson*, pp. 9-11; Warner, *Representative Families*, 1, pp. 81-84.

135. Frank L. Stearns, *The Life and Public Services of George Luther Stearns* (Philadelphia, 1907), p. 352; G. L. Stearns to F. C. Cabell, Sept. 29, 1865, in Boston *Daily Advertiser*, Oct. 25, 1865; James M. McPherson, *The Struggle for Equality: Abolitionists and the Negro in the Civil War and Reconstruction* (Princeton, N.J., 1964), p. 413.

136. Knox, *Camp-Fire*, pp. 319, 323-24; *Report of the Joint Committee*, 4, p. 144.

137. Perry, *Life and Letters*, p. 248. See also [Benham], *A Year of Wreck*, p. 131; Newton H. Winchell Diary, vol. 13, May 16, 1864, MiHS; D. D. Haskell to Gov. Lewis

Parsons, Nov. 4, 1865, Gen. Corr., and James M. Shute to Gov. Robert Patton, Feb. 10, 1866, Gov.'s Corr., A.A.

138. H. M. Crydenwise to parents, Nov. 28, 1863 (for the quotation), Mar. 13 and 21, 1862, Aug. 19, 1862, and June 2, 1864, Crydenwise Papers, EU.

139. H. M. Crydenwise to parents, Apr. 3 [1866] (for the quotation), and Nov. 11, 1866, Crydenwise Papers, DU; see also H. M. Crydenwise to parents, May 14, 1865, June 4, 1865, July 12, 1865, and Aug. 23, 1865, Crydenwise Papers, EU.

140. [Benham], *A Year of Wreck*, p. 234.

141. Garth W. James to Henry James, Sr., Apr. 7, 1866, in possession of Prof. William Childers, University of Florida.

142. Anna R. Burr, ed., *Alice James. Her Brothers. Her Journal* (New York, 1934), pp. 7-9, 22, 28-30, 33-35; the quotations are on pp. 9 and 34. F. O. Matthiessen, *The James Family* (New York, 1948), pp. 69-70.

143. Burr, ed., *Alice James*, pp. 28, 43; see also William Childers, "Garth Wilkinson and Robertson James in Florida" (unpublished paper, University of Florida, 1970); Fredrickson, *Inner Civil War*, pp. 68-69; Matthiessen, *James Family*, p. 266.

144. *Makers of America* (Florida ed.), 2 (Atlanta, 1909), pp. 382-87; J. M. Hawks, *The Florida Gazetteer* (New Orleans, 1871), pp. 127-28; [George] Dewhurst to Edwin Stoeber, Dec. 22, 1865, E. M. Stoeber Papers, SCL.

145. Quoted in Wilson, *Crusader in Crinoline*, p. 515; Catherine Beecher to Gov. J. L. Orr, July 13, 1868, Orr-Patterson Papers, SHC; Catherine E. Beecher and Harriet Beecher Stowe, *The American Woman's Home, or, Principles of Domestic Economy* (New York, 1869), pp. 41-42.

146. James M. McPherson, *The Abolitionist Legacy: From Reconstruction to the NAACP* (Princeton, N.J., 1975), pp. 76-77; Overy, *Wisconsin Carpetbaggers*, pp. 39-45. See also David Montgomery, *Beyond Equality: Labor and the Radical Republicans, 1862-1872* (New York, 1967), pp. 436-37.

147. Charles Stearns to William Lloyd Garrison, Jan. 31, 1840, Apr. 25, 1841, in the *Liberator*, Feb. 14, 1840, June 18, 1841; "Minutes of the Board of Trustees Meetings," Oct. 7, 1854, NEEACo Papers, KSHS; Charles Stearns, *The Black Man of the South and the Rebels* (Boston, 1872), pp. 20-28; Lewis Perry, *Radical Abolitionism: Anarchy and the Government of God in Antislavery Thought* (Ithaca, N.Y., 1973), pp. 240-49.

148. Stearns, *The Black Man*, p. 20; see also Charles Stearns to W. L. Garrison, Jan. 21, 1863, Mar. 27, 1865, in the *Liberator*, Mar. 20, 1863, Apr. 21, 1865.

149. Stearns, *The Black Man*, pp. 31-32, 49; Perry, *Radical Abolitionism*, p. 242; McPherson, *Struggle for Equality*, pp. 414-16.

150. *The Ku-Klux Conspiracy, Testimony Taken by the Joint Select Committee to Inquire into the Condition of Affairs in the Late Insurrectionary States*, vol. 2, pt. 7 (Washington, D.C., 1872), p. 717.

151. The respective quotations are in C. C. Parker to Gov. Lewis Parsons, July 25, 1865, Misc. Corr., Gov.'s Corr., AA; and A. L. Gurney to Edwin D. Morgan, June 1, 1866, Records of the U.S. Senate, NA. See also Petition of Citizens of Alabama Remonstrating Against an Increase of the Tax on Cotton, June 1, 1866; Citizens of Natchez, Mississippi, Remonstrating Against an Increase in the Tax on Cotton, May 11, 1866, all in the Records of the U.S. Senate, NA.

152. George M. Fredrickson, *The Black Image in the White Mind: The Debate on Afro-American Character and Destiny, 1817-1914* (New York, 1971), pp. 165-97; Eric Foner, *Free Soil, Free Labor, Free Men: The Ideology of the Republican Party before the Civil War* (New York, 1970), pp. 290-93.

153. Foner, *Free Soil*, p. 39.

154. Henry Lee Higginson to Horatio Woodman, Nov. 2, 1865, H. Woodman Papers, MHS; C. C. Parker to Lewis Parsons, July 25, 1865, Misc. Corr., Gov.'s Corr., AA; [Benham], *A Year of Wreck*, p. 21; Olsen, *Carpetbagger's Crusade*, p. 29; A. L. Gurney to E. D. Morgan, June 1, 1866, Records of the U.S. Senate, NA. Garth James informed his father, "We have [given] a great impetus to labor immediately, for in less than a month most of the planters about us were hiring Negroes themselves and starting their own farms." (Burr, ed., *Alice James*, p. 45.)

155. Morse, *Sketch*, p. 25; see also [Benham], *A Year of Wreck*, p. 14; Overy, *Wisconsin Carpetbaggers*, p. 11; Thomas Montgomery to Alexander Montgomery, Jan. 30,

1866, T. Montgomery Papers, MiHS; F. W. Bardwell to Eben Loomis, Aug. 31, 1866, Box 44, Todd Family Papers, YU.

156. G. W. James to "Willy" [James], March 10, 1866, in possession of Prof. William Childers, University of Florida; [Benham], *A Year of Wreck*, pp. 14, 137; Stearns, *The Black Man*, pp. 90-91; Reid, *After the War*, pp. 290-91; J. F. B. Marshall to T. B. Forbush, Mar. 14, 1867, SEC, NEEACo Papers, KSHS; D. D. Haskell to Gov. L. Parsons, Nov. 4, 1865, Gov.'s Corr., AA; Rose, *Rehearsal*, p. 226.

157. Sea Island Cotton Company, circular to stockholders, Sept. 15, 1866, Markham-Puffer Papers, CU; see also Smith, "Some Northern Wartime Attitudes," p. 261.

158. R. M. Moore to Gen. Wager Swayne, Apr. 15, 1867, Recon. Corr. of W. Swayne, AA.

159. Morgan, *Yazoo*, p. 25; John Hope Franklin, *Reconstruction After the Civil War* (Chicago, 1961), p. 95; *The Ku-Klux Conspiracy*, vol. 2, pt. 7, pp. 1081-82.

160. J. Y. Cantwell to John Sherman, Dec. 11, 1865, vol. 88, Sherman Papers, LC; Henry C. Thomas to J. D. Waters, May 20, 1865, Box 11, folder 7, Waters Family Papers, Essex Inst.

161. N. L. Williams to G. G. Klapp, May 21, 1865, Box 13, folder 7; see also N. L. Williams to the "Boys," Apr. 20, 1865, and Nov. 16, 1865, Box 11, folder 7, Waters Family Papers, Essex Inst.

162. Harris, *Presidential Reconstruction*, pp. 170-71; J. D. Waters to mother, Mar. 27, 1864, Box 12, folder 5, Waters Family Papers, Essex Inst.; J. F. B. Marshall to T. B. Forbush, Mar. 4, 1867, SEC, NEEACo Papers, KSHS; Morgan, *Yazoo*, p. 83; Shoalmire, "Carpetbagger Extraordinary," pp. 96-97.

163. [Benham], *A Year of Wreck*, pp. 16 and 21.

164. A. Winchell to F. A. Blades, Dec. 14, 1863, A. Winchell Letterbook, MiHS; see also A. B. Swayne to Gen. Wager Swayne, Jan. 15, 1866, Reid Papers, LC; Eben Loomis to Eliza, Jan. 10, 1866, Box 8, Todd Family Papers, YU; H. M. Crydenwise to parents, July 11, 1866, Crydenwise Papers, DU; *Harvard College Report of the Class of 1860* (Cambridge, Mass., 1866), p. 45; Chicago *Tribune*, Aug. 14, 1866; [n.n.] to editor, Feb. 27, 1866, in Boston *Daily Advertiser*, Mar. 12, 1866.

165. F. P. Blair, Jr., to Montgomery Blair, Jan. 14, 1866, Box 8; see also F. P. Blair, Jr., to wife, Nov. 21, 1865, Box 3; F. P. Blair, Jr., to F. P. Blair, Sr., Nov. 10, 1864, Box 1; F. P. Blair, Jr., to M. Blair, Mar. 29, 1865, and F. P. Blair, Jr., to F. P. Blair, Sr., Nov. 2, 1865, Box 7, Blair Family Papers, LC. His father, Frank Blair, Sr., was never keen on his son's plantation venture and thought it amounted to "throwing himself away." Nonetheless, he hoped his son's "cotton will in two years bring you $100,000 in gold and then you will put it in bonds and mortgages and live on the interest, and give your head and heart to the country." (F. P. Blair, Sr., to F. P. Blair, Jr., Feb. 1, 1867, Box 53, Blair Family Papers, LC.)

166. Marie B. Jones to Mary Loomis, Mar. 25, 1866, Box 8, Todd Family Papers, YU.

167. John Wilder to Mary Loomis, Mar. 27, 1866, Box 8, Todd Family Papers, YU; Blanche B. Ames, comp., *Chronicles from the Nineteenth Century: Family Letters of Blanche Butler and Adelbert Ames* ([n.p.], 1957), pp. 217-18. See also F. G. W. John to D. D. Slauson, Sept. 19, 1866, D. D. Slauson Papers, LSU; George S. Dennison to H. C. Warmoth, Oct. 21, 1865, Warmoth Papers, SHC.

168. J. D. Waters to H. F. Waters, Jan. 23, 1865, Box 8, JDW folder, H. F. Waters Papers; see also C. C. Waters to E. S. Waters, Apr. 6, 1865, Box 4, folder 3; N. L. Williams to Gill Klapp, May 21, 1865, Box 13, folder 7, Waters Family Papers, Essex Inst.

169. C. C. Waters to H. F. Waters, May 8, 1866, Box 8, CCW folder, H. F. Waters Papers, Essex Inst. Alexander Winchell of the University of Michigan had similar notions. He planned only a one-year sabbatical. "I expect that I may train some other person to manage the plantation thereafter in my absence and that I shall make only one or two visits in the year." (A. Winchell to F. A. Blades, Dec. 14, 1863, A. Winchell Letterbook, MiHS.)

170. For evidence of northern absenteeism, see W. Reid to Anna E. Dickinson, Mar. 27, 1867, A. E. Dickinson Papers, LC; W. L. McMillen to H. C. Warmoth, June 12, 1871, June 8, 1873, Warmoth Papers, SHC; New York *Herald*, May 23, June 13, 1866; *Ku-Klux Conspiracy*, vol. 2, pt. 7, pp. 1081-82; and William J. Barbee, *The Cotton Question* (New York, 1866), pp. 102 and 251.

171. Frederick J. Williams to Salmon P. Chase, Feb. 27, 1864, Gen. Corr., Record of the Direct Tax Commission for S.C., NA.

172. Overy, *Wisconsin Carpetbaggers,* pp. v-vi, 25-26, 56-57; the quotation is on p. vi. See also Richard N. Current, "Carpetbaggers Reconsidered," in David H. Pinkney and Theodore Ropp, eds., *A Festschrift for Frederick B. Artz* (Durham, N.C., 1964), p. 148.

173. J. D. Waters to W. D. Waters, Feb. 21, 1864, Box 10, folder 3, Waters Family Papers, Essex Inst.

174. Eugene Genovese, *The World the Slaveholders Made: Two Essays in Interpretation* (New York, 1969), p. 28.

175. A. Winchell Diary, Jan. 17, 1864, MHC.

Chapter 3

1. The variation in the figures is owing to the discrepancy between the amount of land listed in the "Sales Certificate" registers and the amount reported in the "Minutes" of the Direct Tax Sales Commission for South Carolina. The "Minutes" of December 1, 1863, note that 5,800 acres of plantation land were sold to private individuals, but I located no certificates for them in the records of transactions. My estimates derive from the following sources: "Tax Sales Certificates," Feb. 25, 1863-Apr. 17, 1865; "Army, Navy, or Marine Land Certificates," Jan. 19, 1864-Mar. 25, 1865; "Cash Sale Land Certificates," Jan. 21, 1864-Jan. 16, 1865; "Land Sale Certificates," Nov. 1, 1866-Jan. 12, 1876, all bound volumes. See also A. D. Smith to Salmon P. Chase, Apr. 2, 1863; William H. Brisbane to Joseph J. Lewis, Mar. 2, 1864, and Apr. 2, 1864, in "Minutes." Records of the Direct Tax Commission for South Carolina, NA. Also, William E. Wording to E. A. Rollins, Feb. 26, 1867, vol. 116, John Sherman Papers, LC; and William E. Wording to Thomas Harland, Mar. 25, 1867, Gen. Corr., Records of the Direct Tax Commission for South Carolina, NA.

2. Charles B. Wilder, the superintendent of contrabands at Fortress Monroe, was part of a group of Bostonians who bought six plantations in the area of Hampton, Virginia. Louis Gerteis, *From Contraband to Freedman: Federal Policy Toward Southern Blacks, 1861-1865* (Westport, Conn., 1973), pp. 46-47; "Letter From the Secretary of the Treasury," *House Executive Documents,* no. 47, 39 Cong., 1 sess. (Ser. 1255); see also copy of Direct Tax Sales for Fernandina, Florida, 1864-65, in the Samuel A. Swann Papers, FU.

3. Katherine M. Jones, ed., *Port Royal Under Six Flags* (New York, 1960), p. 301; Charleston *Daily Courier,* Feb. 23, 1866.

4. There were, of course, advertisements for sheriffs' sales of plantations. See, for example, Boston *Daily Advertiser,* Jan. 5, 1866.

5. Jimmy G. Shoalmire, "Carpetbagger Extraordinary: Marshall Harvey Twitchell, 1840-1905" (Ph.D. diss., Mississippi State University, 1969), pp. 93-4, 105; also Jerrell H. Shofner, *Nor Is It Over Yet: Florida in the Era of Reconstruction, 1863-1877* [Gainesville, Fla., 1974], p. 233.

6. John T. Trowbridge, *The South: A Tour of its Battle Fields and Ruined Cities* (New York, 1969), p. 580.

7. Trowbridge, *The South,* p. 191.

8. The quotation is in J. F. B. Marshall to E. E. Hale, Jan. 12, 1867, SEC, NEEACo Papers, KSHS; see also Boston *Daily Advertiser,* Oct. 30, 1865; Walter L. Fleming, *Civil War and Reconstruction in Alabama* (New York, 1905), p. 323; farewell address of William A. Marvin in *A Journal of the Proceedings of the House of Representatives of the General Assembly of the State of Florida at its Fourteenth Session* (Tallahassee, 1865), p. 24.

9. "Letter from New Orleans," Boston *Daily Advertiser,* May 7, 1866.

10. "The Southern Eldorado," *DeBow's Review,* AWS 1 (Mar. 1866), pp. 253-55; and Paul M. Gaston, *The New South Creed: A Study in Southern Mythmaking* (New York, 1970), p. 27.

11. Gainesville *New Era,* June 22, 1866 (for the quotation), and July 8, 1865. See also Selma *Daily Messenger,* Feb. 28, 1866; Macon *Journal and Messenger,* Nov. 28, 1865; Vicksburg *Weekly Herald,* Jan. 20, Mar. 3, 1866; Natchez *Democrat,* Oct. 10, 1865; Charleston *Daily Courier,* Mar. 3, 1866; Shofner, *Nor Is It Over Yet,* p. 259.

12. Henry Watson, Jr., to James Dixon, Dec. 27, 1865, Henry Watson, Jr., Papers, DU.

13. Augusta *Daily Constitutionalist*, July 29, 1865; Selma *Daily Messenger*, Sept. 25, Nov. 22, 1866; Gainesville *New Era*, Aug. 17, 1866; and Gaston, *New South Creed*, pp. 17-42.

14. Boston *Daily Advertiser*, Oct. 2, 1865; Roger P. Leemhuis, "James L. Orr: The Civil War and Reconstruction Years" (Ph.D. diss., University of Wisconsin, 1970), pp. 140-41; Gaston, *New South Creed*, p. 23.

15. James L. Sellers, "The Economic Incidence of the Civil War in the South," in Ralph Andreano, ed., *The Economic Impact of the American Civil War*, 2d ed. (Cambridge, Mass., 1967), p. 101.

16. Ibid., pp. 101-03.

17. Ibid., pp. 104-05; Robert P. Sharkey, *Money, Class and Party: An Economic Study of Civil War and Reconstruction* (Baltimore, 1959), p. 235; George L. Anderson, "The South and Problems of Post-Civil War Finance," *Journal of Southern History* 9 (May 1943): 181-95.

18. Pierce Butler to P. C. Hollis, May 29, 1866, and July 3, 1866, Box "O," folder 4, Butler Family Papers, Hist. Soc. of Pa.; Nicholas B. Wainwright, ed., *A Philadelphia Perspective: The Diary of Sidney George Fisher Covering the Years 1834-1871* (Philadelphia, 1967), p. 507; James L. Roark, *Masters Without Slaves: Southern Planters in the Civil War and Reconstruction* (New York, 1977), p. 137.

19. J. T. McMurran to Stephen Duncan, July 22, 1865, Stephen Duncan Papers, LSU; William C. Harris, *Presidential Reconstruction in Mississippi* (Baton Rouge, La., 1967), p. 77; Charleston *Daily Courier*, Feb. 24, 1866; see also John R. Dennett, *The South As It Is, 1865-1866*, ed. Henry M. Christman (New York, 1965), p. 311.

20. One example is the blanket mortgage, which, by covering everything movable and immovable on a plantation, guaranteed that such estates that changed hands by process of foreclosure did so as undivided units. (Roger Shugg, *Origins of Class Struggle in Louisiana* [Baton Rouge, La., 1939], pp. 250-51.)

21. Harold D. Woodman, *King Cotton and His Retainers: Financing and Marketing the Cotton Crop of the South, 1800-1925* (Lexington, Ky., 1968), pp. 247-51.

22. See, for example, Boston *Daily Advertiser*, Jan. 2, 1866; New York *Tribune*, Oct. 11, 1865; and Smallwood-Hodgkins & Company to William H. Branch, Aug. 4, 1866, folder 11, Branch Family Papers, SHC.

23. Florida *Union*, Oct. 14, 1865, and July 22, 1865; Selma *Daily Messenger*, Nov. 25, 1866; Natchez *Democrat*, Dec. 5, 1865; Charleston *Daily Courier*, Jan. 30 and 31, 1866; C. Mildred Thompson, *Reconstruction in Georgia: Economic, Social, Political, 1865-1872* (New York, 1915), p. 89.

24. Charles Stearns, *The Black Man of the South and the Rebels* (Boston, 1872), p. 161; see also Whitelaw Reid, *After the War: A Tour of the Southern States, 1865-1866*, ed. C. Vann Woodward (New York, 1965), pp. 343-44.

25. Reid, *After the War*, p. 381; Dennett, *The South As It Is*, p. 307.

26. Benjamin P. Colburn to E. W. Bonney, Nov. 1866, Eli W. Bonney Papers, DU; "Description of a Plantation for Sale," Oct. 7, 1865, Thomas Affleck Papers, LSU; A. H. Cole to Edward Atkinson, Jan. 11, 1867, Edward Atkinson Papers, MHS; John Murray Forbes's notes on southern lands [c. Nov. 1866], SEC, NEAACo Papers, KSHS; Gainesville *New Era*, Aug. 12, 1865; Boston *Daily Advertiser*, Jan. 2, 1866.

27. J. Floyd King to Lin [Caperton], Nov. 21, 1865, Series A, Thomas Butler King Papers, SHC; J. Parsons to Mrs. David Yulee, Oct. 10, 1865, David Yulee Papers, FU.

28. William Clifford to John A. Andrew, Sept. 27, 1865, John A. Andrew Papers, MHS; "The Southern Eldorado," *DeBow's Review*, AWS 1 (Mar. 1866), pp. 253-55.

29. Boston *Daily Advertiser*, Dec. 4, 1865, Jan. 18, 1866; William H. Quincy to Lewis Parsons, Oct. 16, 1865, and Samuel C. Reed to Robert Patton, June 14, 1866, both in Gov.'s Corr.; and J. L. Register to Lewis Parsons, July 29, 1865, Gov.'s Misc. Corr., all in AA.

30. New York *Tribune*, Oct. 11, 1865; Flory & DeFrance to C. D. Hamilton, Mar. 28, 1866, C. D. Hamilton Letterbooks, MA; Trowbridge, *The South*, pp. 380-81.

31. J. M. Heck to K. P. Battle, Sept. 4, 1865, Battle Family Papers, SHC; Gainesville *New Era*, Oct. 7, 1865; Boston *Daily Advertiser*, Sept. 12, 1865. Battle and Heck relinquished their interests in the General Southern Land Agency in Oct. 1865, to New

York capitalists in order to devote full time to their North Carolina Land Agency, which seemed to be doing a good business. ("General Southern Land Agency Circular," Nov. 22, 1865, Battle Family Papers, SHC.) See also the Florida *Union*, Oct. 14, 1865, for an account of the Southern Real Estate and Emigration Company.

32. Augusta *Daily Constitutionalist*, Feb. 2, 1866; Reid, *After the War*, p. 211; Kenneth M. Clark to Lewis Thompson, Aug. 27, 1865, Lewis Thompson Papers, SHC.

33. Henry Watson, Jr., to Sereno Watson, Dec. 10, 1865, and H. Watson, Jr., to [Sereno Watson?], Jan. 2, 1866, both in Henry Watson, Jr., Papers, DU.

34. George J. Kollock to wife, May 15, 1866, folder 10, Kollock Family Papers, Ga. Hist. Soc.; J. Parsons to Mrs. David Yulee, Oct. 10, 1865, David Yulee Papers, FU; Boston *Daily Advertiser*, Jan. 5, 1866; Mary Granger, ed., *Savannah River Plantations* (Savannah, Ga., 1947), p. 160.

35. J. Floyd King to Lin [Caperton], Dec. 24, 1865, Jan. 18, 1866, Series A, Thomas Butler King Papers, SHC.

36. *DeBow's Review*, AWS 2 (Sept. 1866), pp. 335-36, AWS 3 (Apr. and May 1867), pp. 453-54; Harris, *Presidential Reconstruction*, pp. 168-69; "Circular of the American Land Company and Agency" [1866], MHS; W. Hutchinson to C. D. Hamilton [n.d.], Charles D. Hamilton Papers, MA; Charles S. Wylly, *The Seed That Was Sown in the Colony of Georgia: The Harvest and the Aftermath* (New York and Washington, D.C., 1910), p. 82; John Q. Anderson, ed., *Brokenburn: The Journal of Kate Stone, 1861-1868* (Baton Rouge, La., 1955), p. 368.

37. Walter Goodman to Gov. Benjamin G. Humphreys, Dec. 11, 1865, vol. 77, Gov.'s Corr., MA; Boston *Daily Advertiser*, Dec. 4, 1865.

38. The agent whom the association sent to Europe was also the overseas representative of the United States Cotton Company, the northern firm that had sizable interests in the South Carolina Sea Islands. Mary Wilkin, ed., "Some Papers of the American Cotton Planters' Association, 1865-1866," *Tennessee Historical Quarterly* 7 (Dec. 1948):335-61, 8 (Mar. 1949), pp. 49-62; Woodman, *King Cotton*, p. 252.

39. Charleston *Daily Courier*, Mar. 9, 1866; Ralph S. Elliott to Emmie, Jan. 28, 1866, Elliott-Gonzales Papers, SHC.

40. Reid, *After the War*, pp. 414-15; Dennett, *The South As It Is*, p. 307; *DeBow's Review*, AWS 3 (Apr. and May 1867), p. 453; entry of Nov. 16, 1865, diary, "1862," Whitelaw Reid Papers, LC; entry of Mar. 9, 1866, John Berkeley Grimball Diaries, SHC; J. Floyd King to Mallory [King], Jan. 18, 1866, Series A, Thomas Butler King Papers, SHC; Boston *Daily Advertiser*, Dec. 30, 1865; Harris, *Presidential Reconstruction* pp. 168-69.

41. "Circular of the American Land Company and Agency" [1866], MHS; Gainesville *New Era*, Feb. 17, 1866; 1857-58 Diary, pp. 95-97, John Fripp Diaries, SHC; Arney R. Childs, ed., *The Private Journal of Henry William Ravenel, 1859-1887* (Columbia, S.C., 1947), p. 257.

42. J. Floyd King to Mallory [King], Jan. 18, 1866, Series A, T. B. King Papers, SHC; Wilkin, ed., "Some Papers of the American Cotton Planters' Association," pp. 344-47.

43. Quoted in Harris, *Presidential Reconstruction*, p. 169; *DeBow's Review*, AWS 2 (Sept. 1866), p. 336; Reid, *After the War*, pp. 414-15; P. M. Nightingale to John Murray Forbes, Oct. 1, 1866, SEC, NEEACo Papers, KSHS; Charleston *Daily Courier*, Jan. 30, 1866.

44. Ralph S. Elliott to Emmie, Jan. 28, 1866, Elliot-Gonzales Papers. See also R. H. Colcock to James [Gregorie], Oct. 8, 1865, Gregorie-Elliott Papers, both in SHC.

45. James B. Heyward to William Heyward, Mar. 16, 1866, Heyward-Ferguson Papers, SHC; [Benham], *A Year of Wreck*, p. 152.

46. Battle, Heck & Company to "Dear Sir," June 26, 1865, Battle Family Papers, SHC; E. C. Cabell to editor, New York *Tribune*, Sept. 29, 1865; *DeBow's Review*, AWS 2 (July 1866), p. 40; Chicago *Tribune*, Aug. 14, 1866.

47. William H. Heyward to James B. Heyward, Apr. 17, 1866, Heyward-Ferguson Papers, SHC; Robert M. Myers, ed., *The Children of Pride* (New Haven and London, 1972), p. 1307.

48. Amos Whitehead to William H. Branch, Aug. 16, 1866, folder 11, Branch Family Papers, SHC. A Florida businessman wrote of his fears "for the state of society at the South" and thought "t'would be well for those of us who can, to emigrate if not entirely

from the country at least to one of the original free states." (Samuel A. Swann to D. McRae, June 23, 1865, Samuel A. Swann Letterbooks, FU.)

49. Francis P. Fleming to Aunt Tilly, May 3, 1865, Francis P. Fleming Papers, University of South Florida; F. F. L'Engle to E. M. L'Engle, June 26, 1867, folder 7, E. M. L'Engle Papers, SHC.

50. Reid, *After the War*, pp. 211 and 291; Augusta *Daily Constitutionalist*, Dec. 13, 1865; Savannah *Republican*, June 16, 1865; Rose, *Rehearsal*, p. 351; Roark, *Masters Without Slaves*, pp. 122-23.

51. John H. Parrish to Henry Watson, Jr., July 30, 1865, Henry Watson, Jr., Papers, DU; a committee of citizens, "The Future of South Carolina—Her Inviting Resources," *DeBow's Review*, AWS 2 (July 1866), p. 40; Boston *Daily Advertiser*, July 24, 1865; Reid, *After the War*, p. 291; John Murray Forbes's notes on southern lands [c. Nov. 1866], SEC, NEEACo Papers, KSHS.

52. Gainesville, *New Era*, Nov. 11, 1865.

53. Chicago *Tribune*, Aug. 14, 1866. The Charles Colcock Jones family of Liberty County, Georgia, were among those extensive planters who tried to sell part of their land, but only those places where the freedmen were giving the most trouble. (Myers, ed., *The Children of Pride*, p. 1311.)

54. Joel Williamson, *After Slavery: The Negro in South Carolina During Reconstruction, 1861-1877* (Chapel Hill, 1965), pp. 69-70; Vernon L. Wharton, *The Negro in Mississippi, 1865-1890* (New York, 1965), pp. 48-49; Roark, *Masters Without Slaves*, pp. 111-55.

55. Hugh Lawson Clay to Clement C. Clay, Apr. 23, 1866, Clement C. Clay Papers, DU.

56. Mrs. C. C. Eustis to William Minor, Dec. 4, 1865, William J. Minor and Family Papers, LSU; D. C. Clark to Lewis Thompson, Dec. 23, 1865, Lewis Thompson Papers, SHC.

57. Williamson, *After Slavery*, pp. 34-38; Eugene D. Genovese, *Roll, Jordan, Roll: The World the Slaves Made* (New York, 1974), pp. 97-112; Roark, *Masters Without Slaves*, pp. 106, 123-24.

58. Augusta *Daily Constitutionalist*, Dec. 13, 1865, Feb. 2, 1866.

59. J. C. Delavigne, "The Future of the South," *DeBow's Review*, AWS 5 (Apr. 1868), p. 393; "A Friendly Kentuckian to the Planters of Montgomery County, Alabama," Augusta *Daily Constitutionalist*, Sept. 8, 1865; Selma *Daily Times*, Aug. 7, 1865; Joe Gray Taylor, *Louisiana Reconstructed, 1863-1877* (Baton Rouge, La., 1974), pp. 315-16; Reid, *After the War*, p. 151.

60. Reid, *After the War*, p. 564.

61. Reid, *After the War* pp. 374 and 427; Gainesville *New Era*, Aug. 12, 1865; Boston *Daily Advertiser*, Aug. 3, 7, 1865; Rufus Barringer to K. P. Battle, July 18, 1865, Battle Family Papers, SHC; *The Report of the Joint Committee on Reconstruction*, 39 Cong., 1 sess. (Ser. 1273), 3, pp. 6, 19.

62. Reid, *After the War*, p. 397.

63. Reid, *After the War*, pp. 382, 414-15, 454-55, 480; [Benham], *A Year of Wreck*, p. 138; Albert T. Morgan, *Yazoo; Or, On the Picket Line of Freedom in the South* (Washington, D.C., 1884), pp. 26-27; E. McBurrus to C. D. Hamilton, Nov. 3, 1866, C. D. Hamilton Letterbooks, MA; D. M. Hayden to [n.n.], Oct. 2, 1866, Gay Family Papers, LSU; William D. Waters to Clifford C. Waters, Jan. 24, 1865, Box 13, folder 1, and Clifford C. Waters to Edward S. Waters, Jan. 24, 1866, Box 4, folder 3, both in Waters Family Papers, Essex Inst.; agreement between Alfred V. Davis and George Gilson Klapp, Feb. 16, 1864, Good Hope Plantation Papers, LSU; F. King to Mallory [King], Jan. 18, 1866, Series A, T. B. King Papers, SHC; C. W. Walker to Whitelaw Reid, Apr. 14, 1869, Reid Papers, LC; Gainesville *New Era*, Feb. 17, 1866.

64. Agreement between William H. Trescot and Henry S. Sanford, Jan. 1, 1868, Box 33, folder 3, Henry S. Sanford Papers, Sanford Memorial Library, Sanford, Fla.

65. Stephen Elliott to cousin, Aug. 2, 1865, Elliott-Gonzales Papers, SHC.

66. Alex R. Lawton to father, Nov. 27, 1865, Alexander R. Lawton Papers, SHC.

67. Selma *Daily Messenger*, Mar. 13, 1866; Reid, *After the War*, p. 382; entry of Nov. 12, 1865, diary, "1862," Whitelaw Reid Papers, LC; A. Warren Kelsey to Edward Atkinson, Nov. 20, 1865, Atkinson Papers, MHS; *Report of the Joint Committee*, 3, p. 29. It is likely that some of the new men were Confederate veterans from other parts of the South.

68. [Benham], *A Year of Wreck*, p. 138. See also "Cotton and the Cotton Trade," *DeBow's Review*, AWS 3 (Apr. and May 1867), p. 451; (Greensboro) *Alabama Beacon*, Feb.

16, 1866; see, for example, the advertisement of W. Dix & Company in the Natchez *Democrat*, Dec. 5, 1865.

69. Trowbridge, *The South*, p. 384; *Report of the Joint Committee*, 3, p. 44.

70. Shofner, *Nor Is It Over Yet*, p. 133.

71. Harris, *Presidential Reconstruction*, pp. 165-66; Shugg, *Origins of Class Struggle*, pp. 245-46.

72. Quoted in Barbee, *The Cotton Question*, p. 250. A recent study of the wealthiest planters in five black-belt counties in Alabama for the period 1850-70 shows that over 40 percent of this class maintained their elite status through the decade of war, defeat, emancipation, and Reconstruction. The rate of persistence was only slightly less than that for the same group during the 1850s. Whether these rich planters did as well in the decade of the 1870s, especially following the Panic of 1873, is another question. A good guess is that they probably did persist to the same degree, though in greatly depressed circumstances. Jonathan M. Wiener, "Planter Persistence and Social Change: Alabama, 1850-1870," *Journal of Interdisciplinary History* 7 (Autumn 1976): 235-60; see also Roark, *Masters Without Slaves*, pp. 170-80.

73. *Report of the Joint Committee 3*, p. 29.

74. Reid, *After the War*, pp. 455 (for the quotation) and 579; Harris, *Presidential Reconstruction*, pp. 165-66; Shofner, *Nor Is It Over Yet*, p. 132; [Benham], *A Year of Wreck*, p. 152.

75. J. Floyd King to Lin [Caperton], Dec. 24, 1865, Series A, Thomas Butler King Papers, SHC; Boston *Daily Advertiser*, Oct. 26, 1865; Vicksburg *Weekly Herald*, Dec. 23, 1865.

76. Reid, *After the War*, p. 382. See also Chicago *Tribune*, Jan. 16, 1866; New York *Times*, July 2, 1866.

77. "Whitelaw Reid," *Scribner's Monthly* 8 (Aug. 1874): 447; for more on absentee lessees see G. Colhoun to Stephen Duncan, Apr. 15, 1865, Stephen Duncan Papers, LSU; and Barbee, *The Cotton Question*, pp. 102 and 251.

78. R. J. H., "Trip to Northern Alabama," *The Nation*, Aug. 17, 1865, p. 208.

79. This estimate is based on an analysis of the "Mississippi Plantation Register–1864," vol. 330 (entry 2385), BRFAL Records, NA.

80. "Circular" from General Lorenzo Thomas, Oct. 27, 1863, in "Applications for Lease of Abandoned Plantations" (entry 2383), BRFAL Records, NA.

81. The quotation is in William J. Minor to Stephen Duncan, Aug. 16, 1865, Stephen Duncan Papers, LSU; see also *Report of the Joint Committee 4*, p. 142. For an illuminating economic portrait of the great planters of Natchez, see Morton Rothstein, "The Antebellum South as a Dual Economy: A Tentative Hypothesis," *Agricultural History* 41 (October 1967): 373-82.

82. Stephen Duncan, Jr., to father, Dec. 23, 1863, Stephen Duncan Papers, LSU. The Duncan papers from 1862 to 1865 contain cotton accounts with merchants in Liverpool, England. See also John Minor to father, Mar. 1, 1864, William Minor Papers, LSU.

83. James D. Waters to mother, Feb. 12, 1864, Box 12, folder 5, Waters Family Papers, Essex Inst.; see also Wainwright, ed., *A Philadelphia Perspective*, p. 467.

84. Knox *Camp-Fire and Cotton-Field*, pp. 342-44; "Mississippi Plantation Register–1864," vol. 330 (entry 2385); "Register of Leased Plantations– 1865" (entry 532), pp. 1-9; both in BRFAL Records, NA.

85. Agreement between Alfred V. Davis and George Gilson Klapp, Feb. 16, 1864, Good Hope Plantation Papers, LSU; Stephen Duncan to General [James B.] McPherson, Dec. 14, 1863, filed under John Heath application in "Applications for Lease of Abandoned Plantations" (entry 2383), BRFAL Records, NA.

86. James D. Waters to mother, Feb. 12, 1864, Box 12, folder 5, Waters Family Papers, Essex Inst.; Knox, *Camp-Fire and Cotton-Field*, p. 339; David H. Overy, Jr., *Wisconsin Carpetbaggers in Dixie* (Madison, Wis., 1961), p. 19.

87. Entry of Mar. 24, 1864, Isaac Shoemaker Diary, DU; H. Brown to J. P. Williston, Feb. 16, 1864, Atkinson Papers, MHS; Knox, *Camp-Fire and Cotton-Field*, pp. 317, 324, 339, 340-42; Horace S. Fulkerson, *A Civilian's Recollections of the War Between the States*, ed. by P. L. Rainwater (Baton Rouge, La., 1939), pp. 173-75.

88. Entries of May 2, 4, 1864, Shoemaker Diary, DU; Knox, *Camp-Fire and Cotton-Field*, pp. 317, 448-49; Bell I Wiley, *Southern Negroes, 1861-1865* (New Haven, Conn.,

1938 [1965]), p. 242; Fulkerson, *A Civilian's Recollections*, pp. 178-87, and especially pp. 172-77, for an amusing story of how a Confederate mother secured the release of her Yankee lessee from guerrilla captivity.

89. Entries of May 9, 10, 1864, June 4, 5, 1864, Nov. 15, 1864 (where the quotation appears), and an unidentified newspaper clipping (c. May 1864), Alexander Winchell Diary, and A. Winchell to Zachariah Chandler, May 2, 1864, A. Winchell and Family Papers, all in the MHC. See also A. Winchell to C. A. Montross, Dec. 16, 1864, Alexander Winchell Letterbook, MiHS.

90. Entry of May 10, 1864, A. Winchell Diary, MHC; A. Winchell to Captain Bestwick, Dec. 12, 1864, and A. Winchell to C. A. Montross, Dec. 16, 1864, A. Winchell Letterbook, MiHS; Knox, *Camp-Fire and Cotton-Field*, pp. 329, 402-03; Wiley, *Southern Negroes*, pp. 242-44.

91. Stephen Minor to William Minor, March 21, 1864, William J. Minor and Family Papers, LSU; *Report of the Joint Committee*, 4, pp. 140-41; Lorenzo Thomas to Edwin M. Stanton, Sept. 5, 1863, L. Thomas Letterbook, AGO-Generals Papers, NA.

92. Henry C. Minor to father, Mar. 23, 1864; and R. A. Minor to William Minor, March 30, 1864, William J. Minor and Family Papers, LSU.

93. Knox, *Camp-Fire and Cotton-Field*, p. 329. In 1864 Henry Thomas, the general's son, leased Arnandalia plantation, just across the river from Natchez, while his companions, James D. Waters and G. G. Klapp, leased the neighboring Tacony plantation. Both places were considered highly desirable from the standpoint of safety and repair. (James D. Waters to Edward S. Waters, Feb. 1, 1864, Box 4, folder 5; and J. D. Waters to mother, Feb. 12, 1864, Box 12, folder 5, Waters Family Papers, Essex Inst.)

94. Lorenzo Thomas to Edwin M. Stanton, Sept. 5, 1863, Oct. 24, 1863, L. Thomas Letterbook, AGO-Generals Papers, NA. On the functioning of military governors in the occupied Confederacy, see William B. Hesseltine, *Lincoln's Plan of Reconstruction* (Chicago, 1960 [1967]), pp. 48-72.

95. Lorenzo Thomas to William P. Mellen, Feb. 22, 1865, Box 8, letters received, W. P. Mellen Papers, Civil War Special Agency Records, NA; *Report of the Joint Committee*, 4, p. 144.

96. Henry C. Thomas to James D. Waters, Sept. 16, 1865, Box 11, folder 7, Waters Family Papers, Essex Inst.

97. William E. Smith, *The Francis Preston Blair Family in Politics*, 2 vols. (New York, 1969), 2, pp. 334-35; William Polk to Francis P. Blair, Jr., July 3, 1866, Box 3, Blair Family Papers, LC. At least two other Union generals had plantation interests in the area—Francis J. Herron and Elias S. Dennis. (Ezra J. Warner, *Generals in Blue: Lives of the Union Commanders* [Baton Rouge, La., 1964], pp. 118-19, 228-29.)

98. C. Peter Ripley, *Slaves and Freedmen in Civil War Louisiana* (Baton Rouge, La., 1976), pp. 22-23. Exemption from the provisions of the Confiscation Act of 1862 and the Emancipation Proclamation was no great relief for the slaveholders in federally occupied Louisiana. The slaves would settle for nothing less than compensation in one form or another.

99. Stephen Duncan, Jr., to father, Dec. 23, 1863, and Jan. 11, 1863 [1864]; Z. Preston to Stephen Duncan, Dec. 28, 1865, Stephen Duncan Papers, LSU.

100. William J. Minor to Stephen Duncan, Aug. 16, 1865, Stephen Duncan Papers, LSU.

101. Z. Preston to Stephen Duncan, Aug. 16, 1865, Stephen Duncan Papers, LSU. See also James D. Waters to mother, Feb. 12, 1864, Box 12, folder 5, Waters Family Papers, Essex Inst.; Overy, *Wisconsin Carpetbaggers*, p. 19.

102. Stephen Minor to William Minor, Mar. 21, 1864, William J. Minor and Family Papers, LSU; Knox, *Camp-Fire and Cotton-Field*, p. 325.

103. G. G. Klapp to James D. Waters, Oct. 8, 1865, Box 11, folder 7, Waters Family Papers, Essex Inst.

104. Charles E. Cauthen, ed., *Family Letters of the Three Wade Hamptons, 1782-1901* (Columbia, S.C., 1953), p. 118; "Mississippi Plantation Register—1864," vol. 330 (entry 2385), BRFAL Papers, NA.

105. Edward C. Anderson to Robert Gourdin, Oct. 18, 1865, Robert Newman Gourdin Papers, EU; Armistead Burt to wife, Jan. 20, 1866, Armistead Burt Papers, DU.

106. Boston *Daily Advertiser,* Dec. 20, 1866. See also "Report of the Commissioner of the Bureau of Refugees, Freedmen and Abandoned Lands," November 1, 1866, *House Executive Documents,* no. 1, 39 Cong., 2 sess. (Ser. 1285), p. 276.

107. J. Floyd King to Lin [Caperton], Feb. 28, 1866, Series A, Thomas Butler King Papers, SHC; application of Robert C. and Charles H. Nichols, Jan. 13, 1866, "Applications for Restoration of Property" (entry 1022), BRFAL Papers, NA.

108. John Murray Forbes's notes on southern lands [c. Nov. 1866], SEC, NEEACo Papers, KSHS; W. D. Holden to Gov. Benjamin G. Humphreys, Feb. 16, 1866, vol. 78, Gov.'s Corr., MA; Fleming, *Civil War and Reconstruction,* p. 717; John Wilder to Eben Loomis, Dec. 29, 1865, Box 8, Todd Family Papers, YU.

109. Dennett, *The South As It Is,* p. 265; see also Trowbridge, *The South,* p. 365.

110. Reid, *After the War,* pp. 362-63; Henry Watson, Jr., to Walter S. Pitkin, Dec. 22, 1865, Henry Watson, Jr., Papers, DU; see also Georgia Smith to Lin [Caperton], Jan. 15, 1866, Series A, Thomas Butler King Papers, SHC.

111. Stephen Elliott to cousin, Aug. 2, 1865, Elliott-Gonzales Papers; see also Alexander R. Lawton to father, Nov. 27, 1865, Alexander R. Lawton Papers, both in SHC.

112. John M. Bonner to S. Lafayette Bonner, Jan. 28, 1866, S. C. Bonner Papers, LSU; Morgan, *Yazoo,* pp. 75-6; Trowbridge, *The South,* p. 365.

113. [Benham], *A Year of Wreck,* p. 137.

114. [Benham], *A Year of Wreck,* pp. 338-39; *Report of the Joint Committee,* 3, p. 98; Benjamin C. Truman Report, *Senate Executive Documents,* no. 43, 39 Cong., 1 sess. (Ser. 1283), p. 7.

115. Reid, *After the War,* p. 559; Harris, *Presidential Reconstruction,* p. 98.

116. Henry M. Crydenwise to parents, Apr. 3 [1866], and Feb. 11, 1866, in the Henry M. Crydenwise Papers at DU and EU, respectively.

117. [Benham], *A Year of Wreck,* pp. 180 and 234; Clifford C. Waters to mother, Mar. 1, 1866, Box 12, folder 4, Waters Family Papers, Essex Inst. Some officers of black troops who became planters on their own account simply used their former soldiers as hands. See Truman Report, *Senate Executive Documents,* p. 7; John Wilder to Eben Loomis, Dec. 29, 1865, Box 8, Todd Family Papers, YU; and Edward M. Main, *The Story of the Marches, Battles, and Incidents of the Third U.S. Colored Cavalry* (New York, 1970), p. 55.

118. New York *Times,* Feb. 4, 1866. A cotton grower in Louisiana agreed to give a Union officer one-tenth of the crop for supplying his plantation with fifteen first-class hands. (D. D. Slauson and W. H. Carroll to J. N. Chambers, Dec. 23, 1866, and J. N. Chambers to F. A. Stickle, Jan. 7, 1867, D. D. Slauson Papers, LSU.)

119. New York *Herald,* Aug. 28, 1865. Discharged soldiers were also in demand as overseers in Montgomery County, Alabama. See Wager Swayne to A. F. Perry, Aug. 2, 1865, ibid.; also July 17, 1865.

120. R. S. E[lliott] to Emmie, Dec. 19, 1866, Elliott-Gonzales Papers, SHC; *Report of the Joint Committee,* 3, p. 6.

121. A. W. Kelsey to Edward Atkinson, Jan. 7, 1866, Edward Atkinson Papers, MHS; Dennett, *The South As It Is,* pp. 307 and 354; Sidney Andrews, *The South Since the War,* ed. David Donald (Boston, 1971), pp. 385, 390-91.

122. Boston *Daily Advertiser,* Dec. 24, 1866, and Aug. 3, 7, 1865.

123. *Report of the Joint Committee,* 2, p. 125, and 3, p. 20.

124. E. C. Johnston to Susan, Feb. 25, 1866, folder 10, Kollock Family Papers, Ga. Hist. Soc.; [Benham], *A Year of Wreck,* p. 37.

125. George Torrey to Gov. Benjamin G. Humphreys, Mar. 29, 1866, vol. 78, Gov.'s Corr., MA. Before the war some plantation owners feared that emancipation would result in their being "crushed by the superior force of northern capital or absorbed into them." (Eugene D. Genovese, *The Political Economy of Slavery* [New York, 1965], p. 268.)

126. M. A. Thomas to Mrs. Gay, June 9, 1866, Gay Family Papers, LSU.

127. Bammie to Ema, June 14, 1866, S. C. Bonner Papers, LSU; Ella Lonn, *Reconstruction in Louisiana After 1868* (New York and London, 1918), pp. 11-12; R. S. E[lliott] to Emma, Dec. 19, 1866, Elliott-Gonzales Papers, SHC.

128. Richmond *Times,* quoted in Boston *Daily Advertiser,* Dec. 22, 1866; T. P. Neale to R. N. Gourdin, July 20, 1865, Robert Newman Gourdin Papers, EU.

129. Stephen R. Mallory to Ruby [Mallory], June 15, 1866, Stephen R. Mallory

Papers, SHC; Reid, *After the War*, p. 378. Mallory eventually underwent a change of heart, taking on as a law partner a carpetbagger from Vermont. (*Makers of America: Florida Edition* [Atlanta, 1909], 1, pp. 281-83.)

130. The quotation is in the Boston *Daily Advertiser*, Dec. 30, 1865; Selma *Daily Messenger*, Feb. 28, 1866; Williamson, *After Slavery*, p. 118; Gainesville *New Era*, Aug. 12, 1865.

131. John L. Helm to Gov. Charles J. Jenkins, Nov. 10, 1866, Charles Jones Jenkins Folder, GA. See also [Benham], *A Year of Wreck*, p. 139; *Florida Union*, quoted in *DeBow's Review*, AWS 4 (July and Aug. 1867), pp. 134-35; Selma *Daily Messenger*, Feb. 28, 1866.

132. William H. Trescot to wife, Feb. 9, 1866, William H. Trescot Papers (typescript), SCL.

133. R. H. Colcock to cousin James [Gregorie], Oct. 8, 1865, Gregorie-Elliott Papers, SHC; Earl S. Miers, ed., *When the World Ended: The Diary of Emma LeConte* (New York, 1957), p. 112.

134. Randall Croft to Gov. James L. Orr, Nov. 3, 1866, Gov. James L. Orr Papers, SCA; Harris, *Presidential Reconstruction*, p. 176.

135. Reid, *After the War*, pp. 343, 372-73.

136. Edward C. Anderson to Robert N. Gourdin, Oct. 18, 1865, Robert N. Gourdin Papers, EU; see also Stephen Elliott to cousin, Aug. 2, 1865, Elliott-Gonzales Papers, SHC.

137. G. Calhoun to Stephen Duncan, Oct. 21, 1865, Stephen Duncan Papers, LSU. See also Gainesville *New Era*, July 22, 1865; New York *Herald*, June 24, 1866; Morgan, *Yazoo*, p. 60.

138. Florida *Union*, quoted in *DeBow's Review*, AWS 4 (July and Aug. 1867), pp. 134-35; Gainesville *New Era*, July 22, 1865.

139. Armistead Burt to wife, July 2, 1866, Armistead Burt Papers, DU; see also Hiram Cassedy to William N. Whitehurst, Dec. 16, 1866, William N. Whitehurst Papers, MA.

140. Henry Watson, Jr., to Walter S. Pitkin, Dec. 22, 1865, Henry Watson, Jr., Papers, DU. See also Andrews, *The South Since The War*, pp. 389-400; Eliza F. Andrews, *The Wartime Journal of a Georgia Girl, 1864-1865* (New York, 1908), p. 278; Trowbridge, *The South*, p. 573; Reid, *After the War*, pp. 343-44.

141. *DeBow's Review*, AWS 2 (Oct. 1866), pp. 354-55; Roark, *Masters Without Slaves*, pp. 95-96.

142. *DeBow's Review*, AWS 4 (July and Aug. 1867), pp. 134-35, 150.

143. The quotation is in ibid., AWS 2 (Oct. 1866), p. 354; Gainesville, *New Era*, July 8 and 22, 1865; Richmond *Times*, in Boston *Daily Advertiser*, Dec. 22, 1866; Reid, *After the War*, p. 346.

144. [Benham], *A Year of Wreck*, p. 139. See also Vicksburg *Weekly Herald*, Dec. 23, 1865, Jan. 13, 1866, Feb. 10, 1866, and Mar. 3, 1866; Augusta *Daily Constitutionalist*, Jan. 27, 1866; Gainesville *New Era*, Dec. 9, 1865, and Jan. 27, 1866; *DeBow's Review*, AWS 2 (July 1866), p. 91.

145. Selma *Daily Messenger*, Feb. 28, Apr. 15, 1866; see also "Letter From Jackson," Vicksburg *Weekly Herald*, Mar. 10, 1866; Natchez *Democrat*, Oct. 10, 1865.

146. Some of the most unreconstructed "rebels" Whitelaw Reid talked with were antebellum Yankee settlers. "I'm tired of this crowd of Yankees that is pouring down here," one of them told Reid. "The more I see of them, the more I am convinced that they are a totally different class of people, and can never assimilate with us Southerners." (Reid, *After the War*, p. 378; see also [Benham], *A Year of Wreck*, pp. 44-45.) For a useful survey of some distinguished prewar northern settlers, see Fletcher M. Green, *The Role of the Yankee in the Old South* (Athens, Ga., 1972).

147. Entry of Nov. 8, 1865, Diary, "1862," Whitelaw Reid Papers, LC; see also Reid, *After the War*, pp. 345-46; Selma *Daily Messenger*, Feb. 28, 1866.

148. Quoted in Harris, *Presidential Reconstruction*, p. 168. The fact that Albert T. Morgan avowedly came south to make money seemed to assuage the apprehensions of his southern landlord. (Morgan, *Yazoo*, p. 31.)

149. Not enough attention has been given to the practice in the New South of leasing land to white men who in turn sublet it to black tenants. For evidence of this arrangement, which may have originated in the leasing of plantations to northerners during and shortly

after the war, see Peter Kolchin, *First Freedom: The Responses of Alabama's Blacks to Emancipation and Reconstruction* (Westport, Ct., 1972), p. 47; Theodore Rosengarten, ed., *All God's Dangers: The Life of Nate Shaw* (New York, 1974), passim.

Chapter 4

1. Quoted in Howard K. Beale, *The Critical Year: A Study of Andrew Johnson and Reconstruction* (New York, 1958), p. 161.

2. Northern settlers in the South during presidential Reconstruction have not received nearly the scholarly attention paid to carpetbagger politicians, who, all historians agree, were not well-treated by their neighbors. But this has not kept students of Reconstruction from generalizing about the South's attitude toward northern men. Earlier historians who saw a Radical conspiracy to subjugate the South for partisan or economic reasons, or both, generally gave the impression that all Yankee immigrants, save for a few "troublemakers," experienced no worse than some social coolness from their southern neighbors. These scholars made their point by the simple method of assuming that only favorable opinions of the South were "trustworthy"; anything else was Radical propaganda. See Beale, *The Critical Year*, pp. 69, 93-96, 150-56, 165; William A. Dunning, *Reconstruction, Political and Economic, 1865-1877* (New York, 1962), pp. 50, 93, 94, 110; Claude G. Bowers, *The Tragic Era* (Boston, 1962), pp. 91, 125-26; Walter L. Fleming, *Civil War and Reconstruction in Alabama* (New York, 1905), pp. 318-19; C. Mildred Thompson, *Reconstruction in Georgia* (New York, 1915), pp. 127-28; William W. Davis, *Civil War and Reconstruction in Florida* (New York, 1913), p. 450. Changing racial values and the discrediting of the economic conspiracy theory, however, have disposed most modern historians to regard Radical Reconstruction more favorably, and they therefore tend to take seriously evidence that southern misbehavior, including mistreatment of northern settlers, justified further federal intervention. The idea that Andrew Johnson encouraged southern intransigence and therefore impeded sectional reconciliation has helped the new view win wider acceptance. But a more flexible attitude regarding the evidence has also influenced the change in perspective. (Eric McKitrick, *Andrew Johnson and Reconstruction* [Chicago, 1960], pp. 14, 39-40, 210-12; Kenneth M. Stampp, *The Era of Reconstruction, 1865-1877* [New York, 1965], p. 75; William C. Harris, *Presidential Reconstruction in Mississippi* [Baton Rouge, La., 1967], p. 171*n*.)

3. William R. Brock, *An American Crisis: Congress and Reconstruction, 1865-1867* (New York, 1963), pp. 124, 157 (the quotation is on p. 157); also see Beale, *The Critical Year*, pp. 150-51; Avery Craven, *Reconstruction: The Ending of the Civil War* (New York, 1969), pp. 59, 127, 156-59; E. Merton Coulter, *The South During Reconstruction, 1865-1877* (Baton Rouge, La., 1947), pp. 115-18.

4. John R. Dennett, *The South As It Is, 1865-1866*, ed. Henry M. Christman (New York, 1965), p. 361.

5. Abolitionists seldom had a better weapon in their arsenal than the charge that northerners could not travel in the South unmolested unless they kept their opinions and even their identities to themselves. See, for example, [William Lloyd Garrison], *The "New Reign of Terror" in the Slaveholding States, for 1859-1860* (New York, 1860).

6. See Eric McKitrick's suggestion that cordiality to Yankees was one of the "symbolic requirements" of the surrender. (*Andrew Johnson and Reconstruction*, pp. 21-31.)

7. Lawrence N. Powell, "The American Land Company and Agency: John A. Andrew and the Northernization of the South," *Civil War History* 21 (Dec. 1975): 293-308.

8. The months during which the more well-known northern correspondents traveled in the South are as follows: John Dennett, July 1865-Mar. 1866; Sidney Andrews, Sept.-Nov. 1865; Whitelaw Reid, May 1865-Feb. 1866; and John T. Trowbridge, early summer of 1866. Trowbridge's account was later updated to include the years 1867 and 1868. See also Michael Perman, *Reunion Without Compromise: The South and Reconstruction: 1865-68* (London, 1973), pp. 19-20.

9. Whitelaw Reid, *After the War: A Tour of the Southern States, 1865-1866*, ed. C. Vann Woodward (New York, 1965), p. 220.

10. Ibid., p. 440.

11. Ibid., p. 412. It was not only northern travelers who noted a reversal in the southern

mood. Yankee settlers who had been in the South since Appomattox also felt the change. In Mobile, Alabama, the new men were at first "entirely captivated" by southern hospitality. But after the president's policy took effect, some of them said they were "turned upon like hyenas" and given "notice to leave the country." (*Report of the Joint Committee on Reconstruction*, 39 Cong., 1 sess. [Ser. 1273], 4, p. 55; see also Henry Clay Warmoth, *War, Politics and Reconstruction: Stormy Years in Louisiana* [New York, 1930], pp. 30-31; Fred H. Wilson to Lewis Parsons, Dec. 24, 1865, Gov. Patton Papers, AA.)

12. *Report of the Joint Committee*, 3, pp. 40-41; Frank S. Hesseltine to Thaddeus Stevens, Apr. 26, 1866, vol. 7, Stevens Papers, LC.

13. Even northern travelers who were friendly to Andrew Johnson's policy complained that certain southern politicians and malcontents were behaving badly. (*Report of the Joint Committee*, 3, p. 113.)

14. John A. Andrew to F. P. Blair, Sr., Apr. 12, 1866, Andrew Papers, MHS. See also Powell, "The American Land Company and Agency," pp. 302-03.

15. "Letter from Charleston," Boston *Daily Advertiser*, Dec. 20, 1865; Dennett, *The South As It Is*, pp. 348, 362.

16. Dennett, *The South As It Is*, pp. 348, 362; Albert T. Morgan, *Yazoo; Or, On the Picket Line of Freedom in the South* (Washington, D.C., 1884), pp. 69-71, 77-78; [George Benham], *A Year of Wreck* (New York, 1880), pp. 140-41; C. C. Waters to E. S. Waters, Jan. 24, 1866, Box 4, folder 3, Waters Family Papers, Essex Inst.; Charles Stearns, *The Black Man of the South and the Rebels* (Boston, 1872), pp. 161-62, 165-68.

17. Dennett, *The South As It Is*, p. 362; [Benham], *A Year of Wreck*, p. 140.

18. A. Warren Kelsey to Edward Atkinson, Nov. 13, 1865, Atkinson Papers, MHS.

19. A future carpetbagger congressman from Louisiana tells of the difficulties he encountered when he tried to organize the Republican party in Donaldsonville in the spring of 1866: "It is impossible to convey even a slight suspicion of the dread which prevails among our little party. The object seems to be to drive out of the parish and state every loyal man in the country, by incessant lawsuits and exorbitant taxation." He was later forced to leave the parish. (J. P. Newsham to Henry Clay Warmoth, Apr. 5 and 26, 1866, and Mar. 19, 1867, Warmoth Papers, SHC.) For more details, see Dennett, *The South As It Is*, pp. 334-36.

20. *Report of the Joint Committee*, 3, p. 22; see also pp. 6 and 20.

21. Morgan, *Yazoo*, p. 21; Dennett, *The South As It Is*, pp. 273, 354.

22. For evidence that southerners were apt to boycott northern merchants, see Augustus Watson to Thaddeus Stevens, Dec. 9, 1865, vol. 5, Stevens Papers, LC; William L. Peabody to John A. Andrew, Dec. 26, 1866, Andrew Papers, MHS; Dennett, *The South As It Is*, pp. 264-65; *Report of the Joint Committee*, 4, p. 55; and 3, pp. 101 and 150.

23. S. S. Boyd to Gov. William L. Sharkey, July 13, 1865, vol. 70, Gov.'s Corr., MA. The state Freedmen's Bureau commissioner overturned one such verdict and had the defense attorney and judge in the case arrested. He thought the case was an attempt to provoke a conflict between military and civilian authorities, and he declared that if the owner of the property had claims against anyone for the seizure of his property, "that party is the United States." (Col. Samuel Thomas to Gen. H. W. Slocum, Aug. 21, 1865; see also R. S. Buck to Gov. William L. Sharkey, July 27, 1865; A. Burwell to Gov. W. L. Sharkey, July 27, 1865; Gov. W. L. Sharkey to Gen. H. W. Slocum, July 31, 1865, all in vol. 70, Gov.'s Corr., MA.) See also John T. Trowbridge, *The South: A Tour of Its Battle Fields and Ruined Cities* (New York, 1969), p. 377.

24. Quoted in Edward Atkinson to Hugh McCulloch, Feb. 28, 1866, Atkinson Letterbooks, MHS; *Report of the Joint Committee* 4, p. 52; and 3, p. 4; Boston *Daily Advertiser*, Jan. 15, 1866; Chicago *Tribune*, Jan. 15, 1866.

25. [?] to Thaddeus Stevens, Feb. 23, 1866, vol. 7, Stevens Papers, LC; Robinson to John Wilder, Feb. 22, 1866, Box 47, Todd Family Papers, YU; Boston *Daily Advertiser*, Aug. 2, 1866. One such report concerned the assassination of General Thomas O. Osborn on his Mississippi plantation after a citizen's committee told him to leave the county within twenty-four hours. But Osborn lived until 1904, serving as ambassador to Argentina under Presidents Rutherford B. Hayes and Chester A. Arthur. Exaggerations and falsehoods cling to this subject. (Ezra J. Warner, *Generals in Blue: Lives of the Union Commanders* [Baton Rouge, La., 1964], pp. 351-52; Chicago *Tribune*, Jan. 10, 1866; Boston *Daily Advertiser*, Jan. 22, 1866.)

26. Gainesville *New Era*, Feb. 3, 17, 1866; Boston *Daily Advertiser*, Jan. 15, 1866.

27. J. F. B. Marshall to T. B. Forbush, Feb. 23, 1867, SEC, NEEACo Papers, KSHS; *Report of the Joint Committee* 3, p. 4; W. J. Epperson to Gov. Benjamin G. Humphreys, June 30, 1866, Gov.'s Corr., MA; Henry Warren, *Reminiscences of a Mississippi Carpet-bagger* (Holden, Mass., 1914), pp. 25-28. Gen. Wager Swayne, the Freedmen's Bureau commissioner for Alabama, scoffed at reports of southern hostility to Yankees, but he conceded more than he meant to when he said he knew of "no case in Alabama in which a Northern man was subjected to greater inconvenience than the attentions of a horse-thief." (*Report of the Joint Committee*, 3, p. 141.)

28. Roger L. Ransom and Richard Sutch, *One Kind of Freedom: The Economic Consequences of Emancipation* (Cambridge, Eng., 1977), pp. 44-47; Peter Kolchin, *First Freedom: The Responses of Alabama's Blacks to Emancipation and Reconstruction* (Westport, Conn., 1972), p. 39; R. P. Brooks, *Agrarian Revolution in Georgia, 1865-1912* (Madison, Wis., 1914), pp. 28-29. Gen. Davis Tillson, the Freedmen's Bureau commissioner of Georgia, was under heavy fire from old planters for insisting on a minimum $15 monthly wage for first-class hands and for aiding freedmen to move west to get higher wages. He later reversed his policy on out-of-state transportation. (Gen. Davis Tillson to Gov. C. J. Jenkins, Feb. 3, 1866, Davis Tillson Papers, GA.)

29. Trowbridge, *The South*, p.498n. See also M. L. Bonham to Gov. James L. Orr, Jan. 27, 1866, Gov.'s Corr., SCA; W. H. Mattox to Gov. C. J. Jenkins, Feb. 16, 1866, Exec. Dept. Corr., Charles Jones Jenkins Papers, GA.

30. New York *Herald*, July 1, 1866.

31. Reid, *After the War*, p. 558.

32. James P. Ashford to Gov. Benjamin G. Humphreys, Jan. 14, 1866, vol. 78, Gov.'s Corr., MA.

33. Morgan, *Yazoo*, pp. 47 and 73.

34. Samuel L. James to commander of U.S. forces in Mississippi, Jan. 12, 1866; S. L. James to Gov. Benjamin G. Humphreys, Jan. 12 and 17, 1866, both in vol. 78, Gov.'s Corr., MA. See also Trowbridge, *The South*, p. 374; Dennett, *The South As It Is*, p. 354; Boston *Daily Advertiser*, Jan. 22, 1866.

35. Robert Higgs, *Competition and Coercion: Blacks in the American Economy, 1865-1914* (Cambridge, Eng., 1977), pp. 47-49; James L. Roark, *Masters Without Slaves: Southern Planters in the Civil War and Reconstruction* (New York, 1977), pp. 135-36.

36. M. L. Bonham to Gov. J. L. Orr, Jan. 27, 1866, Gov.'s Corr., SCA; Ira Taylor to Gov. Benjamin G. Humphreys, Apr. 18, 1866, Gov.'s Corr., MA.

37. Dan T. Carter, "The Anatomy of Fear: The Christmas Day Insurrection Scare of 1865," *Journal of Southern History* 42 (Aug. 1976): 345-64. For more on the slave-insurrection psychology, see Steven A. Channing, *Crisis of Fear: Secession in South Carolina* (New York, 1970), pp. 38-41; Clarence L. Mohr, "Georgia Blacks During Secession and Civil War, 1859-1865" (Ph.D. diss., University of Georgia, 1975), pp. 52-55, 59.

38. [Benham], *A Year of Wreck*, p. 90. See also A. W. Kelsey to Edward Atkinson, Aug. 12, 1865, Atkinson Papers, MHS.

39. F. Salter to Gov. Benjamin G. Humphreys, Mar. 29, 1866; F. Salter to Gen. [Thomas J. Wood?], Apr. 3, 1866, both in vol. 78, Gov.'s Corr., MA.

40. Charles A. Smith to Gov. Benjamin G. Humphreys, Apr. 4, 1866, vol. 78, MA.

41. Craven, *Reconstruction*, pp. 61-62; Beale, *The Critical Year*, pp. 150-51, 161-67; Coulter, *The South During Reconstruction*, pp. 115-18.

42. Warren, *Reminiscences*, p. 25. See also Harris, *Presidential Reconstruction*, pp. 35-36; Eliza J. Andrews, *The Wartime Journal of a Georgia Girl, 1864-1865* (New York, 1908), p. 268; New York *Times*, Feb. 4, 1866; *Report of the Joint Committee*, 3, p. 3; Maj. Gen. Thomas J. Wood to Gov. Benjamin G. Humphreys, July 6, 1866, vol. 79, Gov.'s Corr., MA.

43. Robert S. Hudson to Gov. Benjamin G. Humphreys, Aug. 9, 1866. "Petition of Southern Ladies of Yazoo County to Gov. Benjamin G. Humphreys" [July 31, 1866] contained 355 signatures. Both in vol. 79, Gov.'s Corr., MA.

44. Mrs. John Ray to Gov. Benjamin G. Humphreys, Aug. 9, 1866, vol. 79, MA. For more evidence that public sentiment prevented "combined action" against outbreaks of lawlessness, see *Report of the Joint Committee*, 4, p. 156.

45. A. W. Kelsey to Edward Atkinson, Dec. 6, 1865, Atkinson Papers, MHS.

46. A. W. Kelsey to E. Atkinson, Aug. 25, Nov. 13, 1865, ibid.; Warren, *Reminiscences*, pp. 254, 348; Dennett, *The South As It Is*, pp. 302, 354; *Report of the Joint Committee*, 3, p. 114, 4, pp. 52-53; Shofner, *Nor Is It Over Yet*, p. 90.

47. Joseph D. Geiger to John Sherman, Nov. 24, 1865, vol. 87, Sherman Papers, LC.

48. John A. Andrew to John Binney, Sept. 10, 1867, Andrew Papers, MHS; Powell, "The American Land Company and Agency," pp. 302-07.

49. Henry L. Higginson to Horatio Woodman, Nov. 2, 1865, Woodman Papers, MHS; J.Y. Cantwell to John Sherman, Nov. 24, 1865, vol. 87, Sherman Papers, LC.

50. Trowbridge, *The South*, p. 380; Dennett, *The South As It Is*, p. 333.

51. Montgomery (Ala.) *Daily Advertiser*, Feb. 16, 1866; Vicksburg *Weekly Herald*, Dec. 9, 1865; Oscar J. E. Stuart to Gov. Benjamin G. Humphreys, Dec. 8, 1865, vol. 77, Gov.'s Corr., MA; Beale, *The Critical Year*, pp. 165-66.

52. Vicksburg *Weekly Herald*, Feb. 17, 1866.

53. Selma *Daily Messenger*, Feb. 28, 1866.

54. Augusta (Ga.) *Daily Constitutionalist*, Nov. 16, 1865.

55. A. H. Bradford to J. D. B. DeBow, July 9, 1866, DeBow Papers, DU; see also Charles Phillips to Kemp P. Battle, Sept. 20, 1865, Battle Family Papers, SHC.

56. Charleston *Courier*, Jan. 18, 1866; Thompson, *Reconstruction in Georgia*, p. 164.

57. Susan Dabney Smedes, *Memorials of A Southern Planter*, ed. Fletcher M. Green (New York, 1965), pp. 223-26; Roark, *Masters Without Slaves*, pp. 149-50, 180.

58. Thompson, *Reconstruction in Georgia*, pp. 163-64; Coulter, *The South During Reconstruction*, p. 188; Paul H. Buck, *The Road to Reunion, 1865-1900* (New York, 1937), pp. 38-39; Joe Gray Taylor, *Louisiana Reconstructed, 1863-1877* (Baton Rouge, La., 1974), pp. 64-65, 409.

59. One thinks of the ease with which the proslavery and antislavery forces in "bleeding Kansas" joined hands in various schemes of land speculation and railroad-charter manipulation, and this so soon after they had been at each others' throats. (See David M. Potter, *The Impending Crisis, 1848-1861*, ed. Don E. Fehrenbacher [New York, 1976], pp. 216-17.)

60. Dennett, *The South As It Is*, p. 317; [Benham], *A Year of Wreck*, p. 146; "Cotton Lands," Selma *Daily Messenger*, Mar. 14, 1866. The tendency to avoid political discussions was particularly strong among commercial men. (*Report of the Joint Committee*, 3, p. 38; Robert H. McKenzie, "Reconstruction Historiography: The View From Shelby," *The Historian* 36 [Feb. 1974]: 207-23.)

61. [Benham], *A Year of Wreck*, pp. 42, 44.

62. Willard Warner to John Sherman, Apr. 15, 1866, vol. 99, Sherman Papers, LC; also see Garth W. James to father, Mar. 2, 1866, G. W. and R. James Papers, in the possession of Prof. William Childers, University of Florida; Anna R. Burr, ed., *Alice James. Her Brothers. Her Journal* (New York, 1934), pp. 44-45.

63. Memphis *Commercial*, quoted in Gainesville *New Era*, Jan. 27, 1866; Macon *Telegraph*, in ibid., Jan. 20, 1866; *Florida Union* (Jacksonville), July 21, 1866; "Affairs in South Carolina," Boston *Daily Advertiser*, Mar. 5, 1866; "From Charleston to the North," Boston *Daily Advertiser*, May 1, 1866; *DeBow's Review*, AWS 2 (Dec. 1866), p. 664; Selma *Daily Messenger*, May 2, 1867; Dennett, *The South As It Is*, p. 307; Henry M. Crydenwise to parents, Mar. 13, 1866, Crydenwise Papers, DU; Forrest Wilson, *Crusader in Crinoline: The Life of Harriet Beecher Stowe* (Philadelphia, 1941), p. 603; *The Ku-Klux Conspiracy: Testimony Taken by the Joint Select Committee to Inquire into the Condition of Affairs in the Late Insurrectionary States*, vol. 2, pt. 7 (Washington, D.C., 1872), p. 1092.

64. Reid, *After the War*, p. 449; [Benham], *A Year of Wreck*, pp. 95, 94-98.

65. Kemp P. Battle to wife [summer of 1865], Battle Family Papers, SHC. Henry Lee Higginson and his associates discovered that the man who sold them their place included in the deal land that he did not own. (Charles F. Morse, *A Sketch of My Life* [Cambridge, 1927], p. 32.)

66. Morgan, *Yazoo*, p. 85.

67. Dennett, *The South As It Is*, p. 307.

68. Morgan, *Yazoo*, pp. 26-27, 30, 46-51. The Col. J. J. U. Black in Morgan's autobiography appears to have been a pseudonym for Col. J. J. B. White, who owned the Tokeba plantation that Morgan rented. (Harriet DeCell and Joanne Prichard, *Yazoo: Its Legends and Legacies* [Yazoo City, Miss., 1976], p. 318.)

69. "From Charleston to the North," Boston *Daily Advertiser*, May 1, 1866; Henry M. Crydenwise to parents, Mar. 3, 1866, Crydenwise Papers, DU; Ambrose B. Hart to Mary Hart, Mar. 20, 1867, A. B. Hart Papers, FU; [Benham], *A Year of Wreck*, p. 339.

70. The quotation is in "Letters from the South," Boston *Advertiser*, Aug. 8, 1865; see also Harriet Beecher Stowe, "Our Florida Plantation," *Atlantic Monthly* 43 (May 1879): 645-46; *Ku-Klux Conspiracy*, vol. 2, pt. 7, p. 1092; McKitrick, *Andrew Johnson and Reconstruction*, pp. 155-56; Taylor, *Louisiana Reconstructed*, pp. 68-70; [Benham], *A Year of Wreck*, pp. 220-30. One northern woman who lived in Alabama in 1866 wrote that "no words can tell the contemptuous manner in which a southern *female* treats a northern lady when she meets her." (Selma *Daily Messenger*, Apr. 17, 1867.)

71. Sidney Andrews, *The South Since the Civil War* (Boston, 1971), p. 176; see also A. W. Kelsey to Edward Atkinson, Jan. 7, 1866, Atkinson Papers, MHS; *Report of the Joint Committee*, 3, pp. 3, 19; Joe M. Richardson, *The Negro in the Reconstruction of Florida, 1865-1877* (Tallahassee, Fla., 1965), pp. 3-4; [Benham], *A Year of Wreck*, pp. 222-30.

72. Morgan, *Yazoo*, pp. 26-27, 46-51, 63. Governor John A. Andrew's land company made it a policy to interest influential southerners in "the pecuniary results" of the plantations that northerners leased or bought through its agency. The rationale was that the southern man would feel in "honor bound to protect those engaged with him" against trouble with the "poor white population," who might otherwise harass the Yankee newcomers. (William L. Burt to J. A. Andrew, May 10, 1866, Andrew Papers, MHS.)

73. Macon *Telegraph*, quoted in Gainesville *New Era*, Jan. 20, 1866; see also Sarah W. Wiggins, "Social Ostracism of White Republicans in Alabama During Reconstruction," *Alabama Review* 28 (Jan. 1974): 55.

74. Morgan, *Yazoo*, p. 64.

75. Henry Lee Higginson to Horatio Woodman, Nov. 2, 1865, Woodman Papers, MHS.

76. *DeBow's Review*, AWS 2 (Feb. 1866), pp. 218-19; Frances Butler Leigh had a Yankee for a neighbor who went to "the greatest expense to stock [his plantation] with mules and farming implements of all sorts, insisting upon it that we Southerners don't know how to manage our own places or negroes, and he will show us. . . ." (*Ten Years On A Georgia Plantation Since the War* [London, 1883], pp. 53-54.) See also Selma *Daily Times*, Jan. 31, 1866.

77. [Benham], *A Year of Wreck*, p. 137; Gainesville *New Era*, Dec. 9, 1865.

78. Wetumpka (Ala.) *Standard*, quoted in Gainesville *New Era*, Nov. 9, 1866; Leigh, *Ten Years*, p. 54n. It was said in Florida that the mules had become unruly because the Yankees did not "know how to manage mules in a latitude so close to the equator." (*Florida Union*, July 14, 1866.) See also Stearns, *The Black Man*, pp. 90-91; [Benham], *A Year of Wreck*, pp. 270-75.

79. Selma *Daily Messenger*, Sept. 25, 1866; see also "European and Northern Immigrants at the South," *DeBow's Review*, AWS 2 (Dec. 1866), p. 644.

80. Leigh, *Ten Years*, p. 54.

81. [Benham], *A Year of Wreck*, p. 138.

82. Morgan, *Yazoo*, p. 35; Clifford C. Waters to Edward S. Waters, July 7, 1865, Box 4, folder 3, Waters Family Papers, Essex Inst. The wife of an Alabama planter with whom Whitelaw Reid had a joint plantation investment said she did not consider Reid a Yankee. "You are a Western man and have no right to call yourself a Yankee," her husband explained to Reid. (John A. Jacques to W. Reid, July 3, 1869, Reid Papers, LC.) See also *When the World Ended: The Diary of Emma LeConte*, ed. Earl S. Miers (New York, 1957), p. 116.

83. Macon *Telegraph*, quoted in Gainesville *New Era*, Jan. 20, 1866; Selma *Daily Times*, Oct. 18, 1865; Morgan, *Yazoo*, p. 46; William J. Barbee, *The Cotton Question* (New York, 1866), p. 102.

84. Cleveland (Ohio) *Herald*, quoted in Selma *Daily Messenger*, June 23, 1866; Selma *Daily Messenger*, Mar. 14, 1866; Selma *Daily Times*, Jan. 31, 1866; "Personal Safety in South Carolina," Boston *Daily Advertiser*, Jan 18, 1866; "European and Northern Immigrants at the South," *DeBow's Review*, AWS 2 (Dec. 1866), p. 644; [Benham], *A Year of Wreck*, p. 159; Dennett, *The South As It Is*, p. 266; Bliss Perry, *The Life and Letters of Henry Lee Higginson* (Boston, 1921), p. 251.

85. Morgan, *Yazoo*, pp. 81-82; Henry Lee Higginson to Horatio Woodman, Nov. 2, 1865, Woodman Papers, MHS.

86. Memphis *Commercial*, quoted in Gainesville *New Era*, Apr. 27, 1866.

87. Dennett, *The South As It Is*, pp. 294-97. See also Reid, *After the War*, p. 560; [Benham], *A Year of Wreck*, p. 139.

88. George W. Colby, et al., to the Senate and House of Representatives of the United States, June 1, 1866; A. S. Gurney to Edwin D. Morgan, June 1, 1866; Citizens of Natchez to the Senate and House of Representatives, May 11, 1866; all in the Records of the U.S. Senate, NA. See also Boston *Daily Advertiser*, June 8, 1866.

89. Gainesville *New Era*, Oct. 17, 1866.

90. Reid, *After the War*, p. 560; [Benham], *A Year of Wreck*, pp. 156-68, 461; Boston *Daily Advertiser*, Mar. 7, 1867.

91. J. M. Gilman to Isaac Crowe, June 30, 1865, Crowe Papers, MiHS.

92. Loomis's family had been among the northern colonists who settled for a short while in Fairfax County, Virginia, in the 1840s. Eben Loomis to wife, Feb. 5, 1866, Box 8, Todd Family Papers, YU.

93. The northern practice of assuming a border-state identity was apparently an old one among people of the Northwest who had regular business dealings in the South. Men who had farms in Indiana, say, often took up "their residence in Kentucky" in order to say that they hailed from that state when they took their drops south. ([Benham], *A Year of Wreck*, p. 462.)

94. Reid, *After the War*, p. 560.

95. Walter Hart to mother, Jan. 15, 1867, Walter and Edmund Hart Papers, FU.

96. Dennet, *The South As It Is*, pp. 235-36; Memphis *Commercial* quoted in Gainesville *New Era*, Apr. 27, 1866.

97. W. N. Hart to sister, Feb. 18, 1867; W. N. Hart to mother, Mar. 16, 1867, Walter and Edmund Hart Papers, FU.

98. Dennett, *The South As It Is*, pp. 327-28; *Report of the Joint Committee*, 3, pp. 155-56.

99. [Benham], *A Year of Wreck*, pp. 139-40; *Report of the Joint Committee*, 3, p. 156.

100. Selma *Daily Times*, Oct. 18, 1865.

101. T. H. Thurston to T. B. Forbush, Feb. 1, 1867, SEC, NEEACo Papers, KSHS; [Benham], *A Year of Wreck*, p. 461; Reid, *After the War*, p. 560.

102. Morgan, *Yazoo*, pp. 60, 61-67.

103. Willard Warner to John Sherman, Apr. 15, 1866, vol. 99, Sherman Papers, LC; see also J. Y. Cantwell to John Sherman, Jan. 23, 1866, vol. 91, ibid.

104. Garth W. James to Henry James, Sr., Mar. 27 and June 26, 1866, G. W. and R. James Papers, in possession of Prof. William Childers, University of Florida.

105. J. H. Norwood to Gov. James L. Orr, July 12 and 24, 1866, Gov. Orr Papers, SCA.

106. C. J. Elford to Gov. J. L. Orr, July 23, 1866; see also E. W. Kingsland to Gov. Orr, July 5, 1866; R. D. Crittenden to Gov. Orr, July 6, 1866, Gov. Orr Papers, SCA.

107. [?] Robinson to John Wilder, Feb. 22, 1866, Box 47, Todd Family Papers, YU; A. W. Kelsey to Edward Atkinson, Aug. 12, 1865, Atkinson Papers, MHS; J. Y. Cantwell to John Sherman, Jan. 23, 1866, vol. 91, Sherman Papers, LC.

108. C. J. Elford to Gov. J. L. Orr, July 23, 1866; R. D. Crittenden to Gov. Orr, July 6, 1866, Gov. Orr Corr., SCA; Perman *Reunion Without Compromise*, pp. 27-28.

109. Morgan, *Yazoo*, p. 195.

110. John W. A. Sanford to [Dwight Foster?], Apr. 28, 1866, Foster Family Papers, Amer. Antiquar. Soc.

111. William L. Burt to John A. Andrew, Feb. 21, 1866, John A. Andrew Papers, MHS.

112. "Instead of a feeling of distrust or surprise at finding men fresh from the North who sympathize with them, and who denounce as they denounce," George C. Benham quickly discovered, white southerners "seem rather to be surprised at not finding it." (*A Year of Wreck*, p. 159.)

113. Morgan, *Yazoo*, pp. 45, 69-70, 71; Ambrose B. Hart to Mary Hart, Mar. 20, 1867, A. B. Hart Papers, FU; [Benham], *A Year of Wreck*, pp. 414-16, 463.

114. [Benham], *A Year of Wreck*, p. 146.

115. Selma *Daily Messenger*, Feb. 28, 1866.

Chapter 5

1. [George C. Benham], *A Year of Wreck* (New York, 1880), p. 234.

2. A. Warren Kelsey to father, Sept. 29, 1865, Edward Atkinson Papers, MHS. See also John Wilder to Eben Loomis, Nov. 2, 1865, Dec. 28, 1865, Jan. 4, 1866, Box 8, Todd Family Papers, YU; F. H. Thurston to T. B. Forbush, Feb. 1, 1867, SEC, NEEACo Papers, KSHS; Hiram McCollam to Andrew McCollam, Feb. 23, 1867, Andrew McCollam Papers, SHC; Whitelaw Reid Diary, "1862," Nov. 16, 1865, LC.

3. J. Floyd King to Mallory [King], Jan. 18, 1866, J. Floyd King to Lin [Caperton], Dec. 24 and 29, 1865, Jan. 7, 1866, Series A. Thomas Butler King Papers, SHC. See also Gainesville *New Era*, Jan. 20, 1866; *Florida Union* (Jacksonville), July 21, 1866.

4. [Benham], *A Year of Wreck*, pp. 98-99, 121, 120-23.

5. Ibid., p. 78.

6. Ibid., p. 101.

7. Ibid., pp. 101-02, 121.

8. Rowland T. Berthoff, "Southern Attitudes Towards Immigration," *Journal of Southern History* 17 (Aug. 1951): 328-60.

9. Eben Loomis to Eliza, Apr. 15, 1866, Box 8, Todd Family Papers, YU; James D. Waters to mother, Mar. 27, 1864, Box 12, folder 5, Waters Family Papers, Essex Inst.; see also Garth W. James to father, Mar. 27, 1866, G. W. and R. James Papers, in possession of Prof. William Childers, University of Florida.

10. [Benham], *A Year of Wreck*, pp. 190-93, 197, 268-69; Mary Loomis to Eben Loomis, July 4, 1866, Box 8, Todd Family Papers, YU; James D. Waters to Edward S. Waters, May 29, 1864, Box 4, folder 5, Waters Family Papers, Essex Inst.; Wetumpka (Ala.) *Standard*, quoted in Gainesville *New Era*, Nov. 9, 1866.

11. Robert W. Fogel and Stanley L. Engerman, *Time on the Cross: The Economics of American Negro Slavery* (Boston and Toronto, 1974), pp. 208-09.

12. William J. Barbee, *The Cotton Question* (New York, 1866), pp. 100-01. See also John T. Trowbridge, *The South: A Tour of Its Battle Fields and Ruined Cities* (New York, 1969), p. 379.

13. Charles Stearns, *The Black Man of the South and the Rebels* (Boston, 1872), pp. 32-33; Albert T. Morgan, *Yazoo; Or, On the Picket Line of Freedom in the South* (Washington, D.C., 1884), p. 98; New York *Herald*, May 23, 1866; Garth W. James to mother, Jan. 27, 1868, Garth W. and Robertson James Papers, in possession of Prof. William Childers, University of Florida.

14. James D. Waters to mother, Apr. 24, 1864, Box 12, folder 5. See also J. D. Waters to Edward S. Waters, Feb. 25, 1864, and Mar. 16, 1864, Box 4, folder 5, Waters Family Papers, Essex Inst.; Whitelaw Reid, *After the War: A Tour of the Southern States, 1865-1866*, ed. C. Vann Woodward (New York, 1965), p. 504; Stearns, *The Black Man*, p. 330.

15. Henry W. Warren, *Reminiscences of a Mississippi Carpetbagger* (Holden, Mass., 1914), p. 33. See also Willie Lee Rose, *Rehearsal for Reconstruction: The Port Royal Experiment* (New York, 1964), pp. 79-81; Harold F. Williamson, *Edward A. Atkinson: The Biography of an American Liberal* (Boston, 1934), pp. 12-13; Harriet Beecher Stowe, *Palmetto Leaves* (Boston, 1873), pp. 289-90; Thomas W. Knox, *Camp-Fire and Cotton-Field: Southern Adventure in Time of War* (New York, 1865), p. 413; entry of Mar. 30, 1864, Isaac Shoemaker Diary, DU.

16. New York *Times*, Jan. 17, 1866.

17. "Letters from the South," Boston *Daily Advertiser*, Aug. 9, 1865.

18. [Benham], *A Year of Wreck*, p. 131. See also "Letters From the South," Boston *Daily Advertiser*, July 31, 1865, Aug. 18, 1865; New York *Daily Tribune*, May 24, 1865; New York *Times*, June 18, 1865; Philadelphia *Public Ledger*, Jan. 12, 1866; James M. Shute to Gov. R. Patton, Feb. 10, 1867, Gov.'s Corr., AA; George L. Stearns to F. C. Cabell, Sept. 29, 1865, Boston *Daily Advertiser*, Oct. 25, 1865.

19. "Letters From the South," Boston *Daily Advertiser*, July 31, 1865.

20. Sarah F. Hughes, ed., *Letters (Supplementary) of John Murray Forbes*, 3 vols. (Boston, 1905), 2, p. 172; Trowbridge, *The South*, p. 573; Elizabeth W. Pearson, ed., *Letters from Port Royal* (New York, 1969), pp. 107, 228; Boston *Daily Advertiser* Oct. 25, 1865.

21. Quoted in Rose, *Rehearsal*, p. 223.

22. Boston *Daily Advertiser*, June 9, 1865; Chicago *Tribune*, Aug. 14, 1866; John A. Andrew to Lydia M. Child, on the back of L. M. Child's letter to Andrew dated Aug. 8, 1867, John A. Andrew Papers, MHS. For an excellent discussion of the major tenets of laissez faire capitalism as understood by the more thoughtful northern planters, see Rose, *Rehearsal*, pp. 223-29.

23. James McKaye, *The Mastership and Its Fruits: The Emancipated Slave Face to Face with His Old Master* (New York, 1864), pp. 26-27.

24. Stearns, *The Black Man*, p. 16.

25. Edward Atkinson to Octavius Cohen, May 6, 1867, and E. Atkinson to J. H. Black, Dec. 11, 1867, Atkinson Letterbooks, MHS. See also Joel Williamson, *After Slavery: The Negro in South Carolina During Reconstruction, 1861-1877* (Chapel Hill, N.C., 1965), p. 73; George M. Fredrickson, *The Black Image in the White Mind: The Debate on Afro-American Character and Destiny, 1817-1914* (New York, 1971), pp. 181-83.

26. Rose, *Rehearsal*, p. 223. See also Edward Atkinson to John Murray Forbes, Aug. 30, 1865; E. Atkinson to David A. Wells, Apr. 11, 1866; E. Atkinson to John A. Andrew, Dec. 9, 1865, Atkinson Letterbooks, MHS.

27. Edward Atkinson to Charles Sumner, July 8, 1867, Atkinson Letterbooks, MHS. It was the conviction that government intervention was unnecessary, as much as the disdain for gift-giving, that made him opposed to confiscation.

28. Bliss Perry, *Life and Letters of Henry Lee Higginson* (Boston, 1921), pp. 252-54; the quotation is on page 254; Henry M. Crydenwise to Charles [Crydenwise], Mar. 21, 1866, H. M. Crydenwise Papers, DU.

29. New York *Times*, Jan. 4, 1866. See also Rose, *Rehearsal*, p. 310.

30. Edward Atkinson to John A. Andrew, Dec. 9, 1865, Atkinson Letterbooks, MHS; Lawrence N. Powell, "The American Land Company and Agency: John A. Andrew and the Northernization of the South,:" *Civil War History* 21 (Dec. 1975): 303-04; James M. McPherson, *The Struggle for Equality: Abolitionists and the Negro in the Civil War and Reconstruction* (Princeton, N.J., 1964), pp. 412-13.

31. McPherson, *Struggle for Equality*, p. 413.

32. Philbrick asked $5 an acre from the blacks and $10 from the whites. William D. Waters to Clifford C. Waters, Nov. 3, 1865, Box 13, folder 1, Waters Family Papers, Essex Inst.; Rose, *Rehearsal*, pp. 308-310.

33. Clifford C. Waters to Edward S. Waters, Jan. 28, 1876, Box 4, folder 3, Waters Family Papers, Essex Inst.

34. Clarence H. Danhof, "Farm-Making Costs and the 'Safety Valve': 1850-1860," *The Journal of Political Economy* 49 (June 1941): 323; *National Anti-Slavery Standard* (New York), Sept. 4, 1845.

35. Warren, *Reminiscences*, p. 18; Stearns, *The Black Man*, pp. 267-72, 276-77, 305-06, 323; the quotation is on page 272. McPherson, *Struggle for Equality*, pp. 414-16; and idem, *The Abolitionist Legacy: From Reconstruction to the NAACP* (Princeton, N.J., 1975), p. 77.

36. William D. Waters to Abigail Waters, Jan. 28, 1865, Box 12, folder 1, Waters Family Papers, Essex Inst.; see also *Report of the Joint Committee on Reconstruction*, pt. 3, p. 157.

37. Fredrickson, *Black Image*, pp. 178-83.

38. "Letters From the South," Boston *Daily Advertiser*, Aug. 19, 1865; "A Visit to Port Royal," ibid., Dec. 4, 1865; New York *Herald*, May 23, 1866; Fredrickson, *Black Image*, pp. 176-77.

39. Pearson, ed., *Letters From Port Royal*, p. 275; Reid, *After the War*, pp. 113-14; John R. Dennett, *The South As It Is, 1865-1866*, ed. Henry M. Christman (New York, 1865), pp. 209-10; Rose, *Rehearsal*, p. 226.

40. A. Warren Kelsey to Edward Atkinson, Sept. 4, 1865, Atkinson Papers, MHS.

41. Entry of Apr. 2, 1865, Isaac Shoemaker Diary, DU; Stearns, *The Black Man*, p. 113.

42. A. W. Kelsey to E. Atkinson, Nov. 3, 1865 (for the quotation), Aug. 25, 1865, and Sept. 18, 1865, Atkinson Papers, MHS; H. B. Sargent to John A. Andrew, Apr. 29, 1865, Andrew Papers, MHS; [Benham], *A Year of Wreck*, p. 169.

43. Dennett, *The South*, p. 213. See also New York *Times*, June 18, 1865.

44. Reid, *After the War*, p. 18; Frances B. Leigh, *Ten Years On A Georgia Plantation*

Since the War (London, 1883), pp. 55-56. See also Pearson, ed., *Letters*, p. 137; Williamson, *After Slavery*, p. 88; Daniel T. Rodgers, *The Work Ethic in Industrial America, 1850-1920* (Chicago, 1978), p. 19.

45. Eugene D. Genovese, *Roll, Jordan, Roll: The World the Slaves Made* (New York, 1974), pp. 285-324, esp. p. 286; E. P. Thompson, "Time, Work-Discipline, and Industrial Capitalism," *Past and Present* 38 (Dec. 1967): 56-97; see also Bennett H. Wall, "An Epitaph for Slavery," *Louisiana History* 16 (summer 1975): 238-41 and 244-45, for a thoughtful critique of Genovese's conception of the black work ethic.

46. The quotation is in Perry, *Life and Letters*, p. 252; Genovese, *Roll, Jordan, Roll*, pp. 296-97.

47. Mary Loomis to Eben Loomis, July 4, 1866, Box 8, Todd Family Papers, YU; see also A. W. Kelsey to E. Atkinson, Sept. 4, 1865, and Nov. 3, 1865, Atkinson Papers, MHS; Fogel and Engerman, *Time on the Cross*, p. 172.

48. James E. Yeatman, *A Report on the Condition of the Freedmen of the Mississippi* (St. Louis, 1864), p. 9; Reid, *After the War*, p. 578.

49. Henry L. Higginson to Horatio Woodman, Nov. 2, 1865, Woodman Papers, MHS; Whitelaw Reid to mother, Sept. 11, 1866, Reid Papers, LC.

50. H. L. Higginson to H. Woodman, Nov. 2, 1865, Woodman Papers, MHS; see also Pearson, ed., *Letters*, p. 236.

51. Perry, *Life and Letters*, p. 255.

52. [Benham], *A Year of Wreck*, pp. 103, 131; Stearns, *The Black Man*, pp. 116, 155.

53. McPherson, *Struggle for Equality*, p. 413; Stearns, *The Black Man*, pp. 54, 85; Perry, *Life and Letters*, p. 257; Stowe, *Palmetto Leaves*, pp. 298, 306; Eben Loomis to Mary Loomis, June 2, 1866, Box 8, Todd Family Papers, YU.

54. Perry, *Life and Letters*, p. 255; Stearns, *The Black Man*, p. 116; Genovese, *Roll, Jordan, Roll*, pp. 10, 295.

55. Higginson was pleased. He believed that class needed "reforming and educating quite as much as the blacks." (Perry, *Life and Letters*, p. 255; F. W. Loring and C. F. Atkinson, *Cotton Culture and the South Considered with Reference to Emigration* [Boston, 1869], p. 11.)

56. Edward E. Hale to George [?], Feb. 21, 1862, Letterbook of E. E. Hale, NEEACo Papers, KSHS; Rose, *Rehearsal*, pp. 160-61; William D. Waters to Abigail Waters, May 14, 1865, Box 12, folder 1, Waters Family Papers, Essex Inst.; Genovese, *Roll, Jordan Roll*, p. 21.

57. Stearns, *The Black Man*, p. 49; Burr, ed., *Alice James*, p. 45.

58. Labor contract [c.1865], Box 11, folder 7, Waters Family Papers, Essex Inst.

59. Walter Hart to Lucy Hart, Sept 27, 1867, W. N. Hart Papers, FU.

60. Barbee, *The Cotton Question*, pp. 102, 251; Knox, *Camp-Fire and Cotton-Field*, pp. 418, 430-31, 445-57; [Benham], *A Year of Wreck*, pp. 344-45; Jimmy G. Shoalmire, "Carpetbagger Extraordinary: Marshall Harvey Twitchell, 1840-1905" (Ph.D. diss., Mississippi State University, 1969), pp. 65-73.

61. Clifford C. Waters to Henry F. Waters, May 8, 1866, Box 8, C. C. Waters folder, Henry F. Waters Papers; see also C. C. Waters to Edward S. Waters, Jan. 24, 1866, Box 4, folder 3, Waters Family Papers, both in Essex Inst.

62. James D. Waters to mother, Apr. 24, 1864, Box 12, folder 5, Waters Family Papers, Essex Inst.; see also George C. Hardy to F. A. Eustis, Oct. 24, 1870, F. A. Eustis Papers, SCL.

63. Pearson, ed., *Letters*, pp. 176, 179.

64. Rose, *Rehearsal*, pp. 82-83, 300-01, 434; Thompson, "Time, Work-Discipline, and Industrial Capitalism," pp. 60, 91-93. See also Pearson, ed., *Letters*, pp. 108-09; Ulrich B. Phillips, *American Negro Slavery* (Baton Rouge, La., 1966), p. 247.

65. The quotation is in "Letters From the South," Boston *Daily Advertiser*, July 31, 1865; Perry, *Life and Letters*, pp. 251, 256; New York *Herald*, May 23, 1866, and June 13, 1866; "Articles of Agreement . . . ," May 29, 1867, E. M. Stoeber Papers, SCL; William D. Waters to Abigail Waters, Jan. 6 [1865], Box 12, folder 1, and W. D. Waters to C. C. Waters, Jan. 14, 1865, Box 13, folder 1, Waters Family Papers, Essex Inst.; Geo. C. Hardy to F. A. Eustis, July 25, 1870, F. A. Eustis Papers, SCL; William Markham to Fairchild Andrews, Feb. 3, 1865, and "Estimates for Lemington Plantation in 1867," Markham-Puffer Papers, CU; Dennett, *The South As It Is*, p. 205. It should not be overlooked, however, that one

reason for the spread of the task system in the Port Royal vicinity was regulations promulgated by Gen. Rufus Saxton, the military governor of the Department of the South. In December, 1862, he stipulated that the freedmen were to "plant and cultivate a certain number of tasks ... of cotton for the government." (Bell I. Wiley, *Southern Negroes, 1861-1865* [New Haven, 1965], pp. 198-99.)

66. Stearns, *The Black Man*, pp. 126, 170, 516-17; the quotations are on page 516.

67. Ambrose Hart to Willy [Hart], Apr. 19, 1868, A. B. Hart to Lou [Hart], May 24, 1868, and A. B. Hart to father, July 7, 1871, A. B. Hart Letters, FU; J. F. B. Marshall to T. B. Forbush, Mar. 4, 1867, SEC, NEEACo Papers, KSHS; sharecropping contract, Mar. 17, 1875, D. D. Slauson Papers, LSU; G. G. Klapp to J. W. Waters, Dec. 8, 1869, Box 11, folder 8, Waters Family Papers, Essex Inst.

68. The quotation is in Louis S. Gerteis, *From Contraband to Freedman: Federal Policy Toward Southern Blacks, 1861-1865* (Westport, Conn., 1973), pp. 75, 72-77; see also Wiley, *Southern Negroes*, pp. 189, 211-12; C. Peter Ripley, *Slaves and Freedmen in Civil War Louisiana* (Baton Rouge, La., 1976), pp. 40-48.

69. Orders, no. 9, Mar. 11, 1864, "Applications for Leasing Abandoned Plantations" (entry 2383), BRFAL Records, NA; see also Ripley, *Slaves and Freedmen*, pp. 40-68, 90-101; Wiley, *Southern Negroes*, pp. 211-12.

70. Wiley, *Southern Negroes*, p. 200; Pearson, ed., *Letters*, pp. 261-62; Plantation Leasing Regulations, Apr. 20, 1864, in "Minutes," Records of the Direct Tax Commission for S.C., NA; Gerteis, *From Contraband to Freedman*, p. 66; William S. McFeeley, *Yankee Stepfather: General O. O. Howard and the Freedman*, (New Haven, 1968), pp. 130-89: see especially page 149 for his observation that the Bureau's labor agreements "were charters for an involuntary labor system dressed in liberty of contract."

71. The quotation is in [Benham], *A Year of Wreck*, pp. 118-19. See also "Notes of a Plantation Experience" [1866], Box 207, W. Reid Papers, LC; James D. Waters to mother, Apr. 24, 1864, and June 5, 1864, Box 12, folder 5, labor contract [c. 1865 or 1866], Box 11, folder 1, Waters Family Papers, Essex Inst.; H. M. Crydenwise to parents, Apr. 3 [1866], H. M. Crydenwise Papers, DU; entry of Apr. 4, 1864, Isaac Shoemaker Diary, DU; Harriet Beecher Stowe, "Our Florida Plantation," *Atlantic Monthly* 43 (May 1874): 648; Stearns, *The Black Man*, pp. 46-48; Knox, *Camp-Fire and Cotton-Field*, pp. 382-84.

72. Wiley, *Southern Negroes*, pp. 186, 211-12, 214-15; Gerteis, *From Contraband to Freedman*, pp. 74-77; Perry, *Life and Letters*, p. 261; application of Wesley Ditts, Jan. 30, 1865, "Applications for Leasing Abandoned Plantations" (entry 2383), BRFAL Records, NA. For a helpful discussion of the distinction between share wages and share rentals, see Williamson, *After Slavery*, p. 128, especially note 8.

73. Ripley, *Slaves and Freedmen*, pp. 51-52; Vernon Lane Wharton, *The Negro in Mississippi, 1865-1890* (New York, 1947), p. 65; Wiley, *Southern Negroes*, p. 236; Pearson, ed., *Letters*, p. 246; Knox, *Camp-Fire and Cotton-Field*, p. 354. Dennett tells of a case in which the freedmen on a Port Royal plantation refused to contract because the planter insisted on paying cash wages instead of dividing the crop. This was a rare incident. (*The South As It Is*, p. 203.)

74. Wiley, *Southern Negroes*, pp. 186, 189, 211-12, 214-15; F. W. Bardwell to J. F. B. Marshall, Feb. 22, 1867, Marshall to T. B. Forbush, Dec. 29, 1866, H. B. Scott to Marshall, Feb. 14, 1867, all in SEC, NEEACo Papers, KSHS; H. M. Crydenwise to parents, Apr. 3 [1866], Crydenwise Papers, DU; Stowe, "Our Florida Plantation," p. 648; [Benham], *A Year of Wreck*, p. 118; Reid, *After the War*, p. 490. "Letter From New Orleans," Boston *Daily Advertiser*, Apr. 28, 1866. Dennett, *The South As It Is*, pp. 270, 328-29.

75. Wiley, *Southern Negroes*, pp. 211-12; Orders, no. 9, Mar. 11, 1864, in "Applications for Leasing Abandoned Plantations" (entry 2383), BRFAL Records, NA; Knox, *Camp-Fire and Cotton-Field*, p. 354; Dennett *The South As It Is*, pp. 321-22.

76. Reid, *After the War*, p. 534.

77. William D. Waters to Abigail Waters, Mar. 26, 1865, Box 12, folder 1, James D. Waters to mother, June 5, 1864, Box 11, folder 7, Waters Family Papers, Essex Inst.; Plantation Journal for 1867, D. D. Slauson Papers, LSU; Gen. N. P. Banks to Gen. Halleck, Oct. 15, 1863, Banks Papers, LSU; Eben Loomis to Mary Loomis, Feb. 13, 1866, Box 8, Todd Family Papers, YU; "Articles of Agreement Between E. M. Stoeber of Edisto Island, S.C. and The Freedman & Women on his Place," May 29, 1867, E. M. Stoeber Papers, SCL; Perry, *Life and Letters*, p. 252; Gerteis, *From Contraband to Freedman*, p. 163.

78. Ripley, *Slaves and Freedmen*, pp. 25-68; Orders, no. 9, Mar. 11, 1864, in "Applications for Leasing Abandoned Plantations" (entry 2383), BRFAL Records, NA.

79. Perry, *Life and Letters*, p. 255; Knox, *Camp-Fire and Cotton-Field*, p. 354; Mary Loomis to Eben Loomis, July 4, 1866, Box 8, Todd Family Papers, YU; [Benham], *A Year of Wreck*, p. 120; Stearns, *The Black Man*, p. 126; New York *Herald*, May 23, 1866; James D. Waters to mother, June 5, 1864, Box 12, folder 5, Waters Family Papers, Essex Inst.; Reid, *After the War*, p. 526.

80. Stearns, *The Black Man*, p. 116; Reid, *After the War*, p. 505; H. M. Crydenwise to parents, Oct. 2, 1866, Crydenwise Papers, DU; G. G. Klapp to J. D. Waters, June 17, 1865, Box 11, folder 7, Waters Family Papers, Essex Inst.

81. "Articles of Agreement . . . ," May 29, 1867, E. M. Stoeber Papers, SCL; labor contract [c. 1865], Box 11, folder 1, Waters Family Papers, Essex Inst.; Stearns, *The Black Man*, p. 363; Orders, no. 9, Mar. 11, 1864, in "Applications for Leasing Abandoned Plantations" (entry 2383), BEFAL Records, NA; Gerteis, *From Contraband to Freedman*, pp. 162-63. Joe Gray Taylor, *Louisiana Reconstructed, 1863-1877* (Baton Rouge, La., 1974), p. 332.

82. Labor contract [c. 1865], Box 11, folder 6, Waters Family Papers, Essex Inst.; see also Stearns, *The Black Man*, pp. 46-48; Warren, *Reminiscences*, p. 18.

83. "Articles of Agreement . . . ," May 29, 1867, E. M. Stoeber Papers, SCL.

84. [Benham], *A Year of Wreck*, p. 311.

85. Elmore (Ala.) *Standard*, May 15, 1867. See also Knox, *Camp-Fire and Cotton-Field*, p. 313; Yeatman, *A Report*, p. 10; H. B. Scott to J. F. B. Marshall, Feb. 14, 1867, SEC, NEEACo Papers, KSHS.

86. "Letters From New Orleans," Boston *Daily Advertiser*, Sept. 21, 1866. See also C. C. Waters to mother, Mar. 12, 1865, Box 12, folder 4, Waters Family Papers, Essex Inst.; A. B. Hart to mother, May 11, 1868, A. B. Hart Letters, FU.

87. Rose, *Rehearsal*, p. 226.

88. [Benham], *A Year of Wreck*, p. 394.

89. New York *Herald*, as quoted in Henry L. Swint, "Northern Interest in the Shoeless Southerner," *Journal of Southern History* 16 (Nov. 1950): 464; see also Rose, *Rehearsal*, pp. 164-65, 227; Charles Nordhoff, *The Freedmen of South Carolina* (New York, 1863), p. 20.

90. Pearson, ed., *Letters*, pp. 93, 228, 246.

91. McKaye, *The Mastership*, p. 28.

92. McKaye, *The Mastership*, pp. 27-28; James E. Yeatman, *Suggestions of a Plan for Free Labor . . .* (St. Louis, 1864), p. 5; Wiley, *Southern Negroes*, pp. 219-20, 224, 226-27; Gerteis, *From Contraband to Freedman*, pp. 148-49, 163; Ripley, *Slaves and Freedmen*, p. 61.

93. Rose, *Rehearsal*, p. 301. Military authorities at Port Royal closely regulated plantation stores during the war. (Pearson, ed., *Letters*, p. 280.)

94. "Letter from Charleston," Boston *Daily Advertiser*, Dec. 9, 1865; see also Dennett, *The South As It Is*, pp. 264-65; S. F. Dewey to John A. Wilder, Apr. 22, 1866, Box 45, Todd Family Papers, YU.

95. James D. Waters to Edward S. Waters, Feb. 25, 1864, Box 4, folder 5, Waters Family Papers, Essex Inst.

96. J. D. Waters to E. S. Waters, Mar. 16, 1864, Box 4, folder 5, Waters Family Papers, Essex Inst. For a less colorful account of an active opening day, see Knox, *Camp-Fire and Cotton-Field*, p. 410.

97. J. D. Waters to E. S. Waters, Mar. 16, 1864, Box 4, folder 5, Waters Family Papers, Essex Inst.

98. Ibid.

99. J. D. Waters to mother, Mar. 27, 1864, and Apr. 24, 1864, Box 12, folder 5, Waters Family Papers, Essex Inst.

100. Clifford C. Waters to mother, Mar. 12, 1865, Box 12, folder 4, Waters Family Papers; C. C. Waters to Henry F. Waters, Apr. 29, 1867, and Aug. 31, 1867, Box 8, C. C. Waters folder, H. F. Waters Papers, Essex Inst.

101. New York *Tribune*, May 24, 1865.

102. New York *Herald*, May 23, 1866; Perry, *Life and Letters*, p. 254; Reid, *After the War*, pp. 527-31; F. E. Wilder to [William] Markham, May 20, 1867, Markham-Puffer

Papers, CU; Clifford C. Waters to Edward S. Waters, Dec. 9, 1873, Box 4, folder 3, Waters Family Papers, Essex Inst.; J. Floyd King to Lin [Caperton], Jan. 1, 1866, Series A, Thomas Butler King Papers, SHC.

103. Wiley, *Southern Negroes*, p. 234.

104. Montgomery had operated a store on Davis Bend, Mississippi, since 1842. (Benjamin Montgomery to Joseph E. Davis, June 27, 1866, J. E. Davis Papers, MA.)

105. Knox, *Camp-Fire and Cotton-Field*, p. 411; Perry, *Life and Letters*, p. 258; Reid *After the War*, p. 527.

106. Reid, *After the War*, p. 257.

107. Perry, *Life and Letters*, pp. 257-58, 261; the quotation is on page 258.

108. William D. Waters to Abigail Waters, Feb. 22, 1864, Box 12, folder 1, Waters Family Papers, Essex Inst.; [Benham], *A Year of Wreck*, p. 353; John Eaton, *Grant, Lincoln and the Freedmen* (New York, 1907), p. 160.

109. Gerteis, *From Contraband to Freedman*, p. 163; Yeatman, *A Report*, p. 9; Wiley, *Southern Negroes*, p. 240; Eaton, *Grant, Lincoln and the Freedmen*, p. 158; J. Floyd King to Lin [Caperton], Jan. 1, 1866, Series A, Thomas Butler King Papers, SHC; New York *Herald*, May 23, 1866; Reid, *After the War*, pp. 498-99; Trowbridge, *The South*, p. 392.

110. Ambrose B. Hart to mother, May 11, 1868 ("old clothes"), and A. B. Hart to Lou Hart, May 24, 1868, A. B. Hart Papers, FU; Reid, *After the War*, pp. 498-99 ("watered down"). See also [Benham], *A Year of Wreck*, pp. 276-77, 330-31, 389; Plantation Journal, 1866, D. D. Slauson Papers, LSU; shipping invoice, Sept. 28, 1867, Box 3, Blair Family Papers, LC; F. W. Bardwell to Eben Loomis, July 30, 1866, Box 44, Todd Family Papers, YU; George C. Hardy to F. A. Eustis, Oct. 24, 1870, F. A. Eustis Papers, SCL; bill of sale, Feb. 6, 1865, and E. Smith to Waters and Klapp, Apr. 18, 1865, Good Hope Plantation Papers, LSU; Clifford C. Waters to Edward S. Waters, Apr. 16, 1865, Box 4, folder 3, Waters Family Papers, Essex Inst.; Trowbridge, *The South*, p. 392.

111. Reid, *After the War*, p. 528. See also William D. Waters to Edward S. Waters, June 4, 24, 1866, Waters Family Papers, Essex Inst.

112. Clifford C. Waters to Henry F. Waters, Aug. 31, 1867, Box 8, C. C. Waters folder, Henry F. Waters Papers, Essex Inst.; see also Ambrose B. Hart to mother, May 11, 1868, A. B. Hart Papers, FU.

113. *The Report of the Joint Committee on Reconstruction*, 39 Cong., 1 sess. (Ser. 1273), 4, p. 144. See also Reid, *After the War*, pp. 565-66; Henry L. Higginson to Horatio Woodman, Nov. 2, 1865, H. Woodman Papers, MHS; New York *Tribune*, May 24, 1865; New York *Herald*, June 13, 1866.

114. F. E. Wilder to [William] Markham, May 15, 1867, Markham-Puffer Papers, CU; James D. Waters to George G. Klapp, May 11, 1865, Good Hope Plantation Papers, LSU.

115. Clifford C. Waters to Edward S. Waters, Dec. 9, 1873, and Feb. 22, 1876, Box 4, folder 3, C. C. Waters to James D. Waters, Mar. 30, 1869, Box 11, folder 2, Waters Family Papers, Essex Inst.; New York *Herald*, May 23, 1866, and July 1, 1866.

116. Computed from Slauson and Carroll Plantation Journal, 1866, D. D. Slauson Papers, LSU; for a comparable estimate, see Gerteis, *From Contraband to Freedman*, pp. 164-65.

117. Reid, *After the War*, pp. 529-30.

118. J. Floyd King to Lin [Caperton], Jan. 1, 1866, Series A, Thomas Butler King Papers, SHC; Knox, *Camp-Fire and Cotton-Field*, p. 316; Yeatman, *A Report*, pp. 7-8.

119. Quoted in Eaton, *Grant, Lincoln, and the Freedmen*, p. 158.

120. Clifford C. Waters to Henry F. Waters, Apr. 29, 1867, and Aug. 31, 1867, Box 8, C. C. Waters folder, H. F. Waters Papers, Essex Inst.; see also H. B. Scott to J. F. B. Marshall, Feb. 14, 1867, SEC, NEEACo Papers, KSHS.

121. Robert T. Turnbeck to [A. W.] Kelsey, Jan. 9, 1869, E. Atkinson Papers, MHS.

122. Clifford C. Waters to Edward S. Waters, Nov. 14, 1873, Nov. 15, 1874, Jan. 28, 1876, and Feb. 7, 1876, Box 4, folder 3, Waters Family Papers, Essex Inst. A former surgeon with the Corps d'Afrique also made the transition from plantation storekeeper to supply merchant fairly easily. See Plantation Journal, 1866; agreement between D. D. Slauson and Richard Walker (col'd.), Jan. 9, 1871, Plantation Journal, 1876; and Gabe Posey in account with D. D. Slauson, Nov. 6, 1875, D. D. Slauson Papers, LSU. For accounts of the growth of supply merchants, see Harold Woodman, *King Cotton and his Retainers* (Lexington, Ky., 1968), pp. 308-09; C. Vann Woodward, *Origins of the New*

South, 1877-1913 (Baton Rouge, La., 1951), pp. 180-84; Jonathan M. Weiner, *Social Origins of the New South: Alabama, 1860-1885* (Baton Rouge, 1978), pp. 77-83; Taylor, *Louisiana Reconstructed*, pp. 382-406; and especially Michael Wayne's dissertation "Antebellum Planters in a Postbellum World: Natchez District, 1860-1880," in progress at Yale University.

123. Clifford C. Waters to James D. Waters, 1873, Box 11, folder 2; C. C. Waters to Edward S. Waters, Mar. 9, 1873, Nov. 14, 1873, and July 10, 1876, Box 4, folder 3, Waters Family Papers, Essex Inst.

124. George C. Hardy to F. A. Eustis, Oct. 28, 1870, F. A. Eustis Papers, SCL; see also John Davis to E. M. Stoeber, Mar. 2, 1867, E. M. Stoeber Papers; and Nat. L. Thompson to Reuben G. Holmes, Feb. 18, 1874, R. G. Holmes Papers, both in SCL.

125. C. C. Waters to E. S. Waters, July 10, 1876, Box 4, folder 3, Waters Family Papers, Essex Inst.; see also A. B. Hart to father, June 18, 1868, and Sept. 19, 1869, A. B. Hart Papers, FU; G. C. Hardy to F. A. Eustis, Oct. 28, 1870, F. A. Eustis Papers, SCL. There was an element of gamble in these speculations, for one had to borrow heavily and continually to keep his shelves stocked.

126. One southern planter told John Trowbridge in 1866: "I have neighbors who keep stores of plain goods and fancy articles for their people; and, let a nigger work ever so hard, and earn ever so high wages, he is sure to come out in debt at the end of the year." Trowbridge, *The South*, p. 366; see also Dennett, *The South As It Is*, pp. 290-92; Ripley, *Slaves and Freedmen*, pp. 196-97; Williamson, *After Slavery*, p. 175; Jerrell H. Shofner, *Nor Is It Over Yet: Florida in the Era of Reconstruction, 1863-1877* (Gainesville, 1974), p. 124.

127. Entry of Nov. 8, 1865, Diary, "1862," Whitelaw Reid Papers, LC; see also Reid, *After the War*, pp. 343, 372-73. The plantation stores established by the old planters in Natchez did not aim strictly at enlarging profits but at protecting them from the competing claims of the merchants for a share of the tenants' crops. See the dissertation in progress by Michael Wayne at Yale University. Also Wiener, *Social Origins*, pp. 77-133.

128. Quoted in Rose, *Rehearsal*, p. 216; Alexander Winchell to H. Brown, Jr., May 16, 1864, A. Winchell Letterbooks, MiHS; A. Winchell Diary, June 4, 1864 (pp. 18-20, MHC; Clifford C. Waters to Henry F. Waters, Apr. 29, 1867, Box 8, C. C. Waters folder, H. F. Waters Papers, Essex Inst.; E. O. Haven to A. Winchell, Aug. 13, 1864, A. Winchell and Family Papers, MHC.

129. William D. Waters to Abigail Waters, Apr. 1, 1865, Box 12, folder 1, Waters Family Papers, Essex Inst.

130. Perry, *Life and Letters*, p. 261; see also Stearns, *The Black Man*, p. 153.

131. [Benham], *A Year of Wreck*, p. 331.

132. See Willie Lee Rose's observations in *Rehearsal*, p. 229.

133. Morgan, *Yazoo*, pp. 89-90, 112.

134. Rose, *Rehearsal*, pp. 32-62, 154.

135. William H. Brisbane to Joseph J. Lewis, Dec. 2, 1864, in "Minutes," Records of the Direct Tax Commission for South Carolina, NA.

136. Rose, *Rehearsal*, p. 229; William D. Waters to Abigail Waters, May 27, 1866, Box 12, folder 1, and Clifford C. Waters to James D. Waters, Nov. 8, 1872, Box 11, folder 2, Waters Family Papers, Essex Inst.

137. Quoted in Eaton, *Grant, Lincoln and the Freedman*, p. 160; see also Ripley, *Slaves and Freedmen*, pp. 126-45; Wiley, *Southern Negroes*, pp. 265-70, 275; Knox, *Camp-Fire and Cotton-Field*, p. 365. The correspondence of the Waters family makes no mention of a school on the Thomas plantation during the war, and James Waters was in a position to know.

138. *Report of the Joint Committee*, 4, p. 144; D. D. Haskell to Gov. Lewis Parsons, Nov. 4, 1865, and James M. Shute to Gov. Robert Patton, Feb. 10, 1866, in Gov.'s Corr., AA; Boston *Daily Advertiser*, Aug. 23, 1866; *The Nation*, Aug. 17, 1865, p. 208; Shoalmire, "Carpetbagger Extraordinary," pp. 95-97; Perry, *Life and Letters*, p. 253; Morgan, *Yazoo*, pp. 103-04, 112; [Benham], *A Year of Wreck*, p. 304; Stearns, *The Black Man*, pp. 116, 276-77.

139. Clifford C. Waters to Henry F. Waters, Apr. 29, 1867, Box 8, C. C. Waters folder, H. F. Waters Papers, Essex Inst.

140. Stearns, *The Black Man*, pp. 197-99; Eben Loomis to wife, June 2, 1866, Box 8,

Todd Family Papers, YU; Garth W. James to father, Apr. 14, 1866, G. W. and R. James Papers, in possession of Prof. William Childers, University of Florida.

141. Clifford C. Waters to Henry F. Waters, Apr. 29, 1867, Box 8, C. C. Waters folder, H. F. Waters Papers, Essex Inst.; H. M. Crydenwise to parents, July 24, 1865, H. M. Crydenwise Papers, EU.

142. Garth W. James to parents, Apr. 8, 1868, James Family Papers, HU; Francis S. Thacher to T. B. Forbush, Mar. 30, 1867, SEC, NEEACo Papers, KSHS; Lt. Erastus W. Everson to Maj. James E. Cornelius, May 27, 1866, in Boston *Daily Advertiser*, June 19, 1866; Shoalmire, "Carpetbagger Extraordinary," pp. 95-97; entry of Apr. 22, 1864, Shoemaker Diary, DU.

143. H. M. Crydenwise to parents, June 25, 1866, H. M. Crydenwise Papers, DU; Stearns, *The Black Man*, pp. 116, 193-96; Perry, *Life and Letters*, p. 259; Stowe, "Our Florida Plantation," pp. 648-49.

144. H. M. Crydenwise to parents, June 25, 1866, H. M. Crydenwise Papers, DU; Francis S. Thacher to T. B. Forbush, Mar. 30, 1867, SEC, NEEACo Papers, KSHS; Rose, *Rehearsal*, pp. 87-88.

145. Stearns, *The Black Man*, p. 117.

Chapter 6

1. Quoted in Bliss Perry, *Life and Letters of Henry Lee Higginson* (Boston, 1921), p. 247.

2. Whitelaw Reid, *After the War: A Tour of the Southern States, 1865-1866*, ed. C. Vann Woodward (New York, 1965), p. 386.

3. Peter Kolchin, *First Freedom: The Responses of Alabama's Blacks to Emancipation and Reconstruction* (Westport, Conn., 1972), pp. 8-9; [George C. Benham], *A Year of Wreck* (New York, 1880), p. 329. See also Robert Higgs, *Competition and Coercion: Blacks in the American Economy, 1865-1914* (Cambridge, Eng., 1977), pp. 38-55.

4. Henry W. Warren, *Reminiscences of a Mississippi Carpetbagger* (Holden, Mass., 1914), p. 19; Henry Lee Higginson to Horatio Woodman, Nov. 2, 1865, H. Woodman Papers, MHS; Clifford C. Waters to mother, Mar. 1, 1866, Box 12, folder 4, Waters Family Papers, Essex Inst. See also Boston *Daily Advertiser*, Apr. 28, 1866.

5. John T. Trowbridge, *The South: A Tour of Its Battle Fields and Ruined Cities* (New York, 1969), p. 364.

6. *Report of the Joint Committee on Reconstruction*, 39 Cong., 1 sess. (Ser. 1273), 4, p. 143. Whitelaw Reid gives some indication of how the freedmen in the Mississippi Valley may have gained sophistication after one or two seasons of working for government lessees. Black people regarded a northern man, he tells us, "either as an adventurous swindler, without any money at all, or as a Croesus, made of money." (*After the War*, p. 506.)

7. Perry, *Life and Letters*, p. 254; Charles Stearns, *The Black Man of the South and the Rebels* (Boston, 1872), pp. 47, 262; see also entry of Mar. 21, 1864, Isaac Shoemaker Diary, DU.

8. Reid, *After the War*, p. 546.

9. "Notes of a Plantation Experience" [1866], Box 207, W. Reid Papers, LC.

10. Albert T. Morgan, *Yazoo; Or, On the Picket Line of Freedom in the South* (Washington, D.C., 1884), pp. 46, 90-96; see also Reid, *After the War*, p. 549; Elizabeth W. Pearson, ed., *Letters from Port Royal* (New York, 1969), p. 81.

11. Willie Lee Rose, *Rehearsal for Reconstruction: The Port Royal Experiment* (New York, 1964), p. 213.

12. William D. Waters to Edward S. Waters, Feb. 3, 1866, Box 4, folder 2, Waters Family Papers, Essex Inst.; see also Reid, *After the War*, pp. 503-04, 547-48; New York *Herald*, June 26, 1866.

13. Rufus Saxton, as quoted in Martin Abbott, *The Freedman's Bureau in South Carolina* (Chapel Hill, N.C., 1967), p. 8; New York *Herald*, June 13, 1866. For a discussion of the plantation restoration program, see William S. McFeely, *Yankee Stepfather: General O. O. Howard and the Freedmen* (New Haven, 1968), pp. 130-48.

14. General Howard amended this provision in June, 1865. (McFeely, *Yankee Stepfather*, pp. 97-98.)

15. Gainesville *New Era*, Feb. 24, 1866; Charleston (S.C.) *Daily Courier*, Feb. 1, 1866.

See also Augusta (Ga.) *Daily Constitutionalist*, Feb. 4, 1866; Brig. Gen. J. C. Beecher to Lt. M. N. Rice, Jan. 31, 1866, J. C. Beecher Papers, DU; J. Fraser Mathewes to editor, Charleston (S.C.) *Daily Courier*, Feb. 16, 1866.

16. Joel Williamson, *After Slavery: The Negro in South Carolina During Reconstruction* (Chapel Hill, S.C., 1965), pp. 82-83; J. Floyd King to Lin [Caperton], Feb. 13, 1866, Series A, Thomas Butler King Papers, SHC.

17. Brig. Gen. J. C. Beecher to Maj. Smith, Jan. 31, 1866, Beecher Papers, DU.

18. Brig. Gen. J. C. Beecher to H. H. Evans, Feb. 4, 1866; see also J. C. Beecher to Lt. M. N. Rice, Jan. 31, 1866, and Feb. 2, 1866; Beecher to Maj. Smith, Jan. 31, 1866, J. C. Beecher Papers, DU; New York *Herald*, May 23, 1866.

19. Sworn testimony of Toby Maxwell, T. G. Campbell Papers, GA. See also Remus Ellroth testimony, ibid.; New York *Herald*, June 2, 1866. For an unfriendly treatment of Campbell's administration, see E. Merton Coulter, *Negro Legislators in Georgia During the Reconstruction Period* (Athens, Ga., 1968), pp. 121-76.

20. Sworn testimony of Toby Maxwell, T. G. Campbell Papers, GA; New York *Herald*, June 2 and 13, 1866. See also W. F. Eaton to Gen. Davis Tillson, May 27, 1866, letters received, Records for Assistant Commissioners for Georgia, BRFAL Papers, NA.

21. New York *Herald*, June 2 and 13, 1866; Tunis G. Campbell, *Sufferings of the Rev. T. G. Campbell and his Family in Georgia* (Washington, D.C. 1877), pp. 7-8. The Campbell story has an unhappy sequel. Following his dismissal from the Freedmen's Bureau, he purchased a plantation on the mainland and persuaded many freedmen from St. Catherines to join him. He was immensely popular with the blacks, but not with the local whites, who feared his political power; he went from Reconstruction registrar to constitutional convention delegate, and finally to state senator. After years of harassment and attempted assassination, his enemies finally convicted him on trumped-up charges. He spent eleven months in a plantation prison camp. (Campbell, *Sufferings*, pp. 8-9, 15-27.)

22. Boston *Daily Advertiser*, Apr. 28, 1866. Some of these islands did become a resort for northern wealth, beginning in the 1880s. (Caroline C. Lovell, *The Golden Isles of Georgia* [Boston, 1933], pp. 274-75.)

23. Edward Barnwell Heyward to Jim [?], Jan. 22, 1866, E. B. Heyward Papers, SCL.

24. C. C. Drew to Clifford C. Waters, Jan. 10, 1864, Box 13, folder 2, Waters Family Papers, Essex Inst.

25. Pearson, ed., *Letters*, p. 255. See also "Minutes," Apr. 24, 1864; and William H. Brisbane to Joseph J. Lewis, Dec. 13, 1864, Gen. Corr., Records of the Direct Tax Commission for S.C., NA.

26. William D. Waters to Abigail Waters, Jan. 10, 1865, Box 12, folder 1, Waters Family Papers, Essex Inst.; Pearson, ed., *Letters*, pp. 165, 171, 250-51, 303-04; Rose, *Rehearsal*, p. 313.

27. Reid, *After the War*, p. 564.

28. Harriet B. Stowe, *Palmetto Leaves* (Boston, 1873), pp. 289-90, 300; H. B. Stowe, "Our Florida Plantation," *Atlantic Monthly* 43 (May 1879): 648; Stearns, *The Black Man* pp. 76-78.

29. The quotation is in Stearns, *The Black Man*, pp. 326-28, 334-35, 339; [Benham], *A Year of Wreck*, pp. 274-75; Charles F. Morse, *A Sketch of My Life* (Cambridge, 1927), p. 30; J. F. B. Marshall to T. B. Forbush, Feb. 9, 1867, SEC, NEEACo Papers, KSHS; William D. Waters to Abigail Waters, Feb. 22, 1864, Box 12, folder 1, Waters Family Papers, Essex Inst.; Eugene D. Genovese, *Roll, Jordan, Roll: The World the Slaves Made* (New York, 1974), p. 115.

30. Perry, *Life and Letters*, p. 265. Charles Stearns voiced the same complaint. He said that the freedmen's "self esteem" was "the most formidable obstacle in the way of their improvement. They cannot be made to realize that they are spiritually 'poor and blind and naked,' but they believe they are 'rich in goods and have need of nothing' spiritually." *The Black Man*, p. 327.

31. William D. Waters to Abigail Waters, Jan. 10, 1865, Box 12, folder 1. See also W. D. Waters to Clifford C. Waters, Jan. 14, 1865, Box 13, folder 1, Waters Family Papers, Essex Inst.; Pearson, ed., *Letters*, pp. 300-01; Rose, *Rehearsal*, pp. 307-13.

32. Reid, *After the War*, p. 506; Morse, *A Sketch*, p. 30; see also F. W. Bardwell to Eben Loomis, Aug. 31, 1866, Box 44, Todd Family Papers, YU.

33. James D. Waters to mother, June 5, 1864, Box 12, folder 5, Waters Family Papers,

Essex Inst.; see also Stearns, *The Black Man*, p. 189; Reid, *After the War*, p. 527; [G. W. James] to parents, Apr. 6, 1867, G. W. and R. James Papers, in possession of Prof. William Childers, University of Florida.

34. Edward Stetson to Clifford C. Waters, June 5, 1864, Box 13, folder 2, Waters Family Papers, Essex Inst.

35. "Notes of a Plantation Experience" [1866], W. Reid Papers, LC.

36. Reid, *After the War*, p. 508.

37. John R. Dennett, *The South As It Is, 1865-1866* (New York, 1965), p. 205.

38. Thomas Knox, *Camp-Fire and Cotton-Field: Southern Adventure in Time of War* (New York, 1865), p. 374.

39. The quotation is in Reid, *After the War*, p. 547; Pearson, ed., *Letters*, pp. 294-95; Rose, *Rehearsal*, p. 313.

40. William D. Waters to Abigail Waters, Jan. 10, 1865, Box 12, folder 1; George C. Klapp to James D. Waters, Aug. 17, 1865, Box 11, folder 7, Waters Family Papers, Essex Inst. See also Perry, *Life and Letters*, p. 256; Reid, *After the War*, pp. 547-48.

41. [Benham], *A Year of Wreck*, p. 353; "Notes of a Plantation Experience" [1866], W. Reid Papers, LC.

42. James D. Waters to mother, June 5, 1864, Box 12, folder 5, Waters Family Papers, Essex Inst.; Reid, *After the War*, p. 506.

43. Reid, *After the War*, p. 517. See also Stearns, *The Black Man*, p. 75; entry of Apr. 2, 1864, Shoemaker Diary, DU.

44. Stearns, *The Black Man*, pp. 121-22; *The Ku-Klux Conspiracy: Testimony Taken by the Joint Select Committee to Inquire into the Condition of Affairs in the Late Insurrectionary States* (Washington, D.C., 1872), vol. 2, pt. 7, p. 717; C. C. Waters to J. D. Waters, Dec. 19, 1865, Box 11, folder 2, Waters Family Papers, Essex Inst.; H. B. Scott to J. F. B. Marshall, July 22, 1868, SEC, NEEACo Papers, KSHS.

45. William D. Waters to Edward S. Waters, June 4, 1866, Box 4, folder 2, Waters Family Papers, Essex Inst.; [Benham], *A Year of Wreck*, p. 213. See also A. B. Hart to Mary Hart, July 31, 1870, A. B. Hart Papers, FU; H. B. Scott to J. F. B. Marshall, July 22, 1868, SEC, NEEACo Papers, KSHS; entry of May 6, 1864, Shoemaker Diary, DU; and John Ficklen, *The History of Reconstruction in Louisiana* (Baltimore, 1910), p. 137.

46. James D. Waters to mother, Apr. 24, 1864, Box 12, folder 5; see also Abigail D. Waters to William C. and Susan Waters, Oct. 25, 1865, Box 13, folder 6, Waters Family Papers, Essex Inst.; Perry, *Life and Letters*, p. 264.

47. Stearns, *The Black Man*, p. 55.

48. William D. Waters to Abigail Waters, Aug. 12, 1866 (for the quotation), and Oct. 12, 1866, Box 12, folder 1; James D. Waters to Edward S. Waters, Feb. 25, 1864, Box 4, folder 5; George G. Klapp to James D. Waters, June 29, 1865, and July 21, 1865, Box 11, folder 7; J. D. Waters to G. G. Klapp and C. C. Waters, July 19, 1865, Box 13, folder 7, Waters Family Papers, Essex Inst.; Pearson, ed., *Letters*, pp. 320-23; Rose, *Rehearsal*, p. 368; *DeBow's Review*, AWS 4 (Oct. 1867), p. 336.

49. [Benham], *A Year of Wreck*, p. 213; Stearns, *The Black Man*, pp. 122-23; Knox, *Camp-Fire and Cotton-Field*, pp. 351-52.

50. Stearns, *The Black Man*, pp. 122, 236. See also John Blassingame, *The Slave Community* (New York, 1972), p. 92.

51. Knox, *Camp-Fire and Cotton-Field*, p. 351. Eugene Genovese offers this explanation of the slave ethic regarding stealing: "The slaves made a distinction: they stole from each other but merely took from their masters. . . . If they belonged to their masters, if they were in fact his chattels—how could they steal from him?" (*Roll, Jordan, Roll: The World the Slaves Made* [New York, 1974], p. 602.)

52. William D. Waters to Abigail Waters, July 23, 1866, Box 12, folder 1, Waters Family Papers, Essex Inst., *italics mine.*

53. Stearns, *The Black Man*, p. 341. See also Perry, *Life and Letters*, p. 259; "Notes of a Plantation Experience" [1866], W. Reid Papers, LC.

54. [Benham], *A Year of Wreck*, p. 213; see also Knox, *Camp-Fire and Cotton-Field*, p. 351; Stearns, *The Black Man*, p. 121.

55. Stearns, *The Black Man*, p. 343; [Benham], *A Year of Wreck*, p. 202; Pearson, ed., *Letters*, p. 287; Rose, *Rehearsal*, p. 368.

56. Stearns, *The Black Man*, pp. 120, 355-56, 363; Perry, *Life and Letters*, p. 259; William D. Waters to Abigail Waters, Jan. 10, 1865, Box 12, folder 1; labor contract [c.

1865], Box 11, folder 1, Waters Family Papers, Essex Inst.; Orders, No. 9, Mar. 11, 1864, "Applications for Leasing Abandoned Plantations" (entry 2383), BRFAL Records, NA. See also Knox, *Camp-Fire and Cotton-Field*, p. 428; entry of Apr. 24, 1864, Shoemaker Diary, DU.

57. Proceedings of the "High Court of Pains and Penalties," Sept. 16, 28, and 29, 1865, Oct. 11 and 16, 1865, Good Hope Plantation Papers, LSU.

58. Perry, *Life and Letters*, p. 264.

59. Reid, *After the War*, p. 504; *The Ku-Klux Conspiracy*, vol. 2, pt. 7, p. 717; E. L. Devereaux to James D. Waters, May 17, 1866, Box 11, folder 8, Waters Family Papers, Essex Inst.

60. "Letters From the South," Boston *Daily Advertiser*, Aug. 5, 1865. See also Stearns, *The Black Man*, pp. 334-38; Frances B. Leigh, *Ten Years on a Georgia Plantation Since the War* (London, 1883), p. 53; Pearson, ed., *Letters*, p. 227; Perry, *Life and Letters*, p. 257; William D. Waters to Abigail Waters, Mar. 8, 1864, and Oct. 12, 1866, Box 12, folder 1; G. G. Klapp to J. D. Waters, July 31, 1864, Box 11, folder 7; C. C. Waters to E. S. Waters, Jan. 24, 1866, Box 4, folder 3, Waters Family Papers, Essex Inst.; A. B. Hart to Mary Hart, July 31, 1870, A. B. Hart Papers, FU; J. N. Chambers to Capt. F. A. Stickel, Mar. 28, 1867, D. D. Slauson Papers, LSU.

61. Robert W. Fogel and Stanley L. Engerman's criticism of the racial bias of most free-soil critics of the slave South is well taken. (*Time on the Cross: The Economics of American Negro Slavery* [Boston, 1974], pp. 177-81, 209-23.)

62. Two modern economists estimate that "The number of man-hours per capita supplied by the rural black population fell by an amount between 28 and 37 percent of the quantity of labor that had been extracted through the coercion of slavery." They attribute this decline to the voluntary withdrawal of women and children from the work force and to the determination of the freedmen in general to work fewer days and shorter hours. (Roger L. Ransom and Richard Sutch, *One Kind of Freedom: The Economic Consequences of Emancipation* [Cambridge, Eng., 1977], pp. 5-6, 46.)

63. [Benham], *A Year of Wreck*, pp. 202-03; Stearns, *The Black Man*, pp. 516-17. See also George G. Klapp to James D. Waters, June 17, 1865, Box 11, folder 7, Waters Family Papers, Essex Inst.

64. Stearns, *The Black Man*, p. 171. In a sense the freedmen were indulging old habits here too. The converting of privileges into rights, Eugene Genovese tells us, was the slaves' way of turning the paternalistic code to their advantage. (*Roll, Jordan, Roll*, pp. 146-47.)

65. [Benham], *A Year of Wreck* pp. 198-99.

66. Ibid., p. 119. See also Stearns, *The Black Man*, pp. 170-71; Pearson, ed., *Letters*, p. 48; "Letters From the South," Boston *Daily Advertiser*, Aug. 5, 1865; William D. Waters to Abigail Waters, June 9, 1866, Box 12, folder 1; James D. Waters to Edward S. Waters, Mar. 16, 1864, Box 4, folder 5, Waters Family Papers, Essex Inst.; entry of Apr. 2, 1864, Shoemaker Diary, DU.

67. Stearns, *The Black Man*, p. 171.

68. Ibid.

69. A.B. Hart to Mary Hart, July 31, 1870, A. B. Hart Papers, FU. See also Genovese, *Roll, Jordan, Roll*, p. 198, for an explanation of this aspect of slave funerals.

70. [Benham], *A Year of Wreck*, p. 263; Rose, *Rehearsal*, p. 74.

71. Genovese, *Roll, Jordan, Roll*, p. 201.

72. Stearns, *The Black Man*, p. 170.

73. Selma *Daily Messenger*, Mar. 3, 1866; H. M. Crydenwise to parents, Apr. 3 [1866], H. M. Crydenwise Papers, DU; Herbert G. Gutman, *The Black Family in Slavery and Freedom* (New York, 1976), pp. 167-68.

74. Pearson, ed., *Letters*, pp. 52, 126, 160; [Benham], *A Year of Wreck*, p. 333; Stowe, *Palmetto Leaves*, pp. 311-14.

75. Blassingame, *Slave Community*, p. 94; Genovese, *Roll, Jordan, Roll*, pp. 495-501.

76. Louis S. Gerteis, *From Contraband to Freedman: Federal Policy Toward Southern Blacks, 1861-1865* (Westport, Conn., 1973), p. 157; "Register of Leased Plantations-1865" (entry 532), BRFAL Records, NA. Conscription of male hands at Port Royal had also placed the burden of fieldwork on the women. (Rose, *Rehearsal*, pp. 268-69.)

77. James D. Waters to William D. Waters, Jan. 22, 1865, Box 10, folder 3, Waters Family Papers, Essex Inst.

78. James D. Waters to mother, Mar. 27, 1864 (for the quotation), Apr. 24, 1864, June

5, 1864, Box 12, folder 5, Waters Family Papers, Essex Inst.; Knox, *Camp-Fire and Cotton-Field*, pp. 426-28; Gerteis, *From Contraband to Freedman*, p. 161. The method occasionally achieved even more than the intended result. Whitelaw Reid gave this account of the effect of the ticket system on a plantation near Natchez, Mississippi: "Under this arrangement the overseer said he had very few sick people on the plantation. Sometimes in fact they went to the fields when really too sick to work, lest they should lose their wages for the day. In unpleasant weather too, . . . they were far less anxious to quit work than formerly." (*After the War*, p. 488.)

79. George G. Klapp to James D. Waters, July 31, 1864 (for the quotation), Aug. 3, 1864, Box 11, folder 7, Waters Family Papers, Essex Inst.; Report on Laborers [n.d.], Good Hope Plantation Papers, LSU.

80. Pearson, ed., *Letters*, pp. 53, 56, 250, 303-04. Whitelaw Reid may have revealed more than he intended in this sardonic statement: "An abolitionist making women work in the fields, like beasts of burden—or men!" (Whitelaw Reid to Anna E. Dickinson, June 18, 1866, A. Dickinson Papers, LC.)

81. Morgan, *Yazoo*, pp. 82-83; Warren, *Reminiscences*, p. 18.

82. Chicago *Tribune*, Aug. 14, 1866.

83. The quotation is in "Trip to Northern Alabama," *The Nation*, Aug. 17, 1865, p. 208; Stowe, *Palmetto Leaves*, pp. 314-17; *The Ku-Klux Conspiracy*, vol. 2, pt. 7, p. 1089; see also "Letters From the South," Boston *Daily Advertiser*, Aug. 19, 1865; J. F. B. Marshall to T. B. Forbush, Mar. 4, 1867, SEC, NEEACo Papers, KSHS.

84. Stearns, *The Black Man*, p. 334; [Benham], *A Year of Wreck*, pp. 282-83; Genovese, *Roll, Jordan, Roll*, pp. 321-22.

85. C. C. Waters to Henry F. Waters, May 8, 1866; see also J. D. Waters to H. F. Waters, Apr. 20, 1868, Box 8, H. F. Waters Papers, Essex Inst.; *Report of the Joint Committee*, 4, p. 141. Black veterans may have been more reliable laborers, but they had no strong attachment to plantation labor. When the army came to his neighborhood to recruit troops for the Indian Wars, George Benham had to call in the Freedmen's Bureau in order to prevent the ex-soldiers from breaking their contracts in order to enlist. ([Benham], *A Year of Wreck*, pp. 217-18.)

86. H. M. Crydenwise to Charles Crydenwise, Mar. 21, 1866 (for the quotation), and April 3 [1866], H. M. Crydenwise Papers, DU.

87. Stearns, *The Black Man*, p. 517. For more examples of successful black husbandry see Rose, *Rehearsal*, pp. 314-15; Gerteis, *From Contraband to Freedman*, pp. 171-79; C. Peter Ripley, *Slaves and Freedmen in Civil War Louisiana* (Baton Rouge, La., 1976), pp. 76-83.

88. The respective quotations are in Pearson, ed., *Letters*, pp. 112-13; and Stearns, *The Black Man*, p. 336. See also Perry, *Life and Letters*, p. 255.

89. Leigh, *Ten Years*, pp. 55-56.

90. Boston *Daily Advertiser*, Nov. 4, 1865 (for the quotation), Jan. 4, 1867; Thomas Affleck to wife, Dec. 19, 1865, Thomas Affleck Papers, LSU.

91. Quoted in Genovese, *Roll, Jordan, Roll*, p. 312.

92. Stearns, *The Black Man*, p. 85; Whitelaw Reid to Anna Dickinson, Nov. 11, 1866, A. Dickinson Papers, LC. See also Reid, *After the War*, p. 506; [Benham], *A Year of Wreck*, p. 244; Eben Loomis to Mary Loomis, June 2, 1866, Box 8, Todd Family Papers, YU; William D. Waters to Abigail Waters, Feb. 2, 1865, Box 12, folder 1; W. D. Waters to E. S. Waters, Feb. 3, 1866, Box 4, folder 2; C. C. Waters to E. S. Waters, Jan. 24, 1866, Box 4, folder 3; and C. C. Waters to mother, Mar. 1, 1866, Box 12, folder 4, Waters Family Papers, Essex Inst.

93. Pearson, ed., *Letters*, p. 144.

94. Harriet Beecher Stowe to O. O. Howard, May 1868, O. O. Howard Papers, Bowdoin College; Mary Boykin Chesnut, *A Diary From Dixie*, ed. Ben Ames Williams (Boston, 1949), p. 163.

95. Stowe, *Palmetto Leaves*, pp. 298, 306-09, 311-13, 314 (the quotation is on p. 314). Southerners were no more successful with similar efforts. Williamson, *After Slavery*, pp. 35, 40.

96. Stearns, *The Black Man*, pp. 44-45.

97. Ibid., pp. 44-46, 54-55, 56, 85; the quotation is on p. 56.

98. Ibid., pp. 44-45.

99. Ibid., pp. 44-46, 54-55, 56, 85; the quotation is on p. 56.

100. Perry, *Life and Letters*, p. 262.

101. Leigh, *Ten Years,* p. 53. See also J. Floyd King to Mallory King, Jan. 18, 1866, Series A, Thomas B. King Papers, SHC; Rose, *Rehearsal,* pp. 370-71; James L. Roark, *Masters Without Slaves: Southern Planters in the Civil War and Reconstruction* (New York, 1977), pp. 160-61.

102. Frederick Law Olmsted, *The Cotton Kingdom,* ed. Arthur M. Schlesinger (New York, 1970), p. 615. See also Genovese, *Roll, Jordan, Roll,* pp. 301-02.

103. *The Ku-Klux Conspiracy,* vol. 2, pt. 7, p. 717.

104. Stearns, *The Black Man,* p. 337.

105. Pearson, ed., *Letters,* pp. 137 and 316.

106. William D. Waters to Abigail Waters, Mar. 8, 1864, Box 12, folder 1, Waters Family Papers, Essex Inst.; Perry, *Life and Letters,* p. 259; Stearns, *The Black Man,* p. 395.

107. Stearns, *The Black Man,* pp. 328, 332-33. See also Pearson, ed., *Letters,* pp. 217-18; James D. Waters to mother, June 5, 1864, Box 12, folder 5, Waters Family Papers, Essex Inst.; Perry, *Life and Letters,* pp. 262-63; Rose, *Rehearsal,* pp. 363-77; *The Ku-Klux Conspiracy,* vol. 2, pt. 7, p. 716, entry of Apr. 28, 1864, Shoemaker Diary, DU.

108. William D. Waters to Abigail Waters, Feb. 2, 1865, Box 12, folder 1, Waters Family Papers, Essex Inst.

109. James D. Waters to Edward S. Waters, Mar. 16, 1864, Box 4, folder 5, Waters Family Papers, Essex Inst.

110. [Benham], *A Year of Wreck,* p. 337; Leigh, *Ten Years,* p. 53; F. W. Bardwell to Eben Loomis, May 21, 22, and 23, 1866, Box 44, and Mary Loomis to Eben Loomis, July 4, 1866, and Aug. 7, 1866, Box 8, Todd Family Papers, YU. See also Stearns, *The Black Man,* p. 170; Francis B. Simkins and Robert H. Woody, *South Carolina During Reconstruction* (Gloucester, Mass., 1966), p. 243.

111. Trowbridge, *The South,* p. 386.

112. A. B. Hart to Emily Hart, Apr. 7, 1871, A. B. Hart Papers, FU; George C. Hardy to F. A. Eustis, July 7, 1870, F. A. Eustis Papers, SCL; William D. Waters to Edward S. Waters, June 24, 1866, Box 4, folder 2; James D. Waters to E. S. Waters, Feb. 25, 1864, Box 4, folder 5, Waters Family Papers, Essex Inst.; G. G. Klapp to Lee, Apr. 1, 1866, Good Hope Plantation Papers, LSU; Eliza J. Andrews, *The Wartime Journal of a Georgia Girl, 1864-1865* (New York, 1908), p. 278.

113. Stearns, *The Black Man,* p. 45. See also Pearson, ed., *Letters,* pp. 112-13; Trowbridge, *The South,* p. 367; "Notes of a Plantation Experience" [1866], W. Reid Papers, LC.

114. James D. Waters to Henry F. Waters, Apr. 20, 1868, Box 8, H. F. Waters Papers, Essex Inst.

115. William D. Waters to Edward S. Waters, Apr. 6, 1865, Feb. 3, 1866, and June 24, 1866, Box 4, folder 2, Waters Family Papers, Essex Inst.

116. Dennett, *The South As It Is,* p. 205. See also "Letters From the South" and "A Visit to Port Royal," Boston *Daily Advertiser,* Aug. 19, Dec. 4, 1865.

117. William D. Waters to Abigail Waters, Feb. 2, 1865, Box 12, folder 1, Waters Family Papers, Essex Inst.

118. W. D. Waters to E. S. Waters, Apr. 6, 1865, Box 4, folder 3, Waters Family Papers, Essex Inst. Apparently the black farmers at various times became overextended in cotton. See William D. Waters to Edward S. Waters, June 4 and 24, 1866, Box 4, folder 2, ibid.; Pearson, ed., *Letters,* p. 331.

119. Eben Loomis to Mary Loomis, July 21, 1866, Mary Loomis to Eben Loomis, July 4, 1866 (two letters), and Aug. 7, 1866, Box 8, Todd Family Papers, YU; Clifford C. Waters to James D. Waters, Sept. 20, 1865, Box 11, folder 2; George G. Klapp to J. D. Waters, June 16, 1865, Box 11, folder 7, Waters Family Papers, Essex Inst.; C. C. Waters to Capt. S. H. West, Oct. 12, 1865, Report on Laborers [n.d.], Good Hope Plantation Papers, LSU; see also Leigh, *Ten Years,* p. 54n.

120. Stearns, *The Black Man,* 363; see also pp. 56, 86 and 338.

121. George C. Hardy to F. A. Eustis, July 4, 1870, F. A. Eustis Papers, SCL.

122. Pearson, ed., *Letters,* p. 332.

123. Ibid., p. 258; see also Stearns, *The Black Man,* pp. 105, 108, and 170; Morgan, *Yazoo,* p. 98; [Benham], *A Year of Wreck,* p. 263; Gerteis, *From Contraband to Freedman,* pp. 160 and 166. See also Genovese, *Roll, Jordan, Roll,* pp. 17-23.

124. James D. Waters to mother, Sept. 10, 1865, Box 12, folder 5, Waters Family Papers, Essex Inst. For more on the disruptive influence of black troops on plantation

discipline, see John S. Purviance to David Yulee, Dec. 3, 1865, D. Yulee Papers, University of Florida; A. W. Kelsey to Edward Atkinson, Aug. 18 and 25, 1865, Atkinson Papers, MHS; Boston *Daily Advertiser*, Dec. 25, 1865; and Reid, *After the War*, p. 298.

125. Stearns, *The Black Man*, p. 170; George C. Hardy to F. A. Eustis, Sept. 12, 1870, F. A. Eustis Papers, SCL; entry of Apr. 20, 1864, Shoemaker Diary, DU, where the quotation appears.

126. Reid, *After the War*, p. 514; see also Gerteis, *From Contraband to Freedman*, p. 166.

127. Stearns, *The Black Man*, p. 236.

128. James D. Waters to George G. Klapp, June 30, 1865, Box 11, folder 7, Waters Family Papers, Essex Inst.

129. Ibid.

130. Elizabeth H. Botume, *First Days Among the Contrabands* (Boston, 1893), p. 121.

131. Reid, *After the War*, pp. 549-50.

132. [Benham], *A Year of Wreck*, p. 202.

133. John H. Kenneway, *On Sherman's Track; Or, The South After the War* (London, 1867), p. 69. See also Ambrose B. Hart to mother, June 8, 1868, A. B. Hart Papers, FU; George C. Hardy to F. A. Eustis, Sept. 12, 1870, F. A. Eustis Papers, SCL; [Benham], *A Year of Wreck*, pp. 198-99; Selma *Daily Messenger*, Aug. 28, 1866; Gainesville *New Era*, Dec. 16, 1865, and Sept. 14, 1866; Clifford C. Waters to James D. Waters, Aug. 2, 1869, Box 11, folder 2, Waters Family Papers, Essex Inst.; William C. Harris, *Presidential Reconstruction in Mississippi* (Baton Rouge, La., 1967), pp. 99-100.

134. James D. Waters to mother, Mar. 27, 1864 (for the quotation), and Apr. 24, 1864, Box 12, folder 5, Waters Family Papers, Essex Inst.

135. William D. Waters to Abigail Waters, June 9, 1866 (for the quotation), and Oct. 12, 1866, Box 12, folder 1, Waters Family Papers, Essex Inst.

136. Quoted in Ficklen, *Reconstruction in Louisiana*, p. 136; Gerteis, *From Contraband to Freedman*, p. 164; Wiley, *Southern Negroes*, pp. 244-45.

137. The quotation is in William D. Waters to Abigail Waters, June 9, 1866, Box 12, folder 1, Waters Family Papers, Essex Inst.; Pearson, ed., *Letters*, 138; [Benham], *A Year of Wreck*, pp. 218-19.

138. Stearns, *The Black Man*, pp. 49 and 415.

139. Ibid., p. 53. A Yankee lessee in the Mississippi Valley during the war made a similar transition within the space of three months: "I find it necessary to be very decided and commanding; . . . I tried at first mild means—persuasion and reason—but that will not answer yet awile [*sic*]; they have been so long used to obedience to positive commands, that the change must be gradual, and in proportion to their education in their new sphere." (Entry of Apr. 28, 1864, Shoemaker Diary, DU.)

140. Stearns, *The Black Man*, p. 54.

141. C. Peter Ripley, *Slaves and Freedmen in Civil War Louisiana* (Baton Rouge, La., 1976), pp. 90, 93-95. See also Gerteis, *From Contraband to Freedman*, pp. 92-93; Proceedings of the "High Court of Pains & Penalties," Sept. 16 and 29, 1865, Good Hope Plantation Papers, LSU.

142. John M. Gould, *History of the First—Tenth—Twenty-ninth Maine Regiment* (Portland, Me., 1871), pp. 586-89. The freedmen in Liberty County, Georgia, were astonished that the bluecoats used rawhide on them. "Very soon they began to whisper that the said Yankees were only Southern men in blue clothes—that the true Yankee had not yet come." (Robert M. Myers, ed., *The Children of Pride* [New Haven, 1972], p. 1292; see also Earl S. Miers, ed., *When the World Ended: The Diary of Emma LeConte* [New York, 1957], pp. 115-16.)

143. Kate Stone recorded an incident in her diary shortly after the war that is very revealing about the social changes occasioned by emancipation. Her brother had shot a freedman in the field and was mobbed and nearly killed by the rest of the gang. For his safety he was sent away to school and returned a few months later thoroughly broken of his habit of speaking loosely about "killing people." (John Q. Anderson, ed., *Brokenburn: The Journal of Kate Stone, 1861-1868* [Baton Rouge, La., 1955], pp. 368-69.) For other

examples of black armed resistance to impositions of one sort or another, see New York *Herald*, Apr. 22, 1866; Boston *Daily Advertiser*, Sept. 16, Dec. 27, 1865, Apr. 2, May 10, Dec. 5, 23, 1867.

144. Ripley, *Slaves and Freedmen*, p. 91; James D. Waters to mother, June 5, 1864, Box 12, folder 5; Geroge G. Klapp to J. D. Waters, June 1 and 4, 1865, Box 11, folder 7; order of Maj. George D. Reynolds, June 10, 1865, Box 11, folder 1, Waters Family Papers, Essex Inst.; order of Capt. D. L. Jones, May 29, 1865, Capt. S. H. West to J. D. Waters, Sept. 25, 1865, Clifford C. Waters to Capt. S. H. West, Oct. 12, 1865, Report on Laborers [n.d.], Good Hope Plantation Papers, LSU.

145. George G. Klapp to James D. Waters, May 26, 1865, Box 11, folder 7, Waters Family Papers, Essex Inst.

146. Reid, *After the War*, p. 515.

147. Stearns, *The Black Man*, pp. 108–09; Maj. J. Rainy Smith to Maj. W. W. Deane, Aug. 30, 1866, letters received, Records of the Assistant Commissioners for Georgia, BRFAL Records, NA. [Benham], *A Year of Wreck*, pp. 218-21; Reid, *After the War*, pp. 530 and 556; Harris, *Presidential Reconstruction*, pp. 93-95, 99-100. See McFeely, *Yankee Stepfather*, pp. 3, 158-59, and passim, for an excellent account of how the agents generally came to share the planters' view of all things.

148. Elmore (Ala.) *Standard*, Jan. 17, 1868. See also A. B. Hart to Louisa Hart, Oct. 7, 1870, A. B. Hart Papers, FU.

149. Stearns, *The Black Man*, pp. 108–09.

150. Stearns, *The Black Man*, pp. 76-81, 170, 355; [Benham], *A Year of Wreck*, pp. 221, 304; Pearson, ed., *Letters*, p. 87; Gainesville *New Era*, Sept. 14, 1866; Warren, *Reminiscences*, p. 30.

151. Rose, *Rehearsal*, p. 327.

152. "We none of us think that if left to themselves they would have energy enough to be really thrifty and prosperous, no matter how much help they should get in the way of lands," Henry Lee Higginson's wife wrote of the freedmen. (Perry, *Life and Letters*, p. 257.)

153. Rose, *Rehearsal*, p. 366; Pearson, ed., *Letters*, pp. 327-28.

154. [Benham], *A Year of Wreck*, p. 276.

155. Rose, *Rehearsal*, p. 366, and pp. 363-77.

156. Quoted in ibid., p. 365.

157. William D. Waters to Abigail Waters, Mar. 8, 1864 (for the quotation), and Sept. 16, 1865, Box 12, folder 1; Clifford C. Waters to James D. Waters, Aug. 2, 1869, Box 11, folder 2, Waters Family Papers, Essex Inst.

158. Garth W. James to William James, Sept. 29, 1866; G. W. and Robertson James Papers, in possession of Prof. William Childers, University of Florida; G. W. James to Alice James, Apr. 28, 1869, James Family Papers, HU; Perry, *Life and Letters*, p. 265.

159. Whitelaw Reid to Anna E. Dickinson, June 18, 1866, Anna E. Dickinson Papers, LC.

160. Stearns, *The Black Man*, pp. 173-74.

161. Herbert G. Gutman, *Work, Culture, and Society in Industrializing America* (New York, 1976), pp. 71-73.

162. *DeBow's Review*, AWS 4 (Oct. 1867), p. 336; Selma *Daily Messenger*, Aug. 28, 1866; Eben Loomis to wife, July 3, 1866, Box 8, Todd Family Papers, YU; Ambrose Hart to Louisa Hart, Nov. 17, 1868, A. B. Hart Papers, FU; James D. Waters to mother, Mar. 27, Apr. 24, 1864, Box 12, folder 5, Waters Family Papers, Essex Inst.

163. Gainesville *New Era*, Sept. 14, 1866.

164. *DeBow's Review*, AWS 4 (Oct. 1867), p. 336.

165. William D. Waters to Edward S. Waters, June 24, 1866, Box 4, folder 2, Waters Family Papers, Essex Inst.

166. Ambrose B. Hart to Mary Hart, July 31, 1870, A. B. Hart Papers, FU.

167. Stearns, *The Black Man*, p. 279.

168. *The Ku-Klux Conspiracy*, vol. 2, pt. 7, p. 724; Leigh, *Ten Years*, p. 54*n*; Gainesville *New Era*, Dec. 16, 1865; Eben Loomis to sister Eliza, Jan. 9, 1867, Box 9, Todd Family Papers, YU.

169. Perry, *Life and Letters*, pp. 265-66.

Chapter 7

1. Anna R. Burr, ed., *Alice James. Her Brother. Her Journal* (New York, 1934), p. 45. See also Bliss Perry, *Life and Letters of Henry Lee Higginson* (Boston, 1921), p. 250; Clifford C. Waters to Edward S. Waters, Jan. 24, 1866, Box 4, folder 3, Waters Family Papers, Essex Inst.

2. James D. Waters to mother, Sept. 10, 1865, Box 12, folder 5; see also J. D. Waters to G. G. Klapp and C. C. Waters, July 19, 1865, Box 13, folder 7; and C. C. Waters to mother, Mar. 12, 1865, Box 12, folder 4, Waters Family Papers, Essex Inst.; [George C. Benham], *A Year of Wreck* (New York, 1880), pp. 141, 159-60; Jimmy G. Shoalmire, "Carpetbagger Extraordinary: Marshall Harvey Twitchell, 1840-1905" (Ph.D. diss., Mississippi State University, 1969), pp. 29-30.

3. Francis S. Thacher to T. B. Forbush, Mar. 30, 1867, SEC, NEEACo Papers, KSHS.

4. Journal of Ambrose B. Hart, Dec. 19, 1866, FU.

5. Clifford C. Waters to Edward S. Waters, Jan. 24, 1866, Box 4, folder 3, Waters Family Papers, Essex Inst.; [Benham], *A Year of Wreck*, p. 162. See also Charles Stearns, *The Black Man of the South and the Rebels* (Boston, 1872), pp. 159-64; Sarah Crydenwise to mother, Oct. 29, 1865 [c. 1866], H. M. Crydenwise Papers, EU.

6. Ambrose B. Hart to mother, Apr. 30, 1867, A. B. Hart Papers, FU. See also Shoalmire, "Carpetbagger Extraordinary," pp. 62-63; Sarah Crydenwise to mother, Oct. 29, 1866 [c. 1865], H. M. Crydenwise Papers, EU.

7. Henry Warren, *Reminiscences of a Mississippi Carpetbagger* (Holden, Mass., 1914), p. 48; Robertson James to Mrs. J. M. Forbes, Dec. 30, 1866, James Family Papers, HU.

8. Shoalmire, "Carpetbagger Extraordinary," p. 63; Stearns, *The Black Man*, pp. 190-92; [Benham], *A Year of Wreck*, pp. 69, 109-11.

9. C. C. Waters to E. S. Waters, Jan. 24, 1866, Box 4, folder 3, Waters Family Papers, Essex Inst.; see also Stearns, *The Black Man*, pp. 396-97.

10. A. W. Kelsey to Edward Atkinson, Oct. 4, 1865, Atkinson Papers, MHS.

11. James D. Waters to Henry F. Waters, Dec. 10, 1865, Box 13, folder 4, Waters Family Papers, Essex Inst.; see also Shoalmire, "Carpetbagger Extraordinary," pp. 62-64.

12. Albert T. Morgan, *Yazoo; Or, On the Picket Line of Freedom in the South* (Washington, D.C., 1884), p. 72.

13. Garth W. James to William James, Sept. 29, 1866, G. W. and R. James Papers, in possession of Prof. William Childers, University of Florida. See also C. F. Morse to father, Jan. 31, 1865, C. F. Morse Papers, MHS; entry of Mar. 5, 1864, Isaac Shoemaker Diary, DU; C. C. Waters to E. S. Waters, Jan. 24, 1866, Box 4, folder 3, Waters Family Papers, Essex Inst.; Shoalmire, "Carpetbagger Extraordinary," pp. 63-64; John T. Trowbridge, *The South: A Tour of its Battle Fields and Ruined Cities* (New York, 1969), p. 484; Harriet Beecher Stowe, "Our Florida Plantation," *Atlantic Monthly* 43 (May 1874): 645.

14. Stearns, *The Black Man*, p. 81.

15. The quotation is in Garth W. James to William James, Mar. 10, 1866, G. W. and R. James Papers, in possession of Prof. William Childers, University of Florida; [Benham], *A Year of Wreck*, pp. 148-51, pp. 370-71; see also A. B. Hart to mother, Apr. 30, 1867, A. B. Hart Papers, FU; H. L. Higginson to Horatio Woodman, Nov. 2, 1865, Woodman Papers, MHS; Walter Hart to William Hart, Apr. 12, 1867, W. N. Hart Papers, FU; Henry C. Thomas to J. D. Waters, May 20, 1865, Box 11, folder 7, Waters Family Papers, Essex Inst.

16. John Clark to Horatio Woodman, Nov. 11, 1865, Woodman Papers, MHS.

17. Walter Hart to William Hart, Apr. 12, 1867, W. N. Hart Papers; A. B. Hart to Emily Hart, Feb. 6, 1867, and A. B. Hart to father, Mar. 29, 1867, A. B. Hart Papers; both in FU; [Benham], *A Year of Wreck*, pp. 125-26.

18. Walter Hart to mother, Feb. 25, 1867, Walter Hart Papers, FU.

19. William Barbee, *The Cotton Question* (New York, 1866), p. 103. See also E. Merton Coulter, *The South During Reconstruction 1865-1877* (Baton Rouge, La., 1947), p. 201. In January, 1866, Edward Atkinson thought he saw in the South "the signs of an absolute social revolution in the last 60 days." Among the changes he considered noteworthy was the fact that "every white man is at work. . . ." (Edward Atkinson to Maurice Williams, Jan. 6, 1866; and E. Atkinson, to Epping, Hansard & Co., Feb. 27, 1868, Atkinson Letterbooks, MHS.)

20. Susan D. Smedes, *Memorials of a Southern Planter*, ed. Fletcher M. Green (New York, 1965), pp. 224-25.

21. J. Floyd King to Lin [Caperton], Aug. 10, 1865 (for the quotation), and June 8, 1866, Series A, Thomas Butler King Papers, SHC.

22. C. Vann Woodward, "The Southern Ethic in a Puritan World," in his *American Counterpoint: Slavery and Racism in the North-South Dialogue* (Boston, 1971), pp. 30-32.

23. William A. Percy, *Lanterns on the Levee: Recollections of a Planter's Son* (Baton Rouge, La., 1973), p. 62.

24. A. DePuy Van Buren, *Jottings of a Year's Sojourn in the South* (Battle Creek, Mich., 1859), pp. 88-94. The quotations are on pages 89 and 94.

25. Woodward, "Southern Ethic," p. 13.

26. Barbee, *The Cotton Question*, p. 103.

27. Henry M. Crydenwise to parents, Mar. 13, 1866, H. M. Crydenwise Papers, DU; Eben Loomis to Mary Loomis, Mar. 27, 1866, Box 8, Todd Family Papers, YU.

28. Garth W. James to Henry James, Sr., Mar. 27, 1866, G. W. and R. James Papers, in possession of Prof. William Childers, University of Florida; Ralph Barton Perry, *The Thought and Character of William James*, 2 vols. (Boston, 1935), vol 1, pp. 232-33, where the William James letter appears.

29. Perry, *Life and Letters*, pp. 254-55; C. C. Waters to mother, Mar. 12, 1865, Box 12, folder 4, Waters Family Papers, Essex Inst.

30. J. A. Brown to Charles D. Hamilton, Oct. 11, 1866, C. D. Hamilton Letterbook, MA; see also J. Floyd King to Lin [Caperton], June 8, 1866, Series A, Thomas Butler King Papers, SHC.

31. [Benham], *A Year of Wreck*, p. 146.

32. Morgan, *Yazoo*, p. 73.

33. Ibid., pp. 87, 351-53, 357.

34. [Benham], *A Year of Wreck*, pp. 160 and 289; see also Shoalmire, "Carpetbagger Extraordinary," p. 55.

35. Morgan, *Yazoo*, p. 84; [Benham], *A Year of Wreck*, p. 31; Shoalmire, "Carpetbagger Extraordinary," pp. 6-26.

36. J. F. McCaw to Whitelaw Reid, Dec. 22, 1869, W. Reid Papers, LC; Frank P. Blair, Jr., to wife, Sept. 2, and 23, 1867, Box 3, Blair Family Papers, LC.

37. Garth W. James to mother, Jan. 27, 1868, G. W. and R. James Papers, in possession of Prof. William Childers, University of Florida.

38. C. C. Waters to E. S. Waters, Jan. 24, 1866, Box 4, folder 3, Waters Family Papers, Essex Inst.

39. Sidney Andrews, *The South Since the War* (Boston, 1971), p. 290.

40. [Benham], *A Year of Wreck*, p. 28.

41. Morgan, *Yazoo*, pp. 35-36, 64.

42. Ibid., p. 83, especially the note.

43. Whitelaw Reid, *After the War: A Tour of the Southern States, 1865-1866*, ed. C. Vann Woodward (New York, 1965), pp. 513, 517-19. See also Morgan, *Yazoo*, p. 98; Stearns, *The Black Man*, pp. 51-52; George M. Alexander to Frank P. Blair, Jr., July 5 [c. 1866], Box 54, Blair Family Papers, LC; [Benham], *A Year of Wreck*, p. 99.

44. Morgan, *Yazoo*, pp. 46, 90-96; see also [Benham], *A Year of Wreck*, pp. 136-37.

45. William H. Powell, ed., *Officers of the Army and Navy (Volunteers) Who Served in the Civil War* (Philadelphia, 1892), p. 168. See also James L. Roark, *Masters Without Slaves: Southern Planters in the Civil War and Reconstruction* (New York, 1977), pp. 160-61.

46. Morgan, *Yazoo*, pp. 46, 90-96; see also Thomas Affleck to wife, Dec. 19, 1865, T. Affleck Papers, LSU.

47. Willie Lee Rose, *Rehearsal for Reconstruction: The Port Royal Experiment* (New York, 1964), p. 361.

48. Morgan, *Yazoo*, p. 57; see also *DeBow's Review*, AWS 2 (July 1866), p. 91.

49. Morgan, *Yazoo*, p. 49.

50. Ibid., p. 46.

51. Ibid., p. 92.

52. Ibid., pp. 75-76; see also pp. 49-51.

53. Ibid., pp. 90-96, especially pp. 93-94.

54. Ibid., pp. 95-96.

55. Ibid., pp. 97-99.

56. Ibid., pp. 107-09, 112-13.

57. Henry L. Swint, *The Northern Teacher in the South, 1862-1870* (New York, 1967), pp. 94-142.

58. [Benham], *A Year of Wreck*, p. 137; Swint, *The Northern Teacher*, p. 120; "From Charleston to the North," Boston *Daily Advertiser*, May 1, 1866; H. M. Crydenwise to parents, June 25, 1866, H. M. Crydenwise Papers, DU; unidentified newspaper obituary of Martin E. Winchell [n.d.], Newton H. Winchell Papers, MiHS.

59. *House Miscellaneous Documents*, no. 52, 40 Cong., 3 sess. (Ser. 1385), pt. 1, p. 110,

60. Stearns, *The Black Man*, pp. 67-69, 70, 145-51, 156; the quotation is on page 69.

61. [Benham], *A Year of Wreck*, p. 336.

62. Edward Atkinson to John A. Andrew, Dec. 9, 1865, Atkinson Letterbooks, MHS; John Paul Baldwin, "Fifty Years in Louisiana: Views of a Northern White Settler in the South," *The Crisis* 13 (Dec. 1916): 72; Stearns, *The Black Man*, p. 515; John R. Dennett, *The South As It Is, 1865-1866*, ed. Henry M. Christman (New York, 1965), p. 344. For an interesting fictional account of how land sales to black people antagonized local whites, see Albion W. Tourgee, *A Fool's Errand* (New York, 1966), pp. 98-99.

63. [Benham], *A Year of Wreck*, p. 226.

64. Morgan, *Yazoo*, p. 113; see also pp. 121, 104.

65. [Benham], *A Year of Wreck*, pp. 318-19, 415; Stearns, *The Black Man*, pp. 166-67; Selma *Daily Messenger*, Apr. 17, 1867.

66. Stearns, *The Black Man*, pp. 159, 161-62; Morgan, *Yazoo*, pp. 12, 101; [Benham], *A Year of Wreck*, pp. 319, 323; see also Journal of Ambrose Hart, Dec. 30, 1866, FU.

67. Stearns, *The Black Man*, p. 156; see also Morgan, *Yazoo*, p. 105; [Benham], *A Year of Wreck*, pp. 133-34.

68. Garth W. James to William James, Sept. 29, 1866, G. W. and R. James Papers, in possession of Prof. William Childers, University of Florida.

69. [Benham], *A Year of Wreck*, pp. 319-20.

70. Ibid., p. 325.

71. Ibid., p. 416.

72. Michael Perman, *Reunion Without Compromise: The South and Reconstruction, 1865-1868* (Cambridge, Eng., 1973), pp. 201-11; Jerrell H. Shofner, *Nor Is It Over Yet: Florida in the Era of Reconstruction, 1863-1877* (Gainesville, Fla., 1974), pp. 92-94.

73. Morgan, *Yazoo*, p. 333.

74. [Benham], *A Year of Wreck*, p. 220. When he first arrived in Florida one northerner "came in contact with a strong element and being Col. of a very gallant regiment, his colors were not hid and the result was 3 or 4 duels or fights as he termed them in which he came out ahead and thus won himself a place in the community and made himself felt." (George W. Parsons Diary, Sept. 11, 1873, FU.)

75. Ulrich B. Phillips throws some light on this seeming paradox. He quotes to good effect a northern tutor's account of a conversation with Wade Hampton: "He wishes to be two or three miles at least from any neighbors. He utterly disapproves of the custom of farmers in Connecticut who for the sake of society cluster together in villages or hamlets. . . . He thinks the tendency of these village settlements is to make people more contracted, less hospitable and less friendly." As Phillips explained, "Seclusion was valued not only for the sake of serenity but as heightening the welcome and grace of social contacts on occasion." (*Life and Labor in the Old South* [Boston, 1963], p. 365.)

76. Warren, *Reminiscences*, pp. 19-23; Whitelaw Reid to C. W. Walker, Sept. 29, 1869, Reid Private Letterbook, vol. 3, LC; H. M. Crydenwise to parents, Mar. 13, 1866, H. M. Crydenwise Papers, DU; James D. Waters to mother, Apr. 24, 1864, Box 12, folder 5, Waters Family Papers, Essex Inst.; Ambrose Hart to Molly Hart, May 1868, A. B. Hart Papers, FU; Robertson James to Alice James, June 8, 1867, James Family Papers, HU.

77. Garth W. James to parents, Feb. 1, 1867, G. W. and R. James Papers, in possession of Prof. William Childers, University of Florida; C. C. Waters to Henry F. Waters, Box 8, C. C. Waters folder, Henry F. Waters Papers, Essex Inst.

78. G. W. James to mother, Jan. 27, 1868, G. W. and R. James Papers, in possession of Prof. William Childers, University of Florida.

79. The respective quotations are in Eben Loomis to wife, June 2, 1866 and Mar. 11,

1866; see also ibid., Feb. 22, 1866, May 11, 1866, and June 21, 1866, Box 8, Todd Family Papers, YU.

80. Millicent Todd, *Eben Jenks Loomis* (Cambridge, Mass., 1913), pp. 28-30.

81. Stearns, *The Black Man*, p. 82.

82. Mary Boykin Chesnut, *A Diary From Dixie*, ed. Ben Ames Williams (Boston, 1949), p. 163; Stearns, *The Black Man*, p. 171.

83. The quotation is in Elizabeth W. Pearson, ed., *Letters From Port Royal* (New York, 1969), p. 182; William D. Waters to Abigail Waters, Mar. 26, 1865, Box 12, folder 1, Waters Family Papers, Essex Inst. See also entries of Apr. 16, 28, 1864, Shoemaker Diary, DU.

84. Eben Loomis to sister Eliza, Apr. 15, 1866, Box 8, Todd Family Papers, YU.

85. Stearns, *The Black Man*, p. 143.

86. Ambrose B. Hart to Mary Hart, July 31, 1870, A. B. Hart Papers, FU.

87. Trowbridge, *The South*, p. 498*n*; see also Reid, *After the War*, p. 579.

88. Reid, *After the War*, p. 579; see also Report of Benjamin C. Truman, *Senate Executive Documents*, no. 43, 39 Cong., 1 sess. (Ser. 1238), p. 7; *Report of the Joint Committee on Reconstruction*, 39 Cong., 1 sess. (Ser. 1273), 4, p. 141.

89. Vicksburg *Weekly Herald*, Feb. 10, 1866, Aug. 11, 1866.

90. Ibid., Dec. 2, 1865.

91. Whitelaw Reid to Anna Dickinson, Nov. 25, 1866, A. Dickinson Papers, LC.

92. "Notes on a Plantation Experience," Feb. 27 [1866], Box 207, W. Reid Papers, LC.

93. James D. Waters to mother, Feb. 12, 1864, Box 12, folder 5, Waters Family Papers, Essex Inst.

94. J. D. Waters to mother, Mar. 27, 1864, Box 12, folder 5; J. D. Waters to father, Feb. 21, 1864, Box 10, folder 3; J. D. Waters to E. S. Waters, Feb. 25, 1864, Mar. 16, 1864, and Oct. 1, 1864, Box 4, folder 5, Waters Family Papers, Essex Inst.

95. Mrs. M. W. Dunbar to J. D. Waters, Mar. 13, 1865, Box 11, folder 7, Waters Family Papers, Essex Inst.

96. J. D. Waters to Edward S. Waters, Mar. 16, 1864, Box 4, folder 5, Waters Family Papers, Essex Inst.

97. J. D. Waters to Edward S. Waters, Mar. 16, 1864, Box 4, folder 5, Waters Family Papers, Essex Inst.

98. J. D. Waters to E. S. Waters, Apr. 10, 1864, and Oct. 1, 1864, Box 4, folder 5; see also J. D. Waters to father, Mar. 19, 1865, Box 10, folder 3, Waters Family Papers, Essex Inst. Planters in the Department of the Gulf also knew something about courting the authorities. (See George Hepworth, *The Whip, Hoe, and Sword* [Boston, 1864], pp. 61-68.)

99. J. D. Waters to E. S. Waters, Mar. 16, 1864, Box 4, folder 5, Waters Family Papers, Essex Inst.

100. Clifford C. Waters to E. S. Waters, Jan. 24, 1866, Box 4, folder 3; Henry C. Thomas to J. D. Waters, Sept. 6, 1865, Box 11, folder 7, Waters Family Papers, Essex Inst.

101. C. C. Waters to E. S. Waters, July 7, 1865, Box 4, folder 3, Waters Family Papers, Essex Inst.

102. J. Floyd King to Lin [Caperton], Feb. 19, 1866, Series A; see also J. Floyd King to Virginia King, Mar. 28, 1866, Series C, Thomas Butler King Papers, SHC.

103. C. C. Waters to E. S. Waters, Jan. 24, 1866, Box 4, folder 3; and C. C. Waters to mother, Mar. 1, 1866, Box 12, folder 4, Waters Family Papers, Essex Inst.

104. C. C. Waters to E. S. Waters, Apr. 16, 1865, and Jan. 24, 1866, Box 4, folder 3; J. D. Waters to E. S. Waters, Sept. 30, 1866, Box 4, folder 5; G. G. Klapp to J. D. Waters, Apr. 23, 1868, Box 11, folder 8; J. D. Waters to Joseph Linton Waters, May 26, 1866, J. L. Waters folder, Waters Family Papers, Essex Inst.

105. G. Griffing Wilcox, "War Times in Natchez," *Southern Historical Society Papers* 30 (1902): 137-38.

106. Pierce Butler, *The Unhurried Years: Memories of the Old Natchez Region* (Baton Rouge, La., 1948), p. 177; see also New York *Herald*, May 21, 1866; Vicksburg (Miss.) *Weekly Herald*, Mar. 10, 1866; William C. Harris, *Presidential Reconstruction in Mississippi* (Baton Rouge, La., 1967), p. 112.

107. *Florida Union* (Jacksonville), June 16, 1866.

108. Stowe, "Our Florida Plantation," pp. 644-45; Forrest Wilson, *Crusader in Crinoline: The Life of Harriet Beecher Stowe* (Philadelphia, 1941), p. 603; Eben Loomis to

Mary Loomis, Apr. 28, 1866, Box 8, Todd Family Papers, YU. One Yankee visitor to Jacksonville reported that though the general population was "rude and violent toward each other," they were not "disposed to ill treat a northerner who is well disposed, and does not fall into their ways." (J. F. B. Marshall to Gov. Andrew, Mar. 21, 1867, Andrew Papers, MHS.)

109. Henry Lee Higginson to Edward Atkinson, Dec. 16, 1866, Atkinson Papers, MHS.

110. Frances B. Leigh, *Ten Years On a Georgia Plantation Since the War* (London, 1883), pp. 51, 53-56, 61-62.

111. "Letter From Charleston," Boston *Daily Advertiser*, Apr. 12, 1866. See also *Report of the Joint Committee*, 3, pp. 33-34, 40-41.

112. Rose, *Rehearsal*, p. 211.

113. Rupert S. Holland, ed., *Letters and Diary of Laura M. Towne* (Cambridge, Mass., 1912), pp. 176-78; Frank H. Williams to J. D. Waters, Oct. 8, 1865, Box 11, folder 7; William D. Waters to Abigail Waters, Mar. 17, 1865, and Aug. 10, 1866, Box 12, folder 1, Waters Family Papers, Essex Inst.

114. Holland, ed., *Letters and Diary*, p. 167.

115. W. D. Waters to Edward S. Waters, June 4, 1866, Box 4, folder 2, Waters Family Papers, Essex Inst.

116. W. D. Waters to Abigail Waters, July 23, 1866, Box 12, folder 1, Waters Family Papers, Essex Inst.; see also Gainesville *New Era*, Apr. 7, 1866.

117. W. H. Trescot to [wife], Jan. 6, 1867, W. H. Trescot Papers, SCL.

118. Katherine M. Jones, comp., *Port Royal Under Six Flags* (Indianapolis, Ind., 1960), pp. 300-01; Rose, *Rehearsal*, pp. 360-61.

119. W. H. Trescot to Gov. James L. Orr, Nov. 4, 1866, Gov. Orr Papers, SCA.

120. A. F. Crosman to commissioner of Public Lands, May 10, 1864, Gen. Corr., Records of the Direct Tax Commission for S.C., NA; Charleston *Daily Courier*, Feb. 22, 1866; "A Visit to Port Royal," Boston *Daily Advertiser*, Dec. 4, 1865; W. H. Trescot to Gov. J. L. Orr, Nov. 4, 1866, Gov. Orr Papers, SCA; Virginia C. Holmgren, *Hilton Head: Sea Island Chronicle* (Hilton Head, S.C., 1959), p. 107; Holland, ed., *Letters and Diary*, pp. 175, 188.

121. The "heads of families" provision of the Direct Tax laws, under which the freedmen were able to buy land, continued in effect until 1870. (Guion G. Johnson, *A Social History of the Sea Islands* [Chapel Hill, N.C., 1930], p. 187.)

122. Holland, ed., *Letters and Diary*, p. 178; see also Pearson, ed., *Letters*, pp. 288, 327-28.

123. C. C. Waters to E. S. Waters, Dec. 18, 1872, Box 4, folder 3, Waters Family Papers, Essex Inst.

124. William D. Waters to E. S. Waters, June 4, 1866, Box 4, folder 2. See also Edward Stetson to C. C. Waters, Jan. 22, 1865, Box 13, folder 2; W. D. Waters to Abigail Waters, Feb. 2, 1865, and May 6, 1865, Box 12, folder 1, Waters Family Papers, Essex Inst.

125. H. M. Stuart and E. G. Dudley to Gov. J. L. Orr, Jan. 5, 1866 (for the quotation), and Feb. 5, 1866, Gov. Orr Papers, SCA; E. L. Devereaux to J. D. Waters, May 17, 1866, Box 11, folder 8, Waters Family Papers, Essex Inst.; Holmgren, *Hilton Head*, p. 83.

126. John T. Trowbridge offered familiar advice to prospective northern emigrants: "Just now I should not advise Northern men to settle far back from the main routes of travel, unless they go in communities, ... forming societies independent of any hostile sentiment that may be shown by the native inhabitants." (*The South*, p. 584.) See also Reid, *After the War*, p. 401; Boston *Daily Advertiser*, Dec. 16, 1865, Jan. 2, 1866, Nov. 8, 1866.

127. William L. Burt to John A. Andrew, May 10, 1866, Andrew Papers, MHS; *DeBow's Review*, AWS 2 (Dec. 1866), pp. 664-65.

128. G. W. James to father, July 9, 1866 (for the quotation), June 26, 1866, and Aug. 6, 1866, G. W. and R. James Papers, in possession of Prof. William Childers, University of Florida; "Cotton Planting in Florida," Boston *Daily Advertiser*, Oct. 30, 1866.

129. G. W. James to father, July 9, 1866, G. W. and R. James Papers, in possession of Prof. William Childers, University of Florida.

130. G. W. James to William James, Sept. 29, 1866; see also G. W. James to mother, Aug. 20, 1866, ibid.

131. Chicago *Tribune*, Aug. 14, 1866.

132. Selma *Daily Messenger*, Nov. 10, 1866 (for the quotation), Mar. 21, 1866, and June 13, 1866; *The Ku-Klux Conspiracy, Testimony Taken by the Joint Select Committee to Inquire into the Condition of Affairs in the Late Insurrectionary States* (Washington, D.C., 1872), vol. 2, pt. 7, pp. 715-17, 830.

133. "From Charleston to the North," Boston *Daily Advertiser*, May 1, 1866. See also Maurice M. Vance, "Northerners in Late Nineteenth Century Florida: Carpetbaggers or Settlers?" *Florida Historical Quarterly* 28 (July 1959): 3-4; Benjamin C. Truman Report, p. 7.

134. Trowbridge, *The South*, p. 409. See also Chicago *Tribune*, Jan. 15, 1866; "Report of the Commissioner of the Bureau of Refugees, Freedmen, and Abandoned Lands," *House Executive Documents*, no. 11, 39 Cong., 1 sess. (Ser. 1255), p. 33.

135. Although he was not in a situation in which white hostility was a matter of constant concern, Clifford Waters illustrates how a northern man's racial asperity mellowed whenever he was irritated with his southern neighbors. "I think that when we are impatient with the negroes we ought to take into consideration the degrading influences to which they have been exposed," he wrote at a time when his indignation with the whites was running high. "I don't know how we can reasonably expect the negroes to be moral, and honest when the whole atmosphere around them was one of immorality, dishonesty, and licentiousness [*sic*]" (C. C. Waters to E. S. Waters, January 24, 1866, Box 4, folder 3, Waters Family Papers, Essex Inst.). For similar instances, see G. W. James to William James, September 29, 1866, G. W. and R. James Papers, in possession of Prof. William Childers, University of Florida.

136. Woodward, "Southern Ethic," 21-25; idem., *The Strange Career of Jim Crow*, 2d rev. ed. (New York, London, and Oxford, 1966), 67-74; Edmund S. Morgan, "The Puritan Ethic and The American Revolution," *William and Mary Quarterly* 24 (Jan. 1967): 20-22.

137. Stearns, *The Black Man*, pp. 162, 239-40, and 368 (where the quotation appears); Chesnut, *Diary From Dixie*, p. 539.

138. Ezra J. Warner, *Generals in Blue: Lives of the Union Commanders* (Baton Rouge, La., 1964), p. 47; see also Swint, *The Northern Teacher*, pp. 13-14; Sarah W. Wiggins, "Ostracism of White Republicans in Alabama During Reconstruction," *The Alabama Review* 27 (Jan. 1974): 52-64.

139. D. P. Holland to John A. Wilder, September 15, 1866, Box 45, Todd Family Papers, YU.

140. Ambrose B. Hart to Mary Hart, March 20, 1867; see also A. B. Hart to father, March 10 and 20, 1867, A. B. Hart papers, FU.

141. H. M. Crydenwise to parents, March 3, 1866, H. M. Crydenwise papers, DU; H. M. Crydenwise to Gov. B. G. Humphreys, March 13, 1866, vol. 78, Gov.'s Corr., MA.

142. H. M. Crydenwise to parents, Dec. 25, 1866 (for the quotation), Aug. 5, 1866, and Nov. 11, 1866, H. M. Crydenwise Papers, DU.

143. [Benham], *A Year of Wreck*, pp. 109-12.

144. Ibid., pp. 106-07.

145. Stearns, *The Black Man*, p. 212.

146. [Benham], *A Year of Wreck*, p. 146.

147. Someone must have profited from the cotton that reached the market in 1865 and 1866. Although the amount of cotton exported in 1866 was approximately one-third of that exported in 1860 (a banner year for southern cotton), it brought a price ($281,000,000) that was nearly 50 percent greater than that of the 1860 crop. Some allowance must be made for the larger costs of production and processing after the war, but it is hard to imagine that they could have eaten up most of the profits. There is probably some basis for the frequent southern complaints against the ubiquitous cotton speculators, military and civilian. (Calculated from table U 73-93, "Exports of Selected U.S. Merchandise: 1790-1957," in *Historical Statistics of the United States, Colonial Times to 1957: A Statistical Abstract Supplement* [Washington, D.C., 1961], p. 547.) See also David A. Wells, *The Recent Financial, Industrial and Commercial Experiences of the United States: A Curious Chapter in Politico-Economic History* (New York, 1872), p. 26, which gives a smaller estimate; and Harris, *Presidential Reconstruction*, p. 181.

148. Rose, *Rehearsal*, p. 434; Reid, *After the War*, p. 500.

149. James D. Waters to mother, Sept. 28, 1864, Box 12, folder 5; see also J. D. Waters

to Edward S. Waters, Oct. 1, 1864, Box 4, folder 5, Waters Family Papers; Tacony Plantation Ledger, 1864-1868, all in Essex Inst.

150. William Walsh to Isaac Crowe, Jan. 5, 1865, Crowe Papers, MiHS. See also Boston *Daily Advertiser*, July 11, 1865; David H. Overy, Jr., *Wisconsin Carpetbaggers in Dixie* (Madison, Wis., 1961), pp. 19-21; Harold F. Williamson, *Edward Atkinson: The Biography of an American Liberal* (Boston, 1934), p. 12; Bell I. Wiley, *Southern Negroes, 1861-1865* (New Haven, Conn., 1965), pp. 242-44.

151. Tacony Plantation Ledger, 1864-1868, Essex Inst.; Harris, *Presidential Reconstruction*, pp. 171-72; Joel G. Taylor, *Louisiana Reconstructed, 1868-1877* (Baton Rouge, La., 1974), pp. 344-45.

152. H. Loney to Henry C. Badger, Nov. 6, 1866, SEC, NEEACo Papers, KSHS.

153. William D. Waters to Abigail Waters, Sept. 30, 1866, Box 13, folder 1, Waters Family Papers, Essex Inst.

154. Henry Lee Higginson to Edward Atkinson, Dec. 16, 1866, Atkinson Papers, MHS; J. Floyd King to Lin [Caperton], Nov. 7, 1866, and Dec. 23, 1866, Series A, Thomas Butler King Papers, SHC; [Benham], *A Year of Wreck*, p. 402.

155. Whitelaw Reid had even managed to make a small profit in 1866, despite his short crops. (W. Reid to Anna E. Dickinson, Nov. 25, 1866, A. Dickinson Papers, LC.)

156. Henry H. Hurlbert to C. A. Montross, Nov. 10, 1864, and Bailey & Little to C. A. Montross, Nov. 9, 1864, "Applications for Lease of Abandoned Plantations" (entry 2383), BRFAL Records, NA. Jerrell H. Shofner gives a nice account of how the continued high price of cotton impelled planters to become more extended in cotton, despite planting losses. (*Nor Is It Over Yet: Florida in the Era of Reconstruction, 1863-1877* [Gainsville, 1974], pp. 126-27.) See also Mary Loomis to Eben Loomis, Jan. 26, 1867, Box 9, Todd Family Papers, YU.

157. Perry, *Life and Letters*, p. 258; [Benham], *A Year of Wreck*, p. 277; Harris, *Presidential Reconstruction*, pp. 171-72; Taylor, *Louisiana Reconstructed*, pp. 344-46; Stearns, *The Black Man*, pp. 96-98; J. D. Waters to Henry F. Waters, Nov. 27, 1867, Box 8, J. D. Waters folder, H. F. Waters Papers, Essex Inst.

158. The respective quotations are in Warren, *Reminiscences of a Mississippi Carpetbagger*, p. 52; John Wilder to Eben Loomis, Dec. 5, 1866, Box 8, Todd Family Papers, YU; F. W. Bardwell to T. B. Forbush, Oct. 29, 1867, SEC, NEEACo Papers, KSHS.

159. Perry, *Life and Letters*, p. 266; Frank P. Blair, Jr., to Montgomery Blair, April 9, 1869, Box 8, Blair Family Papers, LC; Morgan, *Yazoo*, p. 135; [Benham], *A Year of Wreck*, pp. v, 459.

160. J. D. Waters to Henry F. Waters, Dec. 27, 1867, Box 8, J. D. Waters folder, H. F. Waters Papers, Essex Inst.

161. Perry, *Life and Letters*, p. 266; see also Mary Loomis to Eben Loomis, Jan. 3, 1867, Box 9, Todd Family Papers, YU; estimates for Rice Park Plantation for 1867, Markham-Puffer Papers, CU; Martin C. Cooley to Luther R. Smith, Sept. 25, 1866, Smith Papers, Mo. Hist. Soc.; J. Floyd King to Lin [Caperton], Nov. 7, 1866, Series A, Thomas Butler King Papers, SHC; F. A. Stickel to D. D. Slauson, Sept. 14, 1867, Slauson Papers, LSU; "Whitelaw Reid," *Scribner's Monthly* 8 (August 1874): 444; *DeBow's Review*, AWS 3 (Apr. and May, 1867), pp. 448-54.

162. "Minutes," Jan. 1, 1867, Feb. 18, 1867, and May 29, 1867, Records of the Direct Tax Commission for S.C., NA.

163. Ralph E. Elliott to brother, Mar. 13, 1867, Thomas R. S. Eliott Papers; A. Coward to [E. Capers], Feb. 6, 1867, Ellison Capers Papers, both collections at DU; *DeBow's Review*, AWS 3 (Apr. and May 1867), p. 453.

164. J. H. D. Bowman to William E. Johnson, Jan. 1, 1867, Apr. 26, 1867, and Nov. 16, 1867, Johnson Papers, SCL.

165. J. D. Waters to H. F. Waters, Apr. 20, 1868, Box 8, J. D. Waters folder, H. F. Waters Papers, Essex Inst.; J. Floyd King to Lin [Caperton], Dec. 23, 1866, Series A, Thomas Butler King Papers, SHC. See also J. M. Gilman to Isaac Crowe, Dec. 30, 1866, Crowe Papers, MiHS.

166. *Senate Executive Documents*, no. 14, 40 Cong., 1 sess. (Ser. 1308), pp. 62-65, 146-47; Shofner, *Nor Is It Over Yet*, pp. 104, 128; Harris, *Presidential Reconstruction*, pp. 178-80; Morgan, *Yazoo*, pp. 122-28; Frank P. Blair, Sr., to Frank P. Blair, Jr., Dec. 23,

1867, Box 53, Blair Family Papers, LC; J. M. Gilman to Isaac Crowe, Oct. 1, 7, 24, and 28, 1866, and Nov. 18, 1866, Crowe Papers, MiHS.

167. Stephen L. Howard to D. W. Jordan, Dec. 31, 1865 ("a hard set"); Styles & Carter to D. W. Jordan, Mar. 20, 1866, Daniel W. Jordan Papers, DU; [Benham], *A Year of Wreck*, p. 74 ("my word").

168. Morgan, *Yazoo*, pp. 100-01.

169. Stearns, *The Black Man*, pp. 145-50.

170. Lorenzo Thomas to J. D. Waters, Oct. 9, 1867; see also Mrs. Henry C. Thomas to J. D. Waters, July 13, 1867, Oct. 4, 1867, and Jan. 12, 1868; and Henry C. Thomas to James D. Waters, Oct. 12, 1867, Nov. 25, 1867, all in Box 11, folder 8, Waters Family Papers, Essex Inst.

171. J. D. Waters to H. F. Waters, Apr. 20, 1868, Box 8, J. D. Waters folder, H. F. Waters Papers; G. G. Klapp to J. D. Waters, Apr. 23, 1868, Box 11, folder 8; see also J. D. Waters to E. S. Waters, Sept. 30, 1866, Box 4, folder 5, all in Waters Family Papers, Essex Inst.

172. Howard A. White, *The Freedmen's Bureau in Louisiana* (Baton Rouge, La., 1970), p. 34.

173. W. D. Wickersham to Wager Swayne, Apr. 27, 1867, and Oct. 24, 1867; see also statement of Judge F. Bugbee, May 11, 1867, Reconstruction correspondence of W. Swayne, AA. See also Shofner, *Nor Is It Over Yet*, p. 128.

174. Martin C. Cooley to L. R. Smith, Sept. 25, 1866, Luther R. Smith Papers, Mo. Hist. Soc.

175. The quotation is in Stearns, *The Black Man*, p. 148; W. D. Wickersham to W. Swayne, Apr. 25, 1867, Recon. Corr. of W. Swayne, AA.

176. Morgan, *Yazoo*, pp. 122-28; the quotation is on page 125.

177. J. M. Gilman to Isaac Crowe, Oct. 14, 1866, Crowe Papers, MiHS; Stearns, *The Black Man*, p. 151; J. D. Waters to H. F. Waters, Apr. 20, 1868, Box 8, J. D. Waters folder, H. F. Waters Papers, Essex Inst.

178. [Benham], *A Year of Wreck*, pp. 163, 402-03.

179. F. W. Loring and C. F. Atkinson, *Cotton Culture and the South: Considered with Reference to Emigration* (Boston, 1869), p. 79.

180. C. Vann Woodward, *Reunion and Reaction: The Compromise of 1877 and the End of Reconstruction* (Boston, 1951), passim.

Epilogue

1. [George C. Benham], *A Year of Wreck* (New York, 1880), p. 461; Eben Loomis to Eliza, Jan. 8, 1867, Box 9, Todd Family Papers, YU.

2. James D. Waters to Henry F. Waters, Nov. 27, 1867, Box 8, J. D. Waters folder, H. F. Waters Papers, Essex Inst.; Eben Loomis to Eliza, May 5, 1868, Box 9, Todd Family Papers, YU.

3. Henry Thomas to James D. Waters, Dec. 20, 1868, Box 11, folder 8, Waters Family Papers, Essex Inst.; see also Benjamin P. Thomas and Harold M. Hyman, *Stanton: The Life and Times of Lincoln's Secretary of War* (New York, 1962), pp. 581-84, 588-92, 596-98, 608-11.

4. William E. Smith, *The Francis Preston Blair Family in Politics*, 2 vols. (New York, 1969), vol 2, pp. 334-35. Actually, Blair always sought to advance his interests in two fields at once. "My affairs at the plantation are getting on very well," he wrote to his father in May, 1866. "I hope to have a good crop—I am going now to try for a political crop also & will plant good seed. I hope I may win on one string or the other." (Francis P. Blair, Jr., to F. P. Blair, Sr., May 6, 1866, Box 8, Blair Family Papers, LC.)

5. "Whitelaw Reid," *Scribner's Monthly* 8 (Aug. 1874): 447.

6. W. J. Cash, *The Mind of the South* (New York, 1941), p. 143; C. Vann Woodward, *Origins of the New South, 1877-1913* (Baton Rouge, La., 1951), p. 443.

7. [Benham], *A Year of Wreck*, p. 405.

8. Bliss Perry, *Life and Letters of Henry Lee Higginson* (Boston, 1921), p. 267; Charles F. Morse, *A Sketch of My Life* (Cambridge, Mass., 1927), pp. 31, 32-65.

9. *House Reports*, no. 261, 43 Cong., 2 sess. (Ser. 1660), pp. 237, 241; William L. McMillen to Henry Clay Warmoth, Nov. 30, 1869, Warmoth Papers, SHC; see also Morton Rubin, *Plantation County* (New Haven, Conn., 1963), p. 11.

10. There is no reason to quarrel with Walter L. Fleming's observation that "many of the carpet-bag politicians were northern men who had failed at cotton planting." (*Civil War and Reconstruction in Alabama* [New York, 1905], p. 718n.) See also James W. Garner, *Reconstruction in Mississippi* (Baton Rouge, La., 1968), p. 136; Richard N. Current, "Carpetbaggers Reconsidered," in *A Festschrift for Frederick B. Artz*, ed. David H. Pinkney and Theodore Ropp (Durham, N.C., 1964), pp. 139-57.

11. Albert T. Morgan, *Yazoo; Or, On the Picket Line of Freedom in the South* (Washington, D.C., 1884), p. 132.

12. George E. Tuxbury to William Markham, Nov. 10, 1872, Markham-Puffer Papers, CU.

13. Joseph Logsdon, "Yazoo, Mississippi: Race Relations in the Deep South During Reconstruction" (paper delivered at the Conference on the First and Second Reconstructions, University of Missouri, St. Louis, Feb. 15-17, 1978).

14. Charles Stearns, *The Black Man of the South and the Rebels* (Boston, 1872), pp. 267-77, 305-25, 496, 531-38; James M. McPherson, *The Abolitionist Legacy: From Reconstruction to the NAACP* (Princeton, N.J., 1975), p. 77.

15. Garth W. James to father, Oct. 17, 1868, and G. W. James to parents, Nov. 8, 1866, both in G. W. and R. James Papers, in possession of Prof. William Childers, University of Florida; see also S. H. Garvin to T. B. Forbush, July 1867, SEC, NEEACo Papers, KSHS; and Savage & Haile to G. W. James, Aug. 25, 1869, James Family Papers, HU.

16. Anna R. Burr, ed., *Alice James. Her Brothers. Her Journal* (New York, 1934), p. 25.

17. F. O. Matthiessen, *The James Family* (New York, 1948), pp. 267-71; the quotations are on pages 268 and 269.

18. Marie Caskey, *Chariot of Fire: Religion and the Beecher Family* (New Haven, Conn., 1978), pp. 194-95; see also Forest Wilson, *Crusader in Crinoline: The Life of Harriet Beecher Stowe* (Philadelphia, 1941), pp. 527-29, 533, 559-60.

19. George G. Klapp to James D. Waters, Mar. 21, Apr. 23, 1868, June 14, Oct. 22, Dec. 8, 1869, Waters Family Papers, Essex Inst.

20. *Report of the Secretary of the Class of 1863 of Harvard College* 8 (Cambridge, Mass., 1913), p. 113.

21. Clifford C. Waters to Edward S. Waters, Nov. 15, 1874, Box 4, folder 3, Waters Family Papers, Essex Inst.

22. Edward Stanley Waters Diary, Jan. 13, 27, 1880, Waters Family Papers, Essex Inst.

Bibliographical Essay

This is only a selective discussion of the sources that are the basis of this study. For a complete rundown the reader should consult the notes.

Manuscripts

The manuscript sources for this work are widely scattered. The trail begins in Salem, Massachusetts, snakes its way through much of the South, and continues its progress in many of the archives of the Midwest and mid-Atlantic states. Neither time nor money allowed me to pursue the trail along many of its sinuosities, let alone discover all its branches and bypaths. Nor could I visit every manuscript library with useful collections, though I did visit most of them. Some hard-to-get-at material is on microfilm and available on interlibrary loan; a few collections were photocopied and mailed to me.

There is no substitute, however, for a personal inspection of the ground. Some archives are impressively catalogued, and the professionals who run them are extremely cooperative. They can often point out collections that are easy to overlook in thumbing through the published guides to manuscripts. It was while running down a clue to a northern plantation journal at the Essex Institute in Salem, Massachusetts, that I stumbled on one of the most valuable collections of its kind in the history of this period. Consisting of over a dozen boxes, the Waters Family Papers not only give a full picture, in fascinating detail, of the planting activities of this family in Louisiana and South Carolina, but furnish a great deal of revealing information regarding the many Yankee cotton growers within the range of the family's acquaintance. It is doubtful, for example, if the full scope of General Lorenzo Thomas's business involvement in the Mississippi Valley would have ever come to light had the Waters's correspondence not survived. So far as I know, these valuable papers have never before been used by historians. The collection merits the consideration of all students of nineteenth-century social and cultural history, northern and southern. Another useful collection at the Essex Institute are the papers of Henry F. Waters, a cousin of the family.

Although nothing quite compares to the Waters Family Papers, there are several other good collections of papers of northern planters. The Todd Family Papers in the archives of Yale University contain the interesting correspondence of Eben J. Loomis, the astronomer who became a planter, as well as the papers of his brother-in-law, John Wilder, an officer of black troops, who was strongly tempted to follow many of his colleagues into cotton-raising. There are two separate collections for another officer of black troops who was interested in planting, the Yankee overseer, Henry M. Crydenwise. His papers are at Emory University in Atlanta and Duke University in Durham, North Carolina. The first collection, by and large, is for the years of his military service; the second covers his year of cotton-growing in Mississippi. Also at Duke is the valuable diary of Isaac Shoemaker, who was a government lessee in the Southwest during part of 1864. The papers of Whitelaw Reid and Frank P. Blair, Jr. (the latter of which form part of the Blair Family collection) are both in the Manuscripts Division of the Library of Congress, and shed a good deal of light on the affairs of these two lessees in the area of Natchez, Mississippi. The business aspect of northern-operated plantations comes through clearly in the papers of Daniel D. Slauson, a surgeon with the Corps d'Afrique, and in the Good Hope Plantation collection, which pertains to Waters and Klapp's management of one of Alfred V. Davis's plantations. Both collections are in the Department of Archives at Louisiana State University.

There are three interesting manuscript collections at the Minnesota Historical Society in St. Paul. The papers of Isaac Crowe give some particulars regarding the plantation and store speculations of two midwesterners in Port Gibson, Mississippi; the Thomas Montgomery collection sheds more light on the plantation fever among USCT officers; and the Newton H. Winchell and Family Papers yield a clue or two regarding the activities of the Ann Arbor Cotton Company. But the complete story of the latter enterprise, together with the cotton companies and planters associated with it, had to be pieced together from the letters and diaries of Alexander Winchell, which are found in the Michigan Historical Collection at the University of Michigan. The William Markham-C. C. Puffer collection at Cornell University is very revealing regarding the interests and activities of three other cotton companies of the period, all of which operated out of Port Royal: the Sea Island Cotton Company, the Port Royal Cotton Company, and the United States Cotton Company, which gobbled up the other two.

The James Family Papers in Houghton Library at Harvard were somewhat disappointing regarding the planting activities of Garth Wilkinson James and his brother Robertson in Florida. More helpful were the typescript copies of the James brothers' letters that Professor William Childers secured from a descendant of the family and very kindly allowed me to copy. Also at the University of Florida (in the P. K. Yonge Library) are the valuable papers of Ambrose B. Hart, a New Yorker who cut lumber and grew cotton with an ex-Confederate colonel in Florida. Of equal interest were the letters of Hart's brothers, who raised oranges and vegetables in the state at the same time. The Edmund and Walter N. Hart Papers are also in the Yonge Library. There are some small collections of Yankee planters' papers: the Charles F. Morse Papers at the Massachusetts Historical Society; the Charles W. Dustan Papers at the Southern Historical Collection in Chapel Hill; the Edward M. Stoeber and Reuben G. Holmes Papers at the South Caroliniana Library in Columbia, South Carolina; and the Luther R.

Smith collection at the Missouri Historical Society. All yielded at least a few interesting items.

Much of the story regarding northern planters emerges in the manuscript collections of persons who were not planters themselves but were in some way connected with the movement, if only by ties of friendship. Edward Atkinson's papers at the Massachusetts Historical Society were extremely valuable. A major proponent of Yankee cotton cultivation, Atkinson invested heavily in free-labor plantations and stayed in fairly close correspondence with some northern planters; there is also a revealing series of letters in his collection from A. Warren Kelsey, who managed a plantation for him in Mississippi during the war and toured the South as a cotton agent after the war. The John A. Andrew Papers, in the same library, were no less useful, not only for the light they shed on his American Land Company and Agency, but also for the illumination he received from northerners and southerners concerning cotton-growing. Finally, the small collection of Horatio Woodman Papers at the MHS contained some interesting letters from Henry Lee Higginson.

The papers of the New England Emigrant Aid Company, available on microfilm from the Kansas State Historical Society, yielded several important letters from northern planters in Florida (chiefly from the Gordon colony) and a revealing series of reports from the agent it sent on an inspection tour of that state. Some idea of how Yankee planters operated at Port Royal in the 1870s can be gained from George C. Hardy's letters in the Frederick Eustis collection at the South Caroliniana Library. Valuable letters from northern cotton growers and fortune-seekers also turned up in the papers of John Sherman, the papers of Thaddeus Stevens, and the papers of Anna E. Dickinson, all in the Library of Congress; the last collection contains some interesting correspondence from Whitelaw Reid. The Henry Clay Warmoth Papers at the Southern Historical Collection were another source of fruitful information, especially on the northern planters in Louisiana who later became important carpetbaggers. Whoever wishes to learn about Senator William Sprague's cotton speculations must begin with the letters of J. Floyd King, which are in Series A of the Thomas Butler King Papers, also at Chapel Hill. More of this story emerges in George E. Spencer's letters in the Grenville M. Dodge Papers at the Iowa State Department of History and Archives. The John Fox Potter Papers at the State Historical Society of Wisconsin has some interesting items pertaining to government lessees in the Mississippi Valley.

By far the most challenging research involved reconstructing, from a plethora of manuscript sources, the southern response to the northern planter movement. Obviously I could not pursue all the possibilities, but I tried to search out most of the collections of the southern figures that my intuition and a careful reading of secondary sources suggested might contain helpful leads. This work led me down more dead ends than I care to remember, but it also had many rewards, and gradually a picture of southern attitudes began to emerge that is seldom found in historical literature on postwar readjustments in the former Confederacy.

I hit the largest vein of pay dirt in the Southern Historical Collection. The Gregorie-Elliott Papers, the Heyward-Ferguson Papers, the Elliott-Gonzales

Papers, and the diaries of John Fripp and John Berkeley Grimball bare the outlines of southern expectations in South Carolina. The Branch Family Papers, the Stephen R. Mallory Papers, and the E. M. L'Engle Papers do something of the same for Florida. The Andrew McCollam and Lewis Thompson Papers were helpful for Louisiana, while the Alexander R. Lawton collection was valuable for understanding the responses of planters in Georgia to the economic and social crisis following the war. Finally, the Battle Family Papers tell the story of the General Southern Land Agency.

The William Perkins Library at Duke University also has several useful collections. The papers of Henry Watson, Jr., a substantial ex-slaveholder who sat out the war in Europe, make clear the confusion among plantation owners in Greene County, Alabama. The J. D. B. DeBow Papers clarify the connection between southern political attitudes and economic aspirations. A small collection of General James C. Beecher's correspondence, moreover, supplied many items concerning the militancy of black homesteaders in the area of General William T. Sherman's land grants. Other collections at Duke that proved useful were the papers of E. W. Bonney, Clement C. Clay, and Armistead Burt.

The South Caroliniana Library houses the valuable collections of William H. Trescot and E. B. Heyward, two South Carolina planters who were somewhat at sea about their futures. The papers of another South Carolinian, William E. Johnson, are useful for the correspondence from the agent for Johnson's plantations near Vicksburg, Mississippi. The Robert N. Gourdin collection at Emory University was very revealing, while the Kollock Family Papers at the Georgia Historical Society in Savannah yielded a few bits of useful information. There are also some interesting items in the David Yulee and Samuel A. Swann Papers at the University of Florida.

Louisiana State University has a rich collection of manuscripts relating to the activities of the great planters of Natchez and vicinity. Indispensable to this study were the Stephen Duncan Papers, the William Minor Papers, and the William J. Minor and Family Papers. They disclosed a pattern of shrewd maneuvering that supports the picture that emerged in the Waters Family collection. Other useful collections at Baton Rouge are the Thomas Affleck Papers, the S. C. Bonner Papers, and the Gay Family Papers.

The official correspondence of various southern governors, both appointed and elected, were of incalculable value. Not only do they contain illuminating letters from old planters, but in some states they contain a surprising amount of correspondence from Yankee planters who were having difficulties with their new neighbors. At the Georgia Department of Archives and History in Atlanta there are the papers of Charles J. Jenkins and James Johnson; at the Alabama Department of Archives and History, in Montgomery, the correspondence of Lewis E. Parsons and Robert M. Patton, as well as the official papers of General Wager Swayne, the state's Freedmen's Bureau commissioner; at the South Carolina Archives Department, in Columbia, the papers of James L. Orr, Benjamin Perry, and Robert K. Scott; and at the Mississippi Department of Archives and History, in Jackson, the records of William L. Sharkey and Benjamin G. Humphreys.

There are private papers in some of these libraries worth mentioning. The small collection of Tunis G. Campbell Papers in the Georgia Archives reveals more of the outlines of the confused land situation on the Sea Islands. There are also important items in the C. D. Hamilton Letterbooks and William N. Whitehurst Papers at the Mississippi Archives. The papers of Joseph E. Davis, also at Jackson, contain the fascinating correspondence of his remarkable former slave, Benjamin Montgomery, detailing the situation at Davis Bend, Mississippi, shortly after the war.

Federal records housed in the National Archives in Washington, D. C. were indispensable for constructing the collective biography of the wartime northern planting class. The "Applications for Leasing" files, though disappointing in some respects, contain enough informative correspondence to make going through them worth the effort. They are items 2383 and 2384 of the records of the Bureau of Refugees, Freedmen, and Abandoned Lands (RG 105), for which there is a very helpful mimeographed guide. Entry 532, "Register of Leased Plantations," should also be consulted. The same can be said of the "Applications for Restoration of Property" files (entry 1022), which pertain to efforts by southern and northern planters to dispossess the black squatters along the south Atlantic seaboard.

The records of the Direct Tax Commission for South Carolina (RG 58) were a gold mine of information concerning the Yankee purchasers and lessees at Port Royal. The various land-sale certificates (some in bound volumes, some in cartons) gave a relatively complete picture of who got the land on the South Carolina Sea Islands, or at least of who made the first purchases. By consulting the book of "Minutes" one can determine who leased the plantations as well. When these two sets of records are used in conjunction with the "General Correspondence" and "Letters Sent" files of the commissioners, quite a bit of revealing information can be obtained. On the same score, one should also read the "Port Royal Correspondence" section of the records of the Treasury Department's Fifth Special Agency (RG 366). All of these records, furthermore, are invaluable for an understanding of federal policy regarding southern blacks and southern lands. The same is true of General Lorenzo Thomas's Letterbooks, which are found in the "Generals' Papers" of the records of the Adjutant Generals' Office (RG 94).

Official Documents

Not much need be said about the publications of the federal government, except that I used many of them at various points in this study. There are a few that I found particularly useful and that I should mention here. As anyone familiar with the literature of Reconstruction knows, *The Report of the Joint Committee on Reconstruction*, 39 Cong., 1 sess. (Ser. 1273), pays handsome dividends to the careful reader. Though I did not exploit it to the same extent, *The Ku-Klux Conspiracy, Testimony Taken by the Joint Select Committee to Inquire into the Condition of Affairs in the Late Insurrectionary States*, 13 volumes (Washington, D.C., 1872), also has rewards for anyone willing to spend time searching for them. The *Reports to President Andrew Johnson*, submitted by Carl Schurz and Benjamin C. Truman, and found in *Senate Executive Documents*, nos. 42 and 43 (Ser. 1237 and 1238), respectively, 39 Cong., 1 sess., also contain much that is useful.

Newspapers

Reconstruction scholars can scarcely overlook the newspapers of the period. Not only do they reflect fairly well the public opinion of the time (dependent as they largely were on subscriptions for their revenues), but they also carry a great deal of interesting material even outside of their editorial columns, and I do not except their classified sections from these remarks. So many of these journals had exchange agreements among them that it is easy to recover valuable material even from newspapers long since lost, if one reads all of the columns carefully. One advantage was that Yankee planters were often the subjects of these exchange articles.

For the northern states the most useful newspapers were the Boston *Daily Advertiser*, New York *Tribune*, New York *Herald*, New York *Times*, Chicago *Tribune*, and the Philadelphia *Public Ledger*. Many of these journals, notably the *Daily Advertiser* and the New York *Herald* and *Tribune*, had correspondents in the South who sent back valuable reports on conditions there. The jumping-off point for southern journals is *DeBow's Review*, which is filled with useful information of an industrial nature. It was impossible to consult all the extant newspapers in my theater of operations, but I did try to read at least one newspaper for each state. For Mississippi: the Vicksburg *Weekly Herald* and the Natchez *Democrat*. For Alabama: the Selma *Daily Messenger*, the Selma *Daily Times*, and the Montgomery *Advertiser*. For Louisiana: the New Orleans *Picayune*. For Georgia: the *Savannah Republican* and the Augusta *Daily Constitutionalist*. For South Carolina: the Charleston *Daily Courier*. And for Florida: the Gainesville *New Era* and the *Florida Union* (Jacksonville).

Memoirs and Collections of Letters

This was an important category of material. There is always a self-serving element even in the best of autobiographies, and the memoirs of northern planters and their contemporaries are no exception. But it is precisely because these people were often so conscious of their own rectitude and so largely blind to their own sectional and racial prejudices that their autobiographies—and their letters too—frequently have a factual usefulness not always found in mere briefs for the defense. Autobiographers often divulged facts that a later generation might find damaging to their cases, or at least open to an interpretation different from that which the writers intended. I suppose this is another way of saying that the farther the distance in time from which one writes the history of a period, the easier it is to avoid being taken in by the prejudices of that period.

Although it is largely the battlefield reports of a war journalist, Thomas W. Knox's *Camp-Fire and Cotton-Field: Southern Adventure in Time of War* (New York, 1865) was also the first in the genre of northern planter reminiscences. It tells the story of his cotton-planting experiences in the Mississippi Valley during the war. Charles Stearns, *The Black Man of the South and the Rebels* (Boston, 1872), is about life on a Garrisonian's plantation in Georgia after the war. Harriet Beecher Stowe has left us two accounts of affairs on her son's plantation in Florida: One is a quasi-fictional story concerning "Macintosh Plantation" that appeared in her *Palmetto Leaves* (Boston, 1873); the other is her article, "Our Florida Plantation," *Atlantic Monthly* 43 (May 1874): 641-49.

George Benham's *A Year of Wreck* (New York, 1880), which was published anonymously, and Albert T. Morgan's *Yazoo; Or, On the Picket Line of Freedom in the South* (Washington, D.C., 1884) owe a great deal in style, theme, and format to Albion W. Tourgee's *A Fool's Errand*, with an introduction by George Fredrickson (New York, 1966), a novel of Reconstruction that became an overnight sensation when it first appeared in 1879. Writing from Carroll Parish, Louisiana, where he had settled in as something of a respectable member of the local gentry, Benham devotes most of his memoir to his experiences with free labor in 1866, though he includes a considerable amount of material concerning his relations with local whites. Having fled to Washington, D.C., following Reconstruction, Morgan, on the other hand, says disappointingly little about life on his Yazoo, Mississippi, plantation, but he more than compensates for this omission by his good ear for dialect and his perceptive account of the triangular relationship between newcomers, natives, and freedmen. Though I only cite it once, *A Fool's Errand* helped me to visualize more clearly certain points of conflict between northerners and southerners.

There are some other first-hand accounts by northern planters in the postwar South, but probably because they were written so long after the fact (and at a time when sectional reconciliation was in full bloom), they are not nearly so revealing as the reminiscences of Benham and Morgan. Still, helpful details were gleaned from Henry Warren, *Reminiscences of a Mississippi Carpetbagger* (Holden, Massachusetts, 1914), and Charles F. Morse, *A Sketch of My Life* (Cambridge, 1927). John Eaton's memoirs, *Grant, Lincoln and the Freedmen* (New York, 1907), contain useful facts regarding wartime lessees in the Mississippi Valley.

The collected letters of northern planters and their contemporaries were of great value. There is a good run of letters written by Garth W. James from Florida in Anna R. Burr, ed., *Alice James. Her Brothers. Her Journal* (New York, 1934). Bliss Perry, in his *Life and Letters of Henry Lee Higginson* (Boston, 1921), made a lasting contribution by reproducing some of Higginson's correspondence from Georgia, as well as portions of Ida Agassiz Higginson's diary. None of the material seems to have survived in the Higginsons' extant manuscript collections. Elizabeth W. Pearson, ed., *Letters from Port Royal* (New York, 1969) is a Golconda of information regarding affairs on the South Carolina Sea Islands during and shortly after the war. Rupert S. Holland, ed., *Letters and Diary of Laura M. Towne* (Cambridge, 1912), is helpful on the same score. Sarah F. Hughes, ed., *Letters and Recollections of John Murray Forbes*, 2 vols. (Boston, 1900) is necessary for understanding this Boston philanthropist and businessman's work on behalf of the freedmen, though I found volume 2 of her *Letters (Supplementary) of John Murray Forbes*, 3 vols. (Boston, 1905) of even greater value.

Some southern memoirs that proved interesting were Francis Butler Leigh, *Ten Years on a Georgia Plantation Since the War* (London, 1883); Eliza J. Andrew, *The Wartime Journal of a Georgia Girl, 1864-1865* (New York, 1908); Susan D. Smedes, *Memorials of a Southern Planter*, edited and with an introduction by Fletcher M. Greene (New York, 1965); Mary Boykin Chesnut, *A Diary From Dixie*, ed. Ben Ames Williams (Boston, 1949); Earl S. Miers, ed., *When the World Ended: The Diary of Emma LeConte* (New York, 1957); and John Q. Anderson, ed., *Brokenburn: the Journal of Kate Stone, 1861-1868* (Baton Rouge, La., 1955). No less helpful were editions of collected letters, among the most important of which are Robert M. Myers, ed., *Children of Pride* (New Haven, 1972); and Charles E. Cauthen, ed., *Family Letters of the Three Wade Hamptons* (Columbia, S.C., 1953).

Travelers' Accounts, Pamphlets, and Regimental Histories

Books by northern reporters who toured the South after Appomattox were extremely useful. For the most part they complement the story told by other primary sources of the period and provide a wealth of concrete detail. Whitelaw Reid's *After the War: A Tour of the Southern States, 1865-1866*, edited and with an introduction by C. Vann Woodward (New York, 1965), is the best of the lot. Parts of it are Reid's memoir of life on two of the places he leased in Concordia Parish, Louisiana, in 1866—Scotland and Fishpond plantations. John R. Dennett, *The South As It Is, 1865-1866*, edited and with an introduction by Henry M. Christman (New York, 1965), was also very helpful, as was John T. Trowbridge's *The South: A Tour of its Battle Fields and Ruined Cities*, with a foreword by Otto H. Olsen (New York, 1969). Sidney Andrews, *The South Since the War*, with an introduction by David Donald (Boston, 1971), was not as useful for my purposes as these other accounts, not because Andrews was a poor reporter, but because he generally confined his observations strictly to political affairs. A few interesting items were found in John H. Kenneway, *On Sherman's Track: Or, The South After the War* (London, 1867). In addition, there are two books written in this period that also helped me at various points: William J. Barbee, *The Cotton Question* (New York, 1866); and F. W. Loring and C. F. Atkinson, *Cotton Culture and the South, Considered with Reference to Emigration* (Boston, 1869).

The contemporary pamphlet literature was also of assistance. Two pamphlets by James E. Yeatman of the Western Sanitary Commission supplied pertinent details about the government leasing system in the West: *A Report on the Condition of the Freedmen of the Mississippi* (St. Louis, 1864); and *Suggestions of a Plan for Free Labor, and the Leasing of Plantations under a Bureau or Commission to be Appointed by the Government; Accompanying a Report Presented to the Western Sanitary Commission* (St. Louis, 1864). In the same connection, James McKaye's *The Mastership and its Fruits: The Emancipated Slave Face to Face with His Old Master* (New York, 1864) was also of some help. For an understanding of the suppositions of the northern planter movement, see Edward Atkinson, *Cheap Cotton By Free Labor* (Boston, 1861); Thomas W. Conway, *The Introduction of Capital and Men From the Northern States and From Europe Into the Southern States of the Union* (New York,

1866); and Edward S. Tobey, *The Industry of the South: Its Immediate Organization Indispensable to the Financial Security of the Country* (Boston, 1865).

Most regimental histories were useful merely for biographical information, but some furnished interesting textual material as well. I list only a few of them: John M. Gould, *History of the First-Tenth-Twenty-ninth Maine Regiments* (Portland, Me., 1871); Alfred Roe, *The Twenty-fourth Regiment of Massachusetts Volunteers* (Worcester, Mass., 1907); E. M. Haynes, *A History of the Tenth Regiment Vermont Volunteers* (Rutland, Vt., 1894); and William H. Powell, ed., *Officers of the Army and Navy (Volunteer) Who Served in the Civil War* (Philadelphia, 1893).

Secondary Works

My debt to Willie Lee Rose's *Rehearsal for Reconstruction: The Port Royal Experiment*, with an introduction by C. Vann Woodward (New York, 1964), should be clear from the preface and the notes. It is far and away the best book ever written about northern planters—and abolitionists as well—in the post-emancipation South. David H. Overy, Jr., *Wisconsin Carpetbaggers in Dixie* (Madison, Wis., 1961), has an illuminating discussion of an important group of entrepreneurs who operated in the Mississippi Valley. It is a useful study, though I feel that Overy overstates his "frontier" thesis somewhat. Richard N. Current's "Carpetbaggers Reconsidered," in *A Festschrift for Frederick B. Artz*, ed. David H. Pinkney and Theodore Ropp (Durham, N.C., 1964), falls into the same error; even so, it is a valuable article, as is his book *Three Carpetbag Governors* (Baton Rouge, 1967). James M. McPherson's *The Struggle for Equality: Abolitionists and the Negro in the Civil War and Reconstruction* (Princeton, 1964) and his *The Abolitionist Legacy: From Reconstruction to the NAACP* (Princeton, 1975) provide further particulars on abolitionists who were interested in cotton-planting. George M. Fredrickson's *The Inner Civil War: Northern Intellectuals and the Crisis of the Union* (New York, 1965) has many insights concerning the motives of New England patricians and transcendentalists who became planters in these years. A useful guide to one category of northern immigrants is Henry Swint's *The Northern Teacher in the South, 1862-1870* (New York, 1967). Another group of newcomers is treated in Ezra J. Warner, *Generals in Blue: Lives of the Union Commanders* (Baton Rouge, 1964). There are some good biographies of individual northern planters. Royal Cortissoz, *The Life of Whitelaw Reid*, 2 vols. (London, 1921); William E. Smith, *The Francis Preston Blair Family in Politics*, 2 vols. (New York, 1969); and Forrest Wilson, *Crusader in Crinoline: The Life of Harriet Beecher Stowe* (Philadelphia, 1941), deepened my understanding of three outsiders engaged in planting after the war.

For an understanding of federal programs and policies toward southern blacks during the war, one must begin with Bell I. Wiley, *Southern Negroes, 1861-1865*, with an introduction by C. Vann Woodward (New Haven, 1965); Louis S. Gerteis, *From Contraband to Freedman: Federal Policy Toward Southern Blacks, 1861-1865* (Westport, Conn., 1973); and V. Jacque Voegeli, *Free But Not Equal: The Midwest and the Negro During the Civil War* (Chicago,

1967). Professor Rose's study is useful in this connection, too. Wiley and Gerteis, moreover, also have very good discussions on the Yankee lessees in the Mississippi Valley during the war. In C. Peter Ripley's *Slaves and Freedmen in Civil War Louisiana* (Baton Rouge, 1976) there is finally a first-rate study of affairs in the Department of the Gulf. The sequel to the wartime story of federal policy is best told in the revisionist histories of the Freedmen's Bureau. William S. McFeely's *Yankee Stepfather: General O. O. Howard and the Freedmen* (New Haven, 1968) is indisputably the best of all the accounts, but Martin L. Abbott's *The Freedmen's Bureau in South Carolina, 1865-1872* (Chapel Hill, 1967) and Howard A. White's *The Freedmen's Bureau in Louisiana* (Baton Rouge, 1970) were also helpful.

What life was like in the South during the old regime is at the present writing being hotly debated. I tend to sympathize with the idea that southern slaveholders, for all of their capitalistic characteristics, sustained a relationship to the means of production radically different from that of their northern counterparts, though I am reluctant to accept all of the particulars of this point of view. Nonetheless, all of the major studies of southern slavery informed my understanding of the antebellum order to some degree. Eugene Genovese's *The World the Slaveholders Made: Two Essays in Interpretation* (New York, 1969) helped me to see the parallel between Yankee cotton growers and West Indian sugar planters, while his latest contribution, *Roll, Jordan, Roll: The World the Slaves Made* (New York, 1974), aided my understanding of the conflicts between the new masters and the freedmen. Ulrich B. Phillips, *American Negro Slavery*, with a foreword by Eugene Genovese (Baton Rouge, 1966), was of assistance in the same way, as well as being a source of useful detail. All the same, students of the old order can scarcely overlook Kenneth M. Stampp's *The Peculiar Institution: Slavery in the Ante-Bellum South* (New York, 1956). Neither can they ignore John W. Blassingame's *The Slave Community: Plantation Life in the Ante-Bellum South* (New York, 1972), Leslie H. Owens' *This Species of Property: Slave Life and Culture in The Old South* (Oxford and New York, 1976), and Lawrence W. Levine's *Black Culture and Black Consciousness* (Oxford, London, and New York, 1977), if they would understand the slave plantation as seen from the quarters. Many of Edgar Thompson's essays, moreover, which have been conveniently collected in *Plantation Societies, Race Relations, and The South: The Regimentation of Populations* (Durham, N.C., 1975), have enriched my understanding of plantation culture in general. Despite its methodological flaws, Robert W. Fogel and Stanley L. Engerman, *Time on the Cross: The Economics of American Negro Slavery* (Boston, 1974), has some useful insights. C. Vann Woodward's "The Southern Ethic in a Puritan World," in his *American Counterpoint: Slavery and Racism in the North-South Dialogue* (Boston, 1971), pp. 13-46, has helped me to understand the different ways in which northerners and southerners viewed such basic issues as work and leisure.

How the ex-slaves helped to shape the new order is ably told in Vernon L. Wharton, *The Negro in Mississippi, 1865-1900* (New York, 1965); Joel Williamson, *After Slavery: The Negro in South Carolina during Reconstruction, 1861-1877* (Tallahassee, 1965); and Peter Kolchin, *First Freedom: The Responses of Alabama's Blacks to Emancipation and Reconstruction* (Westport, Conn., 1972). Wharton's study was the pathbreaker in this field; Williamson's work sets very high standards. Herbert G. Gutman's *The Black Family in Slavery and Freedom, 1750-1925* (New York, 1976), moreover, is extremely useful regarding the aspirations of the freedmen, as is Leon F. Litwack's "Free at Last," in Tamara K. Hareven, ed., *Anonymous Americans: Explorations in Nineteenth-Century Social History* (Englewood Cliffs, N. J., 1971), 131-71. E. P. Thompson's various explorations of working class and plebian culture have a great deal of relevance for students of slavery and emancipation. I cite only two of his articles: "Time, Work-Discipline, and Industrial Capitalism," *Past and Present* 38 (Dec. 1967), 56-97; and "The Moral Economy of the English Crowd in the Eighteenth Century," ibid. 50 (Feb. 1971), 76-136. C. Vann Woodward, *The Origins of the New South, 1877-1913* (Baton Rouge, 1951) is indispensable for understanding the new regime in its maturer phases. Some new interpretations of the postbellum South are: Jay R. Mandle, *The Roots of Black Poverty: The Southern Plantation Economy after the Civil War* (Durham, N. C., 1978), and Jonathan M. Wiener, *Social Origins of the New South: Alabama 1860-1885* (Baton Rouge and London, 1978). Roger Shugg, *Origins of Class Struggle in Louisiana* (Baton Rouge, 1968), reminds us of certain outward continuities in the antebellum system of landholding after the war.

General studies of Reconstruction are fairly numerous. The best brief overviews are Kenneth M. Stampp's *The Era of Reconstruction, 1865-1877* (New York, 1965), and John Hope Franklin's *Reconstruction: After the Civil War* (Chicago and London, 1961), but one should not neglect J. G. Randall and David Donald, *The Civil War and Reconstruction*, 2d ed. (Boston, 1961), which is the standard work on the subject, or even E. Merton Coulter, *The South During Reconstruction, 1865-1877* (Baton Rouge, 1947). Eric L. McKitrick, *Andrew Johnson and Reconstruction* (Chicago, 1960), is a brilliant contribution to the study of national policy and southern attitudes during the period immediately preceding Radical rule. All the same, the book that it superseded, Howard K. Beale, *The Critical Year: A Study of Andrew Johnson and Reconstruction* (New York, 1930), still has instructive things to say. Michael Perman's *Reunion Without Compromise: The South and Reconstruction, 1865-1868* (Cambridge, Eng., 1973) is a useful study of southern attitudes for the immediate postwar years. James L. Roark's *Masters Without Slaves: Southern Planters in the Civil War and Reconstruction* (New York, 1977) is an indispensable work on the mind of the old planters during the transition to free labor. Anyone who wishes to see how early the South began its psychological accommodation to postwar realities, should consult Paul M. Gaston's excellent study, *The New South Creed: A Study in Southern Mythmaking* (New York, 1970).

State studies of southern Reconstruction are even more abundant than general works. Although over a half-century old, many of the histories written under William A. Dunning's supervision or influence remain very helpful. The best of them was James W. Garner's *Reconstruction in Mississippi*, with an introduction by Richard N. Current (Baton Rouge, 1968). It has been updated for the early years by William C. Harris, *Presidential Reconstruction in Mississippi* (Baton Rouge, 1967), a work I used very much. Walter L. Fleming's *Civil War and Reconstruction in Alabama* (New York, 1905) still remains the best general treatment of that state, while South Carolina some time ago received a good revisionist study in Francis B. Simkins and Robert H. Woody, *South Carolina During Reconstruction* (Chapel Hill, 1932). Wharton and Williamson, it should be added, are also important revisions of the older literature for their states, as is Richardson's study of the freedmen in Florida. There are new studies of Florida and Louisiana: Jerrell H. Shofner, *Nor Is It Over Yet: Florida in the Era of Reconstruction, 1863-1877* (Gainesville, 1974); and Joel Gray Taylor, *Louisiana Reconstructed, 1863-1877* (Baton Rouge, 1974); both of which are important additions to the literature. Georgia has also received revisionist attention, but C. Mildred Thompson's *Reconstruction in Georgia* (New York, 1915) was more helpful for my purposes.

Three studies in particular helped to clarify my understanding of Republican ideology and of northern ideas of race: Eric Foner, *Free Soil, Free Labor, Free Men: The Ideology of the Republican Party Before the Civil War* (New York, 1970); David Montgomery, *Beyond Equality: Labor and the Radical Republicans, 1862-1872* (New York, 1967); and George M. Fredrickson, *The Black Image in the White Mind: The Debate on Afro-American Character and Destiny, 1817-1914* (New York, 1971), which is an extremely clear-headed treatment of the subject.

Finally, mention should be made of some economic studies of the period that I found useful. These include: Ralph Andreano, ed., *The Economic Impact of the American Civil War*, 2d ed. (Cambridge, Eng., 1967); Robert P. Sharkey, *Money, Class, and Party: An Economic Study of Civil War and Reconstruction*, with a foreword by C. Vann Woodward (Baltimore, 1959); Emerson D. Fite, *Social and Industrial Conditions in the North During the Civil War* (New York, 1910); and relevant sections of Randall and Donald. Econometricians have begun to apply their techniques to the Reconstruction South. I have benefited from the work of three: Robert Higgs, *Competition and Coercion: Blacks in the American Economy, 1865-1914* (Cambridge, 1977); and Roger L. Ransom and Richard Sutch, *One Kind of Freedom: The Economic Consequences of Emancipation* (Cambridge, 1977). An important critique of this literature is Harold D. Woodman's "Sequel to Slavery: The New History Views the Postbellum South," *Journal of Southern History* 43 (Nov. 1977), which also offers several stimulating suggestions on how historians should begin to view the postwar South.

Dissertations

I shall name only a few of the more important dissertations. Jimmy G. Shoalmire, "Carpetbagger Extraordinary: Marshall Harvey Twitchell, 1840-1905" (Ph.D. diss., Mississippi State University, 1969) is a very revealing study of a Freedmen's Bureau agent in northwestern Louisiana who became a planter while on his way to becoming the Republican boss of his parish. Richard J. Amundson, "The American Life of Henry Shelton Sanford" (Ph.D. diss., Florida State University, 1963) is valuable for understanding this capitalist's many southern investments. An important source of biographical information is Richard L. Hume's "The 'Black and Tan' Constitutional Conventions of 1867-1869 in Ten Former Confederate States: A Study of Their Membership" (Ph.D. diss., University of Washington, 1969). Clarence L. Mohr's "Georgia

Blacks During Secession and Civil War, 1859-1865" (Ph.D. diss., University of Georgia, 1974) is an excellent study of how the slaves themselves undermined the institution of bondage. Finally, two dissertations nearing completion at Yale University have strengthened my theoretical grasp of the nature of the changes occasioned by emancipation. They are Michael Wayne's "Antebellum Planters in a Postbellum World: The Natchez District, 1860-1880," and Steven Hahn's "The Roots of Southern Populism: White Yeomen Farmers, Tenants, and Share-croppers in Upper Piedmont, Georgia, 1850-1890."

Index